LANGUAGE AND LANGUAGE LEARNING

Prosodic Analysis

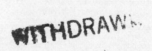

LANGUAGE AND LANGUAGE LEARNING

General Editors: RONALD MACKIN *and* PETER STREVENS

1   Henry Sweet *The Practical Study of Languages*
2   J.R. Firth *The Tongues of Men* and *Speech*
3   Randolph Quirk and A.H. Smith *The Teaching of English*
4   Neile Osman *Modern English*
5   H.E. Palmer *The Principles of Language Study*
6   N.E. Enkvist, J. Spencer and M. Gregory *Linguistics and Style*
7   H.E. Palmer *Curso Internacional de Ingles*
8   J.C. Catford *A Linguistic Theory of Translation*
9   Peter Strevens *Papers in Language and Language Teaching*
10 David Abercrombie *Studies in Phonetics and Linguistics*
11 *Five Inaugural Lectures* edited by Peter Strevens
12 Axel Wijk *Rules of Pronunciation for the English Language*
13 L.A. Hill *Selected Articles on the Teaching of English as a Foreign Language*
14 H.H. Stern *Foreign Languages in Primary Education*
15 Peter Ladefoged *Three Areas of Experimental Phonetics*
16 A.S. Hayes *Language Laboratory Facilities*
17 *Modern Language Teaching* edited by Hans Jalling
18 H.E. Palmer *The Scientific Study and Teaching of Languages*
19 H.S. Otter *A Functional Language Examination*
20 J. Dakin, B. Tiffen and H. Widdowson *Language in Education*
21 *Language Testing Symposium* edited by Alan Davies
22 H.E. Palmer and Sir Vere Redman *This Language-Learning Business*
23 *An Annotated Bibliography of Modern Language Teaching: Books and Articles 1946–1967* compiled by Janet O. Robinson
24 *Languages and the Young School Child* edited by H.H. Stern
25 *Prosodic Analysis* edited by F.R. Palmer
26 Edward M. Stack *The Language Laboratory and Modern Language Teaching*
27 *The Prague School of Linguistics and Language Teaching* edited by V. Fried
28 *The Indispensable Foundation* edited by E.J.A. Henderson
29 J.B. Pride *The Social Meaning of Language*

Prosodic Analysis

Edited by F. R. PALMER

London
OXFORD UNIVERSITY PRESS
1970

Oxford University Press, Ely House, London W. 1

GLASGOW NEW YORK TORONTO MELBOURNE WELLINGTON
CAPE TOWN SALISBURY IBADAN NAIROBI DAR ES SALAAM
LUSAKA ADDIS ABABA BOMBAY CALCUTTA MADRAS KARACHI
LAHORE DACCA KUALA LUMPUR SINGAPORE HONG KONG TOKYO

Handbook edition SBN 19 437111 5
Paperback edition SBN 19 437036 4

Printed in Great Britain by Stephen Austin and Sons, Limited, Hertford

Contents

Editor's and Publisher's note   vii

Introduction   ix

1   Sounds and Prosodies   J.R. Firth (1948)   1

2   Prosodies in Siamese: a study in synthesis   E.J.A. Henderson (1948)   27

3   The phonology of loanwords in some South-East Asian languages   E.J.A. Henderson (1951)   54

4   Some prosodic aspects of retroflexion and aspiration in Sanskrit   W.S. Allen (1951)   82

5   A study of quantity in Hausa   J. Carnochan (1951)   91

6   The phonology of the nasalized verbal forms in Sundanese   R.H. Robins (1953)   104

7   The tonal system of Tibetan (Lhasa dialect) and the nominal phrase   R.K. Sprigg (1955)   112

8   The 'broken plurals' of Tigrinya   F.R. Palmer (1955)   133

9   A phonological analysis of the Szechuanese monosyllable   N.C. Scott (1956)   152

10   'Openness' in Tigre: a problem of prosodic statement   F.R. Palmer (1956)   157

11   Some aspects of the phonology of the nominal forms of the Turkish word   Natalie Waterson (1956)   174

12   Aspects of prosodic analysis   R.H. Robins (1957)   188

13   Phonological (prosodic) analysis of the new Chinese syllable (modern Pekingese)   M.A.K. Halliday (1959)   201

14   Some problems of segmentation in the phonological analysis of Terena   J.T. Bendor-Samuel (1960)   214

15   Vowel harmony in Igbo   J. Carnochan (1960)   222

16   Vowel harmony in Lhasa Tibetan: prosodic analysis applied to interrelated vocalic features of successive syllables   R.K. Sprigg (1961)   230

Bibliography   253

Editor's and Publisher's Note

THE articles contained in this volume are substantially as they were when first published. All the articles have been lithographically reproduced as they originally appeared, except article 12 which has been reset. Minor alterations of three kinds have, however, been made.

First, some of the authors themselves have made minor alterations to the texts.

Secondly, some of the authors have added up-to-date comments on their articles: these are printed in square brackets. When new material has been incorporated, the pagination in some cases has altered.

Thirdly, within any single article page references have been altered to correspond to the pagination of this book, but references to other articles have been left in their original form. In Article 12 alone references are to the bibliography in the book.

Abbreviations:

BSOAS Bulletin of the School of Oriental and African Studies.

DJ In Honour of Daniel Jones, David Abercrombie *et al.*, Eds. (London: Longmans, 1964).

JRF *In Memory of J. R. Firth*, C. E. Bazell *et al.*, Eds. (London: Longmans, 1966).

Papers *J. R. Firth, Papers in Linguistics* (London: Oxford University Press), 1957.

SLA *Studies in Linguistic Analysis*, Special Volume of the Philological Society, 2nd ed., 1962.

TPS Transactions of the Philological Society.

Introduction

THIS is a collection of sixteen articles, all written between the years 1948 and 1961, dealing with what has become known as 'prosodic analysis'. All the authors except two were staff members of the Department of Phonetics and Linguistics at the School of Oriental and African Studies at a time when J. R. Firth, as Professor of General Linguistics in the University of London, was Head of that Department; the exceptions are M. A. K. Halliday and J. I. Bendor-Samuel who worked as research students in the Department.

All the articles raise points of general theoretical interest and all except two deal with problems in specific languages. The two that discuss phonology on a wider basis are Firth's 'Sounds and prosodies', which can fairly be regarded as the article that launched the new theory, and Robins' 'Aspects of prosodic analysis' which is an excellent introductory summary of the whole approach.

The articles are arranged in chronological order. This has the advantage that 'Sounds and prosodies' comes at the beginning. In spite of its historical importance, however, the reader who comes new to prosodic analysis would not be advised to read this article first for it is not easy to understand. He would be advised to begin with Robins' 'Aspects of prosodic analysis' and then to turn to one of the more easily understood of the exemplificatory articles, perhaps Carnochan's 'Vowel harmony in Igbo'.

With the exception of Halliday's contribution, all the articles are taken from journals. Some others that might have seemed appropriate but which have appeared in collections in book form, have not been included. In particular, nothing has been taken from the Special Volume of the Philological Society *Studies in Linguistic Analysis*. The reader should refer to the volume since all the articles except the first three are concerned with prosodic analysis. A full bibliography appears on p. 253–6.

Although 'Sounds and prosodies' was the first explicit statement of the theory and the first to use the term 'prosody' and 'prosodic' in the appropriate sense, some of the notions involved are to be found in earlier articles, notably Firth 1934, 1935, 1936 and 1937.[1] Some of the features of phonology that Firth felt were not clearly accounted for in phonemic analysis had been discussed by American authors and especially by W. F. Twaddell in 'On defining the phoneme' where the

[1] I am grateful to the contributors to the volume and to Professor T. F. Mitchell for their helpful comments on this Introduction, especially to Professor E. J. A. Henderson for pointing out the relevance of many of the early articles by Firth and of articles contemporary with 'Sounds and prosodies'.

notion of 'micro phoneme' is similar to Firth's 'polysystemic' approach,
by C. F. Hockett in 'A system of descriptive phonology' where he dealt
with supra-segmentals, Z. S. Harris in his 'Simultaneous components
in phonology' where he first dealt with 'long components', and by
C. F. Hockett again in 'Problems of morphemic analysis' where he
introduced the concept of 'normalization' which provided a non-
phonemic basis for morphemic analysis.[2] The essential difference,
however, was that while Harris and Hockett sought to deal with these
features within the framework of phonemics, Firth saw clearly that it
was the phonemic theory itself that was deficient. Indeed, it is remarkable that there have never been any significant developments along
the lines suggested by Harris and Hockett. If anything, later phonemics
became more orthodox and rigid than ever, and it is not surprising
that it is again under attack today (see below p. xv).

It is not easy to characterize prosodic analysis, except in a negative
way and say that it is phonological analysis not essentially based on
segmentation and classification of the segments as phonemic analysis
is, but in which explicit recognition is given to features that may in
some sense be regarded as non-segmental, or, to use Firth's own terms,
that were 'syntagmatic' rather than 'paradigmatic'. Within prosodic
analysis the main functions played by these features are of three kinds.
First, there are those features which are characteristic of certain places
in the phonological structure: syllable initial, syllable final, word
initial, word final, etc. Secondly, there are those features which are
characteristic of the 'longer piece': vowel harmony, vowel-consonant
harmony, or what is usually called assimilation or even dissimilation,
etc. Thirdly, there are those features which have morphophonological
value, i.e. which link grammar with all the phonetic exponents; Robins
in 'Aspects of prosodic analysis' does not mention the third of these,
and, indeed, it is not explicitly referred to in the earlier literature.

This is, however, an oversimplified statement. It may be more
illuminating to discuss some of the aspects of prosodic analysis
historically, and with detailed reference to some of the articles contained in this volume.

1) In papers published long before 1948, Firth had established three
principles of phonological analysis, first the polysystemic approach,
secondly, the importance of features such as yotization and labio-
velarization (which reappear later as y and w prosodies) and thirdly the
fact that these features are best regarded as not being 'placed'. The
first clear indication of what was later known as the polysystemic
approach, the refusal to identify terms in one system with terms in
another, is found in Firth 1935 where for the nasals in Marathi he noted

---

[2] All four are to be found in M. Joos, Ed., *Readings in Linguistics* (New York:
American Council of Learned Societies, 1958).

a two-term alternance initially, a three-term alternance finally but, though phonetically there were eight different sounds, one 'unique' homorganic nasal before medial consonants; he comments 'I should not identify all these *n* sounds as linguistically and functionally the same unit' (1935: 51). This clearly stemmed from his insistence on the importance of contextualization which had been stressed the year before (Firth 1934) where contextualization is defined as 'not only the recognition of the various phonetic contexts in which the phonemes occur, but the further identification of phonemes by determining their lexical and grammatical functions' (1934: 5). Firth 1936 developed the theme that 'in the symbolization of the forms of a language by means of an ordered system of letters and signs, the first principle should be the recognition of characteristic recurrent contexts in which an ordered series of phonological substitutions may take place' (1936: 71). In later articles the polysystemic approach is taken to mean that different vowel and consonant systems should be set out (*a*) for different places in the syllable and word structure (e.g. there would be different word initial and final consonant systems), and (*b*) for grammatically different structures. These are briefly suggested in 'Sounds and prosodies': 'We may speak of . . . the phonematic system of the concord prefixes of a Bantu language, or of the monosyllable in English', but they are already implied in Firth 1934.

The function of yotization and labiovelarization as *y* and *w* prosodies is foreshadowed in Firth 1935 where he introduced his notion of 'articulation type'. The initial alterances of Burmese were classified in terms of both 'basic articulations' and yotization, labiovelarization and nasalization (but certain combinations of these). But even earlier (Firth 1934), the plosives of Hindi had been discussed in terms of voice, aspiration and length. It was in Firth 1937 that he pointed out that certain features (glottalization and labiovelarization) were best regarded as 'syllabic diacritica and not as being "placed"'. This is the first suggestion of the importance of the syllable in phonological analysis.

The notion of not being placed is clearly of importance for the understanding of prosodies in the sense of features of the longer piece, but at the time the non-placed features were features of the syllable only. It is interesting to note Firth's own comment on the cover of a copy of the article he gave to Professor Henderson. 'This was the first "non-phonemic" analysis *published in English* and the first to separate the "successive" or "placed" units from those which are not "placed"— or may be described as non-successive. People have passed it by in England, because the principles were lost in the detail—but quite a new theory is here already implied.' And towards the end of the article with reference to the 'aspiration-tensity' and voice difference of consonants and yotization and labiovelarization, he comments in the margin, 'These could be treated as not placed or as syllabic diacritica, or "prosodies" in M. [= modern?] sense.' The year 1948 saw three articles written by Firth's colleagues—Carnochan 1948, Henderson 1948 and Scott 1948. These are clearly based upon the model of Firth 1937; Henderson's article in particular is a clear exposition of the theory as it then stood with its emphasis on the syllable, polysystemicity, 'placed' and 'unplaced' features and analysis into articulation types, while Carnochan's is a remarkable attempt to treat an African language in a model designed primarily for the monosyllabic pattern of Chinese.

2) The main burden of 'Sounds and prosodies' is to make the distinction between syntagmatic and paradigmatic features in phonology. Indeed, the title itself was intended to suggest this, sounds being paradigmatic and prosodies syntagmatic. Like so many of Firth's works, the article is not easy to read and not wholly consistent, but its main aim is clearly set out in two sentences: 'By using the common symbols C and V instead of the specific symbols for phonematic consonant and vowel units, we generalize syllabic structure in a new order of abstraction eliminating the specific paradigmatic consonant and vowel systems as such, and enabling the syntagmatic word structure of syllables with all their attributes to be stated systematically. Similarly, we may abstract those features which mark word or syllable initials and word or syllable finals or word junctions from the word, piece, or sentence, and regard them syntagmatically as prosodies, distinct from the phonematic constituents which are referred to as units of the consonant and vowel systems.' In effect Firth here distinguishes three things: first, the syllabic structure stated in terms of C and V; secondly, features of word final, initial, etc.; and thirdly, the units of consonant and vowel systems. The second are prosodic in the strict sense, but Firth treats the first too, i.e. the features of syllabic structure, also as part of his prosodics. It is important to read no more into the article than this. The remainder of the article is almost entirely concerned with exemplification of prosodies of the two kinds, features of syllabification and how they differ from one language to another, and features that are essentially characteristic in specific languages of positions or junctions. The emphasis here was still upon the syllable, but no longer confined to the characteristics of mono-syllabic languages. In quite a striking passage which may perhaps today no longer seem plausible, he suggested for Cairene colloquial: 'Naturally, therefore, the prosodic features of a word include:

1 The number of syllables
2 The nature of the syllable—open or closed
3 The syllabic quantities

4 The sequence of syllables   ⎫ radical and flexional
5 The sequence of consonants   ⎬ elements separately
6 The sequence of vowels   ⎭ treated
7 The position, nature and quantity of the prominent
8 The clear or dark qualities of the syllables.'

3) A synthesis of most of the ideas is to be found in Henderson's 'Prosodies in Siamese', but although a great deal of emphasis is laid there upon initial and final features of the syllable, the main thesis of the paper is that one can handle phonological analysis in terms of a hierarchy, beginning with those features that are characteristic of the sentence and working down through the features that are characteristic of ever-increasingly smaller pieces. We have, therefore, prosodies of sentence, prosodies of sentence parts, prosodies of polysyllables and sentence pieces, prosodies of syllables, prosodies of syllable parts, and finally, consonant and vowel units. Henderson's article is perhaps the neatest and, in some ways, the most convincing of all the articles written since it does provide an overall analysis for a language in wholly consistent prosodic terms. No similar attempt was ever made for any other language and one perhaps must guess that such a neat statement is feasible only in a few selected languages, perhaps of the 'isolating' type like Siamese.

4) Many of the articles written on prosodic analysis are concerned with what can be called features of the longer piece. One of the most striking examples of this is Carnochan's treatment of vowel harmony in his 'Vowel Harmony in Igbo', though the reader's attention should also be drawn to the treatment of Turkish by Waterson in 'Some aspects of the phonology of the nominal forms of the Turkish word', and to the reinterpretation of this by Lyons 1962. It is worth noting, however, that it is not only features that would traditionally be handled in terms of vowel harmony or assimilation that can be regarded as prosodic in this sense, but even those that are traditionally treated under dissimilation as shown in Allen's 'Some prosodic aspects of retroflection and aspiration in Sanskrit'. That features are different in the longer piece is no less important than that they are the same.

5) Since the polysystemic approach meant that different phonological statements could be made for different grammatical elements, it was a short step to treat features having morphophonological value as prosodies. The interdependence of grammar and phonology which is an essential part of this aspect of the theory, had been foreshadowed as early as Firth 1934. Although he does not mention this characteristic of prosodic analysis in his 'Aspects of prosodic analysis', Robins was the first to provide an example of it. In 'The nasalized verbal forms of

Sundanese', nasality is abstracted because nasalization is 'a fundamental inflectional process'. In 'The "broken plurals" of Tigrinya', I argued the case for assigning phonetic exponents to specific grammatical categories, even when such exponents are non-segmental. And in the phonological analysis that follows, the phonematic and prosodic systems that are set up are designed solely to account for the relations between the singular and plural forms of Tigrinya. Similar statements of the phonological exponents of grammatical categories are to be found elsewhere, especially in Henderson 1960, 1961 and 1965a. I did not see, and still do not see, any objection to a polysystemic approach even if it treats phonetically identical forms as phonologically different. I would not expect, for instance, as Firth did not expect, that English *banned* and *band* should be treated as phonologically identical;. yet Bendor-Samuel, in his 'Problems of segmentation in the phonological analysis of Terena', saw this as the main objection likely to be put forward to prosodic analysis. He says of the prosodic analysis of Terena which he proposes that it attempts to treat phonetically identical forms as phonologically different, but that 'few linguists would accept such an analysis'. But the prosodic analysts *did* accept this and today others too would be prepared to follow suit.

6) Two further ideas that are not explicitly suggested in any of the articles in this volume have been put forward recently by Henderson 1966. First, she aims by a prosodic statement to account for 'uneven consonant and vocalic distribution'. This can certainly be done. One of the clearest examples of which I am aware concerns velars and labiovelars together with central and back rounded vowels in Tigrinya. Phonemically a distinction can be established between, e.g. k and k^w and $ə$ and u. One might expect as possible syllables:

$$k^wək, kək^w, k^wək^w, kuk, k^wuk, kuk^w, k^wuk^w.$$

In fact there is only one form, phonetically [kuk], which might phonemically be interpreted as any one of the seven. In prosodic terms the point is that a w prosody can be stated only once for any one syllable and that although it may be associated in certain cases with initial, medial, or final, w and non-w elements do not co-occur within the same syllable. Secondly, Henderson hopes to account for 'the seemingly irregular patterning of initial aspirated plosives'. These are based in a traditional consonantal matrix; there are many gaps which cannot be accounted for. Like Sapir, Henderson looks for sound patterns, but she suggests a matrix whose co-ordinates are prosodies in the sense that they are not in terms of the traditional phonetic categories. The freedom she attempts in the name of prosodic analysis is, it would seem, from the phonemically based phonetics of the I.P.A., but is clearly reminiscent of Firth's 'articulation types' or of her own 1948' article. (One could similarly argue, I think, in favour of freedom from

Jakobson's distinctive features). Henderson's article is certainly controversial, if not, like 'sounds and prosodies', almost revolutionary; but it should not be ignored by anyone wishing to make a serious study of writers on prosodic analysis.

Two other general points about the prosodic approach should be made. Most important was Firth's emphasis upon theory rather than upon method (1957: 1–5) (what today would be called 'discovery procedures'). It was precisely because of this that his polysystemic approach with its emphasis, especially later, upon the grammatical status of the elements being described was possible. Secondly, it was not believed that simplicity for its own sake, especially simplicity of the kind found in phonemics, should always be sought. More important was what Allen (1957: 83) called 'appropriateness'. These were theoretical attitudes that were wholly out of keeping with the phonemic approach; today, however, they are far less unfashionable.

For comparison between the phonemic and prosodic approach the reader should look at Allen 1957, Lyons 1962, Fromkin 1965 and Bendor-Samuel 1965.

Ironically, today when prosodic analysis is no longer being championed with the fervour that it was in the 1950s, many of the points that were made are now quite widely accepted. The transformational-generative school of linguistics wholly accepts the notion that a phonological statement should be quite explicitly geared to the grammar; my own view (Palmer 1958b) that phonology should be regarded as a 'bridge' between grammar and phonetics, is explicitly referred to with approval by Chomsky.[3] The purely segmental nature of phonemics which Firth regarded as perhaps its greatest weakness, has also come under attack, not only from the transformational-generative school which dismiss it as 'taxonomic', but even from some who still believe that they are champions of phonemic analysis. Lamb,[4] for instance, has proposed to recognize in Russian a phoneme h whose realization is wholly that of voicelessness and which extends over more than one phonemic segment; this is an extension of the notion of suprasegmentals to a feature normally assigned to segmental phonemes, but it lacks the essential features of prosodic analysis—its polysystemicity, and Lamb has therefore to indicate voicelessness wherever it occurs and not merely where it is characteristic of more than one segment. Even the abstraction of such features as frontness and backness, as the correct way of handling vowel harmony, has been proposed by one of Chomsky's disciples—although without a single reference to a prosodic article.[5]

[3] N. Chomsky, *Current Issues in Linguistic Theory* (The Hague: Mouton and Co., 1964) 70.
[4] S. M. Lamb, 'Prolegomena to a theory of language' *Language* 42.2 (1966) 545–7.
[5] T. M. Lightner, 'On the description of vowel and consonant harmony' *Word* 21.2 (1965) 244–50.

If the full importance of prosodic analysis has not been recognized it may be because some of the solutions proposed seemed unnecessarily complex and even perverse. But it was probably due more to the fact that the linguistics world was not yet ready for a change away from phonemics and that many of the articles appeared in journals not familiar to most linguists, especially in America. This volume will at least set the record straight historically and make the more important works more easily available.

F. R. Palmer
Department of Linguistic Science
University of Reading

August 1968

1
SOUNDS AND PROSODIES
By J. R. FIRTH

THE purpose of this paper is to present some of the main principles of a theory of the phonological structure of the word in the piece or sentence, and to illustrate them by noticing especially sounds and prosodies that are often described as laryngals and pharyngals. I shall not deal with tone and intonation explicitly.

Sweet himself bequeathed to the phoneticians coming after him the problems of synthesis which still continue to vex us. Most phoneticians and even the " new " phonologists have continued to elaborate the analysis of words, some in general phonetic terms, others in phonological terms based on theories of opposition, alternances, and distinctive differentiations or substitutions. Such studies I should describe as paradigmatic and monosystemic in principle.

Since de Saussure's famous *Cours*, the majority of such studies seem also to have accepted the monosystemic principle so succinctly stated by Meillet : " chaque langue forme un système où tout se tient." I have in recent years taken up some of the neglected problems left to us by Sweet. I now suggest principles for a technique of statement which assumes first of all that the primary linguistic data are pieces, phrases, clauses, and sentences within which the word must be delimited and identified, and secondly that the facts of the phonological structure of such various languages as English, Hindustani, Telugu, Tamil,[1] Maltese,[2] and

[1] At one of the 1948 meetings of the Linguistic Society of America, Mr. Kenneth Pike suggested that in certain Mexican Indian languages it would be convenient to hypothecate a second or phonemic sub-system to account for all the facts. Taking part in the discussion which followed, I pointed out my own findings in Tamil and Telugu for both of which languages it is necessary to assume at least three phonological systems : non-brahman Dravidian, Sanskrito-dravidian, and Sanskritic.

[2] See J. Aquilina : *The Structure of Maltese*, A Study in Mixed Grammar and Vocabulary. (Thesis for the Ph.D. degree, 1940. University of London Library.)

Source: J. R. Firth, " Sounds and prosodies ", *TPS* (1948), 127–52. Reprinted by permission of The Philological Society and Miss Jean M. Wheeler and Miss Barbara M. Firth.

Nyanja [1] are economically and completely stated on a polysystemic basis. In presenting these views for your consideration, I am aware of the danger of idiosyncrasy on the one
hand, and on the other of employing common words which
may be current in linguistics but not conventionally scientific.
Nevertheless, the dangers are unavoidable since linguistics is
reflexive and introvert. That is to say, in linguistics language
is turned back upon itself. We have to use language about
language, words about words, letters about letters. The
authors of a recent American report on education win our
sympathetic attention when they say " we realize that language is ill adapted for talking about itself ". There is no
easy escape from the vicious circle, and " yet ", as the report
points out, " we cannot imagine that so many people would
have attempted this work of analysis for themselves and others
unless they believed that they could reach some measure of
success in so difficult a task." All I can hope for is your
indulgence and some measure of success in the confused and
difficult fields of phonetics and phonology.

For the purpose of distinguishing prosodic systems from
phonematic systems, words will be my principal isolates. In
examining these isolates, I shall not overlook the contexts
from which they are taken and within which the analyses must
be tested. Indeed, I propose to apply some of the principles
of word structure to what I term *pieces* or combinations of
words. I shall deal with words and pieces in English, Hindustani, Egyptian Arabic, and Maltese, and refer to word
features in German and other languages. It is especially
helpful that there *are* things called English words and Arabic
words. They are so called by authoritative bodies ; indeed,
English words and Classical Arabic words are firmly institutionalized. To those undefined terms must be added the
words *sound, syllable, letter, vowel, consonant, length, quantity,
stress, tone, intonation*, and more of the related vocabulary.

In dealing with these matters, words and expressions have
been taken from a variety of sources, even the most ancient,

[1] See T. Hill : *The Phonetics of a Nyanja Speaker,* With Particular
Reference to the Phonological Structure of the Word. (Thesis for the M.A.
degree, 1948. University of London Library.)

and most of them are familiar. That does not mean that the set of principles or the system of thought here presented are either ancient or familiar. To some they may seem revolutionary. Word analysis is as ancient as writing and as various. We A.B.C. people, as some Chinese have described us, are used to the process of splitting up words into letters, consonants and vowels, and into syllables, and we have attributed to them such several qualities as length, quantity, tone, and stress.

I have purposely avoided the word *phoneme* in the title of my paper, because not one of the meanings in its present wide range of application suits my purpose and *sound* will do less harm. One after another, phonologists and phoneticians seem to have said to themselves " *Your* phonemes are dead, long live *my* phoneme ". For my part, I would restrict the application of the term to certain features only of consonants and vowels systematically stated *ad hoc* for each language. By a further degree of abstraction we may speak of a five-vowel or seven-vowel phonematic system, or of the phonematic system of the concord prefixes of a Bantu language,[1] or of the monosyllable in English.[2]

By using the common symbols c and v instead of the specific symbols for phonematic consonant and vowel units, we generalize syllabic structure in a new order of abstraction eliminating the specific paradigmatic consonant and vowel systems as such, and enabling the syntagmatic word structure of syllables with all their attributes to be stated systematically. Similarly we may abstract those features which mark word or syllable initials and word or syllable finals or word junctions from the word, piece, or sentence, and regard them syntagmatically as prosodies, distinct from the phonematic constituents which are referred to as units of the consonant and vowel systems. The use of spaces between words duly delimited

---

[1] See T. Hill: *The Phonetics of a Nyanja Speaker.*

[2] Miss Eileen M. Evans, Senior Lecturer in Phonetics, School of Oriental and African Studies, has work in preparation on this subject, as part of a wider study of the phonology of modern English.

and identified is, like a punctuation mark or " accent ",
a prosodic symbol. Compare the orthographic example " Is
she ? " with the phonetic transcript iʒʃiy? in the matter of
prosodic signs. The interword space of the orthography is
replaced by the junction sequence symbolized in general
phonetic terms by ʒʃ. Such a sequence is, in modern spoken
English, a mark of junction which is here regarded as a
prosody. If the symbol *i* is used for word initial and *f* for
word final, ʒʃ is *fi*. As in the case of **c** and **v**, *i* and *f* generalize
beyond the phonematic level.

We are accustomed to positional criteria in classifying
phonematic variants or allophones as initial, medial,
intervocalic, or final. Such procedure makes abstraction of
certain postulated units, *phonemes,* comprising a scatter of
distributed variants (allophones). Looking at language
material from a syntagmatic point of view, any phonetic
features characteristic of and peculiar to such positions or
junctions can just as profitably and perhaps more profitably be
stated as prosodies of the sentence or word. Penultimate
stress or junctional geminations are also obvious prosodic
features in syntagmatic junction. Thus the phonetic and
phonological analysis of the word can be grouped under the
two headings which form the title of this paper—sounds and
prosodies. I am inclined to the classical view that the correct
rendering of the syllabic accent or the syllabic prosodies of the
word is *anima vocis,* the soul, the breath, the life of the word.
The study of the prosodies in modern linguistics is in a primitive
state compared with the techniques for the systematic study
of sounds. The study of sounds and the theoretical justification
of roman notation have led first to the apotheosis of the sound-
letter in the phoneme and later to the extended use of such
doubtful derivatives as " phonemics " and " phonemicist ",
especially in America, and the misapplication of the principles
of vowel and consonant analysis to the prosodies. There is
a tendency to use one magic phoneme principle within a
monosystemic hypothesis. I am suggesting alternatives to such
a " monophysite " doctrine.

When first I considered giving this paper, it was to be called " Further Studies in Semantics ". I had in mind the semantics of my own subject or a critical study of the language being used about language, of the symbols used for other symbols, and especially the new idioms that have grown up around the word " phoneme ". Instead of a critical review of that kind, I am now submitting a system of ideas on word structure, especially emphasizing the convenience of stating word structure and its musical attributes as distinct orders of abstractions from the total phonological complex. Such abstractions I refer to as prosodies, and again emphasize the plurality of systems within any given language. I think the classical grammarians employed the right emphasis when they referred to the prosodies as *anima vocis*. Whitney, answering the question " What is articulation ? " said : " Articulation consists not in the mode of production of individual sounds, but in the mode of their combination for the purposes of speech." [1]

The Romans and the English managed to dispense with those written signs called " accents " and avoided pepperbox spelling. Not so the more ingenious Greeks. The invention of the written signs for the prosodies of the ancient classical language were not required by a native for reading what was written in ordinary Greek. They were, in the main, the inventions of the great scholars of Alexandria, one of whom, Aristarchus, was described by Jebb as the greatest scholar and the best Homeric critic of antiquity. The final codification of traditional Greek accentuation had to wait nearly four hundred years—some would say much longer—so that we may expect to learn something from such endeavours. [2] It is interesting to notice that the signs used to mark the accents were themselves called προσῳδίαι, prosodies, and they included the marks for the rough and smooth breathings. It is also

---

[1] Amply illustrated by the patterns to be seen on the Visible Speech Translator produced by the Bell Telephone Laboratories.

[2] See " A Short Guide to the accentuation of Ancient Greek ", by Postgate.

relevant to my purpose that what was a prosody to the Greeks
was treated as a consonant by the Romans, hence the " h "
of hydra. On the relative merits of the Greek and Roman
alphabets as the basis of an international phonetic system of
notation, Prince Trubetzkoy favoured Greek and, when we
talked on this subject, it was clear he was trying to imagine
how much better phonetics might have been if it had started
from Greek with the Greek alphabet. Phonetics and phonology
have their ultimate roots in India. Very little of ancient
Hindu theory has been adequately stated in European
languages. When it is, we shall know how much was lost when
such glimpses as we had were expressed as a theory of the
Roman alphabet.

More detailed notice of " h " and the *glottal stop* in a variety
of languages will reveal the scientific convenience of regarding
them as belonging to the prosodic systems of certain languages
rather than to the sound systems. " h " has been variously
considered as a sort of vowel or a consonant in certain
languages, and the glottal stop as a variety of things.
Phonetically, the glottal stop, unreleased, is the negation
of all sound whether vocalic or consonantal. Is it the perfect
minimum or terminus of the syllable, the beginning and the
end, the master or maximum consonant ? We have a good
illustration of that in the American or Tamil exclamation
ʔaʔa ! Or is it just a necessary metrical pause or rest, a sort
of measure of time, a sort of mora or matra ? Is it therefore
a general syllable maker or marker, part of the syllabic
structure ? As we shall see later, it may be all or any of these
things, or just a member of the consonant system according
to the language.

We have noticed the influence of the Roman and Greek
alphabets on notions of sounds and prosodies. The method of
writing used for Sanskrit is syllabic, and the Devanagari
syllabary as used for that language, and also other forms of
it used for the modern Sanskritic dialects of India, are to
this day models of phonetic and phonological excellence.
The word analysis is syllabic and clearly expressive of the

syllabic structure. Within that structure the pronunciation, even the phonetics of the consonants, can be fully discussed and represented in writing with the help of the prosodic sign for a consonant closing a syllable. For the Sanskritic languages an analysis of the word satisfying the demands of modern phonetics, phonology, and grammar could be presented on a syllabic basis using the Devanagari syllabic notation without the use of the phoneme concept, unless of course syllables and even words can be considered as " phonemes ".

In our Japanese phonetics courses at the School of Oriental and African Studies during the war, directed to the specialized purposes of operational linguistics, we analysed the Japanese word and piece by a syllabic technique although we employed roman letters. The roomazi system, as a system, is based on the native Kana syllabary. The syllabic structure of the word—itself a prosody—was treated as the basis of other prosodies perhaps over-simplified, but kept distinct from the syllabary. The syllabary was, so to speak, a paradigmatic system, and the prosodies a syntagmatic system. We never met any unit or part which *had* to be called a phoneme, though a different analysis, in my opinion not so good, has been made on the phoneme principle.

Here may I quote a few of the wiser words of Samuel Haldeman (1856), first professor of Comparative Philology in the University of Pennsylvania, one of the earlier American phoneticians, contemporary with Ellis and Bell. " Good phonetics must recognize the value for certain languages ' of alphabets of a more or less syllabic character ', in which ' a consonant position and a vowel position of the organs ' are regarded ' as in a manner constituting a unitary element '." [1] Sir William Jones was the first to point out the excellence of what he called the Devanagari system, and also of the Arabic alphabet. The Arabic syllabary he found almost perfect for Arabic itself—" Not a letter," he comments, " could be added or taken away without manifest inconvenience." He adds the remark, " Our English alphabet and orthography are

[1] Cf. " The English School of Phonetics ", *Papers*, 92–120.

disgracefully and almost ridiculously imperfect." I shall later be using Arabic words in Roman transcription to illustrate the nature of syllabic analysis in that language as the framework for the prosodies. Sir William Jones emphasized the importance as he put it of the "Orthography of Asiatic Words in Roman Letters". The development of comparative philology, and especially of phonology, also meant increased attention to transliteration and transcription in roman letters. Sir William Jones was not in any position to understand how all this might contribute to the tendency, both in historical and descriptive linguistics, to phonetic hypostatization of roman letters, and theories built on such hypostatization.

In introducing my subject I began with sounds and the Roman alphabet which has determined a good deal of our phonetic thinking in Western Europe—as a reminder that in the Latin word the letter was regarded as a sound, *vox articulata*. We moved east to Greek, and met the prosodies, i.e. smooth and rough breathings, and the accents. The accents are marks, but they are also musical properties of the word. In Sanskrit we meet a syllabary built on phonetic principles, and each character is əkʂərə, ultimate, permanent, and indestructible. Any work I have done in the romanization of Oriental languages has been in the spirit of Sir William Jones, and consequently I have not underestimated the grammatical, even phonetic, excellence of the characters and letters of the East where our own alphabet finds its origins. On the contrary, one of the purposes of my paper is to recall the principles of other systems of writing to redress the balance of the West.

And now let us notice the main features of the Arabic alphabet. I suppose it can claim the title "alphabet" on etymological grounds, but it is really a syllabary.[1] First, each Arabic letter has a name of its own. Secondly, each one

---

[1] Or rather Arabic writing is syllabic in principle. Professor Edgar Sturtevant has stated this view and recently confirmed it personally in conversation.

is capable of being realized as an art figure in itself. Thirdly, and most important of all, each one has syllabic value, the value or *potestas* in the most general terms being consonant plus vowel, including vowel zero, or zero vowel. The special mark, *sukuun*, for a letter without vowel possibilities, i.e. with zero vowel, or for a letter to end a syllable not begin it, is the key to the understanding of the syllabic value of the simple letter not so marked, and this is congruent with the essentials of Arabic grammar. Like the **hələnt** in Devanagari, **sukuun** is a prosodic sign. The framework of the language and the etymology of words, including their basic syllabic structure, consist in significant sequences of radicals usually in threes. Hence a letter has the potestas of one of these radicals plus one of the three possible vowels **i**, **a**, or **u** or zero. Each syllabic sign or letter has, in the most general terms, a trivocalic potentiality, or zero vowel, but in any given word placed in an adequate context, the possibilities are so narrowly determined by the grammar that in fact the syllable is, in the majority of words, fully determined and all possibilities except one are excluded. The prosodies of the Arabic word are indicated by the letters if the context is adequate. If the syllabic structure is known, we always know which syllable takes the main prominence. It is, of course, convenient to make the syllabic structure more precise by marking a letter specially, to show it has what is called zero vowel, or to show it is doubled. Such marks are prosodic. And it is even possible to maintain that in this system of writing the diacritics pointing out the vowels and consonants in detail are added prosodic marks rather than separate vowel signs or separate sounds in the roman sense ; that is to say, generalizing beyond the phonematic level, **fatħa**, **kasra**, **ðamma**, **sukuun**, **alif**, **waw**, **ya**, **taʃdiid** and **hamza** form a prosodic system.

In China the characters, their figures and arrangement, are designs in their own right. Words in calligraphy are artefacts in themselves of high aesthetic value, for which there is much more general respect than we have in England for the Etonian pronunciation of the King's English. For my purpose Chinese offered excellent material for the study of institutionalized words long since delimited and identified. With the help of Mr. K. H. Hu, of Changsha, I studied the pronunciation and phonology of his dialect of Hunanese.[1] Eventually I sorted out into phonological classes and categories large numbers of characters in accordance with their distinguishing diacritica. Diacritica were of two main types, phonematic and prosodic. The prosodic diacritica included tone, voice quality, and other properties of the sonants, and also yotization and labio-velarization, symbolized by y and w. Such diacritica of the monosyllable are not considered as successive fractions or segments in any linear sense, or as distributed in separate measures of time.[2] They are stated as systematized abstractions from the primary sensory data, i.e. the uttered instances of monosyllables. We must distinguish between such a conceptual framework which is a set of relations between categories, and the serial signals we make and hear in any given instance.[3]

Before turning to suggest principles of analysis recognizing other systems of thought and systems of writing outside the Western European tradition, let me amplify what has already been said about the prosodies by quoting from a grammarian of the older tradition and by referring to the traditional theory of music.

Lindley Murray's English Grammar (1795) is divided in accordance with good European tradition,[4] into four parts,

[1] See my " The Chinese Monosyllable in a Hunanese Dialect (Changsha) ", BSOS., vol. viii, pt. 4 (1937) [with B. B. Rogers].

[2] In the sending of Japanese morse ak = ka, the first signal being the characteristic sonant. (Joos, Acoustic Phonetics, L.S.A., pp. 116–126, and conclusions on segmentation.)

[3] See also N. C. Scott, " A Study in the Phonetics of Fijian," BSOAS., vol. xii, pts. 3–4 (1948), and J. Carnochan, " A Study in the Phonology of an Igbo Speaker," BSOAS., vol. xii, pt. 2 (1948). Eugénie Henderson, Prosodies in Siamese, in Asia Major, N.S. Vol. I, 1949.

[4] Cf. " Arte de Escribir ", by Torquato Torio de la Riva, addressed to the Count of Trastamara, Madrid, 1802. The four parts of grammar are etimología ó analogía, syntaxis, prosódia, or ortografía. Prosódia teaches the

viz. Orthography, Etymology, Syntax, and Prosody. Part IV, Prosody, begins as follows : " Prosody consists of two parts : the former teaches the true PRONUNCIATION of words, comprising ACCENT, QUANTITY, EMPHASIS, PAUSE, and TONE ; and the latter, the laws of versification. Notice the headings in the first part—ACCENT, QUANTITY, EMPHASIS, PAUSE, and TONE."

In section 1 of ACCENT, he uses the expression the *stress of the voice* as distinguishing the accent of English. Tho stress of the voice on a particular syllable of the word enables the number of syllables of the word to be perceived as grouped in the utterance of that word. In other words, the accent is a function of the syllabic structure of the word. He recognizes principal and secondary accent in English. He recognizes two quantities of the syllable in English, long and short, and discusses the syllabic analysis and accentuation of English disyllables, trisyllables, and polysyllables, and notices intonation and emphasis.

The syntagmatic system of the word-complex, that is to say the syllabic structure with properties such as initial, final and medial characteristics, number and nature of syllables, quantity, stress, and tone, invites comparison with theories of melody and rhythm in music. Writers on the theory of music often say that you cannot have melody without rhythm, also that if such a thing were conceivable as a continuous series of notes of equal value, of the same pitch and without accent, musical rhythm could not be found in it. Hence the musical description of rhythm would be " the grouping of measures ", and a measure " the grouping of stress and non-stress ". Moreover, a measure or a bar-length is a grouping of pulses which have to each other definite interrelations as to their length, as well as interrelations of strength. Interrelations of pitch and quality also appear to correlate with the sense of stress and enter into the grouping of measures.

quantity of syllables in order to pronounce words with their due accent. There are three degrees in Spanish, acute or long, grave or short, and what are termed *común* or *indiferentes*.

We can tentatively adapt this part of the theory of music for the purpose of framing a theory of the prosodies. Let us regard the syllable as a pulse or beat, and a word or piece as a sort of bar length or grouping of pulses which bear to each other definite interrelations of length, stress, tone, quality—including voice quality and nasality. The principle to be emphasized is the *interrelation of the syllables*, what I have previously referred to as the *syntagmatic relations*, as *opposed to the paradigmatic or differential relations* of sounds in vowel and consonant systems, and to the paradigmatic aspect of the theory of phonemes, and to the analytic method of regarding contextual characteristics of sounds as allophones of phonematic units.

A good illustration of these principles of word-analysis is provided if we examine full words in the spoken Arabic of Cairo, for which there are corresponding forms in Classical Arabic. Such words (in the case of nouns the article is not included) have from one to five syllables. There are five types of syllable, represented by the formulae given below, and examples of each are given.

SYLLABIC STRUCTURE IN CAIRO COLLOQUIAL [1]

(i)   CV : open short. C + *i*, *a*, or *u*.

    (*a*) **fíhim nízil**

    (*b*) **ẓálamu ʕitláxam ḍárabit**

    (*c*) **ʕindáhaʃu**   (*cvc–cv–cv–cv*)

(ii)   CVV : open medium. C + *i*, *a*, or *u*, and the prosody of vowel length indicated by doubling the vowel, hence VV—the first V may be considered the symbol of one of the three members of the vowel system and the second the mark of the prosody of length. Alternatively **y** and **w** may be used instead of the second **i** or **u**.

[1] See also Ibrahim Anis, *The Grammatical Characteristics of the Spoken Arabic of Egypt*. (Thesis for the Ph.D. degree, 1941. University of London Library.) ţ ḍ ş ẓ = ṱ ḏ ş ẕ (I.P.A.)

(a) fáahim fúulah nóobah*
(b) muʃiibah ginéenah* misóogar*
(c) ʃiʃtaddéenah* (cvc–cvc–cvv–cvc)
(d) ʃistafáad náahum

(iii) CVC : closed medium. C + i, a, or u.

(a) ʃáfham dúrguh
(b) yistáfhim duxúlhum
(c) miʃtalbáxha (cvc–cvc ovo ov)

(iv) CVVC : closed long. C + i, a, or u and the prosody of
vowel length—see under (ii).

(a) naam ɡuum ziid
baat ʃiil xoof *
(b) kitáab yiʃíil yiɡúum
(c) ʃistafáad yistafíid yifhamúuh
(d) ʃistalbaxnáah tistálbaxíih

(v) CVCC : closed long. C + i, a, or u and the prosody of
consonant length in final position only, the
occurrence of two consecutive consonants in
final position.

(a) ʃadd bint
(b) ɖarábt yimúrr
(c) ʃistaɡádd yistaɡídd (cvc–cv–cvcc)

In the above words the prominent is marked by an accent.
This is, however, not necessary since prominence can be stated
in rules without exception, given the above analysis of syllabic
structure.

Though there are five types of syllable, they divide into
three quantities ; short, medium, and long. When vowel
length is referred to, it must be differentiated from syllabic
quantity—vowels can be short or long only. The two prosodies
for vowels contribute to the three prosodies for syllables.

* *The special case of* ee *and* oo.

In most cases Colloquial ee and oo correspond to Classical
ay and *aw*, often described as diphthongs. There are advantages, however, in regarding *y* and *w* as terms of a prosodic

system, functioning as such in the syllabic structure of the word. **xawf** and **xoof** are thus both closed long, though *cvwc* is replaced by *cvvc*. Similarly **gináynah** and **ginéenah**, **náy** and **née** are both medium, one with *y*-prosody and one with vowel length. Though the syllabic quantities are equivalent, the syllabic structure is different. Two more vowel qualities must be added to the vowel system, **e** and **o**, different from the other three in that the vowel quality is prosodically bound and is always long.

There are other interesting cases in which, quite similarly, colloquial C + **ee** or **oo** with the prosody of length in the vowel in such words as **geet** or **ʃuum**, correspond to equivalent classical monosyllables **jiʕt**, **ʃuʕm**. The phonematic constituents of the pairs of corresponding words are different, but the prosody of equipollent quantity is maintained. Many such examples could be quoted including some in which the prosodic function of ʕ (glottal stop) and " **y** " are equivalent.

Classical.		*Cairo Colloquial.*
δiʕb		diib
qaraʕt	[Cyrenaican : **garayt**]	ʕareet
faʕs		faas
daaʕim		daayim
naaʕim		naayim
maaʕil		maayil
ɖaraaʕib		ɖaraayib

The prosodic features of the word in Cairo colloquial are the following :—

In any word there is usually such an interrelation of syllables that one of them is more prominent than the rest by nature of its prosodies of strength, quantity, and tone, and this prominent syllable may be regarded as the nucleus of the group of syllables forming the word. The prominent syllable is a function of the whole word or piece structure.

Naturally therefore, the prosodic features of a word include :—

1. The number of syllables.
2. The nature of the syllables—open or closed.
3. The syllabic quantities.
4. The sequence of syllables ⎫ [radicals and flexional
5. The sequence of consonants ⎬ elements separately
6. The sequence of vowels ⎭ treated.]
7. The position, nature, and quantity of the prominent.
8. The dark or clear qualities of the syllables.

There is a sort of vowel harmony and perhaps consonant harmony, also involving the so-called emphatic or dark consonants.

I think it will be found that word-analysis in Arabic can be more clearly stated if we emphasize the syntagmatic study of the word complex as it holds together, rather than the paradigmatic study of ranges of possible sound substitutions upon which a detailed phonematic study would be based. Not that such phonematic studies are to be neglected. On the contrary, they are the basis for the syntagmatic prosodic study I am here suggesting. In stating the structure of Arabic words, the prosodic systems will be found weightier than the phonematic. The same may be true of the Sino-Tibetan languages and the West African tone languages.

Such common phenomena as elision, liaison, anaptyxis, the use of so-called " cushion " consonants or " sounds for euphony ", are involved in this study of prosodies. These devices of explanation begin to make sense when prosodic structure is approached as a system of syntagmatic relations.

Speaking quite generally of the relations of consonants and vowels to prosodic or syllabic structure, we must first be prepared to enumerate the consonants and vowels of any particular language for that language, and not rely on any general definitions of vowel and consonant universally applicable. Secondly, we must be prepared to find almost any sound having syllabic value. It is not implied that general categories such

as vowel, consonant, liquid, are not valid. They are perhaps
in general linguistics. But since syllabic structure must be
studied in particular language systems, and within the words
of these systems, the consonants and vowels of the systems
must also be particular to that language and determined by
its phonological structure.

Let us now turn to certain general categories or types of
sound which appear to crop up repeatedly in syllabic analysis.
These are the weak, neutral, or "minimal" vowel, the glottal
stop or "maximum" consonant, aitch or the pulmonic
onset—all of which deserve the general name of laryngals.
Next there are such sounds as ħ and ʕ characteristic of the
Semitic group of languages which may also be grouped with
"laryngals" and perhaps the back ɣ. Then the liquids and
semi-vowels l, r, n (and other nasals), y and w.

Not that prosodic markers are limited to the above types
of "sound". Almost any type of "sound" may have prosodic
function, and the same "sound" may have to be noticed
both as a consonant or vowel unit and as a prosody.

First, the neutral vowel in English. It must be remembered
that the qualities of this vowel do not yield in distinctness to
any other vowel quality. The term neutral suits it in English,
since it is in fact neutral to the phonematic system of vowels
in Southern English. It is closely bound up with the prosodies
of English words and word junctions. Unlike the phonematic
units, it does not bear any strong stress. Its occurrence
marks a weak syllable including weak forms such as wəz,
kən, ə.

Owing to the distribution of stress and length in Southern
English words, it is often final in junction with a following
consonant initial. Two of the commonest words in the
language, *the* and *a*, require a number of prosodic realizations
determined by junction and stress, ðə, ði, 'ðiy, ə, ən, 'ey, æn.
In other positions, too, the neutral vowel often, though
by no means always, marks an etymological junction or is
required by the prosodies of word formation, especially the
formation of derivatives. The distribution of the neutral vowel

in English from this point of view would make an interesting study. The prosodic nature of ə is further illustrated by the necessity of considering it in connection with other prosodies such as the so-called " intrusive " r, the " linking " r, the glottal stop, aitch, and even w and y. Examples: *vanilla ice, law and order, cre'ation, behind, pa and ma, to earn, to ooze, secretary, behave, without money*. The occurrence of Southern English diphthongs in junctions is a good illustration of the value of prosodic treatment, e.g. :—

(i) The so-called " centring " diphthongs, iə(r), eə(r), ɔə(r), uə(r).

(ii) What may be termed the " y " diphthongs, iy[1], ey, ay, oy.

(iii) The " w " diphthongs uw, ow, aw.

It may be noted that e, æ, ɔ do not occur finally or in similar junctions, and that ɔ:, a:, and ə: all involve prosodic r.

Internal junctions are of great importance in this connection since the verb *bear* must take *-ing* and *-er*, and *run* leads to *runner up*. Can the r of *bearing* be said to be " intrusive " in Southern English ? As a prosodic feature along with ə and in other contexts with the glottal stop, aitch and prosodic y and w, it takes its place in the prosodic system of the language. In certain of its prosodic functions the neutral vowel might be described temporarily as a pro-syllable. However obscure or neutral or unstressed, it is essential in *a bitter for me* to distinguish it from *a bit for me*. In contemporary Southern English many " sounds "[2] may be pro-syllabic, e.g. tsn̩'apl, tstuw'mʌtʃ, sekr̩tri or sekətri, s'main, s'truw. Even if *'s true* and *strew* should happen to be homophonous, the two structures are different : c'cvw and 'cvw. " Linking " and " separating " are both phenomena of junction to be considered as prosodies. In such a German phrase as ʔin ʔeinem ʔalten 'Buch, the glottal stop is a

---

[1] It is, I think, an advantage from this point of view to regard English so-called long *i* : and *u* : as *y*-closing or *w*-closing diphthongs and emphasize the closing termination by writing with Sweet *ij* or *iy*, and *uw*.

[2] In the general phonetic sense, not in the phonematic sense.

junction prosody. I suppose Danish is the best European
language in which to study the glottal stop from the prosodic
point of view.[1] Unfortunately, I am not on phonetic speaking
terms with Danish and can only report. The Danish glottal
stop is in a sense parallel with tonal prosodies in other
Scandinavian languages. It occurs chiefly with sounds said
to be originally long, and in final position only in stressed
syllables. If the word in question loses its stress for rhythmical
or other reasons, it also loses the glottal stop. It is therefore
best considered prosodically as a feature of syllabic structure
and word formation. The glottal stop is a feature of monosyllables, but when such elements add flexions or enter compounds, the glottal stop may be lost. In studying the glottal
stop in Danish, the phonematic systems are not directly
relevant, but rather the syllabic structure of dissyllabic and
polysyllabic words and compounds. In Yorkshire dialects
interesting forms like ˈfɔʔti occur. Note however ˈfɔwər
and ˈfɔwəˈtiyn. A central vowel unit occurs in stressed
positions in these dialects, e.g. ˈθəʔti, ˈθəʔˈtiyn.

There may even be traces of a prosodic glottal stop in
such phrases as t ˈθədʔˈdɛɛ, t ˈθədʔˈtaym. Junctions of
the definite article with stressed words having initial t or
d are of interest, e.g. ɔntʔˈtɛɛbl, itʔˈtram, tətʔˈtɛytʃə,
fətʔˈdɔktə, witʔˈtawil. These are quite different
junctions from those in ˈgud ˈdɛɛ or ˈbad ˈtaym. Compare
also Yorkshire trɛɛn (cvvc) tˈrɛɛn (cˈcvvc), tətˈʃɔp, tə ˈtʃɔp,
and especially witʔˈtak (with the tack) and wid ˈtak (weˈd
take), also witəˈtak (wilt thou take). In London one hears
ˈθəːʔˈtsiyn and ˈθəːtˈʔiyn, where the two glottal stops
have somewhat different prosodic functions.

The glottal stop as a release for intervocalic plosives is
common in Cockney, and is a medial or internal prosody
contrasting with aspiration, affrication, or unreleased glottal
stop in initial or final positions. Such pronunciations as ˈkɔpʔə,

---

[1] See Sweet, " On Danish Pronunciation " (1873), in *Collected Papers*,
p. 345, in which he makes a prosodic comparison with Greek accents.
(On p. 348 he uses the term " tonology ".)

'sapʔə, 'wintʔə, dʒampʔə are quite common. I would like
to submit the following note of an actual bit of conversation
between two Cockneys, for prosodic examination : i 'ʔoːʔ ʔə
'ʔɛv iʔ 'ʔoːf, baʔ i "wawᷞ ʔɛv iʔ oːf.

I have already suggested the *y* and *w* prosodies of English,
including their effect on the length prosody of the diphthongs
and their function in junctions when final. After all, human
beings do not neglect the use of broad simple contrasts when
they can combine these with many other differentiations and
in that way multiply phonetic means of differentiation. In
the Sino-Tibetan group of languages the *y* and *w* element is
found in a large number of syllables—there are many more
y and *w* syllables than, say, *b* or *d* or *a* syllables. In the many
Roman notations used for Chinese, these two elements are
variously represented and are sometimes regarded as members
of the paradigm of initials, but, generally as members of the
paradigm of finals. They can be classified with either, or can
be simply regarded as syllabic features. Sounds of the **y** or **w**
type, known as semi-vowels or consonantal vowels, often have
the syllable-marking function especially in initial and intervocalic position. In Sanskrit and the modern languages
affiliated to it, it is clear that prosodic *y* and *v* must be kept
distinct from similar " sounds " in the phonematic systems.
The verbal forms **aya, laya, bənaya** in Hindustani are not
phonematically irregular, but with the *y* prosody are regular
formations from **a-na, la-na,** and **bəna-na**. In Tamil and other
Dravidian languages *y* and *v* prosodies are common, as markers
of initials, for example, in such Tamil words as **(y)enna,
(y)evan, (y)eetu, (v)oor, (v)oolai, (v)ooṭṭu**. However, the prosodies of the Dravidian languages present complicated
problems owing to their mixed character.

Other sounds of this semi-vowel nature which lend themselves to prosodic function are **r** and **l**, and these often correspond or interchange with *y* or *w* types of element both in
Indo-European and Sino-Tibetan languages. Elements
such as these have, in some languages, such pro-syllabic or
syllable-marking functions that I think they might be better

classified with the syntagmatic prosodies rather than with the overall paradigmatic vowel and consonant systems. Studies of these problems in Indo-European and Sino-Tibetan languages are equally interesting.

The rough and smooth breathings are treated as prosodies or accentual elements in the writing of Greek. It is true that, as with accents in other languages, the rough breathing may imply the omission of a sound, often s, or affect the quality and nature of the preceding final consonants in junction. " h " in French is similarly connected with junction and elision. Even in English, though it has phonematic value in such paradigms as *eating, heating; eels, heels; ear, hear; ill, hill; owl, howl; art, heart; arming, harming; anchoring, hankering; airy, hairy; arrow, Harrow;* and many others, it is an *initial signal* in stressed syllables of full words having no weak forms. English h is a special study in weak forms, and in all these respects is perhaps also to be considered as one of the elements having special functions, which I have termed prosodic. In English dialects phonematic " h " (if there is such a thing), disappears, but prosodic " h " is sometimes introduced by mixing up its function with the glottal stop. I have long felt that the aitchiness, aitchification, or breathi-ness of sounds and syllables, and similarly their creakiness or " glottalization " are more often than not features of the whole syllable or set of syllables. Indeed, in some of the Sino-Tibetan languages, breathiness or creakiness or " glottaliza-tion " are characteristic of prosodic features called tones. In a recent article, Mr. J. Carnochan [1] has a few examples of aspiration and nasalization in Igbo as syntagmatic features of a whole word, rather like vowel harmony, which is prosodic.

Apart from the fact that nasals such as m, n, η are often sonants—that is to say, have syllabic function—they are also quite frequently initial or final signals, and in Bantu languages such signals have essentially a syntagmatic or syllable or word-grouping function. In a restricted prosodic sense, they can be compared with the glottal stop in German.

[1] J. Carnochan, *Bulletin of the School of Oriental and African Studies* (1948).

In bringing certain types of speech sound into consideration of the prosodies, I have so far noticed the neutral or weak vowel, the minimal vowel, which often becomes zero; the glottal stop, the maximal consonant which unreleased is zero sound; aitch, the pulmonic onset, and the liquids and nasals. The first two, I suggest, deserve the name of laryngals, and perhaps h. There remain such sounds as ħ, ʕ, ɣ, and χ, characteristic of the Semitic group of languages. These sounds are certainly phonematic in Classical Arabic. But in the dialects they are often replaced in cognate words by the prosody of length in change of vowel quality, generally more open than that of the measure of comparison.

When words containing these sounds are borrowed from Arabic by speakers of non-Semitic languages, they are usually similarly replaced by elements of a prosodic nature, often with changes of quality in the vowels of the corresponding syllable.

Hindustani and Panjabi provide interesting examples of phonematic units in one dialect or style being represented in another by prosodies. Instances of interchanges in cognates between phonematic units of the vowel system and units of the consonant system are common, and examples and suggestions have been offered of interchanges and correspondences between phonematic units of both kinds and prosodies. The following table provides broad transcriptions to illustrate these principles.

TABLE I
h

Hindustani, Eastern, careful.	Hindustani, Western, quick.	Panjabi, (Gujranwala).
pəhyle	pəyhle	pêylle
bəhwt	bəwht	bâwt
pəhwŋcna	pəwhŋcna	pâwŋc
bhəi		ḅəi
kər rəha həy	kərrahəyh	
rəhta (ræhta)		rêynda

In **pǝhyle** we have a three-syllable word in which **h** is phonematic (*cvcvcv*). In **pǝyhle** there are two syllables by a sort of coalescence in which **ǝyh** indicates an open " h "-coloured or breathy vowel of the æ-type (*cvhcv*). Similarly in the phrase **bǝhwt‿ǝccha** there are four syllables (*cvcvc‿vccv*), in **bǝwht‿ǝccha** three, the vowel in the first of which is *open* back and " h "- coloured (*cvhcvccv*).

In Panjabi **pâylle** the open vowel carries a compound high falling tone and the structure is prosodically quite different (*ĉvccv*) which, I think, is equipollent with *cvhcv* (**pǝyhle**). **bâwt** similarly is *ĉvc*, reduced to a monosyllable with initial and final consonant and a tonal prosody. In Hindustani verbal forms like **rǝhna, rǝhta ; kǝhna, kǝhta** ; the **ǝ** vowel in the h-coloured syllable immediately followed by a consonant is open with a retracted æ-like quality. **yɪh** is realized as **ye, vwh** as **vo**, in both of which there is a similar lowering and potential lengthening in emphasis.

TABLE II

ARABIC ξ IN URDU LOAN-WORDS

Spelling Transliterated.	Transcription of Realization in Speech.
mǝξlum	malum
bǝξd	bad
dǝfξ	dǝfa
mǝnξ	mǝna
mǝξni	mǝani, mani
ystξmal	ystemal

In all these cases the vowel realized is open and fairly long. In Maltese, words which in Arabic have **h** and which still retain **h** in the spelling are pronounced long with retracted quality, e.g. **he, hi, ho, eh, ehe,** as in **fehem, fehmu, sehem, sehmek, qalbhom.** These long vowels may be unstressed. Similarly all the **gh** spellings (transliterated **ɣ**) are realized as long slightly pharyngalized vowels which may also occur in unstressed positions, which is not possible with vowels other than those with the Semitic h and gĥ spellings. E.g. ɣa, aɣ, aɣa, ɣo, oɣ, oɣo, ɣi (ɣey), ɣe, ɣu (ɣəw) in such words as gĥidt, gĥúda magĥmul, bálagĥ. In the phrase balagĥ balgĥa (he swallowed a mouthful) the two forms are pronounced alike with final long a (for form, cf. ĥataf ĥatfa, he snatched). h and gĥ are often realized in spoken Maltese as a prosody of length.

In Turkish the Arabic ع in loan-words is often realized as a prosody of length in such pronunciations as fiil (*verb*, *act*), saat (*hour*), and similarly Arabic ɣ, in iblaa (*communicate*), and Turkish ğ in uultu (*tumult*). We are reminded again of Arabic ع which is also realized as a prosody of length in the colloquials, e.g. Classical jiʕt is paralleled by geet in Cairo, jeet in Iraqi, and ʒiit in Cyrenaican Sa'adi. In Cairo and Iraqi the prosody of length is applied to an opener vowel than in Classical, but this is not always the case.

The study of prosodic structures has bearing on all phonological studies of loan-words, and also on the operation of grammatical processes on basic material in any language. Taking the last-mentioned first, elision or anaptyxis in modern Cairo colloquial are prosodically necessary in such cases as the following : misíkt + ni = misiktíni, where the anaptyctic i is required to avoid the junction of three consonants consecutively which is an impossible pattern. The prominence then falls on the anaptyctic vowel by rule. Pieces such as bint + fariid are realized as bintifaríid. With the vowels i and u, elision is possible within required patterns, e.g. : ɣindíhiʃ + u = ɣindihʃu, titlíxim + i = titlíxmi, but not with a, ʕitlaxam + it = ʕitlaxamit.

Amusing illustrations of the effect of prosodic patterns on word-borrowing are provided by loan-words from English in Indian and African languages and in Japanese. Prosodic anaptyxis produces səkuul in Panjabi and prothesis iskuul in Hindi or Urdu. By similar processes səteʃən and isteʃən are created for *station*. In Hausa *screw-driver* is naturalized as sukuru direba. Treating skr and dr as initial phonematic

units, English *screw-driver* has the structure 'cvw-cvycə, the
prosodies of which Hausa could not realize, hence *cvcvcv-
cvcvcv*, a totally different structure which I have carefully
expressed in non-phonematic notation, to emphasize the fallacy
of saying Hausa speakers cannot pronounce the " sounds ",
and to point to the value of studying prosodic structure by a
different set of abstractions from those appropriate to phonematic structure. It is not implied that there is one all-over
prosodic system for any given language. A loan-word may
bring with it a new pattern suited to its class or type, as in
English borrowings from French, both nominals and verbals.
When completely naturalized the prosodic system of the type
or class of word in the borrowing language is dominant.
In Japanese strange prosodic transformations take place,
e.g. **bisuketto** (biscuit), **kiromeetoru**, **kiroguramu**, **supittohwaia**,
messaasyumitto, **arupen-suttoku**, **biheebiyarisuto**, **doriburusuru**
(to dribble).

Linguists have always realized the importance of the
general attributes of stress, length, tone, and syllabic structure,
and such considerations have frequently been epoch-making
in the history of linguistics. Generally speaking, however,
the general attributes have been closely associated with the
traditional historical study of sound-change, which, in my
terminology, has been chiefly phonematic. I suggest that the
study of the prosodies by means of ad hoc categories and at
a different level of abstraction from the systematic phonematic
study of vowels and consonants, may enable us to take a big
step forward in the understanding of synthesis. This approach
has the great merit of building on the piece or sentence as the
primary datum. The theory I have put forward may in the
future throw light on the subjct of Ablaut which, in spite of
the scholarship expended on it in the nineteenth century from
Grimm to Brugmann, still remains a vexed question and unrelated to spoken language. I venture to hope that some of the
notions I have suggested may be of value to those who are
discussing laryngals in Indo-European, and even to those
engaged in field work on hitherto unwritten languages. The

monosystemic analysis based on a paradigmatic technique of oppositions and phonemes with allophones has reached, even overstepped, its limits ! The time has come to try fresh hypotheses of a polysystemic character. The suggested approach will not make phonological problems appear easier or oversimplify them. It may make the highly complex patterns of language clearer both in descriptive and historical linguistics. The phonological structure of the sentence and the words which comprise it are to be expressed as a plurality of systems of interrelated phonematic and prosodic categories. Such systems and categories are not necessarily linear and certainly cannot bear direct relations to successive fractions or segments of the time-track of instances of speech. By their very nature they are abstractions from such time-track items. Their order and interrelations are not chronological.

An example is given below of the new approach in sentence phonetics and phonology [1] in which the syntagmatic prosodies are indicated in the upper stave and the phonematic structure in the lower stave, with a combination text between. Stress is marked with the intonation indicated.

Prosodies	$\{$	
		cy vcə vcə cəz_mvtʃ_bvcə vy cvcc
		ðy ʌðə [2] ɔfə wəz mʌtʃ betə ay θiŋk
Phonematic Structure	$\{$	ð—ʌð—ɔf—w–z mʌtʃ bet—a—θiŋk
Prosodies	$\{$	
		cvy hvz_ʃvy əccvccic cvc cvc
		way hæz ʃiy əkseptid ðis wʌn

[1] For a fuller illustration of the scope of sentence phonology and its possible applications, see Eugénie Henderson's *Prosodies in Siamese.* (1949).

[2] The use of ə as a prosodic symbol in such final contexts implies potential r or ʔ according to the nature of the junction.

Phonematic
Structure   { wa   æz ʃi   ksept d ðis wʌn

It is already clear that in cognate languages what is a
phonematic constituent in one may be a prosody in another,
and that in the history of any given language sounds and
prosodies interchange with one another. In the main, however, the prosodies of the sentence and the word tend to be
dominant.

To say the prosodies may be regarded as dominant is to
emphasize the phonetics and phonology of synthesis. It accords
with the view that syntax is the dominant discipline in grammar and also with the findings of recent American research
in acoustics. The interpenetration of consonants and vowels,
the overlap of so-called segments, and of such layers as voice,
nasalization and aspiration, in utterance, are commonplaces
of phonetics. On the perception side, it is improbable that we
listen to auditory fractions corresponding to uni-directional
phonematic units in any linear sense.

Whatever units we may find in analysis, must be closely
related to the whole utterance, and that is achieved by
systematic statement of the prosodies. In the perception of
speech by the listener whatever units there may be are
prosodically reintegrated. We speak prosodies and we listen
to them.

2

PROSODIES IN SIAMESE
A STUDY IN SYNTHESIS

by EUGÉNIE J. A. HENDERSON

The term "prosodic feature" is applied in this paper to certain properties of modern spoken Siamese which may be regarded as abstractions apart from the consonant and vowel systems.[1] Such abstractions may be made at the syllable, word, or sentence level. Syllable prosodies include tone, quantity, and those properties which mark the beginning or end of a syllable. Word prosodies include tonal and quantitative features, stress, and the means whereby syllable is linked with syllable. Sentence prosodies include sentence tone, and the means used to mark the beginnings and ends of phrases and sentences, and to connect phrase with phrase or sentence with sentence. Italic type is used to show the consonant and vowel units, and to name the prosodies, while heavy roman is used for phonetic transcription in general terms.

The phonetic structure of Siamese is based primarily upon the monosyllable. A high proportion of words is monosyllabic, and all polysyllables may be pronounced as a succession of monosyllables, each conforming in structure to the pattern appropriate to monosyllables uttered in isolation. I have called this style of speech the "isolative style". It is that commonly used for monosyllabic words and for the slow, deliberate pronunciation of polysyllables, and is that shown in dictionaries.[2] The structure of the syllable, which is also that of the monosyllabic word, is determined by reference to the isolative style only. A study of words of more than one syllable shows that in connected speech, or what may be called the "combinative style", the syllable structure proper to the isolative style is modified in some degree. This degree of modification is a prosodic feature, since it characterises a connected group, whether compound word, polysyllable, or phrase. Such prosodies are appropriate to the combinative style, and clearly cannot be a feature of the isolative style. In addition to "isolative style" and "combinative style", it is sometimes necessary when examining certain

---

[1] See *Sounds and Prosodies*, by J. R. Firth, in the 1948 volume of the Transactions of the Philological Society of Great Britain.

[2] *e.g.*, McFarland's *Thai-English Dictionary*, to which I am indebted for much linguistic material, and the ปทานุกรม .

Source: E. J. A. Henderson, "Prosodies in Siamese", *Asia Major* (New Series) 1 (1949). 189–215. Reprinted by permission of Lund Humphries and the author.

word and sentence prosodies to take into account yet another style, which I have called "rapid combinative style".

TYPES OF CONSONANT SOUND

The types of consonant sound which may be heard at the beginning of a syllable may be represented in general phonetic terms, as follows:—

	Glottal and Pre-Glottal	Velar	Alveolar and Alveolo-Palatal	Labial
Voiceless Plosive	ʔ	k	t	p
,, Aspirated Plosive		kh	th	ph
Voiced Plosive			d	b
Voiceless Affricate			tɕ	
,, Aspirated Affricate			tɕh (or ɕh)	
,, Fricative	h		s	f
Nasal		ŋ	n	m
Semi-vowel		(w)	l, r, j (often dj)*	w

The following consonant clusters are also heard initially: **kr, kl, kw, khr, khl, khw, tr, pr, pl, phr, phl.**

The types of consonant sound which may be heard at the end of a syllable are as follows:—

	Glottal	Velar	Alveolar	Labial
Stop (without voice or plosion) ..	ʔ′	k′	t′	p′
Nasal		ŋ	n	m

It will be seen that *plosion, aspiration, affrication, friction, voice* (except when accompanied by nasality), and the presence of the sounds **r** or **l**, are properties of the syllable initial only, and mark the beginning of a syllable whenever they occur. These features may, therefore, be regarded as belonging to the prosodic system, while what is common to both syllable parts, initial and final, may be postulated as the consonant system.

THE CONSONANT SYSTEM

The units of this consonant system will be represented by the symbols k, t; p, η, n, m, ζ,[3] the last being used to indicate *zero* consonant unit. The

---

[3] The symbol ζ has been chosen as being less likely to cause confusion than Z or O.

* [I now believe that the sound I heard preceding the *j* was not *d* but a weak glottal stop (see "Marginalia to Siamese Phonetic Studies", *DЯ*, 419). If I had recognized this at the time, I should almost certainly have modified the presentation offered in this paper.—Author 1968]

glottal plosive is regarded as being the realization of ζ accompanied by *plosion*. Initial l and **r** are held to be realizations of ζ accompanied by prosodic features which may, for lack of better terms, be called *lateralization* and *rhotacization*. Initial **j** is not regarded as the realization of ζ with *yotization*, since it has been found convenient to postulate *yotization* as a feature of the syllable as a whole. Initial **j**, which is often pronounced with alveolo-palatal closure, is treated as the phonetic expression of *t* accompanied by *voice* and *affrication*. The **w**-element of **kw** and **khw** is a feature of the syllable rather than of the initial since these consonant clusters are never heard before the back vowels **u**, **o**, **ɔ**, **ɯ**, and **ɤ**. This syllabic feature, which is distinct from what is in this paper regarded as *labio-velarization* of the syllable,[4] may be termed *labialization*, and is restricted to syllables beginning with the consonant unit *k*. Initial *w* cannot be regarded as a feature of the syllable as a whole, since it is heard before all vowels except **ɯ**.[5] I have regarded it as a prosody of syllable beginning, restricted to syllables beginning with zero consonant unit.[6] The distribution among the consonant units of the prosodies of syllable-beginning and syllable-ending is set out in detail when the prosodies of the monosyllable are dealt with.

TYPES OF VOWEL SOUND

The vowel sounds of Siamese may be represented in general phonetic terms, as follows:—

Front		Back			
		Unrounded		Rounded	
Long	Short	Long	Short	Long	Short
iː	i	ɯː	ɯ	uː	u
eː	e	ɤː	ɤ	oː	o
ɛː	ɛ	aː	a	ɔː	ɔ
iə		ɯə		uə	

The front vowels may be heard as the starting point of closing diphthongs moving towards a close back vowel position, which may be represented **iu**, **eu**, **eːu**, **ɛu**, **ɛːu**, **iəu**.

---

[4] See page 30.

[5] McFarland's Dictionary records one instance only, หวือ /wɯː, an onomatope, "from the sound of chips or splinters flying past the ear".

[6] There would be some gain in clarity of exposition if two additional consonant units, *y* and *w*, could be postulated to account for initial **j** and **w** and for the final elements of the closing diphthongs described on pp. 29–30. The limited vowel alternance that would obtain before final *y* and *w*, however, does not tally with what is observed before other final consonant units, and points to some other interpretation of the syllables concerned (see page 30).

The vowels aː and a may be heard as the starting point of closing diphthongs moving towards either a close back or a close front vowel position, which may be represented aːi, ai, aːu, au.

The remaining back vowels may be heard as the starting point of closing diphthongs moving towards a close front vowel position, which may be represented ɤi, ui, oi, ɔi, ɯəi, and uəi.

This distribution clearly suggests the treatment of the i- and u-elements of these diphthongs as prosodic features of the syllable as a whole. Syllables characterized by the i-element are described in this paper as yotized, and those characterized by the u-element as labio-velarized.

Vowel quantity, which is closely bound up with word tone, is also abstracted as a prosodic feature at the syllable level.

The Vowel System

The vowel units postulated for this study are, therefore: *i, e, ε, a, ɯ, ɤ, u, o, ɔ, iə, uə, ɯə.*

These vowel units are of three types, which we may call *front, back,* and *mid,* according to whether they may combine with yotization or labio-velarization of the syllable. Front vowel units, which may form part of a labio-velarized syllable, are *i, e, ε,* and *iə.* Back vowel units, which may form part of a yotized syllable, are *u, uə, o, ɔ, ɯ,*[7] and *ɯə.* The mid vowel unit *a* may form part of both yotized and labio-velarized syllables.[8]

The Structure of Monosyllables

As has been stated above, the prosodic features of the syllable uttered in isolation are shared by single monosyllabic words. These features may be considered in three groups:—

(*a*) prosodies of syllable-beginning;
(*b*) prosodies of syllable-ending;
(*c*) prosodies of the syllable as a whole.

(*a*) It has already been observed that the presence of one or more of the following properties is always the signal of the initiation of a syllable: *plosion, aspiration, voice* (except with nasality), *affrication, friction, lateralization, rhotacization,* and *labialization* (except with velarity). These properties may accompany *k, t, p* or *ʐ* and may be grouped in fifteen

---

[7] uːi does not occur in Siamese. *uː* is, however, assumed to be of the same type as *ɯə* by analogy with *u, uə; i, iə.*

[8] It is possible to reduce the number of vowel units by abstracting such properties as *closeness,* of which there might be said to be three degrees, *roundedness, unroundedness, etc.* These properties would not, however, be features of the syllable but of the vowel alternance only, and it has not, therefore, being thought useful to make such abstractions in this study.

different ways. The possible applications of these fifteen groups are shown below:—

	Initial Prosody or Group of Prosodies					Consonant Units Affected			
(1)	Plosion	..	..	..	..	k	t	p	ζ
(2)	Plosion with *lateralization*		..	..	k		p		
(3)	Plosion with *rhotacization*		..	..	k	t	p		
(4)	Plosion with *aspiration*		..	..	k	t	p		
(5)	,,	,,	and *lateralization*		k		p		
(6)	,,	,,	and *rhotacization*		k		p		
(7)	Plosion with *voice*		..	..	..	t	p		
(8)	*Affrication*		..	..	..	..	t		
(9)	*Affrication* with *aspiration*		..	..		t		
(10)	*Affrication* with *voice*		..	..	..	t		
(11)	*Friction*	..	..	..	..	..	t	p	
(12)	*Aspiration*		..	..	..	..			ζ
(13)	*Lateralization*		..	..	..	..			ζ
(14)	*Rhotacization*		..	..	..	..			ζ
(15)	*Labialization*		..	..	..	..			ζ

It will be noted that ζ is never accompanied by more than one prosodic feature, and that *affrication* is only combined with *t*.

(b) *Closure without plosion* is a prosodic feature marking the end of a syllable. When the final consonant is ζ, the presence or absence of such closure is closely linked with syllable prosodies. If closure is present, its realization is glottal.

(c) The prosodies of the syllable as a whole are *tone, quantity, labialization, labiovelarization,* and *yotization*.[9] There is a maximum of five differentiating tone units,[10] whose phonetic expression may be described as (1) mid-level, as in -kha: "to dangle"; (2) low level, as in ₋kha: "Kha"; (3) falling, as in \kha: "price"; (4) high rise-fall[11], as in ^kha: "to trade," (hereafter called for brevity the "acute" tone); and (5) rising, as in /kha: "leg". These tone units may henceforth be referred to by number.

---

[9] Only prosodies of the syllable in isolation are under discussion here. A syllable in a combinative context may be characterized by other features (see pages 35, 40).

[10] For tone of syllables in combinative contexts, see pages 35, 37, 39.

[11] On short syllables closed by a stop the acute tone comprises a short high rise or a short high-level pitch.

The characteristics of a long syllable are:—
   (1)   length of vowel;
   (2)   the realization of final ζ always as phonetic zero;
   (3)   the reduction of the possible tone alternance to tones 2 and 3
         only, when the final consonant unit is accompanied by
         closure without plosion.[12]

The characteristics of a short syllable are:—
   (1)   shortness of vowel;
   (2)   the realization of final ζ as a glottal stop except in yotized
         and labiovelarized syllables;
   (3)   the reduction of the possible tone alternance to tones 2 and
         4 only, when the final consonant is accompanied by closure
         without plosion.

The great majority of syllables containing the vowel units *iə*, *uə*, and
ɯə exhibit the last two characteristics ascribed to long syllables, and such
syllables are thus held to be long. There are, however, a few words such as
ᴧkhiəʔ, -phluəʔ, -tɕhuəʔ, -phuəʔ which exhibit the last two characteristics proper to short syllables. The last three examples cited above are,
however, onomatopes. The first example is a botanical name, and may be
of foreign origin. A similar phonetic construction is found in another
botanical name, ᴧkiəʔ (-plɯək -baːŋ). I suggest that shortness in syllables
of this pattern may be a special feature proper to onomatopes and certain
foreign words, and not of general application. The special prosodies
appropriate to these two classes of word are discussed later in this study.[13]

It is of some interest to note that quantity is extremely rarely of lexical
significance in syllables containing the vowel units *e*, *ɛ*, or *ɔ*, except where
these precede ζ. The incidence of e, eː, ɛ, ɛː, ɔ, and ɔː appears to correlate
with tone to some degree, the acute and mid-level tones tending to be
combined with vowel length, while with the falling tone there is some
preference for the short series. Systematic examination of the recorded
instances also showed that while syllables ending with the phonetic pattern
long close vowel + stop are of fairly frequent occurrence, there is a
remarkable paucity of words or syllables ending in iːm, iːn, uːm, uːn,
uːŋ. No instances at all were found of iːŋ, only two of iːm, and four of
uːŋ. Examples of iːn, uːn, and uːm were more plentiful, but all occurred
in borrowed words. Historical study of all instances of final complexes **of**
the **close vowel + nasal** type might show that length in such syllables

---

   [12] Long syllables with final ζ and *tone* 4 or 5 are often pronounced with some
final glottal closure. This is, however, a syllabic feature, and is distinct from the
glottal stop, which is frequently the realization in short syllables of final ζ accompanied
by the syllable-ending prosody *closure without plosion*.
   [13] See page 33.

must be interpreted as a term in a special prosodic system appropriate to certain borrowed and "foreign" words.

No such clear relation exists between the syllable initial and the distribution of tone and quantity as between the final complex and these features.[14] There appears to be no correlation between the syllable initial and quantity, but there are indications that there may be some correlation between certain syllable initials and tone. It is rare for a syllable beginning with a consonant unit accompanied by *plosion* only, or by *plosion* with *voice*, or *plosion* with *affrication* to be characterized by either *tone* 4 or *tone* 5. Of those syllables that are so characterized, a high proportion are borrowed words, and others are onomatopes.[15] In others again, the incidence of either of these tone units is to be regarded as the result of sentence tone, and is dealt with in its proper place as a prosody of the sentence.[16]

THE PROSODIC STRUCTURE OF ONOMATOPES AND CERTAIN FOREIGN WORDS

There are certain attributes common to some onomatopes, and to certain monosyllabic foreign words, usually of English origin, which do not conform to the pattern prescribed above for the structure of monosyllables. These properties may be described as "irregular" groupings of *tone, quantity*, and *consonant units*. They serve to single out the onomatope or foreign word from the surrounding words of "regular" pattern in much the same way as English printers may use italic type to show a foreign word, or an exclamation mark to single out an onomatope.

Examples of a possibly "irregular" combination of shortness and certain vowel units have already been commented upon in the discussion of the regular distribution of tone and quantity,[17] and will not be enlarged upon here. Examples of other onomatopes and foreign words are set out below with an indication of the way in which they are "irregular" when their structure is compared with that of the vast majority of monosyllables:

Foreign words:			"Irregularity" of Structure:
เชิ้ต	^tǝhɤːt	"shirt"	The phonetic pattern **long vowel + stop** is not normally pronounced on any but low-level or falling tones.[18]

---

[14] The so-called "high consonants" of Siamese orthography and the use of ห นำ suggest that at some time there may have been a correlation between *aspiration* and *tone* 5.

[15] See next paragraph for a discussion of the special properties of certain onomatopes and foreign words.

[16] See pages 44–48.

[17] See page 32.

[18] See page 32.

Foreign words:

| | | | "Irregularity" of Structure: |

ก๊าส[19] ^kaːt "gas" ⎫
โอ๊ก ^ʔoːk "oak" ⎬

As for tɘhɤːt, except that syllables of this pattern with initial ʔ or k would usually be pronounced on low level tone only.

Onomatopes:

ปี๊ป ^piːp "cheep!" As for ^kaːt and ^ʔoːk

กุ๊ก ^kuːk "(call of a night-bird)" ,, ,, ,, ,, ,,

แจ๊ด ^tɕɛːt "chirrup!" ,, ,, ,, ,, ,,

เจี๊ยวจ๊าว ^tɕiəu "chatter, chatter!" It is rare for syllables with an initial tɕ to be pronounced with the acute tone.[20]
  ^tɕaːu

ตุบตับ \tup \tap "(noise of pounding)" Syllables of the pattern **short vowel + stop** are normally restricted to either the low-level or the shortened acute tone.[21]

โจ๊ง /tɕoːŋ "(noise of Malay drum)" It is rare for syllables with this initial to be pronounced with the rising tone.[20]

เป๊ง /peŋ "(noise of hammering sheet iron)" As for /tɕoːŋ

Figure 1 below shows the relative structures of ˌkaːp "outer fibre", ˌkap "with", and ^kaːp[22] "quack!"

FIGURE 1

"Special Word" Prosodies:			"Irregular" combination of syllable prosodies.				
Prosodies of Syllable as a whole:	*Length Tone 2*		*Length Tone 4*		*Shortness Tone 2*	
Prosodies of Syllable parts:	*Plosion*	*Closure*	*Plosion*	*Closure*	*Plosion*	*Closure*
Consonant and and Vowel Units:	k	a	p	k	a	p	k a p
Realization in general phonetic terms:	ˌkaːp		^kaːp		ˌkap	

---

[19] This word, which is given both in the ปทานุกรม and in McFarland, was unknown to a Siamese informant whom I recently had occasion to ask about it.

[20] See page 33.   [21] See footnote 11.

[22] Usually repeated in utterance, as in English.

PROSODIES OF COMPOUND WORDS

. By compound words are meant words of more than one syllable whose
component syllables are themselves meaningful in isolation. The compound
words whose structure it is proposed to examine in some detail here contain
two such components.

There are certain attributes of compound words which serve in the
combinative style to bind the two components together, creating a transitive
relation between them. These attributes may be termed linking prosodies.[23]
They operate by modifying the prosodic structure which would be proper
to one or both of the components taken by themselves. Such modifications
commonly affect (a) *tone*, or (b) *quantity*, as demonstrated below:—

Word:—		Pronunciation in Isolative Style:—	Pronunciation in Combinative Style:—[24]
ที่ไหน	"where?"	\thiː ∕nɑi	-thiˑ ∕nai
ที่นี่	"there"	\thiː ˄niː	-thiˑ ˄niː
สาวสาว	"young girls"	∕saːu∕saːu	-sau ∕saːu
ว่างว่าง	"at your leisure"	\waːŋ\waːŋ	-waŋ \waːŋ
ต้องการ	"want"	\tɔŋ-kaːn	\tɔŋ-kaːn
เท่าไร	"how much"	\thau -rai	\thau_rai[25]
น้ำชา	"tea"	˄naːm -tɕhaː	˄nam-tɕhaː
น้ำตาล	"sugar"	˄naːm -taːn	˄nam -taːn
สีขาว	"white"	∕siː ∕khaːu	-siˑ ∕khaːu

Another linking prosody proper to compound words affects the
realization of the junction of the two medial consonant units. The word
อย่างไร "how", which in the isolative or in "careful" style is pronounced
-jaːŋ-rai, is pronounced -jaŋ-ŋai in the combinative style. Texts
attempting to show colloquial pronunciation may nowadays indicate this
pronunciation orthographically, *viz.*, ยังไง but the word is even in this

---

[23] See *Sounds and Prosodies*, by J. R. Firth, in the 1948 Transactions of the
Philological Society of Great Britain.

[24] In the rapid combinative style, words of this type may be further modified from
the isolative pattern so as to incorporate such features as stress and the neutral tone
(see page 37). A word like ที่ไหน may in the rapid combinative style exhibit the same
phonetic features in utterance as a disyllable of the second type (see page 37) in the
combinative style.

· [25] It is of interest here to note that in a colloquial text I wrote out recently for
recording purposes the word เท่าไร, which occurred several times, was corrected by
a Siamese informant to เท่าไหร่, a spelling which implies a low level tone in the
second syllable. No such spelling as เท่าไหร่ is, however, recognised by dictionaries
I have consulted.

context still felt to be a compound of ˌjaːŋ and ˉrai.[26] In a more rapid and familiar style of speech ˉjaŋ-ŋai may be replaced by ˉjaŋai, a form which it is no longer possible to split up into two syllables of regular structure. The occurrence of a single consonant sound intervocalically after a short vowel, which is not permitted in the isolative style, must always be regarded as a prosody of junction.

The prosodic behaviour of the three utterances, ˌjaːŋˉrai, ˉjaŋ-ŋai, and ˉjaŋai is demonstrated in Figure 2 on page 38.

Other pronunciations which might be similarly analysed are ˌjaːŋˆniː, ˉjaŋˆŋiː, jaˆŋiː (where the syllable ja is pronounced with neutral tone[27]) for the word อย่างนี้ "this way, like this", and ˌjaːŋˆnan, ˌjaŋˆŋan, jaˆŋan for อย่างนั้น "that way, like that". The form ˆŋiː, however, which was quoted to me by a Siamése informant as a contraction of ˌjaːŋˆniː that might occur in the rapid combinative style, as in ⸍khau ⸜tɔŋˌkaːn ˆŋiː ⸜maːk "he wants as many as this", would probably require to be treated as an independent word.

Attention must be drawn to a special class of compound words of which the first component is of Pali or Sanskrit origin, in which junction is marked by the interpolation of a linking syllable pronounced with a neutral tone:—[28]

Orthography	Meaning	Pronunciation of Components by themselves				Pronunciation in Junction
ชลธาร	"stream, water course"	ˉtɕhon	"water",	ˉthaːn	"stream"	ˉtɕhonla-thaːn[29]
ผลไม้	"fruit"	⸍phon	"fruit"	ˆmai	"wood"	⸍phonlaˆmai[29]
นพเก้า	"set of nine precious stones (e.g., on a ring)"	ˆnop	"stone",	⸜kaːu	"nine"	ˆnopphaˌkaːu
ราชยาน	"royal palanquin, barge, etc."	⸜raːt	"king"	ˌjaːn	"vehicle"	⸜raːttɕha-jaːn
พลรบ	"combatants"	ˉphon	"troops"	ˆrop	"fight"	ˉphonlaˆrop[29]

[26] I have not yet found the form ยังไง in a dictionary, although I have seen it written fairly often. It may be speculated whether the word ทำไม ˉthamˉmai "why", which is always so spelt in dictionaries I have seen, does not represent the combinative pronunciation of a word whose isolative pronunciation was once ˉthamˉrai.

[27] The actual pitch of the neutral tone may vary according to context, but is most commonly mid level.

[28] The initial consonant of the linking syllable can, of course, be predicted by recourse to the spelling, which reflects the foreign original in some degree. A full study of the phonetic treatment of Sanskrit and Pali words in Siamese is needed in order to show how far and how many of such words have been "naturalized" into Siamese. Many still retain two possibilities of utterance, one in accordance with the usual principles of Siamese syllable structure, and one pedantic or "alien" pronunciation.

[29] I have heard these words pronounced ˉtɕholla-thaːn, ⸍phollaˆmai, ˉpholla ˆrop. The gemination here is, of course, a prosody of junction.

PROSODIES OF POLYSYLLABLES

A Siamese polysyllable is separable in the isolative style into a sequence of syllables, each of which fulfils the requirements for the structure of monosyllables. The prosodic features peculiar to polysyllables serve to link the syllables of the word with one another, and cannot, therefore, operate in the isolative style. The operation of the prosodies of polysyllables in the combinative style can most simply be demonstrated by an examination of the prosodic behaviour of disyllables.

Disyllables are of two types.

The first type of disyllable may be split up in the combinative no less than the isolative style into two syllables conforming to the rules for the structure of monosyllables, but excluding the possibility of a short first syllable ending in zero consonant, unless accompanied by labiovelarization or yotization. There is no effective difference between the isolative pronunciation of these words and that of connected speech. Examples are อัมพิล -ʔam-phin, วิชฌา ˆwit-tɕhaː, อัปป -ʔap-paʔ, ชมพู ˉtɕhom -phuː, โกณ -koːˆnaʔ, นารี -naː-riː, ฌัณฎา -khan-taː. It will be seen that where there is a junction of two similar consonant units, a long medial stop or nasal results in pronunciation. There is, however, no need to regard gemination as a special feature here. The structure of words in which it occurs is already adequately accounted for by the analysis of the word into consonant and vowel units, with accompanying prosodies of syllable-beginning or ending. The structure of อิทธิ -ʔitˆthiʔ is illustrated below:—

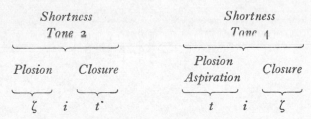

In the second type of disyllable the first syllable is realized in the isolative style as **consonant + short vowel + glottal stop**. In the combinative style, the first syllables of the words of this very numerous class may be joined to the second syllables by the following means:—

(i) A relatively weak stress; that is to say, a stress differentiation is introduced, in which there may be said to be two differential units: *stress* and *lack of stress*.

(ii) What may be called "neutral" tone;[27] this is in effect a one-unit tone system, as contrasted with the usual five-unit tone system. Disyllables

---

[27] The actual pitch of the neutral tone may vary according to context, but is most commonly mid level.

FIGURE 2

	Style I (Isolative)		Style II (Combinative) Realization of $n + \zeta$ as ŋŋ Replacement of Length and Tone 2 (Style I) by Shortness and Tone I.		Style III (Rapid Combinative) Realization of $n + \zeta$ as ŋ (Single intervocalic consonant after short vowel). Replacement of Length and Tone 2 (Style I) by Shortness and Tone I.	
Linking prosodies:						
Prosodies of Syllable ..	Length Tone 2	Shortness Tone I Yotization	Shortness Tone I	Shortness Tone I Yotization	Shortness Tone I	Shortness Tone I Yotization
Prosodies of Syllable Parts ..	Voice Affrication	Rhotacization	Voice Affrication		Voice Affrication	
Consonant and Vowel Units ..	t a ɣ	ζ a ζ	t a ɣ ζ a ζ		t a ɣ ζ a ζ	
Realization in general phonetic terms ..	-jaɳ-rai		-jaŋ-ŋai		-jaɳai	

of this type operate a special tone differentiation of which the two differential units may be said to be *neutral tone* and *five-tone system*. This special tone differentiation is closely bound up with stress, and is always connective. The neutral tone is left unmarked in phonetic transcription.

(iii) The absence of final glottal closure. Whenever a short syllable unaccompanied by labiovelarization or yotization realizes final ζ as phonetic zero, linguistic suspense is created which binds that syllable closely to the following one. Moreover, ⁺his type of pronunciation results in the occurrence of a single intervocalic consonant after a short vowel, which has already been stated as a linking prosody.[30]

(iv) Vowel quality. When the vowel unit of the first syllable is *a*, a vowel sound that is appreciably closer and more centralized than that used in the isolative style is often heard.

Examples of disyllables of the second type are:—

Orthography		Isolative Style	Combinative Style
ทะเล	"sea"	^thaʔ-leː	tha-leː
ถลาย	"destroy"	_thaʔ_laːl	tha_laːl
ระยะ	"interval"	^raʔ^jaʔ	ra^jaʔ
คะเน	"conjecture"	^khaʔ-neː	kha-neː
แขยง	"loathe"	_khaʔ⁄jeːŋ	kha⁄jeːŋ
พระหาม	"dawn"	^phraʔ⁄haːm	phra⁄haːm
สะอาด	"clean"	_saʔ-ʔaːt	sa-ʔaːt[31]
กระทรวง	"Ministry"	_kraʔ-suəŋ	kra-suəŋ
อินัง	"take an interest in"	⁺ʔIʔ-naŋ	ʔI-naŋ
พิธี	"rite"	^phiʔ-thiː	phi-thiː
ธุระ	"business"	^thuʔ^raʔ	thu^raʔ
สุภาพ	"gentle"	_suʔ\phaːp	su\phaːp
อชุ	"honourable"	ʔuʔ^tɕhuʔ	ʔu^tɕhuʔ
อุทาร	"exalted"	_ʔuʔ-thaːn	ʔu-thaːn
กุดั่น	"filigree jewellery"	_kuʔ\dan	ku\dan
กิเลน	"fabulous"	_kiʔ-leːn	ki-leːn

---

[30] See page 36.

[31] It will be noted that the glottal stop, which is in the isolative style the realization of the final ζ of the first syllable, is not present in the combinative style, whereas the glottal plosive, which is the realization of the initial ζ of the second syllable, is common to both styles.

The examples ทะเล, ถลาะ and คะเน, แขยง show that no difference is
made in the combinative style in this context between certain syllables
which in the isolative style are distinguished by tone. คะเน and สุภาพ
have been selected at random to demonstrate the analysis of the prosodic
features of words of this type. (See Figure 3 on page 41.)

Words of more than two syllables may be treated as combinations of
the disyllable types already presented. In general, the prosodic treatment of
short syllables of the type *vowel unit + zero consonant*[32] is aimed at attach-
ing them to the next following "prominent" syllable, which may be a long
syllable, or a short syllable ending in a consonant unit other than zero.
Two or three short syllables may be linked to a following "prominent" one.
Where the last syllable of a word or before a pause is a short one of the type
vowel unit + zero consonant[32] it retains its isolative structure, and functions
as a "prominent" syllable. Examples are:—

Orthography		Isolative Style	Combinative Style
อริยะ	"venerable, sage"	-ʔaʔˆriʔˆjaʔ	ʔariˆjaʔ
อรหะ	"deserving"	-ʔaʔˆraʔ-haʔ	ʔara-haʔ
อุทริยะ	"stomach"	-ʔutˆtaʔˆriʔˆjaʔ	ʔuttariˆjaʔ
อุษณ	"heat"	-ʔuʔ-saʔˆnaʔ	ʔusaˆnaʔ
ศาสนา	"scriptures, religion"	⟋saː-saʔ⟋naː	⟋saːsa⟋naː
เมขลา	"goddess of lightning"	-meː-khaʔ⟋laː	-meːkha⟋laː
กรณ	"act of doing"	-kaʔˆraʔnaʔ	karaˆnaʔ
กิริยา	"verb"	-kiʔˆriʔ-jaː	kiri-jaː

Examples of longer Compound Words (of Pali and Sanskrit origin)
are:—

พระพุทธศาสนา, "the Buddhist religion", isolative: ˆphraʔˆphutˆthaʔ
⟋saː-saʔ⟋naː, combinative: phraˆphutˆthaʔ⟋saːsa⟋naː

ปราซายัดยวิวาหะ, "(a form of marriage)", isolative: -praː-tɕhaː-pat-taʔ
ˆjaʔˆwiʔ-waː-haʔ, combinative: -praː-tɕhaː-pattaˆjaʔwi-waː-haʔ

ชนกาธิบดี, "the father of a King", isolative: -tɕhonˆnaʔ-kaːˆthip-bɔː-diː,
combinative: -tɕhonna-kaːˆthipbɔː-diː

---

[32] Excluding yotized or labiovelarized syllables.

FIGURE 3

Isolative Style

Combinative Style

Linking prosodies: ..

Realization of ζ + n as n.
Stress Relationship.
Relationship of neutral tone and five-tone system.
Centralized quality of a.

Prosodies of Syllable ..

| Shortness Tone 4 | | Length Tone 1 |
| Plosion Aspiration | Closure | |

| Shortness Neutral Tone Lack of Stress | | Length Tone 1 Stress |
| Plosion Aspiration | | |

Prosodies of Syllable Parts ..

Consonant and Vowel Units ..

k a ζ n e ζ

k a ζ n e ζ

Realization in general phonetic terms ..

ˆkha²·ne:

khä·ne:

Linking prosodies: ..

Realization of ζ + p as p.
Stress relationship.
Relationship of neutral tone and five-tone system.

Prosodies of Syllable ..

| Shortness Tone 2 | | Length Tone 3 |
| Friction | Closure | Plosion Aspiration | | Closure |

| Shortness Neutral Tone Lack of Stress | | Length Tone 1 Stress |
| Friction | | Plosion Aspiration | | Closure |

Prosodies of Syllable Parts ..

Consonant and Vowel Units ..

t u ζ p a p

t u ζ p a p

Realization in general phonetic terms ..

-suˀpha:p

suˀpha:p

SENTENCE PROSODIES

Sentence prosodies are of three kinds, namely: (*a*) those affecting small groups or "pieces" within the sentence;[33] (*b*) those relating to the sentence as a whole; and (*c*) those which link one sentence with another, or the part of a sentence with another part.

(*a*) The prosodies affecting pieces within the sentence operate in much the same way as those affecting compound words and polysyllables, serving to bind together certain groups of words within the wider group, which is in turn held together by appropriate sentence prosodies. Among the pieces of a sentence which appear to be regularly linked by prosodic features are the following:—

(i) The future particle จะ -tɕaʔ and the following verbal. A group like จะไป "will go" is bound together by the same prosodic means as disyllables of the second type[34]; that is to say, จะ is pronounced with relatively weak stress, neutral tone, centralized vowel quality, and without final glottal closure: tɕä-pai, as opposed to -tɕaʔ-pai in the isolative style.

(ii) The negative particle ไม่ \mai and the following verbal. ไม่ is usually linked to the following word by relatively weak stress and neutral tone. In rapid combinative style there is also a marked shortening of the utterance in relation to the following word, and the diphthong heard may start from a considerably closer vowel position than would be permissible in the isolative or slower combinative style. In certain contexts it is the verbal form which is pronounced with relatively weak stress and with neutral tone, while ไม่ is pronounced as in the isolative style. The intonation pattern of ไม่ได้หยุด "without stopping", which in the isolative style would be pronounced \mai\daːi-jut, might be represented (\ . .)

(iii) Words in genitival relation. Where this relation is shown by the use of the word ของ/khɔːŋ between two nominals, as in พ่อของเขา "his father", ของ and the following word may be linked by the tonal and quantitative features that serve to link compound words of similar pattern: \phɔː-khɔŋ/khau.[35] In rapid combinative style \phɔːŋ̊/khau may be heard. Where the genitival relation is shown by the juxtaposition of the two nominals the close relation between the two is expressed rhythmically. Thus, the rhythm of the sentence -khrai/khaːi-khai-kai[36] "who is selling hen's eggs?" may be represented ♩ ♩ ♩ ♪♩.

(iv) A numeral and the following classifier. The link here is usually rhythmic.

---

[33] See article by J. R. Firth, quoted above.
[34] See page 37.
[35] See page 35.
[36] A well-known Siamese "tongue-twister".

(b) The prosodies affecting the sentence as a whole include (i) *intonation* and (ii) *sentence tone*.

(i) *Intonation*. In rapid combinative style it is possible to detect certain intonational tendencies which may be mentioned here. A sequence of mid level tones tends to be pronounced on a descending scale, with a fairly marked fall in pitch in the last syllable before a pause. A fall in pitch may be postponed until a word of sufficient semantic import is reached. The words preceding or following an important fall in pitch may, if their content allows it, be pronounced on a fairly low pitch, even if their lexical tone is not low-level. Examples of some of these intonational tendencies in rapid combinative style are given side by side with the pronunciation of the same text in combinative style:—

Orthography	Pronunciation in Combinative Style	Intonation in rapid Combinative Style
เป็นอย่างไร	-pen-jaŋ-ŋai	‾ ‾ ◝
ใจเดียวกันทีเดียว	-tɕai-diəu-kan-thiː-diɔu	‾ ‾ ‾ ◝
แพงเกินไป	-pheːŋ-kɤːn-pai	‾ ‾ ◝
อยู่ในกรุงเทพฯ	-juː-nai-kruŋ\theːp	‾ . ‾ ◝
เราเดินมานานแล้ว	-rau-dɤːn-maː-naːn^lɛːu	‾ ‾ . ‾ ◠
ราคาแปดบาท	-raː-khaː-pɛːt-baːt	‾ ‾ ‾ ◝
ราคาแปดบาทครับ	-raː-khaː-pɛːt-baːt^khrap	‾ ‾ ‾ ◝
คุณกำลังจะไปไหน	-khun-kam-laŋ tɕa-pai/nai ..	‾ ‾ ‾ . ‾ ◞
เรากำลังจะไปกินข้าว	-rau-kam-laŋ tɕa-pai-kin \khaːu	‾ ‾ ‾ . ‾ ◝
ดิฉันไม่ค่อยว่างหมู่นี้	di/tɕhan\mai\khɔi\waːŋ -muː^niː	. ◞ ‾ ◝ ◠

(ii) *Sentence Tone*. When due account has been taken of such intonational tendencies as are described above, however, and of the variations of tone and quantity in isolative and combinative contexts, it becomes clear that on the whole the lexical or isolative patterns remain fairly constant in the phrase and sentence. Nevertheless, spoken Siamese, by the ingenious use of certain particles, commands a flexibility of expression comparable to that achieved in the English sentence by the modulations of stress and intonation. The majority of such particles are used at the end of a phrase or sentence, the most important exception being the anaphoric particle ก็ , which is often found at the beginning of the second part of a two-part sentence, or at the beginning of a sentence which refers back to some earlier one. Such particles serve several purposes. Firstly, by their presence they mark the end of a sentence, or, in the case of ก็, signal the **beginning** of a clause or sentence which is linked with one that has gone before. They also add something to the general meaning of the sentence. They may, for instance, soften a command, indicate a question, or proclaim the sex and social status of the speaker. They have, moreover, the special property of carrying what we may call the *sentence tone*. The sentence tone is a complex of the syllable prosodies of tone and quantity, and is usually realized as one of the five tones proper to monosyllables, combined with either short-ness or length.[37] Particles bearing sentence tone are distinguished from other monosyllables in the sentence in one important respect: the disposition of tone and quantity is determined not by the phonetic structure of the particle itself, but by the requirements of the sentence as a whole.* We thus find as particles such forms as \kha?, \kɔ?, ˉsi, which are inadmissible from the point of view of word-tone.[38] It is not the aim of this study to attempt a detailed statement of the semantic function of the particles themselves, or of the sentence tones they may carry, but some general observations on their use may usefully be made. The following table sets out seven sentence tones, showing the syllable prosodies of which they are a synthesis, and attempting to give some approximate indication of the way in which they may colour the sentences to which they are applied:—

Sentence Tone	Synthesis of Syllable Prosodies	Notes on General Effect
A	*Tone* 1 *and shortness*[39]	The most "neutral" sentence tone. May give impression of casualness.

---

[37] Special effects may, as in other languages, sometimes be obtained by means which are less readily analysed, since they are highly individual. To give an instance: the normal polite way of asking a friend what he said is \phu:t\wa:?a‑rai ˆna ?, but if the polite particle ˆna ? is uttered on an unusually high pitch and with appro-priate voice quality, sarcasm or irony may be implied.

[38] See page 32.

* [I should now add syllable-ending prosodies to the features so determined. Since this paper was written, greater familiarity with the usages of conversational Thai (Siamese) has convinced me that final glottal closure is far less common in particles than I had earlier supposed, and that it is in many situations socially unacceptable. (See "Marginalia to Siamese phonetic studies", 421–422.) If I were re-writing the paper today, many of the final glottal stops shown for particles in the examples that follow would be deleted, with consequent changes in the syllable final prosodies on pp. 51–53.—Author 1968]

[39] This sentence tone is heard as a short open syllable without final glottal closure. Siamese orthography has no way of indicating this pronunciation. Short syllables with zero final consonant, unless realized as diphthongs, are always pronounced with a final glottal stop before a pause, and can never be accompanied by a mid level tone in this position. Written texts I have seen appear to represent this sentence tone by a spelling which indicates a mid level tone, but implies a long final vowel. I have, however, so far not heard a Siamese speaker pronounce a long vowel in this context.

Sentence Tone	Syothesis of Syllable Prosodies	Notes on General Effect
B	*Tone 2 and shortness*	Suggestion of impatience, abruptness, exasperation; or mild command.
C	*Tone 3 and length*	Assertion, or assent. More formal than *D*.
D	*Tone 3 and shortness*	Assertion, or assent, or command.
E	*Tone 4 and length*	Intensity, emphasis, or urgency
F	*Tone 4 and shortness*	Interrogation, invitation; less formal than G.
G	*Tone 5 and length*	Interrogation in slow, careful, or very formal style.

In the following examples the particles that may bear sentence tone are underlined. It will be seen that two such particles can occur together at the end of a sentence. When this happens, it is usually the last of the pair that bears the sentence tone, the first one being bound to the second by appropriate linking prosodies, which may include the neutral tone. Where the first particle of the sentence is felt to have more importance than the second for the sentence as a whole, however, both particles may bear an appropriate sentence tone. Thus, the sentence "How are you?" may be expressed politely by women speakers either by sa‑baːi‑diː ˆkhaʔ or sa‑baːi‑diː ⁄ruːˆkhaʔ. The syllable ˆkhaʔ in both indicates politeness and the fact that the speaker is a woman. It bears sentence tone *F*, to indicate enquiry. The syllable ⁄ruː in the second sentence is an interrogatory particle bearing sentence‑tone *G*, and could be final in the sentence if the speaker did not choose to add the special sign of formal politeness. It should be noted that a sentence may consist solely of a final particle or particles, as:— \khaʔ (indicating polite assent by women); ⁄tɕaː "Yes?" (as to a child, or servant); and ‑thɤʔ‑na "Do (this) for me, please!"; where ‑thɤʔ is a particle expressing a request or mild command, and ‑na a particle expressing polite entreaty or persuasion, here bearing sentence tone *A*.

Examples of Sentence Tone *A*

\khaːu ‑maː ‑<u>si</u>   "Come in!"
\daːi ‑<u>si</u>   "All right!"

ˋtɕiŋ ˉsi	"Indeed!"
ˊkhɔː ˥pai ˥thi	"Please let me pass!"
ˊkhɔː ˥thi	"Give it to me, please" or "Do it for me, please"
˥pɤːt praˉthuːˉthi	"Please open the door!"

Examples of Sentence Tone *B*

ˋthau ˆnan ˍlɛˀ	"That's all"
ˋphuːt ˆsamˍjuːˆnanˍlɛˀ	"You've said all that before!"
ˊphom tɕa-pai-diəu ˆniːˍlɛˀ	"I'm going now"
ˋnan ˍlɛˀ	"That's it!"
ˋphuːt ˥pai ˥jaŋˆŋan ˍlɛˀ	"How you do go on (talking)!"
ˉduː ˋnanˍnɛˀ	"Just look there!"
ˆlɛːu ˥khun ˍlaˀ	"And what about you?"
ˋtɕhaːŋ ˍthɤˀ	"It doesn't matter (= No, thank you)"
ˋnaŋ-loŋˍthɤˀ	"Sit down!"
˥paiˍthɤˀ	"Let's go!"

Examples of Sentence Tone *C*

ˋniːˋnɛː	"Here it is!"
˥tham-pen ˋlen-pai ˋnaː	"Don't play the fool, now"
ˋtɕau ˋkhaː	"Yes, sir" (respectful, used by women)

Examples of Sentence Tone *D*

ˉduː ˋnan ˋnɛˀ	"Just look at that!"
ˋniː ˋkhaˀ	"Here you are" (polite, used by women)
˥tɕhɤːn-khunˍsaŋ-ˀaːˌhaːn siˋkhaˀ	"May I invite you to have something to eat?"
ˆlɛˀ ˀˌˈ raiˍˀiːk ˋlaˀ	"Is there anything more you require?"

Examples of Sentence Tone *E*

ˋkhau ˥maː ˆsiː	"Do please come in!"
ˀaˆrai⁴⁰	"What!"

---

[40] For the use of sentence tone *E* without a final particle, see page 48.

sa‑baːi ‑di: /rɯː^kha?	"How are you?" (used by women)
/khau ‑juː /mai tɕa?	"Is he in, please?"
sa‑baːi ‑di: ^rɯ?	"How are you?"
^phop ‑kan ‑mai ^na?	"We'll be seeing each other again (won't we?)"

Examples of Sentence Tone *F*

‑pai si ^na?	"*Do* go!"
‑loŋ‑kan ‑thi·\ni: ^lɛ?	"Here's where we get down!"
\nan ^lɛ?	"That's quite right!"
\noːn ^nɛ?	"That one over there!"
‑au si ^wa?	"Take it, then!" (vulgar)
‑pai /nai ^wa?	"Where are you going?" (vulgar)
?a ‑rai ^wa?	"What is it, then?" (vulgar)

Examples of Sentence Tone *G*

‑pai si /naː	"Won't you please go?"
\tɕau /khaː	"Yes, sir?" (very respectful)
/tɕaː	"Yes?" (used among intimates)

That the same particle may carry different sentence tones is shown by the following:—

\khaːu‑maː ‑si	"Come in, (please)!"
\kha(ː)u ‑maː ^si?	"Come in, won't you?"
\kha(ː)u ‑maː ^siː	"*Do* come in!"
\khaːu ‑maː ‑si?	"Come in, (please)!"
\khaːu ‑maː si ^kha?	"Won't you come in, please?" (used by women)

In the passage ฉันมาหาคุณดำจ๊ะ เขาอยู่ไหมจ๊ะ "I've come to see Mr. Dam. Is he in, please?" as it might be spoken to a servant answering the door, the particle tɕa is used twice, the first time with a sentence tone appropriate to statements and assertions (*D*), and the second time with one appropriate to enquiries (*F*):— /tɕhan ‑maː /haː‑khun ‑dam \tɕa? /khau ‑juː /mai^tɕa?. Similarly, in a conversation between two women, the answer to sa‑baːi‑di: /rɯː^kha? "How are you?" is sa‑baːi‑di: \kha? "Quite well, thank you".

The sentence tones which may combine with any one particle are restricted in some degree by the semantic function of the particle itself. The interrogative particle rɯ, for instance, may normally be expected to carry one of these sentence tones associated with enquiry, namely, *F* and *G*.

The final particle **^khrap** appears to be subject to a restriction which is not imposed by semantic function. This particle is used by male speakers in the same way as **kha** by women, but in contrast with the variable tone and quantity of the latter, is always pronounced with *Tone* 4. Two factors may here inhibit the working of sentence tone, namely, phonetic form and historical origin. The great majority of final particles have zero final consonant, and it is possible that the presence in this word of final *p* is less conducive to prosodic change. From the historical point of view, **^khrap** has been described as a fairly recent contraction of a two-word expression **/khɔː^rap,**[41] and it may be that awareness of the tone pattern of the original phrase is still acute enough to prevent the acceptance of the contracted form as a particle carrying sentence- rather than word-tone.

It has been observed that where phonetic form and position in the sentence are favourable other words may be characterized by the prosodic features proper to final particles. The pronunciation of รู้ "know", which is ordinarily **^ruː**, may be **^ruʔ** in such expressions as จนอะไรก็ไม่รู้ "Whatever sort of man *is* he?" In certain emphatic contexts อะไร, usually pronounced **ʔa⁻rai** in combinative style, may be heard as **ʔa^rai**. It may be speculated whether the so-called interrogative particle **/mai** may not be regarded as the negative particle **\mai** with a superimposed sentence tone *G*.[42] I am inclined to believe, moreover, that the incidence of *Tone* 4 in certain words expressing notions of distance, size, colour, speed, etc., may properly be accounted for by sentence rather than word tone, and may be referred to the emphatic and intensifying connotation of sentence tone *E*.[43] Among such examples I would include นี้ **^niː** "this", นั้น **^nan** "that", and โน้น **^noːn** "that over there" (as compared with นี่ **\niː**, นั่น **\nan** and โน่น **\noːn**), and the following less familiar words:— ปรี๊ด **^priːt** "extremely (tall or fast)", จ๊วก **^tøuək** "(expressing superlative degree of whiteness)", จิ๊ด **^tøiːt** "smallest", and ล้า **^la** "late", (as compared with ล่า **\laː**, also meaning "late"). Such forms as ปรี๊ด, จ๊วก, จิ๊ด could not

---

[41] Macfarland and the ปทานุกรม only recognize ขอรับ **/khɔː^rap**.

[42] One of my Siamese informants was put to some difficulty to explain how the word for "silk" (the lexical meaning of **/mai**) could come to be used as a sign of interrogation! The relevant entry in MacFarland's *Dictionary* suggests that the interrogative **/mai** is equivalent to **/ruː \mai** "or not".

[43] See in this connection *Techniques of Intensifying in Thai*, by Mary R. Haas, in *Word*, Vol. II, No. 2.

ordinarily be accompanied by Tone 4 as a word-tone.[44] Their prosodic structure may be accounted for either by sentence-tone or by the prosodies for "special words" already examined.[45] My inclination is to treat their "irregular" features as the expression of a sentence prosody comparable with emphatic stress and intonation in English.

The anaphoric function of the particle ก็ has already been mentioned.[46] The lexical pronunciation of ก็ is \kɔː, but this is rarely heard, \kɔʔ being the commoner pronunciation even in the isolative style. The combination in this latter pronunciation of Tone 3 and syllabic shortness, which is "irregular" as monosyllabic structure may, be interpreted as sentence tone. When linking the two parts of a sentence, ก็ is pronounced at the beginning of the second part, being attached to the first word of the second part by prosodies such as obtain for disyllables of the second type.[47] It thus comes about that the function of this particle as a bearer of sentence tone is frequently subordinated to its function as an anaphore. Examples of the use of ก็ as a link between sentence parts are given below:—

\phuːt-diː kɔ-diːꞏpai	"Talking about it will do me no good."
^nɯəꞏrɯəŋ kɔ-phɔːꞏduː	"The *story* (e.g., of a film) is all right."
\phuːt^lɛːu kɔ-cep-cai	"Even talking about it is painful to me."
saꞏbot\hai kɔ\daːi	"I can swear to it."
-khrai\t̠s̠hɯə kɔ\t̠s̠haːŋ	"Let him believe it who can."
-tham ʔa-rai kɔ mai^ruː	"I don't know what to do!"

ก็ may occur at the beginning of a sentence when its function is to refer that sentence back to something that has been said or implied earlier, often by another speaker. Thus, the answer to an enquiry about someone's health may be ก็เรื่อยเรื่อย kɔ\rɯəi\rɯəi "So so". This function of referring back to some earlier utterance leads to the English translation of ก็ as "too" or "also" in many instances. The sentence เขาว่ากับข้าวไทยก็ดี ⸝khau \waːꞏkap \khaːu-thai kɔ-diː may perhaps best be translated "They say Siamese food is good too" (previous conversation having perhaps been about the excellence of Chinese food).

In conclusion, Figures 4 and 5 on pages 51–53 attempt to demonstrate some of the prosodic features discussed in this paper as they apply to a Siamese speaker's pronunciation of the following two short extracts of conversational passages from a Siamese novel:—[48]

[44] See page 32.

[45] See page 33.

[46] See page 43.

[47] See page 37.

[48] *Phu Di*, by Dok Mai Sod.

a) "ˇˀaːu ! wi-mon na-ˀeːŋ.   -maː ˄rot-khrai ˄naˀ ?"

"Ah! There you are, Wimon!   Whose car did you come in?"

"kɔ⁄tɕhan na-si."

"Yes, here I am!"

b) "-rɔŋˇhai kɔ˄rɔːŋ-pai-khon-diəu-si, -thamai ˇtɕŋ

"Go on and cry if you want to, but why must you bang things

kraˇthɛːkˇnan kraˇthɛːkˇniː -nuək ⁄huː maiˇtɕhai ˄rɯˀ ?"

about? The noise is pretty awful, you know!"

"kɔ-khrai ⁄khau ˄tɕhai ˇhai ma-faŋˇlaˀ. ⁄khau -juː

"Who asked you to come and listen to me then? I'm in my

n(a)i ˇhɔŋ -khɔŋ⁄khau."

own room!"

"ˀuˇbaˀ! kɔ⁄khau -nɔːn-juː n(a)iˇhɔŋ."

"But *I* sleep in this room too!"

Reasons of space have made it necessary in Figures 4 and 5 to indicate many prosodic features by abbreviations. A key to the abbreviations used is given below:—

Aff	=	*Affrication*	*NT* =	*Neutral Tone*
Asp	=	*Aspiration*	*P* =	*Plosion*
C	=	*Closure without plosion*	*R* =	*Rhotacization*
			S =	*Stress*
F	=	*Friction*	*Sht* =	*Shortness*
L	=	*Lateralization*	*SC* =	*Single medial consonant after a short vowel*
Lb	=	*Labialization*		
Lv	=	*Labio-velarization*	*T1, etc.* =	*Tone 1, etc.*
Lth	=	*Length*	*V* =	*Voice*
L of S =		*Lack of Stress*	*Y* =	*Yotization*

NT:5 T   =   *Relationship between neutral tone and five-tone system*

L of S:S   =   *Stress relationship*

The abbreviation *T5 > T1 in Syll.* 1 means that the prosodic feature in this case is the fact that in junction the first syllable has *Tone* 1, whereas in isolation it would have *Tone* 5. Other abbreviations of this type are to be similarly interpreted.

FIGURE 4

Prosodies of Sentence	Sentence Tone C	Linked by kɔ				
		Sentence Tone F			Sentence Tone A	

| Prosodies of Polysyllables and Sentence Pieces | | NT:5T L of S:S SC | NT:5T L of S:S SC | | | NT:5T L of S:S SC | NT:5T L of S:S SC |

| Prosodies of Syllables | Lth T3 Lv | Sht NT L of S | Sht T1 S | Sht Sht NT L of S | Lth T1 S | Rhythm Lth T1 | Sht T4 | Sht T4 Y | Sht T1 Y | Sht T4 | Sht NT L of S | Sht T5 S | Sht Sht NT T1 L of S S | Sht T1 S |

| Prosodies of Syllable Parts | P | Lb | P | | R C R | P Asp R | C | P Asp | Aff Asp | P | F |

| Consonant and Vowel Units | ʈaʈ ʔaːru | ʈiʈmounaʈʈeɳ wi‑mon na‑ʔeːŋ | maʈʈotkaʈnaʈ maː‑^rot‑khrai^naʔ | | kɔʈtannaʈtiʈ kɔ/tchan na‑si | |

FIGURE 5

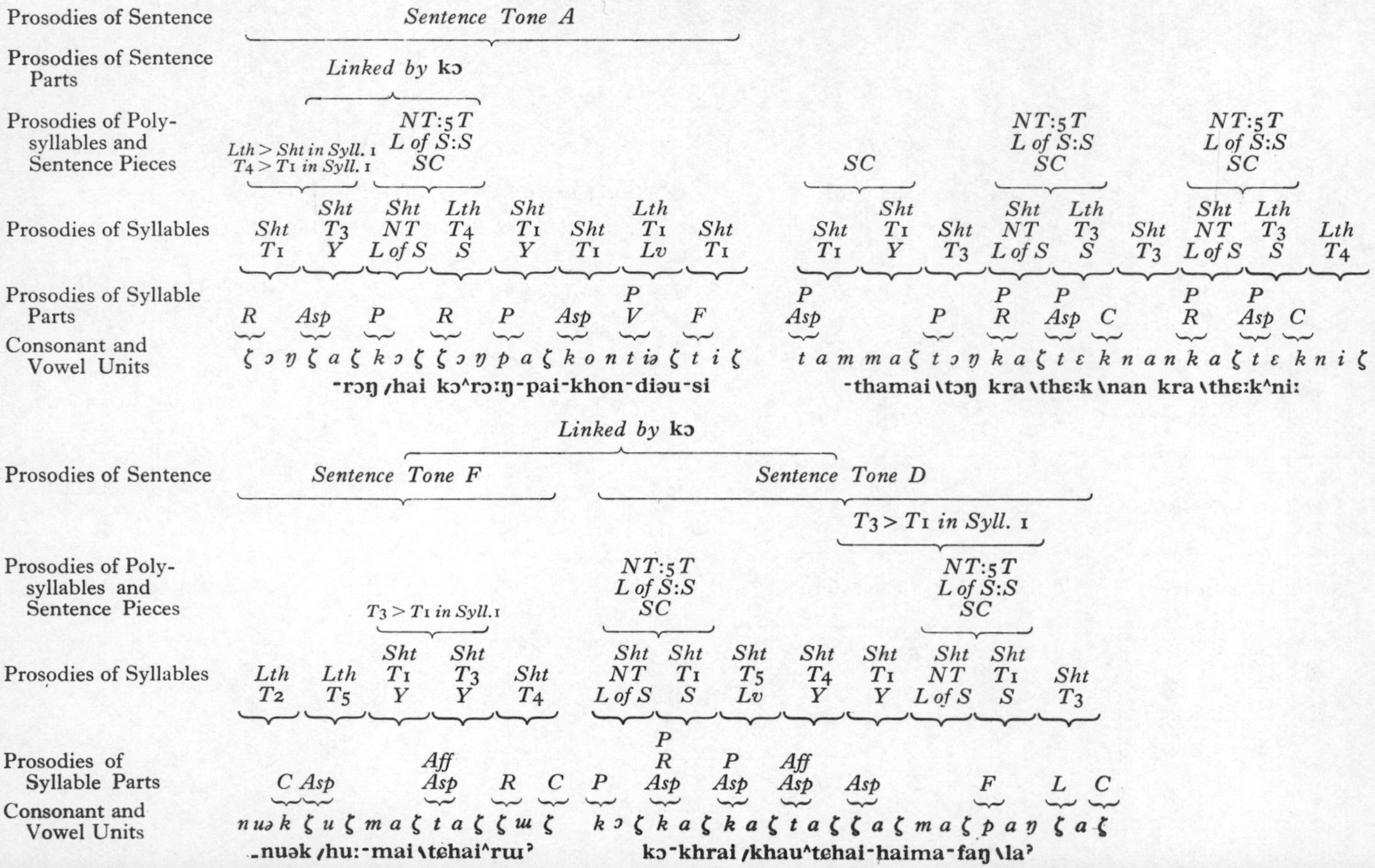
Prosodies of Sentence
Sentence Tone A
Prosodies of Sentence Parts
Linked by kɔ
Prosodies of Poly-syllables and Sentence Pieces
Lth > Sht in Syll. 1
T4 > T1 in Syll. 1
NT:5T
L of S:S
SC
Prosodies of Syllables
Sht T1
Sht T3 Y
Sht NT L of S
Lth T4 S
Sht T1 Y
Sht T1
Lth T1 Lv
Sht T1
Sht T1
Sht T1 Y
Sht T3
Sht NT L of S
Lth T3 S
Sht T3
Sht NT L of S
Lth T3 S
Lth T4
Prosodies of Syllable Parts
R Asp P R P Asp P V F
P Asp P P R P Asp C P R P Asp C
Consonant and Vowel Units
ζ ɔ ŋ ζ a ζ k ɔ ζ ζ ɔ ŋ p a ζ k o n t iə ζ t i ζ
t a m m a ζ t ɔ ŋ k a ζ t ɛ k n a n k a ζ t ɛ k n i ζ
-rɔŋ /hai kɔ^rɔ:ŋ-pai-khon-diəu-si
-thamai \tɔŋ kra \thɛ:k \nan kra \thɛ:k^ni:
Linked by kɔ
Prosodies of Sentence
Sentence Tone F
Sentence Tone D
T3 > T1 in Syll. 1
Prosodies of Poly-syllables and Sentence Pieces
T3 > T1 in Syll. 1
NT:5T
L of S:S
SC
Prosodies of Syllables
Lth T2
Lth T5
Sht T1 Y
Sht T3 Y
Sht T4
Sht NT L of S
Sht T1 S
Sht T5 Lv
Sht T4 Y
Sht T1 Y
Sht NT L of S
Sht T1 S
Sht T3
Prosodies of Syllable Parts
C Asp Aff Asp R C P P R Asp P Asp Aff Asp Asp F L C
Consonant and Vowel Units
n uə k ζ u ζ m a ζ t a ζ ζ ɯ ζ
k ɔ ζ k a ζ k a ζ t a ζ ζ a ζ m a ζ p a ŋ ζ a ζ
-nuək /hu:-mai \təhai^rɯʔ
kɔ-khrai /khau^təhai-haima-faŋ \laʔ

Linked by kɔ

Sentence Tone D

Prosodies of Sentence						

Prosodies of Polysyllables and Sentence Pieces:

$NT:5\ T$ $Lth > S^{ht}$ in Syll.1 $NT:5\ T$ $NT:5\ T$ $NT:5\ T$

$L\ of\ S:S$ $T_5 > T_1$ in Syll.1 $L\ of\ S:S$ $L\ of\ S::S$ $L\ of\ S:S$

SC   SC

Prosodies of Syllables:

Sht Lth Sht NT $L\ of\ S$ Sht Sht NT $L\ of\ S$ Sht Sht NT $L\ of\ S$ Sht

T_5 T_2 T_5 T_1 T_3 T_5 T_3 T_5 T_1 T_2 T_3

Lv S Lv S S Lv S S

Prosodies of Syllable Parts:

P Aff P Asp P P V C P Asp Aff

Asp V Asp Asp V V

Consonant and Vowel Units:

k a ʧ t u ʒ n a ʒ ʊ ŋ k ɔ ˶ k a ʒ   ʧ u ʒ p̣ a ʒ   k ɔ ʒ k a ʒ n ɔ ɪ n u ʒ n a ʒ ɔ ɪ ɲ

ˏkhau. juː naiˋtɕɔŋˏkhɔŋ ˏkhau   ʔu ˎba ʔ   kɔ ˏkhau-nɔːn-juː naiˊthɔŋ

3

THE PHONOLOGY OF LOANWORDS IN SOME SOUTH-EAST ASIAN LANGUAGES

By Eugénie J. A. Henderson

THE expression " loanword " inevitably suggests comparative or historical studies so that it will be as well for me to make my position in the matter clear at the outset. As a phonetician and phonologist my interest lies principally in the present structure of languages ; but the present structure of any language will bear witness to its history. The historical and synchronic approaches are not therefore opposed but complementary. While the language historian is interested in the present for the light it throws upon the past, the descriptive linguist is interested in the past as a key to the present. Fries and Pike have said " The description of a word as a loan is a mixture of approaches ; the mixing of purely descriptive analysis with dialect study, comparative work or historical study ".[1] It is clear that in this field the descriptive linguist owes much to comparativists and historians, but historical and comparative criteria are not the only ones that may lead us to suppose that a word is a loan. A great many of the words discussed in this lecture are well known to be loans on evidence other than that of their phonetic form but my attention was directed to a number of them by the fact that their phonological structure stands apart in some way from what appears to be the regular pattern of the language in which they occur. For some of these words of " irregular " pattern I have not yet found non-phonetic evidence that they are borrowed, but nevertheless feel that the phonetic evidence is in itself strong enough to make this highly probable.

Foreign words may be taken into a language in two ways : (a) they may be recast in a form already acceptable to the borrowing language ; or (b) they may retain some alien

---

[1] C. C. Fries and K. L. Pike. "Coexistent Phonemic Systems," *Language*, vol. 25, No. 1, 1949.

Source : E. J. A. Henderson, ' The phonology of loanwords in some South-East Asian languages ', *TPS* (1951), 131–58. Reprinted by permission of The Philological Society and the author.

features, and so introduce new phonological patterns.[1] In the first case loans will be indistinguishable by phonetic criteria from native words. In the second case alien-introduced patterns of long standing may cease to appear " foreign " to speakers of the language, and may come to form an integral part of the phonological system of the language, forming a new system. The first system will be referred to as primary, and the introduced patterns as secondary systems, which may not be as full as the first. New patterns of more recent introduction than those forming secondary systems may still be felt so alien that they cannot be said as yet to be fully accepted in the language on the same terms as the others, but set up special fragmentary systems, along with some other types of words, as will be discussed later.

This view of language not as monosystemic but as composed of a number of systems is convenient partly, if not principally, on account of the difficulty—if not the impossibility—of dealing adequately and economically with borrowed words, phonaesthetic words, etc., as forming part of one all-embracing system.[2] Professor Firth has pointed out the necessity of postulating at least three phonological systems for Tamil and Telugu, namely non-brahman Dravidian, Sanskrito-Dravidian, and Sanskritic.[3] Fries and Pike have written a paper to show how the presence of Spanish loans in Mazateco led them to assume two " co-existent phonemic systems " for that language.[4]

---

[1] See J. R. Firth, *Sounds and Prosodies*, TPS 1948, p. 150 : " A loan-word may bring with it a new pattern suited to its class or type."

[2] See J. R. Firth, op. cit., where the terms " monosystemic " and " poly-stemic " are first used.

[3] J. R. Firth, op. cit., footnote to p. 127.

[4] C. C. Fries and K. L. Pike, op. cit. It should be pointed out that Fries and Pike's " co-existent phonemic systems " are very different from the primary and secondary systems described in this paper. For example : as I understand the technique applied by F. and P., I believe they would not find it necessary to postulate more than one " phonemic system " for Siamese, whereas I find that a complete structural picture of the language can be most clearly and economically presented by the arrangement of the facts in upwards of a dozen phonological systems and subsystems.

I propose, first, to suggest reasons for regarding Siamese from a polysystemic point of view.

(i) The patterns of the primary [1] system appear to be as follows :—

Monosyllables.	Disyllables.
(1) **CVV** [2]	(1) Combinations of mono-syllable types
(2) **CV(V)C**	(2) **CəCVV**
	CəCV(V)C

(ii) A " naturalized " secondary system expands **CəCVV** and **CəCV(V)C** to **Cⁱ/uCVV** and **Cⁱ/uCV(V)C**

(iii) A fragmentary " alien " system includes **CoCV(V)C**.

Examples of words,[3] presumably of very old borrowing, which conform to the requirements of the primary system are :—

ราช	ˋraːt	king	(rāja)
โลก	ˋloːk	world	(loka)
โทษ	ˋthoːt	fault	(doṣa)
เกิด	ˍkɤːt	to be born	(Cam. **kaɤt**)

---

[1] " Primary " has not necessarily any historical connotation here. I am aware, for instance, that the prosodic structures **CəCVV** and **CəCV(V)C**, whose frequent occurrence as junction forms in phrases and sentences in modern Siamese amply justifies their inclusion in the " primary " phonological system from a synchronic point of view, may perhaps be regarded as " non-Tai " by historians and comparativists, since it appears likely that all *words* of this pattern which are not of foreign (principally Cambodian) borrowing may one day be shown to be, in the historian's view, " derived from " words " originally " compounded of monosyllables.

[2] **C** includes ʔ or initial consonant group.

[3] The examples throughout this paper are shown in the native orthography (with the exception of some recent English borrowings in Siamese which have as yet no fixed spelling) and in phonetic transcription, which must, in a written version of a lecture, take the place of actual utterance. The transcription used is of necessity a general one, which it is hoped will enable those without special knowledge of the languages concerned, but with a knowledge of the International Phonetic Alphabet, to form some idea of what the words sound like, and to compare and contrast them. Neither transliteration nor phonological or phonemic transcriptions would serve this purpose, since they frequently mask the very differences in pronunciation which it was one of the aims of the lecture to demonstrate.

โขม	/kho:m	*linen cloth*	(khoma)
กาล	‾ka:n	*time*	(kāla)
เหตุ	_het	*cause*	(hetu)

None of these words could be detected as a loan on the phonetic evidence.

Of more recent origin, but still conforming to the primary pattern we find :—

‾rim	*ream*	‾biə	*beer*	‾bin	*receipt*
^nɔk	*knockout*	^lit	*litre*	‾bu:\fe:	*buffet*
‾sen	*cent*	‾mai	*mile*	‾baŋkə‾lo:	*bungalow*
_sup	*soup*	^fut	*foot*	‾khre:_dit	*credit*
			(measure)		

‾khɔ:n_kri:t *concrete*   ‾bin\liət *billiards*

‾ka:‾fɛ: or its common variant \khau_fɛ: *coffee.*

The above words are clearly European in origin, though on phonetic grounds alone there would be no reason to suspect them of being loans. Sometimes loans of this type are partnered by native words to form compounds, as for example :—

^nam‾so:‾da: *soda-water,* ^nam mə^net *lemonade,*

while for *alcohol* either ‾ɛn‾kɔ:‾hɔ: or ^nam‾man‾kɔ:‾hɔ: (^nam‾man = *oil*) may be used. Others are :—

\cha:ŋ^fit *fitter* (by analogy with \cha:ŋ‾thɔ:ŋ *goldsmith,*

\cha:ŋ^yep *tailor,* etc.)

sə^wit‾fai^fa: (*electric*) *switch*   (‾fai^fa: = *electricity*)

_pin_pak\phom *hair-pin*   (_pak\phom = *insert in the hair*)

_phak sə_lat *green salad*   (_phak = *vegetable*)

Declared by one of my informants to be Chinese in origin are the following words,[1] some of which are current in spoken but not in written Siamese :—

---

[1] Before the origins and sources of the words here treated as Chinese loans can be stated with any authority, a vast amount of work requires to be done on the Chinese influence, old and new, on Siamese vocabulary. It is felt, nevertheless, that it may be of interest to comparativists to have possible Chinese correspondences noted, even though they are not fully authenticated.   The Chinese words cited in the text are the suggestions of Professor W. Simon and Mrs. K. Whitaker, and range from almost certain identifications to what are for the moment intelligent guesses.

[It has since been pointed out to me that ` **to:** ´ **loŋ** is of Malay origin, and that it is improbable that the particular Chinese form suggested is related to ^ **thu:** ^ **si:**.—Author 1968]

Declared by one of my informants to be Chinese in origin are the following words,[1] some of which are current in spoken but not in written Siamese :—

¯koŋ/si: *firm, com-* ╱khiəm *thrifty* 儉 ╲thuəi *cup*
pany 公 司

¯sin/sɛ: *unqualified* ╲to:/loŋ *please* 勞 動 ˆthu:ˆsi: *come what*
doctor 先 生 *may* 死 都

╲tɤ:i *excellent!* ˆlɯ: *you (fam.)* ¯ta:¯teŋ *scales* 碇

第 一

All of these words conform to the primary pattern.

The secondary system comprising the disyllabic patterns C^i/u CV(V)C, C^i/u CVV may well have been introduced in order to handle Sanskritic loans. The great majority of words of this structural pattern are Pali or Sanskrit loans, many probably of very old standing, e.g. :—

สุภาพ	su'pha:p	*gracious*	(subhāva)
ปิศาจ	pi_sa:t	*demon*	(piśāca)
พินัย	phi¯nai	*discipline*	(vinaya)
พิภพ	phiˆphop	*wealth*	(vibhava)
กุศล	ku/son	*merit*	(kuśala)
ติลก	tiˆlok	*mark on forehead*	(tilaka)

The system once established, new words of any origin may thenceforward be added to it, as for example such manifestly non-Sanskritic borrowings as ku¯daŋ *go-down* (cf. Malay *godong*), siˆrap *syrup*, and the word กุลาบ ku\la:p[1] *rose*, whose non-Sanskritic origin so puzzled King Rama VI that he instituted an inquiry into its history.

Disyllables with short vowels other than ə, i, or u in an open first syllable are still very rare, and are felt to be " alien " in structure. An example is the word โปลิศ poˆlit *police*. It is worth noting that the spelling implies a pronunciation ¯po:ˆlit, there being no way in Siamese of representing a short close o sound without a following stop or nasal in the

---

[1] Compare Persian " gulab " *attar of roses*.

same syllable. Spelling difficulties of this kind are often a pointer to unassimilated phonological patterns.

Let us now consider borrowed words with sounds or tonal behaviour not admitted in the systems so far described.

Foreign Consonant Sounds.

(i) *Initials.*—Siamese is fairly rich in consonantal initials and so does not often introduce foreign sounds at the beginning of syllables. Initial clusters, however, are limited to the following :—kl, khl, kw, khw, kr, khr, pl, phl, pr, phr, tr. It thus comes about that innovations sometimes occur in loans with initial clusters other than these : e.g. \pha:‑blaŋ^ket (*army*) *blanket* ; ^fluk *fluke*. Such words are, however, an exception to the general practice, which is to link the two components of the alien cluster by anaptyxis, e.g. เหล้าบรันดี่ \lau bə‑ran‑di: *brandy*. Compare also such words as สะปอต sə‑po:t *sport*, สถานี sə/tha:‑ni: [1] *station* (used for any kind of stopping place), and the Siamese versions of the English word " station ", which are used to mean a railway station only :—

สเตทั่น sə‑te:\than, สเตแช่น sə‑te:\chɛn or กเตแช่น kə‑te:\chɛn.

(ii) *Finals.*—There is more scope here for foreign innovations, since Siamese normally permits only the following consonant sounds at the end of a syllable :—

three nasals : m n ŋ

four stops : p t k ?

In adapting foreign words to Siamese usage, as a general rule all oral consonants with labial articulation are interpreted by the labial stop p, all velar oral consonants by the velar stop k, all oral pre-velars (except liquids) (i.e. dental, alveolar, palatal, etc.) by the stop t, and the liquids r and l by n. Final consonantal groups are represented by one of the elements concerned. We thus have among Sanskritic loans :—

จล	‑con	*moving*	(cala)
พล	‑phon	*force, troop*	(bala)
ผล	/phon	*fruit*	(phala)
รัฐ	^rat	*country*	(raṭṭha, rāṣṭra)

[1] Cf. Skt. *sthānin.*

As they appear above in isolation, all these words conform perfectly to the primary pattern. In compounds, however, we find l and s as junction finals :—

จลาจล ‾col‾la:‾con *unsteady* (calācala)

พลเทพ ‾phollə\the:p (*name of* (Baladeva)
Krishna's brother)

ผลไม้ /phollə^mai *fruit* (phala + ไม้ *tree*)

รัษฎากร ¹ ^rassə‾da:‾ko:n *national revenue*

Among English borrowings in which alien finals have been adapted to Siamese patterns we find :—‾ho:‾ten *hotel* ; sə‾fiŋ *sphinx* ; ‾bin\liət *billiards* ; ‾ɔp^fit *office* ; ‾po:n sə‾tʁ:‾liŋ *pound sterling*. There are, however, many words in which foreign finals are retained, especially, of course, by speakers with a knowledge of English. Examples are :—^kɔf or ^koφ *golf* ; ‾ɔf^fit *office* ; ‾bas^ket‾bo:n *basket ball*. ‾ɔf^fit is more " learned " than ‾ɔp^fit, which conforms to the primary pattern. It should be remarked that both words conform to the pattern CVCCVC, as contrasted with the English CVCVC. Despite the existence of the secondary systems Cⁱ/uCVC, etc., Siamese remains slow to adopt new forms with short open syllables unless of the type CəCV(V)C, CəCVV. Consider :—^then^nit *tennis* ; ^bɛt‾tʁ:\ri: *battery* ; ^mɛk‾ka:‾si:n *magazine* ; ‾kam‾ma:‾con *commercial*.

It should not be thought that *any* foreign final sounds may be taken over into Siamese by loanwords. Voiced stops are never adopted. Final l is rare, but may sometimes be heard, as in เซลล์ ‾se:l (*electric*) *cell*. It is worth noting here that while voiced stops never occur at the end of a syllable in Siamese, l and s may sometimes occur as junction finals in certain compound words of Sanskritic origin, as we have already seen in /phollə^mai, ^rassə‾da:‾ko:n, etc. It is as if the occurrence of l and s in this context ² has prepared

¹ This spelling, which is transliterated raṣṭākara, is irregular from the Sanskrit point of view.

² The relevant factor here is prosodic. In this context " oral continuance " is no longer a signal of syllable-beginning.

the way for their acceptance and that of other oral continuants as absolute finals in some loanwords. Junction forms of this type are a certain pointer to a Sanskritic loanword, while absolute final l and s are almost certain to be of European origin.

Foreign Vowel Sounds.

Having glanced at the special systems set up for borrowed initial and final consonants, we may now consider what vowel sounds are admitted into special fragmentary systems. We find :—

(a) ai and au before a final consonant, as in ˆpaip (a smoker's) pipe, and ‾paun pound (weight). Compare with แป๊ปน้ำ -ˆpɛːpˆnaːm water pipe, where the sequence pɛːp is primary, but where, as we shall see later, the tone of the first word is " special ".

(b) Short ɤ before a final consonant is completely naturalized in the word เงิน ŋɤn money (silver), but as this appears to be the only word in the language with the sequence ɤC and is of Chinese origin, it may be regarded as the solitary member of a special system all its own.

(c) There are indications that a long close front vowel before a nasal may not be primary. An examination of words of the pattern CVVC shows that there are no words ending in iːŋ, two in iːm, and four in iːn. The four in iːn are จีน -ciːn Chinese, นิล -niːn blue (P.S.), มีน -miːn (a fish) (P.S.), and ตีน -tiːn foot, claw. The pair in iːm are คีม -khiːm[1] pliers, pincers, จีม -ciːm to plug up (e.g. cracks). The first three are thus accounted for as loanwords, and I strongly suspect that the last three are also loans, though I have as yet not

---

[1] With -khiːm, cf. perhaps Cambodian ក្រេប kiəp to pinch.

been able to trace them.[1]　The fact that all these words occur
on a level tone is suggestive, since words ending in a nasal are
commonly found in Siamese on a level tone when borrowed
from a non-tonal language.　(Words ending in stops follow a
different pattern.)

(d) An interesting case of another special vowel system
is that of the diphthongs iəʔ, uəʔ, ɯəʔ.　These sounds are,
I believe, outside the primary phonological system despite
the fact that they are included in the syllabaries set until
recently before a Siamese child learning to read.　Their
inclusion is probably by analogy with the pure vowels,
which are all recited in pairs, one short followed by a
glottal stop, and one long ; e.g. iʔ i: ɯʔ ɯ: uʔ u:.　When
it comes to iə, ɯə and uə, symmetry appears to demand
that here also one should recite iəʔ iə ɯəʔ ɯə uəʔ uə.
Upon investigation, however, one finds that very few words
indeed contain these glottalized diphthongs (I have so far
found no word ending in ɯəʔ), and of these few some are
onomatopoeic words, such as พัวะ _phuəʔ (the noise of
a stick snapping), and พลัวะ _phluəʔ (the sound of a bird
flying out of a thicket).　Other than onomatopoeic words only
three examples have been found, namely :—เดี๊ยะ _diəʔ nimble,
and two botanical names เคี๊ยะ ˆkhiəʔ prickly pear and
ˆkiəʔ in such names of conifers as เกี๊ยะเปิ๊ลกอกบาง
ˆkiəʔ_plɯək-ba:ŋ and เกี๊ยะเปิ๊ลกอกหนา ˆkiəʔ_plɯək/na:.　The
only likely explanation of these last words would appear to
be that they are loans. Of ˆkhiəʔ Macfarland in his dictionary
expressly states that the fruit was " introduced into the
East . . . about the middle of the eighteenth century ".　If he
is right, such a recent borrowing would be consistent with a

[1] Since reading this paper I have learnt from dialect material gathered by
Mr. J. N. Stott and by Mr. E. H. S. Simmonds that in many Tai dialects
there is a word for " foot " that is clearly akin to Siamese ti:n.　It would
thus appear that foreign borrowing is not the explanation of this word,
whose exceptional structure is a challenge to phonologists.

borrowed name. It was only last year that I found some support for the postulation of **ˆkiəʔ** as a loan when a Siamese cited a word **ˆkiəʔ**, which is not in dictionaries I have consulted, but which he used to mean (1) wooden shoes and (2) a kind of fir tree. He described the word as "Chinese" (cf. perhaps 屐), along with a number of other colloquial expressions that he used regularly, but regarded as "spoken" not "written" language. I am still without an explanation of **ˍdiəʔ**, unless it may be classed with phonaesthetic words.[1]

That onomatopoeic words, exclamations, and what may be called phonaesthetic words frequently follow phonological patterns peculiar to themselves has, of course, been pointed out before. I will only refer here to Professor Jakobsen's observation that " ces gestes vocaux [i.e. les exclamations et les onomatopées], qui aussi dans le langage des adultes, tendent à former une couche à part, semblent directement rechercher les sons non admis ailleurs ".[2]

A Siamese device for giving added expressive value to words of an exclamatory or phonaesthetic type is the use of an unorthodox, i.e. non-primary, combination of tone and final. The primary system regulates the tone of syllables ending in stops (which are unexploded in Siamese) in the following way [3] :—

Whereas **CVV** and **CV(V)N** may occur on any one of the five tones, **CVS** and **CVVS** each have a restricted alternance of two only. That is to say, we have :—

$$\mathbf{CVV}_{12345} \quad \text{and} \quad \mathbf{CV(V)N}_{12345}$$

but $\mathbf{CVS}_{24}$ and $\mathbf{CVVS}_{23}$, as in คิด **ˆkhit** *think*, มาก **ˎma:k** *much*, กับ **ˍkap** *with*, จาก **ˍca:k** (*separated*) *from*.

[1] See J. R. Firth, *The Use and Distribution of Certain English Sounds.* English Studies xvii, 1 February 1935.

[2] See *Les Lois Phoniques du Langage Enfantin*, appended to the French translation of Trubetzkoy's *Principes de Phonologie.*

[3] In the formulae in bold capitals **N** = nasal, **S** = stop, **P**ᴷ = unaspirated plosive, and index figures below the line are used to represent the five tones of Siamese.

A further restriction is that words with an initial unaspirated plosive shall occur in the followi᾽ g forms only :
P^kVV_{123}, $P^kV(V)N_{123}$, $P^kV(V)S_2$.

Certain classes of words, however, occur in the shapes
CVS_3, $CVVS_4$, $P^kV(V)S_{34}$, and P^kVV_3. These classes of words
are :—

(a) Onomatopes, such as :—เจื๊อก ^cɯək (*noise of a knife
sticking into a tree*), แป๊ด ^pɛt *honk*, กู๊ก ^kuːk (*call of a bird*),
ก๊าบ ๆ ^kaːp ^kaːp *quack, quack*, ตุบ ตับ \tup \tap (*the sound
of a fist pounding*), จุ๊บ ^cup (*smack of the lips*).

(b) Exclamations and exclamatory expressions. Here we
may include certain particles which may vary their tone in
accordance with grammatical or emotional factors. Examples
are ^baʔ (*an exclamation of surprise*), and the affirmatory
forms of particles such as \khaʔ, \caʔ. Also under this head
are the special words used to express degrees of speed, colour,
distance, size, etc.[1] .

We have for example, ยางปรี๊ด ‾yaːŋ^priːt   *extremely long*

ขาวจั๊วก /khaːu^cɯək   *dazzling white*

There are even varying degrees, as :—

เร็วจี๋   ‾reɯci: *very quick*

เร็วปรี๊ด   ‾reɯ^priːt   *quick as a flash*

แดงแจ๋   ‾dɛːŋ/cɛː   *bright red*

แดงแจ๊ด   ‾dɛːŋ^cɛːt   *vivid red*

แดงแปร๊ด   ‾dɛːŋ^prɛːt   *extremely vivid red*

All these words, /ciː, /cɛː, ^cɛːt, ^priːt, etc., are outside the
primary system.

The fourth tone is sometimes used to intensify the meaning
of a word that is not ordinarily exclamatory, e.g. :—

ə^rai   *what* ! (non-exclamatory form ə‾rai)

^diːˑdiː   *extremely good*

^maːk\maːk   *a very great deal*

[1] Cf. Mary Haas, *Techniques of Intensifying in Thai*, Word, vol. ii, No. 2.

In the last two expressions the second component is the non-exclamatory form. Both ˆdi: and ˆma:k are phonologically "special" forms, and add emphasis to the expression in which they occur.

(c) The same means may also be used to "spotlight" a borrowed word. Loanwords following the pattern $P^kV(V)S_4$ appear to be usually Chinese or English in origin. The allegedly Chinese words appear to occur only in the short form, P^kVS_4, and it is to be noted that this pattern is not in itself felt to be alien by Siamese speakers and many of the words in this form are accepted as Siamese words. The English loans on the other hand are recognized as foreign, and are frequently in the form $CVVS_4$ which is felt by most Siamese to be a "special" pattern, in a way that the pattern P^kVS_4 is not.

E.g. (allegedly Chinese) :—โต๊ะ ˆtoʔ *table* 桌, เก๊ก ˆkek *to chase off*, โป๊ยกั๊ก ˆpoi\kak (*a kind of spice*) (lit. = " 8 angles " 八 角), เจ๊ก ˆcek *a Chinese*, อาเปี๊ะ -a:ˆpeʔ *uncle* 亞 伯, สี่กั๊ก _si:ˆkak *cross-roads* (= " 4 angles " 四 角).

English :—โจ๊ก ˆco:k *'joke*, เท๊ป ˆthe:p *tape-measure*, บุ๊กตั๋ว ˆbuk(/tua) *to reserve a place*, เสื้อเชิ้ต (\sɯə)ˆchɤ:t *shirt*, หมวกแก๊ป (_muək)ˆkɛp *cap*, ไม้แบ๊ต (ˆmai)ˆbɛt *bat*, โป๊สก๊าร์ด ˆpo:səˆka:t *postcard*, ก๊าด ˆka:t, แก๊ส ˆkɛ:t or ˆkɛ:s all meaning *gas*, เทเลแกร๊บ -the:-le:ˆkrɛp, ตะแลบแก๊บ təˆlɛpˆkɛp both meaning *telegraph*.

Now all these words could have been adapted quite easily so as to conform with the primary pattern. Compare, for instance, เท๊ป ˆthe:p *tape-measure*, with เทพ \the:p *god*, *deva* an earlier borrowing. It is as if these recent loans are deliberately kept apart from what is felt to be the indigenous pattern so that they may be marked as " special words ". It may be added that the Siamese sometimes have difficulty in representing what, to borrow Pike's term, we may call " unassimilated loans " in their orthography, which is designed to show only two patterns for syllables closed with a stop.[1]

We have already observed that there appears to be a primary restriction of words of the P^kVV or $P^kV(V)N$ type to tones 1, 2, or 3.[2] In the spoken language, however, there are many words of the patterns P^kVV_{45} and $P^kV(V)N_{45}$. Most of these are not listed in dictionaries I have consulted. Many of them have been described to me by the Siamese themselves as Chinese in origin, as for example :—เก๊ ^ke: *false, counterfeit* 假, เก๋ง ⁄keŋ *a type of building*, เจ๊ง ^ceŋ *rubbish* 髒, เจ๊ ^ce: *sister* 姐, ตุ๋น ⁄tun *steamed* (of fish) 燉, ตุ๊ย ^tui *to blow* 吹, ยี่ปั๊ว \yi:^puə *sufficient*, เจ๊สัว ^ce:⁄suə *rich man*, ไชโป๊ -chai^po: *a kind of cabbage* 白菜, กี๋ ⁄ki: *stool* 几.

Two examples of the exclamatory use of these patterns have already been cited, namely ⁄ci: and ⁄cɛ:.[3] Others are ⁄puɯ: in แดงปื๋อ -dɛːŋ⁄puɯ: *pitch black*, and phonaesthetic words such as เป๋ ⁄pe: *twisted*, เป๋ง ⁄pe:ŋ *straight*, โบ๋ ⁄bo: *perforated*, บุ๋ม ⁄bum or บั๋ม ⁄bam *dented*. It appears likely that all other words in this phonological form are borrowed, possibly from Chinese in the majority of cases, e.g. ปี๋ ⁄pi: and เต๋า ⁄tau *dice*, เจี๋ยน ⁄ciən *a condiment*, เกี๋ยง ⁄kiəŋ *a kind of tree*, ก๋า ⁄ka: *impudent*,[4] เก๋ ⁄ke: *showy, flashy*,[4] กุ๋ย ⁄kui *vagabond, tramp, waif*. There is also the word ป๋อย ⁄bɔi *boy*.

The very common Siamese word เดี๋ยว ⁄diəu meaning *immediately* appears to stand by itself. It is the only word, so far as I can discover, beginning with d and having a rising tone. Perhaps it is to be regarded as belonging to

---

[1] This recalls Fries' and Pike's contention that the basic evidence for what they call the phonemic structure of a language is " the observable reactions of native speakers as they attempt to write or analyse their own language, or to speak a foreign language ", op. cit., p. 50.

[2] See p. 64.

[3] See p. 64.

[4] This word is perhaps to be regarded as phonaesthetic.

the special system for exclamatory or phonaesthetic expressions of time, speed, etc. This is more probable than that it is a loan. It may be compared with ˈtɯː *quick*, *nimble*, and with ˌdiə⁷ *nimble*.[1]

To sum up, before we leave Siamese for the moment, we have so far identified a primary system and ten fragmentary systems. These fragmentary systems are :—

(1) the disyllabic patterns $C^i/nCVV$, $C^i/nCV(V)C$;

(2) the occurrence of l and s in syllable final position in the junction groups -ll-, -ss- ;

(3) the incidence of words on tones 4 and 5 with unaspirated plosive initials ;

(4) the occurrence of short ɤ in ŋɤn ;

(5) the finals iə⁷, uə⁷, ɯə⁷ ;

(6) the admission in initial position of consonants other than voiceless plosives before semi-vowels ;

(7) the admission of l, s and f in absolute final position ;

(8) disyllabic patterns of **CVCVV** or **CVCV(V)C** type, with vowels other than ə, i, u in the first syllable ;

(9) the admission of the diphthongs **ai**, **au** before a final consonant ;

(10) the patterns CVS_3 and $CVVS_4$.

Any word characterized by the features proper to a " special ", i.e. non-primary, system may on the phonetic evidence alone be assumed to be either (a) of a phonaesthetic or exclamatory nature or (b) a loanword. If other linguistic evidence (i.e. of syntax, grammar, meaning, etc.) makes the first assumption appear unlikely, there are strong grounds for believing it to be a loan.

The first two special systems noted above are in use chiefly for Sanskritic loans. The next three appear to deal principally with Chinese, and the remainder with European loans. It must be emphasized, however, that words of European origin may be found in the " Chinese " systems, and in the Sanskrit systems, and words from all three and other sources may be found in the primary system. (Note that words of Chinese

---

[1] See p. 63.

origin do not occur in the Sanskritic systems, since these
accommodate polysyllables.) It is because of this mixing of
words from different sources in the lower layers that I prefer
on the whole not to attach specific names to these groups of
sub-systems which might infer a single origin for the words
found in them. It may be added that the " Sanskritic "
and " Chinese " systems are thoroughly naturalized, i.e. they
are not commonly regarded as alien by the Siamese themselves.
The " European " system on the other hand *is* so regarded.

Turning to Cambodian, we are again confronted with a
language with a large Sanskritic vocabulary but with a native
phonological structure very different indeed from that of
Sanskrit or Pali.

The primary system comprises the following types of
word :—

Monosyllables.	Extended Monosyllables.		Disyllables.
CVV	**C(ə)C** $\begin{cases} \textbf{VV} \\ \textbf{V(V)C} \end{cases}$		
CV(V)C			
	C(əN)C $\begin{cases} \textbf{VV} \\ \textbf{V(V)C} \end{cases}$		(combinations of monosyllables)
	CCə $\begin{cases} \textbf{CVV} \\ \textbf{V(V)C} \end{cases}$		

It will at once be seen that this pattern is much more
elaborate than the corresponding pattern of Siamese. However,
it shares with Siamese an abhorrence of short open syllables
with vowels other than ə. Unlike Siamese, Cambodian does not
admit them in a fully naturalized secondary system, although
there exists a fragmentary system of consciously learned
pronunciations which permits such forms as វិតក្ក **vi'tok**
(P. vitakka) *thought*, ឱសថ **o'sot** (S. auṣadha) *herbs*. The
common practice is to adapt such words to one of the
patterns permitted in the primary system, e.g. :—

(S. putra)	ឬ្ត្រ	ɓot	*son*	**CVC**
(S.P. kapāla)	ក្បាល	kɓa:l	*head*	**CCVVC**
(S.P. bala)	ពល	pùəl	*force*	**CVC**
(S.P. majja)	មជ្	mùc	*to dive*	**CVC**
(S.P. surā)	សុរា	sra:	*alcoholic liquor*	**CCVV**
(S.P. dāna)	ទាន	tìən	*gift*	**CVVC**
(S.P. jīvita)	ជីវិត	cì:vùt	*life*	**CVV–CVC**
(S. krodha)	ក្រោធ	kraot	*anger*	**CCVVC**
(S. vṛddha)	ព្រឌ្	prùv	*old, full-grown*	**CCVC**

Sometimes the Sanskrit **CV-** is transformed into the more acceptable **CVC** by " borrowing " from the initial consonant sound of the following syllable, e.g. :—

(S. putrī)	ឬ្ត្រី	ɓottrəi	*daughter*
(S. ṛṣi)	ឫសី, ឬសី	rùssəi	*hermit, sage*
(S. nidrā)	និទ្រា	nùntrìə	*sleep*
(S.P. devī)	ទេពី	tè:ppì:	*goddess*
(S. tejaḥ)	តេជះ	ɗe:ccèəh	*excellence*

An important feature of Cambodian phonology is the presence of two contrasting voice registers, each with its appropriate vowel alternation. As the Cambodians read their syllabary, those consonant symbols which correspond to Sanskrit voiced sounds imply one register, the consonants corresponding to Sanskrit unvoiced sounds the other, e.g.[1] :—

---

[1] In the phonetic transcription of Cambodian and Mon a grave accent over a vowel or vowel sequence indicates pronunciation with " chest " as opposed to " head " register. In the formulae in bold capitals register is indicated by the figures 1 or 2 below the line. For a description of the phonetic characteristics of the registers, see Henderson (1952) "The Main Features of Cambodian Pronunciation", *BSOAS*.

kɔ   khɔ   kɔ̀   khɔ̀   ŋɔ̀

cɔ   chɔ   cɔ̀   chɔ̀   ɲɔ̀ etc.

I shall refer to the kɔ, cɔ series as being on the first register, the kɔ̀, cɔ̀ series the second register. Thus, while the consonant sounds may be the same on both registers, the consonant symbol will indicate a difference in register and accompanying vowel sound. For example, ก is read ka:, but ก is read kiə. The normal sequence in a syllable is therefore C_1V_1 or C_2V_2, with the appropriate register linked always with the vowel sound (but consonant symbol). There are, however, words containing the sequences C_1V_2 or C_2V_1. For instance, there are a number of words with an initial nasal followed by a vowel of the first register alternance. Some of these appear to be related to Siamese words of the same pattern, and might be worth investigation by language historians. Meanwhile I venture to suggest they are likely to be Siamese loans on the strength of the internal evidence. The words of this type are too numerous for one to be able to say outright, without corroboration from other fields, that C_2V_1 is a foreign pattern, but they are sufficiently few to be suggestive. With the pattern C_1V_2 we appear to be on firmer ground. The consonant sounds normally restricted to the first register are s, h, ɗ, and ɓ. One is not surprised therefore at the obvious foreign origin of the words ยาง ซู้

kau sù: *rubber*, and สาบู่ sa:ɓù: *soap*. The only word I have found with ɗ in a second register syllable is a personal name, as is the only example, other than sa:ɓù:, of ɓ in this context, and personal names frequently follow phonological patterns of their own. Other than kau sù: I have so far found only two other examples of s in a second register syllable, namely, a slang term of abuse ซู่ sù: or เซ่ sÿ:, which is not shown in dictionaries and may be classed as of an exclamatory type; and secondly, the word ซี่ sì: meaning "to eat".[1] This

---

[1] Since reading this paper, I have come across the word ɓù:sì *sparking-plug* ($C_1V_2C_1V_2$) from French "bougie".

word is particularly interesting since the word for " to eat " in Mon diverges from the primary pattern in much the same way. The Mon script links consonant symbol and vowel alternance (with implication of register) much as does the Cambodian, e.g. :—

ka?	kha?	kẹ̀ə?	khèə?	ŋèə?
ca?	cha?	çẹ̀ə?	chèə?	ɲèə? etc.

The spelling of the word " to eat " implies ca?, but the pronunciation is in fact cẹə?, with first register but an accompanying vowel more appropriate to the second register. I understand from colleagues in the S.E. Asian field, who have studied the languages of the area from the historical point of view, that the Mon-Khmer word for " to eat " is not one that they have cause to suspect as a loan. It is not, perhaps, the kind of word one might except to be borrowed, nor does it appear to belong to any of the other classes of words that may be expected to diverge from the primary system. Nevertheless, there must be some explanation why these two words are found in exceptional phonological form in their respective languages, though what it is is as yet undiscovered.

Let us look back for a moment to the Cambodian pattern CəNCVV or CəNCV(V)C. The -əN- has grammatical function as can be seen from the following :—

ទ្រួត	trù:ət	*to supervise*	ទំរួត	tùmrù:ət	*supervision*
កើត	kaʏt	*to be born*	កំនើត	kəmnaʏt	*birth*
ត្រង់	trɔŋ	*straight*	តំរង់	təmrɔŋ	*to straighten*
គ្រុប	krùp	*enough*	គំរុប	kùmrùp	*to suffice*

It will be seen that the register and vowel of the extended form is always the same as that of the simple form. The vowel before the infixed nasal, which is unstressed, may be regarded as anaptyctic, and varies according to the register of the word as a whole.

These infixed words have been classified as extended monosyllables since it is convenient to take the possibility

of two different registers as a mark of a disyllable ; that
is to say we have the formulae [1] :—

Extended

Monosyllable.   *Monosyllable.*   *Disyllable.*

R   R   R   R
⌢   ⌢⌢⌢⌢⌢   ⌢⌢   ⌢⌢

C V C   CəNCVC   C V C   C V C

In Siamese we have, corresponding to **kaʁt, kɔmnaʁt,
tɪùːət, tùmrùːət** the words เกิด **_kʁːt**, กำเนิด ⁻**kam_nʁːt**,

ตรวจ **_truət**, ตำรวจ ⁻**tam_ruət**. Now in a native Siamese word
one would expect the pronunciations ⁻**kam\nʁːt**, ⁻**tam\ruət**, for
the longer forms, since the words would be compounds of
the **CVC–CVVC** type, and, unless special factors intervene, the
spellings เนิด, รวจ imply the pronunciations **nʁːt** and **ruət**

with falling tone. (Compare : จำพวก ⁻**cam\phuək** *assembly.*)
The pronunciation ⁻**kam_nʁːt** can only be satisfactorily
accounted for by regarding the low tones of **_nʁːt** and **_ruət**
as dependent upon the low tone of **_kʁːt** and **_truət**. Tone,
in fact, is regulated in precisely the same way as register
in Cambodian, and not at all according to the rules governing
tone in the primary Siamese pattern. For this reason, if for
no other, one would regard these words as Cambodian loans in
Siamese, rather than the other way about. This special
system for Cambodian loans may be added to the special
systems for Siamese already described.

I now propose to glance briefly at Vietnamese, and in
particular, at the Tonkinese dialect. Here we find a very
different picture from the two languages so far examined,
since the literary language of Vietnamese—that is to say,
the language of the great majority of borrowed words—is
Chinese. We may state the primary phonological pattern of
Tonkinese as :—

(C)V or **(C)VC**, with a range of 6 tones.

---

[1] In these formulae, **R** = register.

The vast majority of Chinese loanwords conform so well to this prosodic pattern that I have so far not discovered any means of extracting them on phonological grounds except in the following case.

The roman orthography in use for Vietnamese represents four nasal initials, and four nasal finals, viz. : *n, m, nh, ng.* The vowels are as follows :—*i, ê, e, ă, a, â, o, ô, u, ơ, ư,* [i e ɛ ă a ɤ ɔ o u ɤ ɯ].

If we look at the distribution of these symbols in dictionaries we find before the various vowels a fairly even distribution of the nasals, but after the vowels we find the following :—

im	*in*	*inh*	—
êm	*ên*	*ênh*	—
em	*en*	—	—
ăm	*ăn*	—	*ăng*
âm	*ân*	—	*âng*
am	*an*	*anh*	*ang*
—[1]	*ôm*	—	*ông*
om	*on*	—	*ong*
um	*un*	—	*ung*
ưm	*ưn*	—	*ưng*
ơm	*ơn*	—	—[1]

From this it appears that *nh* and *ng* are in complementary distribution, i.e. the spelling represents *three,* not *four,* possible final nasals. The spelling *anh* appears to confute this view until it is observed that *enh* is missing ; after which it becomes clear that in *anh* we are dealing with the representation of a front vowel of the 3rd degree of openness before a nasal final, which may be termed non-labial and non-dental. When we examine the pronunciation, we find that the pronunciation of *nh* initially is ɲ, whereas finally it is a palatalized velar, i.e. while *nha* is ɲa, *inh* is iŋ, not iɲ (as can be clearly seen from palatograms). The vowel before final ŋ is usually rather centralized. It is therefore easy to see how the vowel sound in

---

[1] The absence of *ưm* and *ông,* while clearly of importance phonologically, is not relevant to the present discussion.

ë^{i}ŋ came to be interpreted by the symbol *a*, and how the palatal element in the final led to the spelling " *anh* ".

In the primary phonological system therefore, Tonkinese has 3 possible final nasals, with both front and back vowels occurring before each. The spelling *anh* appears, however, to have misled even the Vietnamese themselves, who think of it as representing **a** + **ɲ**. My informants were astonished when the lack of words in *eng* and *enh* was pointed out to them. And in fact further investigation revealed the fact that there are three words spelt *eng*, and pronounced ⁻ɛŋ, i.e. an open front vowel without centralization followed by a fairly back velar nasal. These words are :—

> *keng*—(*the noise of chinking brass*) ;
> *kehg*—(slang) *smart, chic*—said by one of my informants
>   to be from " Américain " ;

and, lastly, *xehg*—*shovel*, or *spade*. I can offer no explanation of this last word except to suggest that it is a loan, possibly from Chinese, and that it must be regarded as belonging to a " special " phonological system.[1]

By the same route that we take to arrive at the phonological interpretation of *anh* as ɛŋ in the primary system, we may conclude that *ach* is the orthographic representation of phonological ɛk, pronounced ë^{i}ḳ. Occasionally one encounters Vietnamese words spelt *ec*, but so far only two have not been accounted for as Cochinchinese spellings (there is great confusion in Cochinchinese of final *c* and *t*) : *léc* in *cù léc* ˌku ′lɛk,[2] *to tickle*, and *kéc* ′kɛk *parrot*. The second of these is possibly to be regarded as an onomatope, while the first may be phonaesthetic.

Another puzzling word—puzzling in form, that is—is *nőu* ′nɤu *gum*, which my informant describes as a word used by the dentists at fairs. It is puzzling because so far as

---

[1] Cf. Fries and Pike, p. 38. For a monosystemic approach to this problem see M. B. Emeneau, *Studies in Vietnamese* (*Annamese*) *Grammar*, p. 16.

[2] In this phonetic transcription the tone marks are used as follows :—
⁻ (bằng) ˍ (nạng) ˇ (hỏi), ˜ (ngã), ′ (sách), ˎ (hùyên).

I can discover it is the only word in the language with *ou* as its final. Once again, borrowing may be the explanation.

Tonkinese borrowings from European languages are usually adapted to the primary system, e.g. :—

cà phê	ˌka⁻fe	*coffee*
mùi xoa	ˌmui⁻swa	*handkerchief* (Fr. *mouchoir*)
sên	⁻sen	*oaktree* (Fr. *chene*)
sơ-mi	ˌsx⁻mi	*shirt* (Fr. *chemise*)
(xe) tăng	⁻(sɛ°)⁻taŋ	*tank*
gi-lê	⁻zi⁻le	*waistcoat, gilet*
mìn	ˌmin	*mine*
bơ	ˋbɤ	*butter* (Fr. *beurre*)
bánh	ˊbëⁱŋ	*bread, cake*
		(possibly < Portuguese [1])
ga	⁻ɤa	*station* (Fr. *gare*)
cao-xu	⁻kau⁻su	*rubber* (Fr. *caoutchouc*)
bi	⁻bi	*marble* (Fr. *bille*)
bia	⁻biə	*beer*
Bà-lê	ˌba‿le	*Paris*
Nữ-ước	˜nɯˊɯək	*New York*
tách	ˊtëⁱk̜	*cup* (Fr. *tasse*)

r is not used in colloquial Tonkinese; but most Tonkinese appear able to pronounce one in very careful or slow style, or when dictating. *Ice-cream* may therefore be *kem* ⁻kɛm or *cà rém* ˌkaˊrɛm, but *cravate* is adopted as *cà-vạt* ˌka‿vat.

A recent example of the setting up of a fragmentary system not conforming to the primary one is the following :—

Vietnamese admits a number of labialised initial consonants—kw, xw, tw, lw, hw, etc., but never admits a labialized labial initial, i.e. we find initial f, b, v, and m, but not fw, bw, vw, mw. However, in the speech of Westernized young Vietnamese, whose political beliefs nowadays often run counter to the traditional status pronoun system, a new pair of pronouns is in current use as between equals (e.g. fellow students) where both status pronouns and those

---

[1] See Dalgado, *Influence of Portuguese Vocables in Asiatic Languages.*

appropriate to the intimacy of the family may be felt to be out of place. These new pronouns are *toa* **twa** for the second person, *moa* **mwa** for the first (French *moi, toi*). **twa** conforms to the primary pattern, but **mwa** stands outside it, and is thereby marked as an " alien " word.

I shall now in conclusion glance very briefly at Mon and Burmese, languages with which I have not yet worked long enough to be able to put forward anything approaching a complete picture of the phonological structure of either. Nevertheless, loanwords in these languages show points of interest. As in Siamese and Cambodian, there appears to be a tendency to adapt Sanskritic words of diverse shapes to a monosyllabic pattern, i.e. **CV**, or **CVC**, the final **C** being a stop, nasal, or h, e.g. :—

	Mon.			Burmese.[1]	
စက်	ca:k	*wheel, machine*	စက်	sɛʔ	(cakkaṃ)
စိုတ်	cɒ:t	*mind*	စိတ်	seiʔ	(citta)
ပါဒ	pɒ:t	*foot*	ပါဒ်	paiʔ	(pāda)
ဘုံ	phù:m	*earth, world*	ဘုံ	boũ	(bhūmi)
ဂြိုဟ်	ḳrɤ̀:h	*planet*	ဂြိုဟ်	jo	(graha)
သိမ်	sɛ:m	*building for ordination*	သိမ်	θeĩ	(sīmā)
ဗိုလ်	bɤ̀:	*force*	ဗိုလ်	bo	(bala)
နဲ	nɒ̀ə	*rule, precept*	နည်း	ˌni	(naya)

In both Mon and Burmese there is a disyllabic pattern **Cə¹CVC**, and foreign words with a similar prosodic structure may be found in this form, as :—

---

[1] The phonetic transcription of the Burmese examples follows the transcription proposed by J. R. Firth, *Alphabets and Phonology in India and Burma*, with the exception that nasalized syllables are marked with ˜ over the vowel symbol, and not with final ŋ, which might be confusing to those comparing Burmese forms with other languages cited here. In the transcription of Mon potential voicing is shown by the mark ◡, e.g. ḳrɤ̀:h.

Mon.			Burmese.	

ပလိက် pəloiᶄ *police* ပလိာ် pəlei?

Also taken into this pattern instead of the monosyllabic one are such words as ṛṣi *Mon.* rĕ(ə)ˡsɔi? (*Bur.* yəðeˡ) *sage*

gati *Mon.* gĕ(ə)ˡtɔi? (*Bur.* gətiˡ) *promise*

In Mon the English words *smart* and *style* also appear in this shape, e.g. သွာတ် səma:t, သတၱိၚ sətaiŋ.

Foreign words of the type ˡCVCVC are, however, reshaped in Mon as combinations of the patterns CV and CVV :—

ၔက်ရိက် lak ᶄet or *luggage* သက်က sak ka? *circus*
lak ᶄoiᶄ

တီက်တ် ti: kɛt *ticket* ဂျာၐန် ja: nè: *journal*

ဗေတ်တရီ bet tri: *battery* သပေၐဟျာ səpɛ: ya: " *spare*",
                                              i.e. *the conductor
                                              of a bus*

Similarly, loanwords of more than two syllables may be handled as combinations of CV, CVC, and CəˡCVC, e.g. :—

ကွၚဆၥိကလိက် (kwaiŋ) chɔ: ᶄelet or ᶄelit *chocolate*, ပၟိသကေၥ bàiŋsəke: *bicycle*, ပၟိသကုက် bàiŋsəkʉ:ᶄ *cinema* (*bioscope*). The Mon loans for *circus*, *luggage*, *journal*, etc., show how un-familiar finals such as dʒ, l, and s are dealt with. Other common examples are ပါတ်ကါ bà:t ka: for *bus*, ဂေတ်(သ) ᶄèət *gas*, ကၥိလိက် kɔ: lɔiᶄ *college*, ၒှုၥမၚေၥါ mənìh mèəŋ gò: *goal-keeper*. The unfamiliar English final consonant groups -nd and -nt are similarly naturalized in ပေၚ pɔiŋ *point*, and ဝၚ pəŋ *pound*. The oddities of Mon spelling and pronunciation, how-ever, are such that one cannot always predict the final of a word borrowed into the language.

Compare :—

(ကွၚ)ကိက်	(kwaiŋ) koiᶄ or	*cake*
	(kwaiŋ) ᶄek	
ဖြိက်	proiᶄ	*brake (of car)*
မၥိတၥိဗုက်	mɔ:tɔ:bʉ̀:ᶄ	*motorboat*
ပၟိသကုက်	bàiŋsəkʉ:ᶄ	*bioscope*
ၐၚတၚိ	phaʉ̀ŋtoiŋ	*fountain pen*

Some of these and similar cases may perhaps be explained as Mon spelling-pronunciations of Burmese orthographic forms. For example, the spelling ဒုက် in Burmese is pronounced **ouʔ**, which is the nearest Burmese can get to **out** or **oup** (in *motorboat* and *bioscope*). This spelling in Mon is regularly pronounced **ɤ:k̬**, and suggests a borrowing via Burmese, since Mon has the possibility of pronouncing **o:t** and **o:p** which would be what one might expect in a direct borrowing (spelling : ဒေါတ် and ဒေါပ်).

Unfamiliar initials, such as **ʃ**, **f**, **fl**, are sometimes naturalized, as in :—ဖ္လေက်ဖံ **phleəkphɔ:m** *platform*, ကဝ်ဖဳ **kɔ: phi:** *coffee*.

More frequently, however, they appear to be taken over in more or less original form, thus starting a new subsystem of syllable initials :—

ဝှလေန်	**flen**	*film* (with metathesis) (or ဖလေန် **phəlen**)
ကဝ်ဖွဲ	**kɔ: fuə**	alternative form of *coffee*
ဖေတ်ယှေန်	**phe:t ʃẹn**	*fashion* (notice " naturalized " absolute initial and " alien " junction initial)
(ပလောံ)ရှာတ်	**(pəlɔʔ)ʃa:t**	*shirt*

It may be noted that the fact that oral continuants (e.g. **s**, **f**) occur in Mon in syllable-initial but not in syllable-final position appears to make it easier for a new sound of this type to be accepted initially than finally, e.g. (ဂ္ၚပ်)ရှူတ် **(gnɔ̀p) ʃu:t** *shoes*.

Unexpected initials or vowel sequences, i.e. which appear not to be the " closest " to the borrowed sounds that the native system allows, may be seen in such forms as :—

(i)	ပါက်တရံင်	**pakkəraun̥**	*patron*
(ii)	မဝ်တဝ်ကါ	**mɔ:tɔ:kɛ:**	*motorcar* (beside more learned **mɔ:tɔ:ka:**)
(iii)	ရေဒီယော	**rè:dì:yɤ̀:**	*radio* (beside more learned **rè:dì:yò:**)

(iv) ဗီဒို   biːdr̀ː   *cupboard* (cf. Burmese ဗီဒို
                                bi do, or bi yo, <*"bureau"*)

(v) ဟောင်မရ   hɤːŋᵐphruː *homerule*
              hɤːŋᵐfruː

The apparent preference for ɤ, when o is permitted in the
system, and the pronunciation kɛː instead of kaː, may perhaps
be indications of what Fries and Pike call "direction of
change".[1] The word **pakkərauŋ** is certainly an illustration of
a *direction of change*, namely, from p(ə)r-, t(ə)r-, t(ə)w-, etc.,
to k(ə)r-, k(ə)w- etc., cf. :—

ကြိုင် ḳ̥ròiŋ *soot*   ကြိပ် ḳ̥rip̆ *to run*   ကြုပ် ḳ̥ròp *property*
                                                  (S. dravya)

ခွေး ḳ̥wèə *door*
     (S. dvār)

I think that hɤːŋᵐphruː and hɤːŋᵐfruː illustrate Mon realizations of the junction *nasal + r*, while biːdr̀ː probably owes the
initial of the second syllable to the fact of its borrowing via
Burmese, which has no r sound.

To sum up : We have seen that by the structural study of
a language it is possible to isolate a number of more or less
complete phonological systems of which one may be regarded
as primary. A system whose prosodic structure conforms to
the primary pattern, may be felt by the native speaker to be
fully naturalized,[2] even though phonematic features may
reveal its non-primary character. Words felt by the speaker
to be of a special kind are marked by special prosodic patterns.
"Special words" are of the following types :—(*a*) exclamations and exclamatory expressions, including certain particles ;
(*b*) phonaesthetic words, including onomatopes ; (*c*) loanwords.[3]

---

[1] op. cit., p. 42.

[2] Firth, p. 150, "When completely naturalized the prosodic system of the
type or class of word in the borrowing language is dominant."

[3] Firth, p. 149, "The study of prosodic structures has bearing on all
phonological studies of loanwords."

COMPARATIVE TABLE SHOWING THE PRONUNCIATION OF SOME SANSKRITIC LOANWORDS

Sanskrit or Pali form.		Siamese.	Cambodian.	Mon.	Burmese.
1. bala	force	˗phon	pùel	bɛ̀ː	bo
2. bhāga	portion	\phaːk	phìeʔ	phêeḳêeʔ	bawaˡ
3. bhāva, bhava	existence	\phaːp	phìep	phêwêeʔ	sei?
4. citta	mind	ˍcit	cɤt	cɐːt	de waˡ
5. deva	god	\theːp	tὲːp	[tewɐtaːo]	do ðaˡ
6. doṣa	fault	\thoːt	tôhˢ	tȷ̊ὸːsaʔ	draʔˡ ¹
7. dravya	property	^sap	trɔ̀ep	ḳrɔ̀p	jo
8. gr̥ha	planet, sign of zodiac	^khrɯʔ_haʔ		ḳrɛ̀ːh	
9. jivita	life	˗chiːʌwit	ciːvùt	çiʷiʔta?	zi waˡ
10. kuśala	merit	kuʌson	kosɔːl	kauʔsoː	kuˡ ðo
11. pati	master	boˑdiː	pɗei		
12. pāda	foot	ˍbaːt	ɓaːt	pɒːt	pai?
13. pitā, pitu-	father	˗biːˑdaː	ɓeiɗàː	poiʔtauʔ	pi taˡ
14. putra, putta	son	ˍbut	ɓot		pouʔtaˡ
15. putrī	daughter	ˍbutˑtriː	ɓottrei		
16. r̥ṣi, isi	sage	rɯ/siː, i/siː	rìessei, rɯssei	rὲsoiʔ	yθθeˡ
17. śapatha	oath, curse	se˗ɓot	sɓot	sɐpɒːt	
18. svasti	fortune	se˗watˑdiː	suːesɗei		
19. velā	time	˗weːˑlaː	[i] pèːl [ii] vèːlie		
20. vinaya	discipline	phiˑnai	piˑnêi	wiʔnὸe	wini
21. vr̥ddha, vuddha	full-grown	^phrut	prɯt	wὺtthêeʔ	wouʔdaˡ

¹ A learned pronunciation. dr is not primary in Burmese.

It follows that while extra-phonetic evidence of the history of words can confirm that our structural studies are on the right lines, the structural evidence itself may be of great importance to the language historian in determining which words *are* loans, and in some cases perhaps even the route by which they were borrowed.

4

Some Prosodic Aspects of Retroflexion and Aspiration in Sanskrit

By W. S. ALLEN

UNDER the traditional titles of Assimilation and Dissimilation, we are presented with two linguistic phenomena apparently involving a principle similar to that which is known in physical science as " action at a distance "— regularly in the latter case, occasionally in the former (under special titles, such as " *dilation* ", " *Fernassimilation* "). The classical example of this type of assimilation is provided by the Sanskrit " cerebralization " (*nati*) of *n*,[1] with reference to which the term " *action à distance* " has, in fact, been used.[2] In connection with the physical principle, it may be of interest to recall Newton's words :—

> " It is inconceivable that inanimate brute matter should, without the mediation of something else which is not material, operate upon and affect other matter without mutual contact."

Speech-sound, of course, is not " brute matter ", and it would be a dangerous and unnecessary principle to submit linguistics to physical criteria, but Newton's uneasiness may at least serve to lead us to a reconsideration of similar postulates of our own science. Amongst these the conception of an articulation A at one point in the temporal dimension [3] exercising a form of " gravitational influence " upon an articulation B at a distant point would appear to be one that is only tolerable *faute de mieux*.

The whole principle of assimilation in descriptive linguistics has already been assailed more than once, on the ground that the implied change is only metaphorical, having reference to a hypothetical " basic " form [4] derived from

[This paper, published in the heyday of the prosodic campaign, displays a typical reaction against traditional and phonemic doctrine. Seventeen years later it still seems to the author a worth-while experiment, and to provide a valid and in some cases preferable alternative ; but some aspects of the rejected doctrines now seem less intolerable than they did. As one example may be cited the ' psychophysical ' explanations of dissimilation ; in fact in a forthcoming publication (*Vox Graeca*, C.U.P.) the following will be suggested as a possible explanation of the apparent anomaly that, whereas by Grassmann's Law, e.g. ἀμφ' + ἔχω → ἀμπέχω (with dissimilation), ἐλειπ + δην → ἐλείφθην (with assimilation) : ' Dissimilation typically involves the avoidance of repetition of an articulatory action, as assimilation involves the extension of an articulatory posture ; aspiration involves a particular posture of the larynx and pharynx [cf. A. C. Sen, *Proc. II ICPS* (1935), 189], and it is only the *adoption* of this posture that constitutes an action ; thus in the examples covered by Grassmann's Law, if both aspirates were preserved, it would involve changing the posture after the first aspirate in order to articulate the immediately following sound(s), and then readopting the posture for the second aspirate. Where there are no intervening articulations, the posture can be maintained and there is thus no case for dissimilation, but rather for assimilation '.—Author 1968]

[1] Cf. Brugmann, *Grundriss*, i, § 973 ; Grammont, *Traité de Phonétique*[3], p. 251, both of which give this example pride of place.

[2] Bloch, *L'Indo-Aryen*, p. 56 ; cf. *Formation de la Langue Marathe*, p. 166.

[3] Or, from the transcriptional point of view, the time-*track* or linear dimension.

[4] Cf. Nida, *Morphology*, p. 26.

Source : W. S. Allen, ' Some prosodic aspects of retroflexion and aspiration in Sanskrit ', *BSOAS*, 13, (1951), 939–46. Reprinted by permission of the School of Oriental and African Studies and the author.

the consideration of other contexts or of earlier stages of the language,[1] and leading to such definitions as " the extension of an element of articulation outside its proper sphere ".[2] However, whilst fully agreeing that we cannot accept the imputation of improper behaviour to any element of utterance, I shall not call upon the support of this general argument in the present discussion, which considers only how, in two particular instances, we may best eliminate the unrealistic postulate of distant influence : such conceptions are especially common in the description of ancient languages, and the two examples here chosen are both from Sanskrit. For assimilation I shall discuss the case already mentioned, and for dissimilation the Sanskrit half of " Grassmann's Law ", approaching each of these in the light of principles suggested by Professor J. R. Firth's article, " Sounds and Prosodies," in *Trans. Phil. Soc.*, 1948.

The law which states the conditions for $n > ṇ$ after $ṛ, ṝ, r, ṣ$ [3]—one of the more imposing " Rules of Internal Sandhi "—is only too well-known ; as stated in the Prātiśākhyas [4] and by Pāṇini,[5] and as perpetuated in our European grammars, it is that (within a word) :—

" $ṛ, ṝ, r, ṣ$, in spite of intervening vowels, gutturals (including h), labials (including v), y and Anusvāra, change n to $ṇ$ if followed by vowels, n, m, y, v." [6]

The complexity of this rule is considerably reduced by a " physiological explanation " such as that of Whitney,[7] namely that " in the marked proclivity of the language toward lingual utterance " the retroflex tongue-position assumed for $ṛ, ṝ, r, ṣ$,[8] is maintained until a following $n (> ṇ)$:—

" unless the proclivity is satisfied by the utterance of a lingual mute, or the organ is thrown out of adjustment by the utterance of an element which causes it to assume a different posture ".

This physiological statement (which, incidentally, is implied by one at least of the ancient Indian treatises [9]) also provides us with a link between the active and the passive members of the assimilation, namely a tongue-position, a

---

[1] Cf. Bloomfield, *Language*, p. 213 ; J. R. Firth, in *English Studies*, xvii, February, 1935 ; R. S. Wells, " Automatic Alternation," in *Language*, xxv, 1949, pp. 99 ff. Similar objections may be made against the Prague concept of " neutralization of oppositions ", applied to the present case by Trubetzkoy, *Principes de Phonologie*, p. 249.

[2] Palmer, *Introduction to Modern Linguistics*, p. 31.

[3] The " dot-and-dash " system of transliteration (n for ṇ, etc.), though highly undesirable in phonetic discussion, is here retained as being in general use by Sanskritists.

[4] *RV.*, v. 42 and 56 ; *AV.*, iii. 75 ; *Tait.*, xiii. 6 ; *Vāj.*, iii. 83 and 94.

[5] VIII. iv. 1 ff.

[6] Macdonell, *Sanskrit Grammar*, § 65. On the apparent *RV.* exceptions *rāṣṭrānām* and *uṣṭrānām* see Wackernagel, *Altind. Gramm.*, § 145b ; Macdonell, *Ved. Gr.*, § 42a.a.

[7] *Sanskrit Grammar*, § 189.

[8] $ṛ, ṝ, r$, being retroflex sounds at the time and place of the crystallization of the rule, as attested by the Pāṇinīya Śikṣā and by the Pāṇinean scheme in general (cf. Varma, *Critical Studies in the Phonetic Observations of Indian Grammarians*, pp. 6 ff.).

[9] *RV. Prāt.*, v. 56 (" *avyavetaṃ . . . vighnakṛdbhiḥ* ").

" point d'articulation ", thus satisfying the Newtonian demand for a mediating factor : as a descriptive statement, however, we shall see that it still has grave shortcomings.

If retroflexion is now abstracted as a prosody it may be stated that the presence of the prosody of retroflexion is marked in the traditional linear transcription by a series of special letters (t, th, d, dh, n, s) ; so that, symbolizing the prosody by R [1] (and eliminating the special "retroflex" letters), we find $\overset{R}{patha}$- orthographically represented by $patha$-, $\overset{R}{upanisad}$ by $upanisad$, etc. $\overset{R}{rtu}$- is denoted simply by rtu- and $\overset{R}{matra}$- by $matra$-, etc., since r, $\bar{r}$, r invariably correlate with the R-prosody.

Sanskrit spelling, in spite of the syllabic basis of the system of writing is, in American terminology, largely " phonemic "—that is to say, if a modern " phonemicist " set out to produce an orthography for Sanskrit, the resulting spellings would show a close parallelism with those attested in Devanāgarī [2] : as such, it is phonetically imprecise (as, of course, any system of transcription must be) and phonologically over-precise : it is this latter fact which is to account for many of the complexities of the ". Rules of Sandhi ", an imposition foreign to the much maligned but often phonologically sound spelling of English.[3] It is thus in the tradition of the Sanskrit orthography that it should mark not only the presence of the prosody but also, to the best of its capabilities, its extension in the linear, phonematic dimension : this it can do where the appropriate special letters are already available—viz. as being units of the monosystemic, phonemic analysis. The result is that in some degree we are enabled to see the extent of the linear projection of the prosody ; thus

$\overset{R}{is\text{-}ta}$-   is represented by $ista$-,   suggesting $\overset{R}{ista}$- ;

$\overset{R}{tad\ dayate}$ „   „ $taddayate$,   „ $\overset{R}{taddayate}$;

$\overset{R}{tan\ dimbhan}$ „   „ $tandimbhan$,   „ $\overset{R}{tandimbhan}$.

The orthography suggests that this extension is particularly wide in the special

---

[1] The use of this symbol may have practical advantages when it comes to considering such changes from linear to prosodic function as are attested by Middle Indian developments of the type Skt. $arta$- > Pkt. $atta$- (cf. Pischel, § 289).

[2] As may be seen in part from Professor M. B. Emeneau's " The Nasal Phonemes of Sanskrit ", *Language*, xxii, 1946, pp. 86 ff., with the findings of which I am in agreement ; cf. also A. H. Fry, " A Phonemic Interpretation of Visarga," *Language*, xvii, 1941, pp. 194 ff.

[3] Cf. J. Vachek, *Acta Linguistica* v, p. 92 f.

case considered, namely where the marker is *ṛ, ṝ, r, ṣ*,[1] i.e. other than a
stop, and is followed by phonological *n*, the *natyakṣara* par excellence,[2] under
the conditions already stated, e.g. :—

R̄ *nisan-na-*,	represented by *niṣaṇṇa-*,		suggesting	R̄ ⌐‾‾‾¬ *nisanna-* ;
R̄ *bṛmh-ana-*,	,, ,,	*bṛmhaṇa-*,	,,	R̄ *bṛmhana-* ;
R̄ *ārabhya-māna-*,	,, ,,	*ārabhyamāṇa-*,	,,	R̄ ⌐‾‾‾‾‾‾¬ *ārabhyamāna-*.

But if we remember that the rules of Sandhi are really rules for Sanskrit spelling,
we shall not expect to find that the orthography tells us the whole story. We
may suspect, for instance, that in *pāṭha-* the retroflexion was present also in the
vowel preceding the *ṭh*,[3] and might be considered as potentially present even
in the initial bilabial stop ; so that such a word could in fact be used to give a
" word-palatogram "[4] in which the retroflex " wipe ", though actually produced
during the phonation of the retroflex stop, would represent a process of the whole
word, the remaining articulations being palatographically non-interfering. But
since it had not been found necessary to have a symbol for a^{τ}, etc., in the
syllabary (in phonemic parlance, since a^{τ} was an allophone, not a phoneme),[5]
this is not represented ; thus the extension of the prosody is, in fact, only
partially marked by spellings such as *iṣṭa-, niṣaṇṇa-*, etc. This is indeed a minor
phonetic imprecision, but in the case of sequences such as *brahmā*, where the
physiological explanation would lead us to expect (probably with justification)

---

[1] Skt. *ṣ* is in many cases the reflex of IE **s* by a process or processes marked at an early
period not only by *ṛ, r*, but also by *i, u, k*, and it might be objected that in examples such as
niṣaṇṇa- the marker is thus not *ṣ* but *i*. There are, however, good reasons for rejecting this
argument : the following facts are relevant :—

(a) From the physiological point of view it is difficult to conceive why a process of retroflexion should be associated with the diverse units *i, u, k*.

(b) Parallel processes, with identical markers, are attested in Iranian and Slavonic.

(c) The reflex of (b) is not, as in Skt., *ṣ* (ꬱ), but Av. *š* (ʃ), O.C.S. *ch* (х).

From (b) it follows that the beginnings of the process(es) are to be put back at least to the
Indo-Iranian period. A possible interpretation of (a) + (c) is that the reflex of IE **s* at this
period varied according to the various markers (? iç, ux^w, rꬱ, kx)—cf. also Morgenstierne,
"The Language of the Ashkun Kafirs," *Norsk Tidsskr. f. Sprogvidenskap*, ii, 1929, p. 199 f.,
Entwistle, *TPS.*, 1944, p. 33 f. The reasons for the ultimate "phonemic divorce" of these
variants from *s*, and their convergence to Skt. *ṣ*, Av. *š*, O.C.S. *ch* (as also the development
*kt > Skt. *ṣṭ*, Av. *št*) are probably to be sought in the total phonological systems of the
respective languages.

Thus, by the time of our attested Skt., the units *i, u, k*, could no longer be treated as markers
of a process : in sequences of the type *iṣ*, etc., *ṣ*, not *i*, was now the marker (viz. of the prosody of
retroflexion), and we may therefore, in the present problem, treat it as parallel to *r*. Where a
process **i + s >iṣ*, etc., appears to be active in the attested language (e.g. in new composition) it
is to be explained as the result of " structural pressure " from inherited forms, intensified by the
canonization of an observed phenomenon to the status of a Sandhi Law ; its lack of physiological
justification is at least hinted at by anomalous forms such as *avaṣṭambh-, pratistambh-*, and the
sandhi *agnis te*, beside Vedic *agniṣ ṭe*, etc.

[2] As shown by its development in Middle Indian (cf. Pischel, § 224).

[3] Cf. the pronunciation of Hindi paṭh, where distinct retroflexion is heard in the vowel.

[4] On word-palatograms and their uses see J. R. Firth, " Word-palatograms and Articulation,"
BSOAS., xii, 1948, pp. 857 ff.

[5] Cf. also Daniel Jones' distinction between assimilation and " similitude " (*Outline*, § 835 ff.).

something in the nature of $\overset{R}{\overbrace{}}$ or even $\overset{R}{\overbrace{}}$ the orthography is very
$brahm\bar{a}$, $\qquad$ $brahm\bar{a}$,

far from specifying the phonetic or the prosodic state of affairs. We have therefore to recognize that in its representation of non-phonematic features the orthography is misleading, its tendency to be over-specific resulting in an erratic and hence unreliable precision. And since it is only in the interests of this orthography that the sandhi rules are operative,[1] any statement which confines itself to explaining those rules adds nothing to the description of the language as spoken.

We may therefore be forgiven for losing a little of the awe which is traditionally accorded to the Sanskrit system of spelling, and in envisaging the possibility of new methods of statement in any phonological reconsideration of the language : for such linguistic purposes the representations (considering only

the R-prosody) $\overset{R}{puspam}$, $\overset{R}{nisanna}$-, $\overset{R}{\bar{a}rabhyam\bar{a}na}$-, $\overset{R}{\bar{\imath}ksaka}$-, $\overset{R}{prakalpana}$- have

the following advantages over $niṣaṇṇa$-, etc. :—

(i) They do not specify, with wholly doubtful fidelity, the linear extension of R, but leave this to study at the proper phonetic level [2] (e.g. the fact that an

example such as $\overset{R}{puspam}$ was utilizable for word-palatography would indicate

the potential extension of the prosody over the whole word—in contrast with,

e.g. $\overset{R}{prakalpana}$-). By generalization from such study rules could be stated for

this extension : e.g. considering r, s, etc., as the focal points of the prosody, and symbolizing a preceding palatographically interfering articulation by T, the maximum possible extension of the prosody in the one direction is

$\overset{R}{\overbrace{}}$
$..T....r..;$ on the other side of the focus the prosody similarly extends

only as far as the first interfering articulation [3] $\overset{R}{\overbrace{}}$ It is, however,
$\qquad\qquad (..r....T..).$

a basic phonological principle that units occurring at one position in a word are

---

[1] In view of the still vexed problem as to the date of the earliest writing of Sanskrit, and hence its relationship to the more ancient grammatical and phonetic treatises, it may be advisable to interpret " orthography " in a wider sense than is usual, i.e. as extending, if such a thing is possible, to a system of phonemic " oral spelling " antedating the use of any script.

[2] In the case of an ancient language such an examination must, of course, be largely hypothetical, and in part based on the very orthographic data which we are rejecting ; however, there is no reason why, having stood on these phonemic stepping-stones whilst building our prosodic bridge, we should any longer tolerate their obstruction of the stream.

[3] The fact that y appears as a *non*-interfering articulation is not unexpected. Intervocalic y in Skt. is in many cases to be treated simply as a prosodic marker of syllable-junction—e.g. in $dhiy\bar{a}$, etc., and probably in many instances of the type $d\bar{a}yaka$- $<$ *$d\bar{a}$-aka- (cf. Wackernagel § 187 ; note also the alternation of y with v, another typical prosodic marker, at all stages of Indo-Aryan) ; as such, it is likely to have involved less constriction than a phonematic y (cf. the " *laghuprayatnatara* " $\dot{y}$ of Jaina Pkt., or of Hindustani aya, etc. As for post-consonantal position, we may remember the frequent alternations of y and i under the conditions of " Sievers' Law ", and the wider extension of the vocalic realization in Vedic Skt., as attested by metrical requirements (-*bhyas* to be realized as -*bhi-as*, etc.).

The weak articulation of y is moreover supported for non-initial position in general by the ancient treatises (cf. Varma, *op. cit.*, pp. 126 ff.).

not to be identified with units in other positions : hence, in the case we are considering, post-focal articulations need not be expected to conform to pre-focal articulations which, for typographical convenience we happen to write with the same letter [1]; it need not therefore occasion any surprise when our phonetic investigations show that an apical nasal in pre-focal position is realized as an interfering (dental) articulation, but that in post-focal position it has a retroflex realization which thus continues the extension of the prosody—hence forms of

the type $\overset{R}{\underset{\textit{nisanna-}}{\rule{1.2cm}{0.4pt}}}$ (*nisanna-*), $\overset{R}{\underset{\textit{nibarhana-}}{\rule{1.2cm}{0.4pt}}}$ (*nibarhaṇa-*), etc.

(ii) The above approach, whilst retaining the ancient and still valuable conception of interfering and non-interfering articulations, no longer gives rise to the unsatisfactory postulate of " action at a distance " ; *r*, etc., no longer change *n* to *ṇ*, but when, by phonetic analysis, R is projected on to the linear plane, both *r* and a following apical nasal are amongst the articulations found to fall within its extension.

The example of dissimilation requires less full discussion, as much of the ground has already been prepared. The statement of the Sanskrit rule, as given by Macdonnell (§ 55), is that :—

" If *gh, dh, bh*, or *h* are at the end of a (radical) syllable beginning with *g, d, b*, and lose their aspiration as final or otherwise, the initial consonants are aspirated by way of compensation."

The customary explanation is then given that :—

" This is an historical survival of the original initial aspiration, which was lost (both in Greek and Sanskrit) by the operation of the later euphonic law that prohibited a syllable beginning and ending with an aspirate. Hence when the final aspirate disappeared the initial returned."

This historical digression also provides an explanation for a rule of reduplication in Sanskrit, viz. (§ 129. 1) :—

" Aspirated letters are represented by the corresponding unaspirated."

Of these statements, the first (descriptive) involves the concept of aspiration being lost by one consonant and " thrown back " upon one preceding it ; the second statement (historical) envisages the aspiration of the first consonant being held in a state of suspended animation against the occasion when a following aspirate shall disappear and so permit its return to life ; and the " euphonic law " characterized by the process of reduplication presents us with the usual conception of dissimilation at a distance, namely the aspiration of one consonant refusing to tolerate the coexistence of another. The " physiological explanations " of the phenomenon are not convincing, and psychological apologiæ even less so.[2]

---

[1] The operation of " Verner's Law " is a case in point. Cf. also Twaddell, *On Defining the Phoneme*, p. 49.

[2] Cf. Grammont, op. cit., pp. 269 ff. ; R. G. Kent, " Assimilation and Dissimilation," *Language*, xii, 1936, pp. 245 ff.

The prosodic treatment rather simplifies the statement, and dispenses with the half-mystic, half-anthropomorphic imagery; it notes simply that the aspiration is a prosody of the potential radical syllable.[1] As such, it requires to be marked once only (in spelling and, in Sanskrit, also in utterance); generally marked by the special (aspirated) form of the second consonant, it becomes necessary to mark it elsewhere if, for reasons connected with interfering junction-prosodies, the second cannot carry it[2]—in Western Hindustani we may observe a prosody of aspiration realized as a breathiness of the vowel, e.g. in the word traditionally spelt **bəhwt**, suggesting a structure CVCVC, but in fact standing for **bəwt** (CVVC) with prosodic aspiration $\overset{H}{(bəwt)}$.[3]

This approach to the present problem, though recent, is not new. It has been used to advantage for a variety of modern languages by members of the Department of Phonetics and Linguistics in the School of Oriental and African Studies, in London[4]; the prosodies abstracted by these treatments have included not only aspiration but also, e.g. yotization, labiovelarization, rhota-cization, affrication, friction, and voice. So far as concerns aspiration, it is also implied by Zellig Harris in his article "Simultaneous Components in Phonology",[5] where, considering the Greek parallel of the present case, he suggests that we might write πέφυκα, etc., in some such way as /'pépūka/, the ' indicating what we should call the prosody of aspiration; by such a representation, as he points out, the reduplicative πε- (not φε-) is entirely what we should expect.

In this article I have tried to show that, in dealing with an ancient language, revered for its orthography but notorious for the complexities of its sandhi-laws, some rationalization, if not simplification, of the latter may be effected by discarding some of our reverence for the former; and that by this approach we avoid the necessity for postulating mysterious gravitational forces whereby one sound influences another. It is perhaps not too much to say that in a large majority of cases the conceptions of assimilation and dissimilation are not only unnecessary but also involve us in the sort of statements that no science can tolerate : in historical and prehistorical linguistics, many examples of so-called

[1] The addition of " potential " is necessary to cover reduplicated forms, such as *babhūva*, where although the *bh*, in fact, belongs to the second syllable, *babh-* is potentially a radical syllable (like *labh-*, *dabh-*, etc.)—cf. the attested secondary root *dadh-* from *da-dhā-ti*. The non-application of the rule in other cases may be illustrated by such a form as *abhi-dhā-bhiḥ*.

[2] E.g. *budh-* : *bhot-syati*. The aspiration may vanish from the syllable altogether if the dominant junction-prosody is such as to involve the transfer of the syllable-prosody to another syllable, as in the case of " Bartholomae's Law " (**budh-ta-* > *buddha-*, etc.). Variations such as *dhug-dhvam* beside *dug-dhi* present a difficulty of interpretation.

[3] Indicated as **bəwht** in Harley's *Colloquial Hindustani* ; cf. also Hoenigswald, " Declension and Nasalization in Hindustani " (*JAOS.*, 68), p. 143 f., n. 15.

[4] E.g. J. R. Firth, " The Structure of the Chinese Monosyllable in a Hunanese Dialect (Changsha)," *BSOAS.*, viii, pp. 1055 ff. ; N. C. Scott, " The Monosyllable in Szechuanese," *BSOAS.*, xii, pp. 197 ff. ; E. J. A. Henderson, " Prosodies in Siamese : A Study in Synthesis," *Asia Major*, I, ii ; J. Carnochan, " A Study in the Phonology of an Igbo Speaker," *BSOAS.*, xii, pp. 417 ff.

[5] *Language*, xx, pp. 181 ff. Cf. also C. F. Hockett, " Peiping Phonology," *JAOS.*, 67, 1947, pp. 253 ff., " Componential Analysis of Sierra Popoluca," *IJAL.*, 13, 1947, pp. 258 ff.

" metathesis " are also probably best reduced to prosodic statement.[1]

The prosodic treatment does not answer problems of phonetic " action at a distance " ; rather like the theory of relativity, it adds a new dimension to the framework within which phenomena are studied and described, and within this framework these problems are found no longer to exist.

In conclusion, I shall briefly consider an issue connected with our first subject (the " cerebralization of n ") which is raised by a notoriously troublesome set of examples. I refer to the type of word which may conveniently be exemplified by the form *parinirviṇṇa-*. By the general laws of sandhi, we should expect **pariṇirviṇṇa-* (cf. *pariniviś-*), whereas, in fact, to use the traditional terminology, the second r, which has an *assimilating* influence on the following **n* ($> ṇ$), has a *dissimilating* influence on the preceding **ṇ* ($> n$) where this stands immediately before the r or separated only by a vowel.[2] As Whitney remarks (*Gr.* § 181b) on observing certain similar cases of s for expected **ṣ* (e.g. *sarsrāṇa-* for **sarṣrāṇa-*)[3] :—

> " The dissimilating influence of a following r, as compared with the invariable assimilating influence of a preceding r, is peculiar and problematical."

The traditional method of statement is here nothing less than ridiculous, and the prosodic approach provides a statement that is linguistically more

acceptable. In a word of the type $\overset{\text{R\ \ \ R}}{\underset{parinirvinna}{\cdots\cdots\cdots}}$ the two " retroflexion-foci "

$(.\,.\,r\,.\,.\,.\,.\,r\,.\,.)$ indicate two R-prosodies ; if the duality thus set up is to be preserved, i.e. if the indicated prosodic structure R-R is not to be reduced in realization to R, there must be an interruption between the two foci : in the cases considered the potential means of such interruption is provided by the intervening apical nasal, which is consequently given its dental realization, i.e.

$\overset{\text{R}\quad\quad\text{R}}{\underset{parinirvinna\text{-}}{\rule{1.2em}{0.4pt}\ \ \rule{1.8em}{0.4pt}}}$. Or we may express the process in slightly different terms by

considering our earlier statement regarding " pre-focal " apical nasals, viz. that they regularly have a palatographically interfering realization (so that in,

e.g. $\overset{\text{R}}{\underset{nibarhana\text{-}}{}}$ the maximum linear extension of the R-prosody is $\overset{\text{R}}{\underset{nibarhana\text{-}}{\rule{3em}{0.4pt}}}$) ;

---

[1] E.g. Skt. *snāna-* > Pkt. *ṇhāṇa-*, etc., IE **ismeros* > Gk. ἵμερος. Note also the Alexandrian prosodic writing of $\acute{\rho}$- (i.e. $\overset{\text{H}}{\underset{r}{}}$) for the Greek sound which was the reflex of *inter alia* IE **sr-* (e.g. ῥέω) : the Gk. $\acute{\rho}$- is transcribed in Latin as *rh-* (e.g. *rhētor*), in Armenian as *hr-* (*hretor*) ; Tsaconian *śinda* < Lac. ῥίδδα, suggests a realization as breathed *r-* (cf. Sturtevant, *Pron. of Gk. and Lat.*[2]. § 67b).

The phonematic s in such cases has been replaced by prosodic breathing, just as the pre-IE phonematic " laryngeal " units are replaced by various prosodies in the attested languages : e.g. length in Gk. τίθημι < **-dheₐ₁-*, aspiration in Skt. *tiṣṭhati* < **-stₐ₂e-*, voice in Skt. *pibati* < **pipₐ₃eti*, hiatus (a prosody of syllabic junction) in Gk. θύος < **dhuₐ₂os* (cf. θυμός, Hitt. *tuḫḫŵis*).

[2] The same peculiarity is shown, as we might expect, by forms such as *pranaṣṭa-* beside *praṇaśati*, or *pariṇiṣṭhā-* for **pariṇiṣṭhā-*, the " dissimilating influence " here extending also to the form *praṇaṅkṣyati* for **praṇaṅkṣyati*.

[3] With a partial parallel in Av. *ⁱⁱⁱⁱayzrāδayeiti* for expected **āyž-*.

we may then say that in *parinirvinna-* the R-R duality is preserved by treating the intervening nasal as related to the second R-prosody rather than the first.

On the basis of this method of statement it might be argued that the interrupting nasal articulation then bears to the two R-prosodies much the same relationship as a prosodic syllable-marker (such as **y** in Hindustani **aya**) bears to the two syllables; and hence that as the syllable-marker belongs to a different dimension from that of the linear syllables, so the " prosody-separator" must belong to yet another dimension outside that of the R-prosodies themselves.[1] We need not be afraid to admit such a possibility: rather should we be prepared to add to our analytical framework just as many dimensions as the material demands. Varro was perhaps not so very far wrong when he stated, some two thousand years ago, that " speech must be recognized as having three dimensions ", of which only one (" longitudo ") is represented on the time-track (" tempore ac syllabis metimur ").[2]

---

[1] The relevant features of the parallelism may be diagrammatically illustrated as follows:—

2nd order prosody of junction:		$\overset{n}{n}$	
1st order prosodies { of junction:	**y**		
of process:		R R	
Syllabic structure:	V V		
Phonematic structure:	**a – a**	*parinirvinna-*	

[2] Ed. Goetz and Schoell, *Frag.* 76. Cf. 200.12 ("*H quod adspiratio sit non littera*").

5

A Study of Quantity in Hausa

By J. CÁRNOCHAN

THE work on which this article is based was done during my visit to the Northern Provinces of Nigeria, 1948–9.[1] Selected material was studied, as spoken by Hausas, first in Zaria, then in Kano, Sokoto, Katsina, Daura, and Damagaram (Zinder). In Zaria I made certain statements from my observation of the utterances, which permitted me to classify the words according to the behaviour of their final syllables. Although there were dialectal differences,[2] my observation of the utterances in other areas gave me no reason to alter my classification. The study of the final open syllable in Hausa has already interested others; in America, J. H. Greenberg[3] and C. T. Hodge,[4] and in this country, Dr. G. P. Bargery and Major R. C. Abraham.[5] In this article I shall consider the final open syllable of the nominal only, by which I understand that class of word in Hausa which can be followed in close syntactical relationship by one of the enclitics, ne[6] or ce. In Zaria it is the form ne which is used after all nominals. In Sokoto, na is used after masculine singular and all plural forms, and ta after feminine singular forms. In Kano and elsewhere ne is used after masculine singular and all plural forms, and ce after feminine singular forms. In examining the final open syllable of the nominal, it is in this context of nominal plus enclitic that I wish first to present it. The enclitics are here given in their Kano forms, and the phrases have the normal Hausa spelling. Some fifteen hundred dictionary examples[7] and a number of proper names were listened to as pronounced by three Zaria speakers. As a result of my observations I arranged the words in two groups according to the behaviour of the final vowel.[8] As mentioned above, it was not found necessary to change this preliminary classification for the utterances of speakers of other Hausa dialects : the classification worked for them all. The examples selected below are typical of those studied, and are arranged in two groups, A and B, to illustrate this classification. All those examples

---

[1] The visit was financed by grants from the University of London Central Research Funds, and from the S.O.A.S.

[2] See footnote 1, p. 1034.

[3] " Hausa verse prosody," *JAOS.*, vol. 69, No. 3, 1949.   " Some problems in Hausa phonology," in *Language*, No. 4 of vol. 17, 1941.

[4] " An Outline Hausa Grammar," supplement to *Language*, vol. 23, No. 4, 1947.

[5] *A Hausa–English Dictionary and English–Hausa Vocabulary*, Rev. G. P. Bargery, 1934. *Dictionary of the Hausa Language*, Major R. C. Abraham and Malam Mai Kano, 1949.
I am referring here to the fact that, in their transcriptions, to indicate the pronunciation of the dictionary entries, both Bargery and Abraham recognize two lengths of final vowel.

[6] Italics are used for examples in Hausa orthography ; heavy type for examples in the special transcription. See footnote to Table 1, p. 1037.

[7] Before I went to Nigeria, Mr. F. W. Parsons of the S.O.A.S. had already listed for a different purpose all the entries of the disyllabic noun in Bargery's *Hausa–English Dictionary*. I am indebted to Mr. Parsons for the use of this list, which saved me a great deal of labour.

[8] There are of course other means of differentiation at other points of the structure but I am treating all these as irrelevant to the present study.

Source : J. Carnochan, ' A study of quantity in Hausa ', *BSOAS*, 13 (1951), 1032–44. Reprinted by permission of the School of Oriental and African Studies and the author.

numbered 1 have their first syllable on a higher pitch than their second, and are referred to as Tone Pattern 1, high–low. Those numbered 2 have both syllables on the same pitch, and are referred to as Tone Pattern 2, high–high. Those numbered 3 have their second syllable on a higher pitch than their first, and are referred to as Tone Pattern 3, low–high. The enclitic syllables *ne* and *ce* are heard on a different pitch from that of the preceding syllable ; so, postulating a two-tone system, they are low after a high tone, and high after a low tone.

CONTEXT 1. NOMINAL PLUS ENCLITIC *ne/ce*. ORTHOGRAPHIC FORM

I. *i* FINAL.

GROUP A.
1. *Zaki ne.*   It's a lion.
2. *Sarki ne.*   He's the emir.
3. *Carki ne.*   It's an ox-bird.

GROUP B.
1. *Koƙi ce.*   It's Koƙi.
2. *Rabi ce.*   It's Rabi.
3. *Audi ne.*   It's Audi.

II. *e* FINAL.

GROUP A.
1. *Arne ne.*   He's a pagan.
2. *Talle ne.*   It's a small soup pot.
3. *Bare ne.*   He doesn't belong to the family.

GROUP B.
1. *Jante ne.*   It's a feverish cold.
2. *Gare ne.*   It's a hoop.
3. *Mage ce.*   It's a cat.

III. *a* FINAL.

GROUP A.
1. *Salla ce.*   It's prayer time.
2. *Wawa ne.*   He's a fool.
3. *Wasa ne.*   It's a game.

GROUP B.
1. *Kulɓa ce.*   It's a skink lizard.
2. *Hausa ce.*   It's Hausa.
3. *Zamba ce.*   It's swindling.

IV. *o* FINAL.

GROUP A.
1. *Ango ne.*   He's the bridegroom.
2. *Tuwo ne.*   It's tuwo, a kind of food.
3. *Baƙo ne.*   He's a stranger.

GROUP B.
1. *Ango ne.*   It's Ango.
2. *Mago ne.*   It's a cream horse.
3. *Baƙo ne.*   It's Baƙo.

V. *u* FINAL.

GROUP A. 1. *Gemu ne.*   It's a beard.
          2. *Hannu ne.* It's a hand.
          3. *Buhu ne.*   It's a sack.

GROUP B. 1. *Shunku ne.*   It's a five-franc piece.
          2. *Cuku ne* [1]   It's cheese.
          3. *Aku ne.*   It's a parrot.

I used the examples as contrasting pairs with my Hausa informants, and made notes on their pronunciation. Below are my findings relevant to this study, with a reference table on page 1037.

I. *i* Final

A-1 and B-1.

1. **Intonation.** The tonal outlines of the two utterances are similar, and are classified as high-low-high. The second high is not on such a high pitch absolutely as the first.

2. **Vowel quality.** The *i* vowels in the two utterances are of different qualities. In A the *i* is a tense close front vowel. In B the *i* is lax, it is not so close as in A, and it is slightly retracted. In A, palatalization is a feature not only of the *ki* but also of the junction of *za* and *ki*. In B the palatalization is not so prominent, the utterance is " coloured " rather by the glottalization of the *ƙ*.

3. **Duration.** The *i* vowels in the two utterances are of different durations, and markedly so. The vowel in A is very much longer than the vowel in B, and tracings made in the laboratory of the S.O.A.S. by Malam M. Tukur Yawuri, confirm this. [2]

4. **Prominence.** In both utterances it seems that it is the first syllable that is the most prominent. It is the highest in pitch, and kymograph tracings show it to be the longest in duration.

A-2 and B-2.

1. **Intonation.** The tonal outlines are similar, and are classified as high-high-low.

2. **Vowel Quality.** The *i* vowels are of different qualities. In A it is a tense close front vowel. In B it is lax, less close and slightly retracted. In A there is strong palatalization of the second syllable.

3. **Duration.** The *i* vowels in the two utterances are of different durations. The vowel in A is very much longer than the one in B.

---

[1] According to the pronunciation of Kano speakers, this word is an example of group A-2, not of group B-2. According to the pronunciation of speakers of the other dialects, it is an example of the group B-2.

[2] [Subsequent to the publication of this article further experimental work with other Hausa speakers gave similar results. Kymograph tracings of the six examples for *i* Final, spoken by M. Jabiru, are included in J. R. Firth, ' Linguistics in the Laboratory ', *Zeitschrift für Phonetik und Allgemeine Sprachwissenschaft*, 12 (1959), 27–35, as well as two oscillograms for *o* Final examples. The reader is referred to pp. 32–4 for these illustrations, and for a discussion on the points raised.—Author 1968]

4. **Prominence.** The final syllable of the noun seems to have greater force or stress than the other syllables in the utterance. This appears to be equally true for A and B. I may add that the impression of my informants on this coincided with mine.

A–3 and B–3.

1. **Intonation.** The tonal outlines are similar and are classified as low-high-low.

2. **Vowel Quality.** The *i* vowels in the two utterances are of different qualities. In A the *i* is a tense close front vowel. In B the *i* is lax, it is not so close as in A, and it is slightly retracted. In A there is palatalization of the second syllable.

3. **Duration.** The *i* vowels in the two utterances are of different durations. The vowel in A is very much longer than the vowel in B.

4. **Prominence.** It is the final syllable of the noun which is the most prominent in both utterances. It may stand out because it is on the highest pitch, but it also seems to carry more force or stress.

Summary of the *i* Final Examples in Context 1

1. In group A, the *i* vowels are tense, close, and front. In group B, they are lax, not so close, and slightly retracted.
2. In group A, the duration of the vowel is long when compared with the examples in group B.
3. Prominence seems to be a feature of the last high tone of the nominal.

What has been stated for the *i* final examples under the headings of intonation and prominence for each contrasting pair applies equally to the pairs of examples for *e, a, o,* and *u* finals also, and will not be repeated.

A–1 and B–1.   **II.** *e* **Final**

1. **Vowel Quality.** The *e* vowels in the two utterances are of different qualities. In A it is a tense half-close front vowel. In B the vowel is lax, much more open, and front. It is important to realize that it is not centralized.[1]

2. **Duration.** The *e* vowels in the two utterances are of very different durations. The vowel in A is much longer than the vowel in B.

A–2 and B–2.

1. **Vowel Quality.** The *e* vowels are of different qualities, and what has been said just above is applicable to these examples too. It is important once more to point out that the *e* vowel in B has a front quality, it is not centralized or retracted, but it is very much more open than the *e* vowel in A.

2. **Duration.** There is a great difference in the duration in the *e* vowels in the two utterances, that for A being very much longer to the ear than that for B.

A–3 and B–3.

1. **Vowel Quality.** The *e* vowels in the two utterances have different

[1] See para. 4, p. 101.

qualities. The one in A is tense, close, and front. That in B is lax, much more open, and front. The junction of the velar stop and the *e* vowel in B is marked by palatalization.

2. **Duration.** The *e* vowel in A is much longer than in B.

III. *a* Final

A–1 and B–1.

1. **Vowel Quality.** The *a* vowels in the final syllables of the nominals in the two utterances have different qualities. In A the vowel is open and slightly retracted from central, but it has not a back quality. In B the *a* vowel is central, and not so open as in A. In addition, the *ɓ* has a constricting effect on it.

2. **Duration.** The *a* vowel in A is much longer than the *a* vowel in B.

A–2 and B–2.

1. **Vowel Quality.** The *a* vowels in the final syllables of the nominals in the two utterances are of different qualities. In A the vowel is open and, although a little retracted from central, it has not a true back quality. In B it is central, and not so open.

2. **Duration.** The *a* vowel in A is much longer than the *a* vowel in B.

A–3 and B–3.

1. **Vowel Quality.** The *a* vowels in the final syllables of the nominals in the two utterances have different qualities. The remarks made for A–2 and B–2 apply to this pair too.

2. **Duration.** The *a* vowel in the final syllable of the nominal in A is much longer than the *a* vowel in the final syllable of the nominal in B.

IV. *o* Final

A–1 and B–1.

1. **Vowel Quality.** The *o* vowels in the two utterances have different qualities. The *o* vowel in A is a tense half-close back vowel with strong lip-rounding. The preceding velar stop is also pronounced with strong lip-rounding. In B the vowel is lax and half-open to open, it is a back vowel, and is said with strong lip-rounding. The preceding consonant is also pronounced with strong lip-rounding. It is important to stress that in B the *o* vowel is not centralized in quality, it has the quality of a back vowel.

2. **Duration.** The *o* vowel in A is very much longer than in B.

A–2 and B–2.

1. **Vowel Quality.** There are differences of quality as for A–1 and B–1. In both utterances the quality of the *o* is a back quality. In A it is much closer than in B. There is strong lip-rounding in both utterances.

2. **Duration.** The *o* vowel in A is much longer than in B.

A–3 and B–3.

1. **Vowel Quality.** In both utterances there is a constricted quality about the *o* vowel, a mark of the junction of the glottalized consonant *ɓ*

with the vowel. A further mark of this junction is the lip-rounding of the consonant and the vowel. There are differences of quality as for A–1 and B–1.

2. **Duration.** The *o* vowel in A is much longer than in B.

V. *u* Final

A–1 and B–1.

1. **Vowel Quality.** The *u* vowels in the two utterances have different qualities. In A the *u* is a tense close back vowel, with strong lip-rounding. In B it is a lax vowel, not so close as in A, and slightly fronted. It has strong lip-rounding, as has the preceding stop. In A the vowel is nasalized.

2. **Duration.** The *u* vowel in A is much longer than in B.

A–2 and B–2.

1. **Vowel Quality.** The observations made were similar to those noted for A–1 and B–1 above.

2. **Duration.** The *u* vowel in A is much longer than the *u* vowel in B.

TABLE 1. REFERENCE TABLE FOR CONTEXT 1 [1]

Intonation and Prominence		Tone Pattern 1 ˈ‿ ‿ ‿	Tone Pattern 2 ‿ ˈ‿ ‿	Tone Pattern 3 ˈ‿ ‿ ‿
i final	Group A	zaakii nee	sarkii nee	carkii nee
	Group B	ƙooƙi cee	raabi cee	audi nee
e final	Group A	arnee nee	tallee nee	baaree nee
	Group B	jante nee	gare nee	maage cee
a final	Group A	sallaa cee	waawaa nee	waasaa nee
	Group B	kulɓa cee	hausa cee	zamba cee
o final	Group A	angoo nee	tuwoo nee	baaƙoo nee
	Group B	ango nee	mago nee	baaƙo nee
u final	Group A	geemuu nee	hannuu nee	buhuu nee
	Group B	shunku nee	cuku nee	aku nee

[1] This special transcription in heavy type focuses attention on the duration differences described in the notes on the contrasting pairs. The " longer " durations are indicated by doubling the letter. The enclitics are written here **nee, cee** because the quality and duration of the vowel are similar to those described under *e* final in group A.

A–3 and B–3.

   1. **Vowel Quality.** There is strong lip-rounding in both utterances for the vowel and for the preceding consonant. The differences in quality are that in A the *u* is a tense close back vowel with strong lip-rounding and in B the *u* is lax, not so close, and a little fronted.

The notes from this study of the fifteen contrasting pairs above may be summarized by saying that in the given context, the quality and duration of the final vowel of the nominal reveal two main patterns ; tense and long, group A ; lax and short, group B. (See Table 1.)

In the second context which I am going to present, two main patterns of behaviour of the final vowel are also found, although the phonetic features are different from those noted in Context 1.

CONTEXT 2. THE NOMINAL IN ISOLATION

Here the same thirty examples are taken as for Context 1, but without the enclitic *ne* or *ce*. In listening to the examples as contrasting pairs, I could detect no difference in quality of the final vowel between the example from group A and the example from group B. Both had a tense quality similar to that

TABLE 2. REFERENCE TABLE FOR CONTEXT 2

Intonation and Prominence		Tone Pattern 1 ⌐—	Tone Pattern 2 ⌐— ⌐—	Tone Pattern 3 ⌐—
i final	Group A	zaakii [1]	sarkii	carkii
	Group B	ƙooƙi' [2]	raabi'	audi'
e final	Group A	arnee	tallee	baaree
	Group B	jante'	₌gare'	maage'
a final	Group A	sallaa	waawaa	waasaa
	Group B	kulɓa'	hausa'	zamba'
o final	Group A	angoo	tuwoo	baaƙoo
	Group B	ango'	mago'	baaƙo'
u final	Group A	geemuu	hannuu	buhuu
	Group B	shunku'	cuku'	aku'

[1] A double final vowel letter indicates those examples in which there was no final glottal closure and release.

[2] A single vowel letter with a following high comma indicates those examples in which there was final glottal closure and release.

described in Context 1 for the examples of group A. There is some difference in duration, the final vowels in A being longer than the final vowels in B: but this difference is not so apparent to the ear as the difference in Context 1, and on kymograph tracings of the words in isolation, it is seldom easy to delimit exactly those parts of the tracings which are judged to correspond to the duration of the vowel in the utterance. There are, however, features of syllable ending which differentiate the two groups. When an example of group B was followed by silence, it ended with glottal closure and release. Examples from group A, uttered under the same circumstances were not glottalized. This was true for all my informants. There were some, however, who devoiced the latter part of the final vowel, so that the utterance ended in breathiness, carrying the characteristic resonance of the particular vowel. In both groups, the prominent syllable of Tone Pattern 1 and Tone Pattern 3 examples is the high tone syllable, and in the examples from Tone Pattern 2, both syllables seem equally prominent.

CONTEXT 3. THE NOMINAL PLUS HIGH-TONE *na/ta*

In Context 3 I am considering the nominal plus the high-tone syllable *na/ta*,[1] " my." Listening to the words in this context gives no guidance at all, so far as I can determine, to the classification of the nominals according to the

TABLE 3. REFERENCE TABLE FOR CONTEXT 3

Intonation and Prominence		Tone Pattern 1 '— — —	Tone Pattern 2 —' — —	Tone Pattern 3 —' — —
i final	Group A	zaakii na'	sarkii na'	carkii na'
	Group B	ƙooƙii ta'	raabii ta'	audii na'
e final	Group A	arnee na'	tallee na'	baaree na'
	Group B	jantee na'	garee na'	maagee ta'
a final	Group A	sallaa ta'	waawaa na'	waasaa na'
	Group B	kulɓaa ta'	hausaa ta'	zambaa ta'
o final	Group A	angoo na'	tuwoo na'	baaƙoo na'
	Group B	angoo na'	magoo na'	baaƙoo na'
u final	Group A	geemuu na'	hannuu na'	buhuu na'
	Group B	shunkuu na'	cukuu na'	akuu na'

[1] In Kano Hausa, *ta* is used after the feminine singular forms and *na* after the others.

behaviour of their final vowels. In all examples from group B as well as from group A the vowel quality and the duration were similar to those described for group A in Context 1. Glottal closure was heard in the pronunciation of *na/ta*, in all the examples and is shown in Table 3 by writing **na'**, **ta'**.

CONTEXT 4. THE NOMINAL PLUS THE OTHER FORMS OF THE *na/ta* PARADIGM

For Context 4 I examined the behaviour of the final vowel of the nominal, when followed by the other forms of the *na/ta* paradigm, and here also could find no guidance to the classification of the words according to the behaviour of their final vowels. In Kano Hausa the forms are : 2nd sg. *-nka/rka, -nki/rki* ; 3rd sg. *-nsa/rsa, -nta/rta* ; 1st pl. *-mmu/rmu* ; 2nd pl. *-nku/rku* ; 3rd pl. *-nsu/rsu*. The *-r-* forms are used after feminine singular nouns ending in *-a*, the *-n-* forms after masculine singulars, after feminine singulars not ending in *-a*, and after all plurals. The *-n/r-* element closes the final syllable of the noun. In all cases the final syllable of the endings is on a low tone. The quality of the final vowel of the noun was not tense in any of the utterances of the examples, but was similar to that described for group B in Context 1, and was " coloured " in the *-n-* forms by nasalization. There was no difference in duration that could be stated. Final glottal closure was heard in all the examples, and is shown in Table 4 by the final high comma.

TABLE 4. REFERENCE TABLE FOR CONTEXT 4

Intonation and Prominence		Tone Pattern 1 ˈ‿ ‿ ‿	Tone Pattern 2 ‿ ˈ‿ ‿	Tone Pattern 3 ˈ‿ ‿ ‿
i final	Group A	zaakinsa'	sarkinsa'	carkinsa'
	Group B	ƙookinsa'	raabinsa'	audinsa
e final	Group A	arnensa'	tallensa'	baarensa'
	Group B	jantensa'	garensa'	maagensa'
a final	Group A	sallarsa'	waawansa'	waasansa'
	Group B	kulɓarsa'	hausarsa'	zambarsa'
o final	Group A	angonta'[1]	tuwonsa'	baaƙonsa'
	Group B	angonsa'	magonsa'	baaƙonsa'
u final	Group A	geemunsa'	hannunsa'	buhunsa'
	Group B	shunkunsa'	cukunsa'	akunsa'

[1] The meaning does not allow the *-nsa'* form here.

From what has been said so far about the behaviour of the final syllable of the nominal in the four contexts described above, it may be seen that certain of the phonetic features are characteristic of certain positions and junctions. "We are accustomed," says Professor J. R. Firth,[1] " to positional criteria in classifying phonematic variants or allophones as initial, medial, intervocalic, or final. Such procedure makes abstraction of certain postulated units, *phonemes*, comprising a scatter of distributed variants (allophones). Looking at language material from a syntagmatic point of view, any phonetic features characteristic of and peculiar to such positions or junctions can just as profitably and perhaps more profitably be stated as prosodies of the sentence or word." My examples in their four contexts are a case in point.

So far as the final open syllable of the nominal is concerned (and I am not going beyond that here), I would postulate a system of vowel units—as units they are not pronounceable—operating in the syllable according to the prosodies of the syllable, which itself is not pronounceable until those prosodies are stated. Let me take two examples from Context 2, the word in isolation. In the orthography they are *zaki* and *koki*. The tonal outline of both words is the same, and the final vowel sounds are not to my ear perceptibly different in closeness, frontness, and tenseness. In *zaki* the final vowel sounds longer than in *koki*. In *koki* it is followed by glottal closure and release, while in *zaki* it is not. I now wish to consider these two final syllables as to their quantity, and would say that *zaki* and the other words of group A have the final syllable long in quantity, while *koki* and the other words in group B have the final syllable short in quantity. The prosody of length in the utterances of group A is marked by the absence of glottal closure and release at the syllable end. The prosody of shortness in the utterances of group B is marked by the presence of glottal closure and release at the syllable end.[2]

In Context 1 also, I would say that the quantity of the final syllable of the nominal is long for the words in group A, and short for those in group B. Here the prosody of length in the utterances of group A is marked by the long duration and tense quality of the vowel. The prosody of shortness in the utterances of group B is marked by the short duration and lax quality of the vowel. Glottal closure and release do not occur in Context 1 ; lax vowels do not occur in Context 2. That is to say, glottalization and laxness do not operate together as final features.

A study of the utterances of the words in Contexts 1 and 2 enabled me to classify them in two groups, according to the behaviour of their final syllables. A study of the utterances in Context 3, however, revealed no differentiating phonetic features by which I could make a similar classification. Here, in junction with the high-tone *na/ta*, the final vowel of the nominal is marked by long duration and tense quality. This is so for the words of both A and B

---

[1] " Sounds and Prosodies," *Transactions of the Philological Society*, 1948, page 130.
[2] See Table 2, on page 97.

groups. It would appear that here the prosody of junction is such that the *na/ta* cannot be immediately preceded by a short lax vowel sound. The final syllable of the nominal has in this context characteristics of a syllable long in quantity. (See Table 3.) No marks of the prosody of shortness associated with examples from group B in Contexts 1 and 2 are found here, and it may be said that in Context 3 the prosody of shortness is non-operative for the group B examples.

In Context 4 the junction of the final vowel of the nominal with what follows is marked by closure of the syllable by means of a nasal or a rolled consonant, and by the lax quality and short duration of the vowel. I generalize this closed syllable as **-CVC-** and note that the second **C** is restricted in this context to the rolled and nasal consonants. The syllable thus differs in its structure from both of those considered so far, the short generalized here **-CV** and the long generalized here **-CVV**. Phonetically the **-CVC-** syllable has vowel quality similar to the **-CV** type in Context 1, and duration similar to the **-CVV** type also in Context 1. For these reasons I consider the **-CVC-** syllable as being of medium quantity.

At this point I wish to make some brief remarks on the vowels *e* and *o* in this type of syllable, which would scarcely be necessary if my treatment of them was traditional among those who have already written on the phonetics of Hausa.[1]

The junction of the velar stops with both the front vowels *i* and *e* is marked by strong yotization, and the exact quality of the vowel sound will vary according to the quantity of the syllable and to other features of its phonetic context.[2] While there may be variation in its degree of tenseness, or in its degree of openness, there is never any doubt that the vowel is a front vowel, and not a central vowel. In syllables of medium quantity, where the closing consonant is a nasal, the *e* vowel may have a quality as open as that for Southern English œ : the quality is essentially a front one, and not a central one. Marked yotization is a feature of the junction of the velar stops with the front vowels, and the more open the quality of the vowel the more marked does the yotization appear to the ear. I give below in Table 5 an illustration using *mage*, a cat, as the example, with alternative systems of transcription.

---

[1] For different treatment of yotization and labialization see :
  (1) p. xxiv of Bargery's " Compiler's introduction " to his dictionary, where he says " A short *e* is rarely heard in a closed syllable, it being usually replaced by a short *a* or when following the letter *k* or *g* by *ya*, e.g. wannan mace, but macan nan ; wannan mage, but magyan nan ; wannan keke, but kekyan nan ".
  (2) Hodge, *Outline of Hausa Grammar*, section 1.14.1, where he says " The vowels /e/ and /o/ are further limited in that they occur only in clusters /ee/ and /oo/. "
  (3) Greenberg, *Some problems in Hausa phonology*, section 4, where he says " Non-pausal short *e* and *o* are replaced by *a* ", and later, " The palatalization and labialization of the velars before *e* and *o* is retained before the *a* in the form with closed syllable."

[2] See notes on *e* final on page 94.

TABLE 5.

Context 1.	Context 2.	Context 3.	Context 4.
ˈ‒	ˈ‒	ˈ‒ ‒	ˈ‒
‒ ‒	‒ ‒	‒ ‒	‒ ‒
maage cee ⎫ maagyɛ cee ⎭	maage' ⎫ maagye' ⎭	maagee na' ⎫ maagyee na' ⎭	maagensa' ⎫ maagyænsa' ⎭

In the second transcription, I am using the symbol **y** to indicate the yotization, **ɛ** to show a more open sort of front vowel, and **æ** a more open variety still. My remarks here do not mean of course that such a phonetic sequence as **-kya** does not occur in Hausa. It does, but the quality of the final vowel is distinctly central. There is an alternance **ka/kya/ke** but not the fourfold possibility **ka/kya/ke/kye**.

A similar problem occurs in studying the junction of the velar consonants with the *o* vowel. The junction of the velar stops with both the back vowels *o* and *u* is marked by strong labialization and the quality of the vowel will vary according to its phonetic context. This has already been mentioned in my notes on the *o* and *u* final.[1] In syllables of medium quantity closed by a nasal consonant, the quality of the *o* vowel is still a back quality, and not a central one. The more open the quality of the vowel, the more marked the labialization appears to the ear. It appears more marked, for instance, in the example **angonta'** from Context 4, than in **ango'** from Context 2. My remarks here do not mean that the phonetic sequence **-gwa** does not occur in Hausa. It does, and there is an alternance **ga/gwa/go** but not the fourfold possibility **ga/gwa/go/gwo**.

It is a commonplace that the vowels in Hausa occur both long and short, and the two dictionaries mentioned above mark this difference in certain cases in their transcriptions. Context 2, the word in isolation, corresponds to the dictionary entries. In the case of words having Tone Pattern 2, high–high, and Tone Pattern 3, low–high, my group A entries agree largely with the dictionary entries having final vowel marked long, and my group B entries with those having final vowel unmarked (considered short), although there are exceptions (e.g. *mago* is shown by Bargery and Abraham with final vowel long, and by me is entered in group B). In the case of the words of Tone Pattern 1, high–low, however, my analysis gives a very different result from that of the dictionaries. Here Bargery and Abraham show nearly all the final low tone vowels as short, by not marking them, while by my criteria the great majority of them have the final syllable long in quantity. It is particularly to the final syllable of the nominal where it is on a low tone that I wish to draw attention, by showing that a classification into long and short syllables can be made for the low tone final syllables as well as for the high tone ones, and by suggesting in this article the criteria for making it.

This is the first time a classification on such criteria has been suggested for Hausa, and I cannot leave this subject without a note on the type of word

[1] See page 95.

found in group B. First there are a large number of proper names, many of them of Arabic origin, e.g. *Hawa, Dauda, Yusufu, Kaduna*. Of the remainder, some are clearly of non-Hausa origin, although they are now regarded as Hausa by the Hausas themselves. Such are *shunku* from French cinq, and *aku*, parrot, some form of which is found in many West African languages. In the case of the nominal, therefore, final glottalization may be a feature of words of non-Hausa origin. In other grammatical categories, however, final glottalization occurs, and is not restricted to words of non-Hausa origin. In a forthcoming paper I propose to examine the whole question of glottalization in Hausa,[1] and to show the importance of this feature, which has, I believe, been up to now only partly appreciated.[2]

[1] See J. Carnochan, ' Glottalization in Hausa ', *TPS* (1952).

[2] [This article had little effect on publications on Hausa phonology until 1965 when Claude Gouffé took up the problems again in ' La Lexicographie du Haoussa et le Préalable Phonologique', *Journal of African Languages*, 4.3. On p. 195 he states the position: ' Il se trouve cependant qu'en 1951 J. Carnochan a publié, sur la quantité de la voyelle finale des nominaux indépendants, une étude qui, dans sa concision et dans sa rigueur, peut être qualifiée de lumineuse,[4] mais dont il semble malheureusement que, depuis, les spécialistes du haoussa n'ont pas toujours fait leur profit.[5] Traitant d'autre part, dans us second article d'inspiration plus doctrinale, de la quantité de la voyelle finale des verbaux,[6] Carnochan a été amené, en 1952, à préciser ou à rectifier implicitement sur certains points les données des dictionnaires. L'ensemble des conclusions de Carnochan, dont les préoccupations sont avant tout celles d'un phonéticien, confirmant de le façon la plus nette le principe méthodologique que nous prétendons appliquer ici à la lexicographie, il convient de reprendre maintenant avec quelque détail la discussion de ces faits.'—Author 1968]

6

The Phonology of the Nasalized Verbal Forms in Sundanese

By R. H. ROBINS

IT is now established practice in descriptive linguistics to treat the subject-matter at separate, and definably separate, levels of analysis. Indeed the traditional categories of Phonology and Grammar represent such an employment of two different levels. Present-day linguists in Great Britain and America recognize the setting up and defining of the various levels of analysis as a basic procedure in handling the utterances of the speakers whose language is being studied.[1]

It is now generally agreed that the grammatical analysis of a language is analysis at a higher level than the phonological analysis ; that is to say, it presupposes, to some extent at least, the results of phonological analysis.[2] In grammar we are dealing with the same material, the utterances of speakers or writers, but organizing and systematizing it by means of different criteria and making use of different terms for its description. Grammar, therefore, rests on, and is conditioned by, the techniques adopted and the methods followed in phonology.

Up to the present a great deal of published grammatical analysis has been built upon phonological analysis made in ' phonemic ' terms. For some years now members of the London group of linguists have been developing techniques of phonological analysis not based on purely ' phonemic ' principles, and to some extent rejecting certain of the tacit assumptions of strictly ' phonemic ' analysis.[3] Such analytic techniques have come to be called ' prosodic ', and it is claimed that they enable a fuller and more convenient phonological statement to be made of the observed and recorded phonetic facts abstracted from utterances.[4]

Since grammatical analysis is built upon the results of phonological analysis, it follows that a different technique of phonology will be likely to simplify or

---

[1] The cardinal importance of establishing separate levels of analysis in the study and description of language and in the statement of linguistic meanings was emphasized by Professor J. R. Firth in ' The Technique of Semantics ', *TPS* 1935, pp. 36–72 (see especially pp. 54–5, 60–1, 63–5) ; cf. ' Personality and Language in Society ', *Sociological Review* Vol. 42, 1950, p. 44, ' General Linguistics and Descriptive Grammar ', *TPS* 1951, p. 76. See also C. F. Hockett, ' A System of Descriptive Phonology ', *Lang.* Vol. 18, 1942, p. 3, G. L. Trager and H. L. Smith, ' Outline of English Structure ', pp. 53–4, 81 ; cf. the use made by R. S. Wells of procedure by levels in his review of recent work by the Danish school (*Lang.* Vol. 27, 1951, pp. 562 ff.).

[2] Firth, ' Technique of Semantics ', pp. 58 ff. ; Trager and Smith. op. cit., p. 53.

[3] See especially Firth, ' Sounds and Prosodies ', *TPS* 1948, pp. 127–152.

[4] A recent bibliography of such work will be found in W. S. Allen, ' Some Prosodic aspects of Retroflexion and Aspiration in Sanskrit ', *BSOAS* Vol. 13, 4, 1951, p. 945, footnote 1.

Source : R. H. Robins, ' The phonology of the nasalized verbal forms in Sundanese ', *BSOAS*, 15 (1953), 138–45. Reprinted by permission of the School of Oriental and African Studies and the author.

complicate, improve or mar, the presentation of the grammar of a language.[1]

In the Sundanese language a considerable simplification can be achieved, and a more coherent account given, of an important part of its grammatical system, when this is based on a phonological analysis not conceived wholly in traditional ' phonemic ' terms.[2] It may be regarded as an additional reason for analysing languages in terms other than purely ' phonemic ' if we find that, as well as providing a better means of stating the phonetic facts, it also simplifies and renders more coherent the statement of grammatical systems.[3]

There is a very large class of stems in Sundanese, mostly dissyllabic, which fulfil the function of verbals as defined within the grammar of the language ; the majority of these are used independently as words (minimal free forms), and also serve as the base for further inflectional processes.

A fundamental morphological process is Nasalization, whereby, from a Root (non-nasalized) form R, a Nasalized form N [4] is derived,[5] with syntactic function as a verbal, and with morphological potentialities as a base for further inflections. This nasalization is achieved, in Root forms beginning with a consonant, either by replacing the initial consonant by a nasal consonant or by prefixing the syllable ŋa-,[6] and in Root forms beginning with a vowel, by prefixing the nasal consonant ŋ.

[1] Cf. Z. S. Harris, *Methods in Structural Linguistics*, pp. 76–8 ; but the discussion here is concerned with the choice between various alternative methods of ' phonemicization ' with an eye on morphemic simplicity. [In rereading what one so confidently asserted sixteen years ago, one is inevitably struck with the transience of methodological dogma and of theoretical controversy, a lesson that needs to be relearned by the enthusiasts of each generation. The first three paragraphs of this article were written, and should now be understood, within the then current debate between the developed phonemic phonology of the Smith-Trager-Harris type and the developing prosodic phonology of the Firthian group.

That grammatical analysis (morphology and syntax) presupposes phonological analysis unilaterally was certainly a central tenet of ' classical ' American phonemics of the so-called ' Bloomfieldian ' era, and it is a matter of historical fact that much of the methodology of morphemics was consciously adapted from the methods of phonemics. In this sense the different analytic method of prosodic phonology led to different grammatical analysis, though it is now clear that in the hierarchical relations between levels, Firthian phonology, like the later Chomskyan phonology, presupposes a prior grammatical analysis, the logical reverse of the ' Bloomfieldian ' situation.—Author 1968]

[2] The Sundanese material here presented has been provided by my research assistant, Mr. Sobaran Nurjaman, from Garut, West Java. It is a pleasure to acknowledge the excellence of his work as my informant in our linguistic collaboration.

[3] Cf. H. Spang-Hanssen, ' On the Simplicity of Descriptions ', *TCLC* 5, 1949, pp. 61–70.

[4] In this article structural elements abstracted at the Grammatical level are symbolized by large capitals, R, N. Structural elements abstracted at the Phonological level are symbolized by small capitals, c, v. Sundanese words are cited in heavy type, **nenǰo**.

[5] The statement that the Nasalized forms are ' derived ' from the non-nasalized Root forms is not intended as a historical statement, but means simply that the morphology of the Sundanese verbals can most easily be stated by treating the non-nasalized form, without any of its possible inflections, as *basic* in the description and the other forms as *derived* from it by the various inflectional processes. Cf. L. Bloomfield, *Language*, p. 217.

[6] And exceptionally ŋə- (see p. 110).

Exx. tenʤo, nenʤo, to see ; pikir, mikir, to think ;
dᵥhᵥs, ŋadᵥhᵥs, to have audience with ;
impi, ŋimpi, to dream.

The morphology of the Sundanese verbals has been treated by several Dutch scholars.[1] Their accounts are made on the basis of the Javanese script as adapted for Sundanese or of the Dutch romanization of this script ; this romanization is now used officially in Indonesia for the Sundanese language. Both these systems of writing may be said to be ' phonemic ' in principle, though the Javanese script is essentially syllabic ; and an adequate ' phonemic ' transcription for Sundanese can be achieved by taking over the Dutch romanization with a few individual changes and with the substitution of single letters for the digraphs. Most of the letters remain unaltered ; taking Coolsma's *Soendaneesch-Hollandsch Woordenboek* as typical (there are a few minor variations among writers in the choice of particular letters to be used), a ' phonemic ' transcription requires the following changes only : ʧ for *tj*, ʤ for *dj*, ɲ for *nj*, ŋ for *ng*, u for *oe* (this letter is now generally preferred to *oe* for written Sundanese in Indonesia), and ᵥ for *eu*. I also use ə for Coolsma's ĕ, and y for his *j*. This transcription is used to identify the Sundanese words cited in this article.

Hitherto the rules for the formation of the Nasalized forms N of verbals have been stated as a set of unconnected procedures of letter changing, and have received little significantly different treatment since Grashuis gave his account in 1873.[2] In reconsidering this process of Ńasalization, a statement of the relevant phonological features of the language must be given.[3]

Sundanese syllables are of the following types : cv, vc, cvc, v, ccv, and ccvc, the latter two types being relatively few in number. If, for descriptive analysis, a zero consonant unit (symbolized by ♯) is posited and included in the consonant system, all syllables may be analysed as c (c) v c structures, with initial, medial, and final elements.

The vowels comprise a seven-term system :—

[1] G. J. Grashuis, ' Over de Verbale Vormen in het Soendaneesch ', Bijdragen, Derde Volgreeks 8, 1873, pp. 4–15 ; H. J. Oosting, *Soendasche Grammatica* ; S. Coolsma, *Soendaneesche Spraakkunst.*

[2] See Grashuis, op. cit., pp. 7–9, Oosting, op. cit., pp. 19–22, Coolsma, *Soendaneesche Spraakkunst*, pp. 66–8.

[3] The phonological details stated here are those necessary for treating the subject of this article. A full study of the phonology and grammar of Sundanese, based on my work with Mr. Nurjaman, is in preparation:

There is commutation [1] of front, central, and back quality, and of open, half-open, and close. With openness (a) the other commutation is not operative. The front vowels, i, e, are articulated with spread lips, and the back vowels, u, o, with rounded lips. From these two classes of vowels we may abstract respectively the prosodic components y (front quality with lip spreading) and w (back quality with lip rounding).[2] ə and ɤ are both central, half-open vowels, without lip rounding or lip spreading, and vary somewhat in quality according to the nature of the preceding and following consonants.

The initial consonants [3] may be divided into two main classes :—

Class 1, Consonants articulated without local supra-glottal closure or constriction :—

h, voiceless ' glottal ' fricative.[4]

#, realized as ʔ initially at word boundaries, between *any* two vowels or between consonant and vowel at the junction of prefixial morpheme and stem, and between two *like* vowels within words (e.g. indit, [ʔindit], to leave, go away ; mi-omoŋan, [miʔomoŋan], to warn ; paŋ-adilna, [paŋʔadilna], the most just ; hees, [heʔes], to sleep). Between *unlike* vowels within words, # is realized as the appropriate transition glide or as phonetic zero, which is also its most general realization in contexts other than the above.

Class 2, Consonants with local supra-glottal articulation, whose utterance involves local closure or constriction within the mouth.

In this class there is commutation in two dimensions, by place of articulation : Bilabial, Dental-alveolar, Palatal or Prepalatal, and Velar, and by method of release : Plosive, Fricative, Nasal, etc. :—

[1] In recent discussions on phonological theory among members of the London group at the School of Oriental and African Studies, Professor J. R. Firth has suggested that the words ' Substitution ' and ' Commutation ' be employed as distinct technical terms in descriptive linguistics.

His suggestion is that ' Substitution ' should be used to refer to the replacement of one element by another at the same level of abstraction (word, morpheme, phonological unit, etc.) in a given place in a text or in a structure abstracted from a text.

' Commutation,' on the other hand, he suggests, should be used of the alternation of terms within a system. When, by abstraction at a particular level of analysis, closed systems of inter-related terms have been set up whereby all the relevant facts can be accounted for, there is Commutation of the terms within such closed and exhaustive systems and their subsystems. Thus in the Sundanese vowel system, as given here, there is a three-term Commutation of Open, Half-open, and Close, and a three-term Commutation of Front, Central, and Back.

Thus Substitution finds order and place within structures, in parallel with texts, whereas Commutation properly applies to systems, which may be multidimensional. In research procedure, substitution in a framework of structure generally precedes the setting up of a Commutation system. The statement of both sets of relations is desirable in linguistic description. See also J. Carnochan, ' Glottalization in Hausa ', *TPS*, 1952, p. 79, footnote 5.

[2] Though the phonetic realization of these prosodic components is most marked in the utterance of a particular vowel (or consonant [see p. 108]) in the syllable, they serve to characterize by their presence, alone or in conjunction with other such components, Sundanese syllables as wholes.

[3] As the inflectional process of Nasalization concerns only the initial consonants of words, and so, in the Sundanese language, the initial consonants of syllables, phonological statements made here are confined to consonants in syllable initial position.

[4] See footnote 1, p. 109.

	Bilabial	*Dental-* alveolar.	Palatal.	Velar.
Voiceless Plosive	p	t	tʃ	k
Voiced Plosive	b	d	dȝ	g
Nasal	m	n	ɲ	ŋ
Semivowel	w		y	
Lateral and Fricative		l, r	s	

The voiceless plosives are unaspirated, and the palatal plosives are affricated.

d is alveolar; t is dental; n is alveolar except when following final t, in which case it is dental (palatograms have been made in confirmation of these observations).

r is an alveolar trill; l is an alveolar lateral.

s is a voiceless sibilant, with tongue-tip down, varying between post-alveolar and prepalatal position, and may be assigned phonologically to the palatal series.

From the bilabial series we may abstract the prosodic component w, as in the case of the vowels u and o, lip rounding being realized in p, b, m as bilabial closure, the extreme form of lip rounding in Sundanese.[1] From the palatal series we may similarly abstract the prosodic component ʏ, as in the case of the vowels i and e.[2]

The dental-alveolar series of consonants in initial position are not markedly back or front in quality as compared with the ʏ and w characterized consonants, and are themselves articulated with neutral lip position, being slightly lip-rounded before w vowels and slightly lip-spread before ʏ vowels. The dental-alveolar consonants may be regarded as the central series.

Consonants of the velar group enjoy the greatest phonetic latitude of any of the Sundanese consonants in their realization, being articulated as pre-velar, mid-velar, or post-velar according to the nature of the preceding or following vowel, with noticeably greater variation than occurs in the Standard English k- and g-sounds in their different phonetic contexts.

The prosodic components mentioned so far are abstractions made from the places of articulation of the c and v units concerned. Apart from such abstractions, if it is observed that certain phonetic features are associated with the release of the initial element of syllables, the presence of such features may be

---

[1] That in Sundanese bilabial closure is the limiting condition of lip rounding is most clearly shown when one of the central, non-lip-rounded vowels precedes or follows one of these consonants, and an off-glide or on-glide is frequently heard (e.g. bʏnaŋ, [bʷʏnaŋ], to get; ŋadʏpa, [ŋadʏʷpa], to measure).

[2] In the vowels, ʏ and w are marked about equally by front quality with lip spreading, and by back quality with lip rounding, respectively. In the consonants, palatal or front articulation is the more prominent feature for ʏ, and lip rounding, or lip closure, is the more prominent feature for w.

separately abstracted and treated in the phonology of the language as a prosodic component of syllable initiality.[1]

Sundanese syllable (and therefore word) initial consonants occur with the following types of release :—

Class 1, Non-local Friction, without Voice, h-,
            Phonological Zero, i.e. ?, at word initial position,

Class 2, Supra- glottal Articulation	Plosion without Voice, p-, t-, ʧ-, k-, Plosion with Voice, b-, d-, ʤ-, g-, Nasal Release, always with Voice, m-, n-, ɲ-, ŋ-, Local Friction without Voice, s-, Local interference, with or without Friction, of the egressive air-stream, always accompanied by Voice, w-, l-, r-, y-.

It will be seen that, besides zero, #, realized as momentary glottal closure, ?, in word initial position, three types of glottal action [2] are involved in syllable initial articulations, and the presence of each may be regarded as a prosodic component of syllable initiality :—

Voicelessness (open glottis, permitting free passage of air during articulation of the consonant),   o

Voice,   z

Voiceless ' glottal ' friction (the glottal action associated with buccal cavity friction)   H

Supra-glottal consonants are orally or nasally released. Oral release, as the largest class of syllable initial articulations may be left unmarked ; nasal release, always accompanied by voice, may be treated as a prosodic component of syllable initiality and symbolized by N.

The derivation of the Nasalized forms, N, from the Root forms, R, may now be stated as depending on the type of glottal action involved in the initial articulation of the syllable. This statement may be simply rendered by means

---

[1] Cf. E. J. A. Henderson, ' Prosodies in Siamese ', *Asia Major*, New Series, Vol. 1, 2, 1949, p. 192.

[2] The traditional designation of h-sounds as ' glottal fricatives ' is now seen to be inadequate (cf. W. S. Allen, *Phonetics in Ancient India*, § 2.00). These sounds are the result of general, non-localized ' cavity friction ' (cf. K. L. Pike, *Phonetics*, p. 71) as the air passes through the buccal cavity under pressure from the lungs ; nevertheless it seems clear that the glottis is not wholly passive, but plays some part in the production of this friction (cf. D. Jones, *Outline of English Phonetics*[6], p. 186, R. K. Potter, G. A. Kopp, and H. C. Green, *Visible Speech*, p. 111, M. Joos, *Acoustic Phonetics*, p. 89), and it is this action of the glottis, as distinct from its non-interference (o) in the utterance of the voiceless supra-glottal consonants, that is here referred to.

of the following formulæ (> = is replaced by) :—

At the Grammatical Level

$$R \quad > \quad N$$

At the Phonological Level

Initial Prosodic Components	$\left\{\begin{array}{l}\text{o}\\\text{z}\\\text{NZ}^1\\\text{H}\end{array}\right\}$ prefix ŋa-		

$$\# \quad > \quad \text{ŋ-}$$

Exx.

o	pake,	make,	to use ;
	tʉŋgʉl,	nʉŋgʉl,	to beat ;
	ʧokot,	ɲokot,	to take ;
	kirim,	ŋirim,	to send ;
	usul,	ɲusul,	to pursue ;
z	boroŋ,	ŋaboroŋ,	to buy (an entire stock) ;
	dahar,	ŋadahar,	to eat ;
	ʤawab,	ŋaʤawab,	to answer ;
	ganti,	ŋaganti,	to change ;
	widaŋ,	ŋawidaŋ,	to dry skins ;
	liwat,	ŋaliwat,	to pass ;
	rawat,	ŋarawat,	to look after ;
	yakti, to be certain,	ŋayakti(kʉn),[2]	to make certain ;
NZ[4]	musuh(an),[3]	ŋamusuh(an)	to oppose ;
	nalaŋsa, to be sad,	ŋanalaŋsa(kʉn),	to make sad ;
	ɲaho, to know,	ŋaɲaho(an),	to inform ;
	ŋʉnah, to be pretty,	ŋaŋʉnah(kʉn),	to make pretty ;
H	hanʧa,	ŋahanʧa,	to work ;
#	ala,	ŋala,	to take ;
	inum,	ŋinum,	to drink ;
	usap,	ŋusap,	to stroke.

There are some exceptions to the formulæ just given. They are the same in number to the exceptions to the 'rules' given in the older statements of the formation of the Nasalized forms. The principal exceptions comprise the following classes [5] :—

Some R forms beginning with z (b-, d-, ʤ-, g-, w-), which form N in NZ without prefixation,

---

[1] See footnote 4.   [2] See footnote 3.

[3] Bracketed forms indicate that the R or N form itself is not used with the function of a verbal, but that it is so used with the inflective suffix given.

[4] R itself may begin with N, but is not thereby counted as N, and must be subjected to a further nasalization for the derivation of N.

[5] The irregular nədəŋ from sədəŋ, and nəʤa from səʤa, given in Coolsma's *Woordenboek* are no longer used and are rejected by Mr. Nurjaman.

e.g. bere, mere, to give ;   dɤlɤ, nɤlɤ, to see ;

ʤiɤn, ɲiɤn, to make ; gegel, ŋegel, to bite (beside ŋagegel) ;

wadaŋ, madaŋ, to eat.

Some R forms beginning with ♯, which add ŋa-, beside the regular form,

e.g. asup, to enter, ŋaasup(an), to put in (beside ŋasupan) ;

oyag, to shake (intr.), ŋaoyag(kɤn), to shake (tr.) (beside ŋoyagkɤn).

Some R forms beginning with н, which replace h by ŋ,

e.g. harti(kɤn), ŋarti(kɤn), to explain (beside ŋahartikɤn).

Monosyllabic R forms, which in all cases prefix ŋa- or ŋə-,

e.g. ʧet, ŋaʧet or ŋəʧet, to paint.

It is now clear from the formulæ and the examples given above that in all the Nasalized forms the prosodic component of syllable initiality is nasal release with voice, nz. In the regular formations, with verbals whose R form begins with o the N form begins with the N consonant of the same phonological series.[1] With verbals whose R form begins with ♯ the N form begins with ŋ. In all other cases the N form is derived by prefixing ŋa- to the R form.

The selection of ŋ and ŋa for this purpose, whatever historical developments may lie behind the process of Nasalization, is seen to bear a particular relation to the phonology of the Sundanese vowel and consonant systems.[2] ŋ, which occurs before vowels of all seven categories in N forms derived from R forms beginning with ♯, belongs to the velar group of consonants, which has the widest phonetic range of variation between front and back articulation (see p. 108, above), and is therefore the most ' neutral ' nasal consonant as between y and w elements and those elements to which the distinction of y and w does not apply. In ŋa, which is prefixed to R forms beginning with consonants belonging to each category in the Sundanese consonant system, ŋ is followed by a, the open vowel, which occupies the position in the Sundanese vowel system in which the commutation of y, w and central is inoperative (see pp. 106 7, above).

The statement of the derivation of the Nasalized forms N from the Root forms R in Sundanese has here been based on certain relevant features in the phonology of the syllables concerned. In this way the regular processes of this derivation can be reduced to three simple rules expressible in short formulæ. By this treatment, in what formerly appeared as the arbitrary substitution of individual letters, there is revealed a certain correspondence of systemic patterning between the grammatical and phonological levels of analysis, when Nasalization, as a process in the morphology of the language, is applied to the phonological structures comprising Sundanese words and syllables.

[1] Dental and alveolar articulations are treated as belonging to the same phonological category.

[2] Cf. L. Hjelmslev, *Principes de Grammaire Générale*, pp. 228 ff., on ' causalité synchronique ' in linguistic systems.

7

THE TONAL SYSTEM OF TIBETAN (LHASA DIALECT) AND THE NOMINAL PHRASE [1]

By R. K. SPRIGG

TONAL CATEGORIES AND UNITS OF STRUCTURE

THE purpose of this article is to re-examine some of the ways in which tone has been stated in certain of the spoken Tibetan dialects, and to apply to the Nominal Phrase [2] in one of them, Lhasa Tibetan (LT), the suggestion that such statements can be more profitably associated not with the *syllable*, as hitherto, but with the *word*.

It is over seventy years since H. A. Jäschke made use of two prosodic categories, termed ' high-toned ' and ' deep-toned ', to account for certain phonetic features of ' words ' as pronounced by speakers of the dialects of the Central Provinces.[3]   Subsequently, and as a result of original research, other phoneticians, notably Dr. Jaw Yuanrenn and the Rev. Mr. P. M. Miller,[4] have found themselves in agreement with Jäschke's two categories to the extent of stating their material in terms of two tonemes. The two tonemes are stated for the *syllable*.[5]

It would be idle to claim that it is anything but difficult to give an account of tone and intonation in any of the Tibetan dialects in question, but it may well be that some of the difficulties in Dr. Jaw's, and in Mr. Miller's, published work result from their technique of statement, which is based on the phoneme theory. In this article material elicited from a Lhasa-born Tibetan, Mr. Rinzin

---

[1] This article is based on a paper, ' The Tonal System of Nouns and Adjectives in the Lhasa Dialect of Spoken Tibetan ', read at the 23rd International Congress of Orientalists, at Cambridge in August, 1954.

[2] A corresponding tonal analysis, relating the two-term Tonal system to the word unit, has been applied to the *Verbal Phrase* in my ' Verbal Phrases in Lhasa Tibetan—I ', *BSOAS*, XVI, 1954, 150–3.

[3] ' Phonetic Table for comparing the Different Dialects ' (H. A. Jäschke, *Tibetan-English Dictionary*, pp. XVI–XVII). An examination of Jäschke's usage with regard to the word ' word ' makes it certain that he is not relating his tonal statement to the word in the sense in which it is used in this article (see below, Delimitation of the Word).

[4] *Love Songs of the Sixth Dalai Lama Tshangs-dbyangs rgyamtsho*, translated into Chinese and English with notes and introduction by Yu Dawchyuan and transcribed by Dr. Jaw Yuanrenn (Y. R. Chao) (Academia Sinica, Series A, no. 5, Peiping, 1930) ; ' The Phonemes of Tibetan (U-Tsang Dialect) with a practical Romanized Orthography for Tibetan-speaking Readers ', by Rev. P. M. Miller, B.S. (*Journal of the Asiatic Society. Letters.* Vol. XVII, No. 3, 1951, 191–216).

[5] ' Tone is a suprasegmental phoneme of the syllable ' (Miller, op. cit., 202) ; though not specifically stated, a corresponding analysis is implied by Dr. Jaw's syllabic system of tone-marking.

Source : R. K. Sprigg, ' The tonal system of Tibetan (Lhasa dialect) and the nominal phrase ', *BSOAS*, 17 (1955), 134–53. Reprinted by permission of the School of Oriental and African Studies and the author.

Wangpo,[1] has been stated in accordance not with an exclusively phonemic analysis but with the polysystemic ' prosodic approach ', promulgated by Professor Firth.[2] The prosodic approach has been adopted in the belief that it disposes of some of the difficulties mentioned above as arising out of the application of the phoneme theory.[3]

The difference in theoretical basis between the prosodic approach and the phoneme theory is reflected firstly in the setting up of a tonal *system* [4] to account for the phonetic material presented here, and secondly in the stating of that system not in relation to the *syllable* but to the *word*.

DELIMITATION OF THE WORD

If the tonal system is to be stated with reference to the word, then the word must be delimited.[5] It is, however, possible to go a long way towards delimiting the word by utilizing for the purpose certain of the phonetic features that characterize the initial and the final consonants of syllables (C-, -C) in intersyllabic junction.[6]

The intersyllabic junction features referred to are best accounted for by setting up a two term prosodic system of Junction, each of the terms having some phonetic exponents that are homophonous and others that are non-

---

[1] Rinzin Wangpo (rig-ḥdzin dbaṅ-po) (R) was employed by the School of Oriental and African Studies as a Research Assistant in London from December, 1948, until September, 1949. The material obtained from R. was checked against the utterances of other Lhasa-dialect speakers in Kalimpong and in Gyantse during the Session 1949–50.

· [2] Firth * (1948 : 127–52). The titles of previous publications in which the ' prosodic approach ' has been used are given in Allen * (1951 : 945). Subsequent publications include Mitchell (1952), Robins * (1953a), Sharp (1954), Carnochan (1952), Robins (1953b), Allen, ' A study in the analysis of Hindi sentence structure ', *Acta Linguistica*, 6 (1950), 2–3, Henderson * (1951).

[3] Jaw makes use of five pitch-levels (op. cit., p. 27) and Miller of four (op. cit., p. 204). Other difficulties attributed to the phonemic technique of analysis may be illustrated from such statements as the following : ' The actual tones in connected speech follow the general principle of one tone being spread over two or more connected syllables. Thus, the high falling tone often becomes a high level tone, the following syllable or syllables, whatever its original tone, taking up a low or falling tone ' (Jaw, pp. 27–8). Miller makes use of the concept of ' Perturbation of Natural Tone ' (p. 206) implied by the quotation from Jaw above : ' a naturally high tone syllable may be perceptually lower than a naturally low tone syllable occurring outside the first named syllable's " intonation phrase " ' (p. 203) ; ' syllables other than the first in a word, and specially postpositionals and terminatives . . . are more susceptible to intonation pressure, and hence do not conform so readily to their inherent tone ' (p. 204).

[4] For the technical specialization of the terms ' structure ' and ' system ', see R. H. Robins, ' Formal Divisions ', 109.

[5] The Tibetan script recognizes the syllable, terminated by the ts'eg ; and a unit, terminated by the śad, comprising an indefinite number of syllables but approximating to the sentence. No intermediate unit is recognized.

[6] Two structures are recognized for the syllable irrespective of grammatical category : CV, CVC. In my ' Verbal Phrases—II ', 320, only one structure was recognized for members of the verb category, viz. CVC ; this statement has proved unsatisfactory.

homophonous. The non-homophonous exponents may be used as criteria for the purpose of delimiting the word, and are consequently termed ' marker ' exponents. One type of marker exponent is held to mark the boundaries of words and hence interverbal syllable relations, including the beginning and end of sentences ; and the other to mark the absence of word boundaries and hence medial, or intraverbal, syllable relations. The two terms of the Junction system may therefore conveniently be termed interverbal and intraverbal, with reference to the function of the marker exponents in the delimitation of words. Since they do not contribute to the purpose of this article, homophonous exponents of inter- and intraverbal junction are not dealt with here; but the marker exponents are treated in detail.

Marker exponents may be stated in relation to (I) the syllable-initial consonant (C-), and (II) the syllable-final consonant (-C).

I. Characterizing C-

A. *Interverbal*

The exponents of inter- and intra-verbal junction that characterize C- cannot be considered independently of the rate of utterance of the sentence ; C- is characterized by one set of phonetic features when the rate of utterance is slow and careful, as when speaking to foreigners, and by other features when the rate of utterance is fast, and no concessions are made to the listener. The marker exponents of the two terms of the junction system in fast and in slow utterances are here considered in terms of a two-term Tempo system, ' fast ' and ' slow ', statable with reference to the sentence unit, hence ' fast tempo ' (ft) and ' slow tempo ' (st).[1]

Some of the exponents of inter- and intra-verbal junction may be stated as criteria for the delimiting of words for both ft and st, while others may be so stated for one of these two prosodic contexts but not the other. First to be stated are those which are valid for both ft and st. They comprise :—

(1) voicelessness (+ lateral occlusion)   ḷ
(2)   ,,   (+ apical friction)   r̥
(3)   ,,   (+ vowel)   h

Voice co-articulated with either lateral occlusion (1) or apical friction (ɹ) is an exponent of both inter- and intra-verbal junction, but *voicelessness* + either of these two types of articulation is a word-initial feature, as also is voicelessness of vowel, e.g. :—

---

[1] Cf. the prosodic statement of Tempo in relation to the Verbal Phrase in ' Verbal Phrases—I ', 149 : ' Rate of Utterance '.

(1)	ˡ	{ lø:lø: ˈtɕhɛ:nɛ:	*(lhod-lhod* [2] byas-nas
		ˈde:gəjĭ: [1]	bsdad-kyi-yin) [3]
		{ ˌlu:lu: ˈɹe:	*(lhug-lhug* red)
(2)	ˌ	ɹɛ:ɹɛ: ˈtɕhɛ:nɛ:	*(hral-hral* byas-nas
		tsu:gydu:	btsug-gi-ḫduṅ)
(3)	h	{ haŋgɔ: ˈkhabɑ: ˈjø:	(lham-k'og ga-bar yod)
		{ hɔ:bə ˈtɕhi: le:ɕa	(hor-pa cig bslebs-ŝag) [4]

The usefulness of the various co-articulations of plosion (voice, voicelessness, etc.) for the delimiting of words is closely related to tempo, but there is, however, one co-articulation of plosion that both marks word-beginning and is also valid for either term of the Tempo system :—

(4) glottality (+ plosion)   ʔ, e.g.

ʔu: thiŋgidu: *(dbugs* ḫt'en-gyi-ḫdug)

but cf. ˈdʑʌu: ˈtɕhi: thɛmbə   (ljags-*dbugs* cig ḫt'en-pa

ᴨʌŋgidu: gnaṅ-gi-ḫdug)

The remaining co-articulations of plosion are the following ; when plosion characterizes C-, it must have one of them as a co-articulation :—

voice	**b/d/g/ɟ/dʑ/dz/dɹ**
voicelessness + aspiration	**ph/th/kh/ch/tɕh/tsh/tʂ**
,, + non-aspiration	**p/t/k/c/tɕ/ts/tʂ**

With one exception (**dʑ**) voice is an exponent of both inter- and intra-verbal junction in ft and st alike, and cannot therefore be utilized for word-delimitation. The degree to which the remaining two co-articulations,

---

[1] The phonetic examples are given in the International Phonetic Alphabet but subject to the same conventions as those stated in ' Verbal Phrases—I ', 142. Two additional symbols have been used in both the phonetic transcriptions and the transliterated text: (I) —/— Pause. (II) - - - Sentence incomplete or interrupted.

[2] Where possible, inter- and intraverbal junction have been illustrated from words having a common constituent in both of these two prosodic contexts ('lhod' in this instance), so that the exponents of either term may be given the maximum prominence.

[3] The task of writing down one of the modern spoken dialects of Tibetan raises problems of some difficulty, for none of the contemporary spoken dialects appears to have an orthography : they all make use of classical Tibetan as their written medium. Thus I have been informed by H. E. Richardson, C.I.E., O.B.E., formerly in charge of the Indian Mission, Lhasa, that ' it is perhaps not strictly correct to say that utterances in Lhasa Tibetan are written down at all. Tibetans do not write what they say except for special purposes such as your research and our sentences ' [i.e. *Tibetan Sentences*, by Sir Basil Gould, C.M.G., C.I.E., and Hugh Edward Richardson, O.B.E. (O.U.P., 1943)].

The Tibetan spellings given in this article are either those of R. himself or of dPal-ḫbyor P'un-ts'ogs. In the main they do not differ from Classical-Tibetan orthography, but the writers have sometimes indulged in phonetic spellings, especially where the phonetic implications of the traditional spelling are markedly different from the phonetic form heard from the recording. Some spellings will therefore look unusual, but then making recordings of spoken Tibetan is not one of the more usual Tibetan activities.

[4] Since marker exponents of inter- and intra-verbal junction have already been stated for certain verb forms, ' Verbal Phrases—I ', 146–9, the examples given in this article have been restricted to words analysable into (I) Noun + Particle, (II) Adjective + Particle.

voicelessness + aspiration and voicelessness + non-aspiration, can be utilized, is bound up with Tempo (ft, st).

For ft the relevant co-articulations of plosion may be exponents of inter- and intraverbal junction as follows :—

	fast tempo (ft)		Inter.	Intra.
(C-) + plosion	voice		X	X [1]
	voicelessness +	aspiration	X	
		non-aspiration	X	

(Examples recorded : X ; no examples recorded : blank.)

Thus in this prosodic context (ft) *voice* is an exponent of either term ; but *voicelessness*, whether co-articulated with aspiration or non-aspiration, is peculiar to interverbal junction, and is thus a marker exponent of interverbal junction, e.g. :—

(5a) Voicelessness (+ plosion)   **p/ph/k/kh/t/th/c/ch/tɕ/tɕh/ts/ tsh/tʂ/tʂ̣**, e.g.

fast tempo (ft)

p	**pɛdʐə**	(*dpe*-c'a)	**ˈkhabɑ: ˈjø:**	
	cf. **tɕhabi** [2]	(p'yag-*dpe*)	(ga-bar yod)	
ph	**ˈphɑ:le:**	(*bag*-leb)	**ˈkhabɑ: ˈɕɑ:bɑ**	
	cf. **ˈɕe:ba**	(bʑes-*bag*)	(ga-bar bʑag-pa)	
t	**ta**	(*rta*)	**tʂi:ɕo:**	
	cf. **ˈʂøndə**	(bʑon-*rta*)	(ḥk'rid-ṣog)	
th	**ˈthɛp**	(*dep*)	che:ɕo:	
	cf. **tɕhadip**	(p'yag-*dep*)	(k'yer-ṣog)	
c	**cɛ:dʐə**	(*skad*-c'a)	**ˈtʂi:gidu:** (dris-kyi-ḥdug)	
	cf. **suŋge:**	(gsuṅ-*skad*)	**ˈjagu ˈdu:** (yag-po ḥdug)	
ch	**chi**	(*k'yi*)	**ˈdi sy: ˈɹɛ:**	
	cf. **ˈsimgi**	(gzim-*k'yi*)	(ḥdi suḥi red)	
tɕ	**tɕu**	(*bcu*)	thambə **ˈjo:əɹe**	
	cf. **sumdʐu**	(gsum-*bcu*)	(t'am-pa yod-pa-red)	
tɕh	**tɕhã:**	(*c'aṅ*)	che:ɕo:	
	cf. **tɕhø:dʐã:**	(mc'od-*c'aṅ*)	(k'yer-ṣog)	

---

[1] When co-articulated with voice friction has been recorded as in free variation with plosion in Intraverbal Junction : **g/ɣ, b/β**.

[2] An advantage of stating a prosodic system of junction is that it enables one to relate the various phonetic forms of a given constituent to a single invariable phonological formula ; differences that there may be between the phonetic forms are stated as exponents of (I) Inter-verbal, or (II) Intraverbal, junction. There is thus no need to give one phonetic form precedence over the others, or dignify it with the title of ' norm '. Cf. A. E. Sharp, ' A Tonal Analysis . . .', 169. Similar advantages are to be gained from a prosodic statement of tempo. From the examples in which a given constituent has been recorded in both Junction contexts it will be seen that Tibetan orthographic usage is not unduly phonetic : the syllable in question in **pɛdʐə** and **tɕhabi** (dpe-c'a, p'yag-dpe) is given the same symbolization in both (dpe) despite considerable phonetic differences.

ts	{ tsɛmu	(*rtsed*-mo)	tse:bəɹe (rtsed-pa-red)
	cf. kɔdzi	(sku-*rtsed*)	tsɛbə naŋaɹe (rtse-ba gnaṅ-ba-red)
tsh	{ tshõ:	(*ts'oṅ*)	'khandɹɛ: 'jna (ga-ḥdras yin-na)
	cf. kudzū:	(sku-*ts'oṅ*)	'khandɹɛ: 'jimbə naŋa (ga-ḥdras yin-pa gnaṅ-ṅa)
tɹ	{ tɹa	(*skra*)	'ɕaɹaɹe (bżar-ba-red)
	cf. ʔudɹə	(dbu-*skra*)	'ɕɑ: naŋaɹe (bżar gnaṅ-ba-red)
tɹ̦	{ 'tɹabə	(*grwa*-pa)	'tɕhi: le:ɕa (cig bslebs-ṡag)
	cf. labdɹɑ:	(slab-*dqra*-la) ¹	'dɹugyjī: (hɡro-gi-yin)

In the st prosodic context, on the other hand, voicelessness may not be stated as a marker exponent of interverbal junction, for the relations of the relevant co-articulations of plosion to inter- and intra-verbal junction are rather different :—

$$
\text{(C-) : Plosion} + \begin{cases} \text{voice} \\ \\ \text{voicelessness} + \begin{cases} \text{aspiration} \\ \\ \text{non-aspiration} \end{cases} \end{cases}
$$

	Inter.	Intra.
voice	X	X
aspiration	X	
non-aspiration	X	X ²

In the st context it is only if accompanied by aspiration that voicelessness marks an interverbal junction context. Here, therefore, it is aspiration that can be distinguished from the other two phonetic features, as being a marker exponent of interverbal junction, while plosion unaccompanied by aspiration is common to both junction contexts. The feature voicelessness (+ plosion) stated at § 5a above as a marker exponent in ft is not valid in st, and should have substituted for it :—

(5b) Aspiration (+ plosion)   ph/th/kh/ch/tɕh/tsh/tɹ̦, e.g.
        slow tempo (st)

ph	{ phɛ̃:	(*p'an*)	tho:gyɹe: (t'ogs-kyi-red)
	cf. thupɛ̃:	(t'ugs-*p'an*)	sugyɹe: (gso-gi-red)
th	{ thaŋgə	(*t'aṅ*-ka)	'kadzɛ: 'jø:na (ga-ts'od yod-na)
	cf. 'ɕɛ:tā:	(żal-*t'aṅ*)	'kadzɛ: 'jø:bə naŋa (ga-ts'od yod-pa gnaṅ-ṅa)
ch	{ chi	(*k'yi*)	'di sy: 'ɹɛ:
	cf. 'simki	(gzim-*k'yi*)	} (ḥdi suhi red)
tɕh	{ tɕhā:	(*c'aṅ*)	che:ɕɔ:
	cf. tɕhø:tɕã:	(mc'od-*c'aṅ*)	} (k'yer-ṡog)

¹ See p. 115, note 3.
² When co-articulated with voicelessness + non-aspiration plosion in the Intraverbal-Junction context is sometimes distinguishable from plosion in the Interverbal-Junction context : it is accompanied by a lax articulation, and might be symbolized in greater detail as ɡ̊, ɖ̣, ḅ.

tsh	{ tsh $\tilde{\text{ɔ}}$:	(*ts'oṅ*)	ˈkhandɹɛ: ˈjina (ga-ḫdras yin-na)
	cf. kutsū:	(sku-*ts'oṅ*)	ˈkhandɹɛ: ˈjimbə naŋa (ga-ḫdras
			yin-pa˘ gnaṅ-ṅa)
tʂ	{ tʂɑ:	(*k'rag*)	thyŋgydu: (ḫt'on-gyi-ḫdug)
	cf. kutɹa	(sku-*k'rag*)	thəmbə nʌŋgidu: (ḫt'on-pa
			gnaṅ-gi-ḫdug)

The five phonetic features given above (1–5) complete the list of exponents of interverbal junction that can also be utilized as criteria for delimiting words with regard to C- ; they all act as markers of word-beginning.

B. *Intraverbal*

The marker exponents of intraverbal junction that may be stated for C-comprise :—

(1) voice (+ apical affrication)   **dz**, e.g.

dz	{ ˈphʌdzi	(ba-*rdzi*)	} ˈɹe: (red)
	cf. ˈziu	(*rdzi*-bo)	
dz	{ ˈdʐʌdzi:	(ljags-*rtsis*)	nʌŋgidu: (gnaṅ-gi-ḫdug)
	cf. tsi:byŋgi	(*rtsis*-dpon-gyi)	tɕhalɛ: nʌŋgidu: (p'yag-las
			gnaṅ-gi-ḫdug).

When co-articulated with apical affrication (**dz**) voice is thus an exception, the sole exception, to the statement made above that voice cannot be utilized for delimiting words. Except in an artificially slow style no word in LT begins with a voiced apical affricate (**dz**), though this type of sound has been recorded medially, in certain types of junction, as exemplified above.

The remaining marker exponents of intraverbal junction are confined to those syllables in which the -V(-) term is characterized by both frontness and spreading. In such syllables velarity, and to some extent dental nasality, is excluded from interverbal, but has been regularly recorded in intraverbal, junction, whence it is possible to add to the list of marker exponents of intra-verbal junction the following :—

(2) velarity   gi(:)/ge:/gɛ(:)/ŋi(:)/ŋe:/ŋɛ(:)

(3) dentality (+ nasality)   ni

Examples as follows :—

(2)	ŋe:	ˈduŋe:	ˈtɕhɛ:bəjī:	(sdug-*bsṅal* byas-pa-yin)
	ŋɛ:	ˈdʐɔ:dʐuŋɛ:		(ḫbyor-byuṅ-*ṅas*)
	gi	sʁbgi ˈdɛndrī:	ˈɕo: nã:sū	(sab-*kyis* gdan-ḫdren ʑu-ba
				gnaṅ-soṅ)
	ge:	{ suŋge: ˈjagu ˈdu:		(gsuṅ-*skad* yag-po ḫdug)
		cf. cɛ:dʐə ˈtʂi:gidu:		(*skad*-c'a dris-kyi-ḫdug)
(3)	ni	{ ˀʌni ˈgo:mbələ tɕhimbəjī		(a-*ni* dgon-pa-la p'yin-pa-yin)
		ˀʌni ˈthu:mədʐū		(a-*ni* thug-ma-byuṅ)

II. Characterizing -C

In addition to the marker exponents of inter- and intra-verbal junction characterizing C- there are also a number characterizing -C that may be used for delimiting words :—

A. *Interverbal*

Absence of oral closure (+ nasality) ĩ:/ɛ̃:/ã:/ɔ̃:/ũ:/ø̃:/ỹ:

Nasality without oral closure is an exponent of certain -C terms in inter-verbal junction, but not, except when the junction-initial C- is characterized by a lateral, an apical-fricative (ɹ) or a semivowel articulation (e.g. ʰmĩ:lə, miṅ-la ; tɕhʌ̃:ɪ̃:, c'aṅ-rin ; ʰtɹũ:ji: ʰla:, druṅ-yig lags) in intraverbal junction. Apart from these and similar examples therefore nasality without oral closure may be considered a marker exponent of interverbal junction, e.g.

ã	{	chɛɹã: ʰkhanɛ: ʰjimba:	(k'yed-*raṅ* ga-nas yin-pa)
	cf.	chɛɹaŋgi tɕhadip ʰkhaba:	(k'yed-*raṅ*-gi p'yag-deb ga-bar bžag
		ʰɕa: naŋajina	gnaṅ-ṅa-yin-na)
ĩ:	{	ʰla ʰji:	(lags *yin*)
	cf.	ʰla ʰjimbədɹa	(lags *yin*-pa-ḥdra)
ỹ:		thyndỹ: ʰɹe:	(*t'uṅ-t'uṅ* red)

B. *Intraverbal*

(1) Oral closure (+ nasality) (except ŋ/n/ɲ, e.g.
              + labiality)

ŋ	{	mɛŋgi ɕe:dʌm ʰtɕhi: ʰgo:jø:	(*sman*-gyi šel-dam cig dgos-yod)
	cf.	mɛ̃: ʰtɕhi: ʰgo:jø:	(*sman* cig dgos-yod)
n	{	ʰjøndɛ̃: (*yon*-tan) }	tɕhimbu ʰɹe:
	cf.	kojø̃: (sku-*yon*) }	(c'en-po red)
ɲ		tɕhyɲdʑỹ: ʰɹe:	(*c'uṅ-c'uṅ* red)

(2) Velarity   k (st) , ɣ/ɤ (ʃt), e.g.

g	{	ʰɹigbə ʰjagu ʰdu:	(*rig*-pa yag-po ḥdug)
	cf.	thuɹi: nobu ʰdu:	(t'ugs-*rig* rno-po ḥdug)
ɣ/k	{	(ʃt) ʰluɣɕa	
		(st) ʰlukɕa }	ʰkhõ: ʰkhadzɛ: ʰɹɛ: (*lug*-ša goṅ ga-ts'od red)
	cf.	ʰlu: ʰmaŋgu ʔajũ:	(*lug* maṅ-po a-yoṅ)

(3) Voice (+ labial plosion)   b
    Friction (+ labiality)   β [1], e.g.

b	{	labdʑũ: ʰɹimbə ʰkhaɹi	(. . . *slab*-sbyoṅs rim-pa ga-re
		ʰkhaɹi ʰtɕhigijø:	ga-re byed-kyi-yod)
	cf.	ʔʌni kʌlʀp ʰɹʀbu ʰɕy:	(a-ni dkaḥ-*slob* ra-po žus)
β	{	ʰjʀβjum ʰɕu:jø:βənɔ:	(*yab*-yum bžugs-yod-pa-no)
	cf.	ʰjʀp ʰɕu:mindu:	(*yab* bžugs-mi-ḥdug)

---

[1] Labial friction has been recorded in interverbal junction, but only when final in the sentence, e.g. khɔɹã:lə ʰduksə ʰlʀβ (k'o-raṅ-la ḥdug-se lab), and is probably best considered as a sentence-final feature.

(4) Apical friction   ɹ¹, e.g.

ɹ ⎰   'ɟagaɹə 'tɕhi: leːɕa   (rgya-*gar*-ba cig bslebs-ṡag)
  ⎱ cf. 'ɟagɑ: 'sɛnə 'lɒɣsø: (rgya-*gar* zer-na lugs-srol ga-ḥdras
           'khandɹɛ: 'ɹɛ: red).

The criteria for setting up the prosodic categories inter- and intra-verbal junction have not thus far required any knowledge of the lexical constituents of words ; they comprise a list of general-phonetic categories, the identification of an instance of any one of which in the speech-stream provides grounds for delimiting words. These exponents could be used for the delimiting of words by anyone with a knowledge of the relevant types of sound irrespective of the constituents of the words concerned. Thus if voiceless plosion should be perceived in listening to an utterance, that feature can be claimed, in fact, as marking the beginning of a word, and similarly with the other marker exponents. The examples given above for these various exponents have, however, gone a step further ; they have been so chosen that it might be possible to illustrate from them some of the phonetic forms ascribable to a constituent in different junction contexts, e.g. *dpe*-c'a (pɛdʑ̊ə), cf. p'yag-*dpe* (tɕhabi) (see p. 116, note 2). Where, however, the constituent and its various contextually distributed phonetic forms are known, it is possible to add to the list of marker exponents characterizing C- a number of others. These further exponents comprise nasal and occlusive articulations that in fact characterize the initial consonant (C-), but would not easily be distinguished from features characterizing the final consonant (-C) by those unfamiliar with the constituents concerned :—

(5)   Inter : Non-nasality   ph/b/th/d/kh/g/ʒ/tʑ̊/dʑ̊/tsh/tɹ̥/dɹ/ɲ
     Intra : Nasality   mb/nd/ŋg/ɲʒ/ɲdʑ̊/nz/ndɹ/md/mdʑ̊/mz/mɲ/ŋɲ

(6)   Inter : Non-occlusion   c/tɕ/tɕh/tɹ/l/s/ɕ̊
     Intra : Occlusion   bʒ/bdʑ̊(ptɕ̊)/bdɹ(ptɹ)/bl/bs(ps)/bɕ̊(pɕ̊) ², e.g.

(5)

Inter. d	{ 'mɛ 'bʌ:gidu:	(*me* ḥbar-gyi-ḥdug)
	'dabȳ: kuɕoːgi 'ɹe:	(*mdaḥ*-dpon sku-gżogs-kyi red)
Intra. nd	'mɛndə cheːɕo:	(*me-mdaḥ* k'yer-ṡog)
Inter. dɹ	{ 'dɹøɲe: tɕhimɔ: 'ɕy:sū	(*mgron*-gñer c'en-mo-la żus-soṅ)
	ku siɹajimbədɹa	(*sku* bsil-ra-yin-pa-ḥdra)
Intra. ndɹ	kundɹȳ: 'tɕhi: pheːɕa	(*sku-mgron* cig p'ebs-ṡag)
Inter. g	{ 'go 'nʌgidu:	(*mgo* na-gi-ḥdug)
	'ɹɑ:	(*ra*)
Intra. ŋg	'ɹaŋgu tagba	(*ra-mgo* btags-pa)

---

¹ Velar and dental nasality, voiceless velar occlusion, and apical friction (ɹ), may be held to mark the absence of word boundaries in some styles of utterance but not in others : in the ' reading ' and ' spelling ' styles these four types of articulation may be final in the word, and cannot therefore be used as criteria for the delimitation of words in these two styles, whereas they can be used as criteria for the style considered here (' speaking style ').

² The exponents appropriate to st are symbolized in brackets.

Inter. b	{	ˈbum ˈjoːəɹe	(ḥbum yod-pa-red)
		ku ɲeːbu ˈmədʑuɳa	(sku mñel-po ma-byuṅ-ña)
Intra. mb		kumbumlə ˈdɹugyɹeː	(sku-ḥbum-la ḥgro-gi-red)

(6)

Inter. tɕ	{	tɕu thambə ˈjoːəɹe	(bcu t'am-pa yod-pa-red)
		ɳa ˈjoːəɹe	(lña yod-pa-red)
Intra. bdʑ		ɳabdʑu thambə ˈjoːəɹe	(lña-bcu t'am-pa yod-pa-red)
Inter. tɕh	{	ˈtɕha ˈdi ˈkhaɹi ˈɹeː	(bya ḥdi ga-re red)
		tɕhu toːdzə ˈgoːjø	(c'u tog-tsam dgos-yod)
Intra. bdʑ		tɕhubdzə ˈɹeː	(c'u-bya red)

In addition to the marker exponents of intraverbal and interverbal junction, which characterize syllable-initial and syllable-final consonants (C-, -C), a further phonetic feature, pause, is a potential marker of word limits :—

ˈjãː ˈdyndɹa ˈɹɛɹeː ˈnãːləjãː thɛ̃ː tɕigi — ˈmaɹeː — thɛ̃ː ɲiː — ˈgiɹiːsi phiɹiːsi phidɹa ˈseɲɛ̃ː ˈtɕhiː ˈduga — khoŋgi phiːge ˈphyːjiː ˈdɹømbyː ˈɹɤbu ˈɕyː

(yaṅ bdun-p'rag re-reḥi naṅ-la-yaṅ t'eṅ gcig-gi — ma-red — t'eṅ gñis — ghi-ri-si p'i-rin-si p'i-ḍar [Greece, Prince Peter] zer-ñan gcig ḥdug-kaṅ —ˈk'oṅ-gi p'a-gas bod-yig sgron-ḥbul ra-po žus.)

The theory that sets up the word and applies the tonal system to it receives further support from the feature sometimes described as vowel harmony,[1] and from the tonal system itself : the exponents of the terms of these two prosodic systems characterize syllables within the limits of the word but not beyond those limits, and may most profitably be stated with reference to the word.[2]

GRAMMATICAL CATEGORIES : DEFINITION

The main categories needed for an adequate description of the word unit at the grammatical level of analysis comprise the following five : Verb, Noun, Adjective, Postposition, Particle. Of these categories the Verb and the Verb Particle have already been defined, on formal grounds (op. cit., pp. 134–140) ; it remains to define the main categories required for an account of tone in the Nominal Phrase : Noun, Adjective, Postposition, Particle (of the following sub-categories : Noun, Adjective, Nominal-Phrase).

This article does not, however, attempt to deal fully with every grammatical type of word in the Nominal Phrase, but takes the words analysable in terms of the categories Noun, Noun Particle, and Nominal-Phrase Particle as examples to which the other grammatical types of word conform with appropriate differences of phonetic exponent. The only grammatical categories to be defined

---

[1] op. cit., pp. 323–8 ; 340–2. ' Prosodic System of Closure.'

[2] A ' word ' unit may be delimited in spoken Burmese by the same technique of analysis as has been applied here to Lhasa Tibetan. Indeed, the similarity even extends to particular marker exponents of inter- and intra-verbal junction.

here are therefore those of (I) Noun, (II) Noun Particle, and (III) Nominal-Phrase Particle.

I. Noun

The criteria for defining the noun category are three in number :—

A. *Number of Syllables*

Like the members of all other grammatical categories, nouns may be monosyllabic, but unlike them, may also be (1) disyllabic, and (2) trisyllabic. The only recorded example of a disyllable that is not a noun, apart from reduplicative adjectives, is the Postposition p'a-gi. Examples as follows :—

(1) *sku-żog p'yags-p'ebs* gnań-byuń
    sku-żog ga-dus c'ibs-bsgyur gnań-ńa-yin-na

(2) *rgya-gar-ba* cig-gi red
    lhas-sa-ba min-na, ḥgrig-gi-ma-red

B. *Colligation*

The Noun may be colligated (1) within word limits, with (a) the Noun-Particle, and (b) the Nominal-Phrase-Particle, categories; and (2) not within word limits, with the Postposition category, e.g. :—

(1) (a) ma-kaḥi yar zla-ba *bcu-rtse* cig ma-kaḥi lon-don-la [London] bsdad-pa-yin :
    Noun + Noun Particle (rtse).

    nor-bu gliń-kaḥi p'yag-las *yun riń-ḥt'uń* ga-gaḥa-tsam gnań-ńa-yin-na :
    Noun + Noun Particle (zero).

(b) *deḥi sńas-la-yań lhas-sa-rań-la* bżugs bżugs-pa-yin-na :
    Noun + Nominal-Phrase Particle (ḥi, la, yań, rań).

    de min-paḥi-yań — lhas-sa *k'ul-la* — *p'yag-las* . . . :
    Noun + Nominal-Phrase Particle (ḥi, yań, la, zero).

(2) ńas ḥdiḥi sńas-ma mt'ar-p'yin sba-bu lags-kyi *tshag-par de* lhas-sa k'ul-la mt'oń-byuń :
    Noun + Particle (ts'ag-par) + Postposition (de).

ḥdas yar me-lon par-k'ań *zer-ńan gcig* ḥdug :
    Noun + Particle (zer-ńan) + Postposition (gcig).

C. *Order of Categories*

(1) *Within the Word*

Within the word the Noun category precedes (a) the Noun Particle, or (b) the Nominal-Phrase Particle, e.g. :

(a) da ñi-ma re-la de rim-pa *ga-gaḥa-tsam* grub-kyi-yod-na, ... :
    Noun (ga-gaḥa) + Noun Particle (tsam).

(b) *ńas deḥi sńas-la ts'ag-par dbyin-jiḥi skor-gyi ḥdi-ḥdras* mases *bod-paḥi ḥdi* mt'oń-ma-myoń :

Noun + Nom.-Phrase Part. ;		Noun + Nom.-Phrase Part.	
ṅa	-s	de	ḥi
ts'ag-par	zero	dbyin-ji	ḥi
skor	gyi	ḥdi-ḥdra	-s [1]
bod-pa	ḥi	ḥdi	zero

(2) *Within the Sentence*

In non-final clauses, and in final clauses in which there is a Verbal Phrase,[2] the Nominal Phrase regularly precedes the Verbal, e.g. :

> *lcags-par de-ḥts'o gaṅ min-mdzad gam gtsaṅ-ma* yin-tsaṅ, *sṅas-maḥi rdo-par-las že-drag gcig-gi gam gtsaṅ-ṅa* ḥdug-ga.
> *da-lta k'o-ḥts'os gnas-don ḥdi* rtogs ma gnaṅ-tsaṅ, *ḥdiḥi rkyen-gyi k'rigs-te* zer-gyi-ḥdug.

In those instances in which a Nominal Phrase is final in a verbal sentence, as it may be in parenthesis, it is characterized by a low level intonation-pattern, e.g. :

da ñi-ma re-la de rim-pa ga-ga-tsam grub-kyi-yod-na, *de ṅa-raṅ-ḥts'os.*

daṅ-po ga-bar slab-pa-yin-gnaṅ, *ṅa-raṅ-ḥtsoḥi lcag-par de bsgrigs-pa gnaṅ-rgyu.*

(3) *In the Nominal Phrase.*

The categories Noun and Noun Particle precede Adjective, Adjective-Particle, Postposition, and Nominal-Phrase-Particle categories in the Nominal Phrase, e.g. :

> da *mt'un-rkyen ra-po cig* gžuṅ-raṅ-nas tog-tsi cig gnaṅ-gi-yod-pas, bzo-lta ra-po :
> Noun (mt'un-rkyen) + Particle (zero) ; Adjective (ra) + Particle (po) ; Postposition (cig) + Nominal-Phrase Particle (zero).

> ṅa-ḥts'oḥi bsam-las rim-pas p'i-nas gcig-gi *mt'un-rkyen ra-po* gnaṅ :
> Noun (mt'un-rkyen) + Particle (zero) ; Adjective (ra) + Particle (po) + Noun-Phrase Particle (zero).

---

[1] Some of these particles have differing phonetic forms, according as the structure of the syllable with which they are in junction is CV or CVC. This phonetic difference is often, and over-phonetically, reflected in the spelling :—

	CVC Junction	CV Junction	
I.	kyi/gyi/gi	ḥi,	e.g. deḥi, dbyin-jiḥi, skor-*gyi*, bod-paḥi.
II.	kyis/gyis/gis	-s,	e.g. ṅas, ḥdi-ḥdras, cf. sba-bu-lags-*kyis*.
III.	la	la/-r/ḥi,	e.g. sṅas-*la* ; cf. luṅ-par, sṅas-maḥi.
IV.	yaṅ	yaṅ/ḥi/-s,	e.g. da-*yaṅ*, suḥi, bsam-las.

[2] See ' Verbal Phrases in Spoken Lhasa Tibetan ', p. 134.

[3] Two distinctive pitch levels are recognized. The symbols used are as follows :—

I. High level ⁻ ; II. Low level _ ; III. Fall \ ; IV. Rise-fall ∧ ; V. Rise ╱.

de *slad-p'yin cig* bod-la yar yaṅ p'a-ges tog rtse cig yag-po yoṅ-gi-red-pa :

Noun (slad-p'yin) + Particle (zero) ; Postposition (cig) + Nominal-Phrase Particle (zero).

par-k' aṅ yod-pas, zer-ñan ra-po :

Noun (par-k'aṅ) + Nominal-Phrase Particle (zero).

II. Noun Particle

(1) All Noun Particles are monosyllabic.

(2) The Noun Particle category is invariably colligated with the Noun, and only with the Noun, category within the limits of the word.

(3) The order of categories within the word is : (*a*) Noun, (*b*) Noun Particle. Only two Noun Particles have been recorded :—

tsam/tse/tsi, zero, e.g.

de-nas ka-lon sbug-la ts'ur p'ebs-ni lo ga-ts'od-*rtse* t'ad-kyi-yod-na :
Noun (ga-ts'od) + Noun Particle (rtse).

k'oṅ de-ni deḥi sṅas-la *sa-skya* k'ul-laḥi cig *c'ibs-bsgyur* gnaṅ :
Noun + Particle (zero).

III. Nominal-Phrase Particle

(1) All Nominal-Phrase Particles are monosyllabic.

(2) The Nominal-Phrase-Particle category is colligated with the final category of the Nominal Phrase, whether (*a*) Noun, or Noun Particle (tsam), (*b*) Adjective Particle, (*c*) Postposition.

(3) This category is final in both word and Nominal Phrase.

The following eleven Nominal-Phrase Particles have been recorded :—

gi/gyi/kyi/ḥi,[1] gis/gyis/kyis/-s,[1] nas/ni, la/-r/ḥi,[1] du/ru/su,[1] ḥts'o, daṅ, las, yaṅ/ḥi/-s,[1] raṅ, zero,[2] e.g. ḥdi da-riṅ ḥdiḥi p'yag-dpe ḥdi ṅa-naṅ-ḥts'oḥi debs-kyi lugs-srol yin-naḥi ṅa-raṅ-ḥts'oḥi bod-paḥi p'yag-dpe-raṅ yin-na.

Noun + Noṁ.-Phrase Part. ;		Noun + Nom.-Phrase Part.	
ḥdi	zero	da-riṅ	zero
ḥdi	ḥi	ḥdi	zero
ṅa-raṅ	ḥts'o + ḥi	debs	kyi
lugs-srol	zero	ṅa-raṅ	ḥts'o + ḥi
bod-pa	ḥi	p'yag-dpe	raṅ + zero

yin-naḥi k'a-seṅ ṅa-raṅ-*ḥts'o* ya-*gaḥi* p'o-braṅ-*la* yar de-ni lo-sar-*la* mdzad-c'en skabs-*su* ya-gaḥi bcar byas, deḥi skabs-*su-yaṅ* ṅa-raṅ-*ḥts'os* gsuṅ-rnam gcig gnaṅ-ṅa-yin-tsaṅ, de zè-drag-*gi* ḥbad . . . gsal-po . . .

---

[1] See p. 123, note 1.

[2] The Particle ni cannot be included in this list : although in some instances the criteria for defining the Nominal-Phrase Particle are applicable to ni, e.g. deḥi rkyen-gyi *de-ni* na-raṅ-ḥts'o bod-yig de-ḥdras-se bris byas . . . : Noun (de) + Particle (ni), other examples have been recorded in which they are not, e.g. med *zer-na-ni* t'on-yod-red-pa : Verb (zer) + Verb Particle (na).

(particles other than zero are in italics; zero, which could not be indicated in this way, would be stated for the following words : k'a-seń, mdzad-c'en, gcig, de).

When the Nominal Phrase is analysed in terms of the grammatical categories enumerated above, any given word, as delimited above (pp. 134–42) can be regarded as comprising any one of the three non-Particle categories (Noun, Adjective, Postposition), represented by a single example, colligated with the Particle category, represented by one or more examples, in the order (I) non-Particle category, (II) Particle category :—

$$\left.\begin{array}{l}\text{Noun}\\\text{Adjective}\\\text{Postposition}\end{array}\right\} + \text{Particle}$$

Thus in every word, at the grammatical level of analysis, the Particle category is represented by at least one example, from one of the three sub-categories (Noun .Particle, Adjective Particle, Nominal-Phrase Particle), but each one of these sub-categories includes zero as a member. The tonal analysis stated below is, however, valid for all three grammatical types of word (Noun + Particle, Adjective + Particle, Postposition + Particle), with appropriate differences of exponent, with the result that it is possible to take any one grammatical type as an example. Words analysable into Noun + Particle have been chosen to illustrate the kind of tonal statement advanced in this article.

TONAL SYSTEM AND WORD

A two-term Tonal system (Tone One, Tone Two) may be stated for LT, and may be associated with the word. A given word may therefore be assigned to one or other prosodic category and termed a Tone-One Word (1W) or a Tone-Two Word (2W), according as the exponents of Tone One or of Tone Two are statable for it.

The criteria for setting up the Tonal system are of four orders:—

        A.   features of pitch.
        B.   features of duration of vowel.
        C.   word-initial features.
        D.   features of voice-quality.

Although the two-term Tonal System may be applied to the word irrespective of the way in which a given word may be analysed grammatically, it is not possible to make a single comprehensive statement of the exponents of the two terms. Not only do differences in grammatical category have to be taken into account, but separate statements of exponents are required by differences in the number and structure of syllables. This article is restricted to a study of words grammatically analysable in terms of the categories disyllabic Noun and Particle, but the type of word studied here will be broadly representative of other types.

In words of the grammatical type disyllabic Noun + Nominal-Phrase Particle the Particle category is represented (I) by the Particle zero, (II) by the Particle la/-r/ẖi.[1]

I. DISYLLABIC NOUN + NOMINAL-PHRASE PARTICLE (ZERO)

The exponents of Tone One and Tone Two with reference to this type of word comprise :—

A. *Pitch Exponents*

The three [2] intonation-patterns of relevant Tone One and Tone Two words are illustrated in the following diagram :—

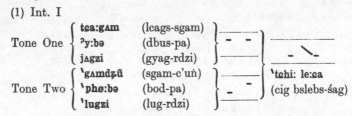

	Intonation I	Intonation II	Intonation III
Tone One:			
Tone Two:			

It will be seen that a relevant Tone One Word does not have one single intonation pattern, but may have any one of three different intonation patterns, as appropriate to a particular intonation context, intonation I, II, or III. A relevant Tone Two Word similarly has three possible patterns, and it is of interest that in one intonation context (intonation III), the exponents of Tone One and Tone Two are identical, and cannot therefore be used as criteria for setting up the Tonal system.[3]

In intonation I, Tone One words are distinguished from Tone Two words by the fact that the pitch of a Tone Two word is higher at the end of the word than at the beginning, while the pitch of the Tone One word is perceived as level, e.g. :—

(1) Int. I

Tone One
- tɕaːgʌm (lcags-sgam)
- ʔyːbə (dbus-pa)
- jʌgzi (gyag-rdzi)

Tone Two
- ˈgʌmdʐũ (sgam-c'uṅ)
- ˈphøːbə (bod-pa)
- ˈlugzi (lug-rdzi)

ˈtɕhiː leːɕa (cig bslebs-śag)

In intonation II both prosodic types of word are characterized by a fall in pitch, but in the case of the Tone Two Word the fall is preceded by a rise, and in the case of the Tone One Word it is not. The intonation-patterns given under intonation II are appropriate to a one-word sentence, e.g. :—

---

[1] See p. 123, note 1.

[2] The intonation-patterns given are in every case exhaustive for the material studied.

[3] In the Intonation-III context therefore a given word cannot be identified as a Tone One or a Tone Two word from exponents of the first order, pitch, but it may well be possible to identify it prosodically from other criteria, i.e. from the third order of exponent, word-initial features (word-initial voice + plosion, voicelessness + non-aspiration + plosion, etc.).

(2) Int. II

Tone One	tɕa:gʌm	(lcags-sgam)	⌐ ‾ ‾ ¹
	ʔy:bə	(dbus-pa)	
	jʌgzi	(gYag-rdzi)	
Tone Two	ꞌgʌmdʐū	(sgam-c'uṅ)	⌐ ‾
	ꞌphø:bɑ:	(bod-pa)	＼
	ꞌlugzi:	(lug-rdzi)	

Finally, as an example of Tone One and Tone Two words in intonation III a sentence was recorded in which k'a-saṅ (1W) and de-riṅ (2W) are heard first with the intonation-pattern appropriate to intonation I, at the beginning of the sentence; and at the end of the sentence, following the verb, with the patterns appropriate to intonation III :—

(3) Int. III

khasā: (k'a-saṅ) (1W) ;   ꞌthiɹī: (de-riṅ) (2W)

ꞌtha ꞌthiɹī: khasā: ꞌbʌbu ꞌlɑ: tɕhalɛ: ŋagū: ꞌkhaɹi nʌŋgijø:nə
(da de-riṅ k'a-saṅ sba-bu lags p'yag-las sña-dgoṅ ga-re gnaṅ-gi yod na,

ꞌthiɹī: khasā:
de-riṅ k'a-saṅ)

It should perhaps be stressed that a given Tone One intonation-pattern is not comparable with any of the Tone Two intonation-patterns other than the one appropriate to the same intonation context ; but all three Tone One intonation-patterns are not only comparable but must be compared in order to establish which of the three Tone One intonation-patterns, the intonation I, the intonation II, or the intonation III, is appropriate to a given Tone One word in a given instance ; similar considerations apply to the Tone Two word. It is not the purpose of this article to deal here with the mutual expectancy of the various possible intonation-patterns, and the implications that they have for each other, except for such brief indications as that, for example, the intonation-I patterns imply at least one succeeding word in the sentence ; the intonation-III patterns imply at least one preceding word.[2]

B. Duration of Vowel

The second-order of exponents of Tone may be stated only with reference to intonation-context II. In this context, where the latter syllable of the noun

---

[1] By using the intonation-pattern given, I have avoided associating the fall in pitch with either the former or the latter of the two syllables. In practice the fall in pitch has been perceived as associated with the latter syllable when that syllable is of a structure CVC, and with the former syllable when the latter syllable is of a structure CV, e.g. tɕa:gʌm (-CVC) : ‾ ＼, but ʔy:bə (-CV) : ＼.

[2] For the sort of statement that would be required for an account of the relevant prosodies of the word (Tone) and the Sentence (Intonation), cf. A. E. Sharp, ' A Tonal Analysis . . .'.

is of a CV structure, the vowel of that syllable is characterized by a greater degree of duration in a Tone Two word than in a Tone One word, and by correlated differences in quality. The difference in exponent may be illustrated from a comparison of such pairs of words as the following :—

yak-herd	(gᵞag-*rdzi*)	(1W)	jʌgzɩ
sheep-herd	(lug-*rdzi*)	(2W)	ˈlɒgzi:
Man of U Province	(dbus-p*a*)	(1W)	ˀy:bə
Man of Bhutan, Bhutanese	(ḫbrug-pa)	(2W)	ˈdɹɒgbɑ:

In the Tone Two word, lug-rdzi, the vowel of the latter syllable is characterized by a greater degree of duration and by a greater degree of closeness (i:) than is phonologically the same vowel in the Tone One word (ɩ). The other pair of examples displays comparable phonetic differences (ə and ɑ:) for a common vowel term.

C. *Word-initial Features*

In much the same way as it was found possible above to treat the exponential features of inter- and intra-verbal junction, characterizing the initial and final consonants of the syllable (C-, -C), into homophonous and non-homophonous according as they might or might not be used as criteria for delimiting the word, so it is also possible to consider those phonetic features which characterize the initial consonant of the word (word-initial C-) as (1) providing, or (2) not providing, criteria for setting up the Tonal system.

(1) *Providing Criteria for setting up the Tonal System*

The exponential features to be considered here, and especially two of the three co-articulations of plosion, i.e. voice, and voicelessness + non-aspiration, may be stated as criteria for establishing (a) Tone One, (b) Tone Two.

(*a*) Tone One

The relevant criteria comprise :—

(i) Voicelessness + non-aspiration (+ plosion) p/t/k/c/tɕ/ts/tɹ

(ii) Voicelessness + vowel

(iii) Glottality (+ plosion) ˀ

    - -

	p	paɹdʑɛ:	(par-chas)	
	t	tɛ:gə	(rta-sga)	
	k	kubɑ:	(sku-par)	
(i)	c	cidu:	(skyid-sdug)	
	tɕ	tɕɑ:gʌm	(lcags-sgam)	
	ts	tsambə	(rtsam-pa)	
	tɹ	traɕɛ:	(skra-ṡad)	
(ii)	h	haŋgo:	(lham-k'og)	
(iii)	ˀ	ˀaɹa	(a-rag)	

_ ＼ _

ˈkhabɑ: ˈjøː:
(ga-bar yod)

Two further criteria may be stated for Tone One. Aspiration when co-articulated with apical affrication (**tsh**), is an exponent of Tone One.

(iii) Aspiration (+ voiceless affrication)   **tsh**, e.g. : –

    tshayɕə (tsʻag-śa)   **ˈkhabɑː ˈjø:** (ga-bar yod).

Finally voicelessness co-articulated with lateral occlusion is also a mark of a Tone One word :—

(iv) Voicelessness + (lateral occlusion)   **l̥**, e.g. :—

    l̥ɛːsə   khyːlə   tɕhalɛ: ˈkhaɹi   naŋajina
    (lhas-sa k'ul-la p'yag-las ga-re gnań-ńa-yin-na)

If the word be characterized by any of the above four initial features, it can only be a Tone One word.

(b) Tone Two

The word-initial features that contribute to the identifying of a word as Tone Two are the following :—

(i) Voice (+ plosion)	**b/d/g/ʒ/dʐ/dɹ**
(ii) Apical friction	**r**

Examples as follows :—

(i)	b	ˈbamɛ̃:	(ḫbam-sman)
	d	ˈdimiː	(lde-mig)
	g	ˈgʌmdʐũː	(sgam-c'uń)
	ʒ	ˈʒãːɕi:	(rgyań-śel)
	dʐ	ˈdʐadzə	(ljags-ts'wa)
	dɹ	ˈdɹampɲɛ̃:	(sgra-bsñan)
(ii)	r	ˈɹɛːdʐə	(ras-c'a)

> **ˈkhabɑː ˈjø:**
> (ga-bar yod)

To the above two exponents may be added a third :—

(iii) Voice (+ friction)   **z**, e.g. :

koŋøː ˈzasa ˈʂuːdɛ̃: ˈdʐɑːjøːβeno   (sku ńos *dza-sag* bżugs-gdan ḫjags-yod-pa-no).

Finally, the word may be characterized by the absence of the features so far stated, plosion, nasality, friction, etc., all of which are at the phonetic level of analysis classified as consonantal, and may thus be perceived phonetically as beginning with a vowel. This feature, the absence of the consonantal articulations referred to, is also a mark of the Tone Two word.

(iv) Absence of plosion, friction, and other consonantal articulations, e.g. :—
    ˈomə (ho-ma)   **cheːɕo:** (k'yer-śog).

D. *Voice Quality*

The fourth criterion cannot be illustrated from examples taken from the disyllabic-Noun category.

(2) *Not providing Criteria for setting up the Tonal System*

Such features as the following may, however, be initial features in Tone One and Tone Two words alike; and give no indication of the tonal category of the word :—

(a) Nasality	m/n/ŋ/ɲ	(b) Voice (+ lateral occlusion) l
(c) Semivowel articulation j		(d) Voicelessness (+ friction) s/ɕ

Tone One.   *Tone Two.*

cf.

		Tone One.		*Tone Two.*		
(a)	m	meyɐe:	(mig-šel)	ˈmɛtɔ:	(me-tog)	
	n	nagzə	(snag-ts'a)	ˈnamsə	(na-bzah̲)	
	ŋ	ŋy:sǎ:	(dṅul-sraṅ)	—	—	
	ɲ	ɲu:gu	(smyu-gu)	ˈɲobdʑə	(ño-c'a)	
(b)	l	luyɕu	(glog-bžu)	ˈʌmji:	(lam-yig)	
(c)	j	jʌgdɹu:	(gYag-p'rug)	ˈjɨgi	(yi-ge)	
(d)	s	sø:dʑə	(gsol-ja)	ˈsimɕa	(gzim-šag)	
	ɕ	ɕʌɳdʑi	(šaṅs-p'yid)	ˈɕɛ:sɛ:	(žal-bzas)	

ˈkhaba: ˈjø:
(ga-bar yod)

Any of the Tone One or Tone Two words may be collocated with
ˈkhaba: ˈjø: (ga-bar yod).

A prominent exponent of Tone One and Tone Two words in addition to the phonetic features already given is the remaining one of the three co-articulations of plosion :—

(e) aspiration (+ plosion)   ph/th/kh/ch/tɕh/tʂ.

While the other two co-articulations of plosion (*voice*, and *voicelessness + non-aspiration*, which can be considered jointly as *non-aspiration*) may be treated as criteria for setting up the Tone system, *aspiration*, with one exception (tsh), may not : it is not possible to identify a word as Tone One or Tone Two from the aspiration feature, e.g. :—

Tone One.   *Tone Two.*

cf.

(e)	ph	phayɕə	(p'ag-ša)	ˈpha:le:	(bag-leb)
	th	thaŋgə	(t'aṅ-ka)	ˈthu:lo:	(dug-log)
	kh	khapsɛ:	(k'a-bzas)	ˈkhʌu	(gahu)
	ch	chibdɹu:	(k'yi-p'rug)		
	tɕh	tɕhø:dʑǎ:	(mc'od-c'aṅ)	ˈtɕhandũ:	(ja-ldoṅ)
	tʂ	tʂombə	(k'ron-pa)	ˈtʂe:gũ:	(drel-k'aṅ)

ˈkhaba: jø:
(ga-bar yod)

II. Disyllabic Noun + Nominal-Phrase Particle (la/-r/-hi)

The statement made for the type of word Disyllabic Noun + Particle (zero) will in the main serve for those other words of that type in which the Particle category is represented by some Nominal-Phrase Particle other than zero, for example the Particle la/-r/ḥi. There will, of course, be certain differences of detail, for example, a difference in the first order of exponent, pitch features, to accommodate an extra syllable. Further, it is not possible to produce criteria in respect of the second order of exponent (vowel duration), as for gYag-rdzi (1W) and lug-rdzi (2W); but the exponents of the third order, word-initial features, may stand for words of this and all types. As an example of minor differences in exponents of the first order the intonation-patterns of relevant words in which the Nominal-Phrase-Particle category is represented by la/-r/ḥi are given :—

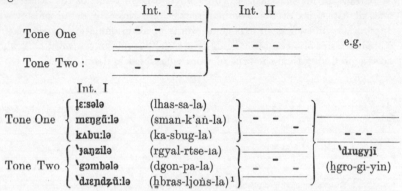

It is submitted that it would be legitimate to give the nouns so far cited a prosodic classification suitable for a dictionary entry : the disyllabic noun lcags-sgam, and all the other disyllabic nouns to be cited in Tone One words, always partake of the features of a Tone One word ; they do not alternate between Tone One and Tone Two ; they could therefore be lexically classified as Tone One *nouns* in the sense that they are to be associated with the *Tone One word*, not the *Tone Two*.

The classification need not, of course, stop short at the disyllabic Noun ; it is equally applicable to all Nouns, to Adjectives, to Postpositions, and to Verbs ; but it is not applicable to the Particle category : Nominal-Phrase Particles are not limited to either Tone One or Tone Two words ; examples of the particle la/-r/ḥi are given in the tonal examples in both Tone

---

[1] As stated above (p. 123, note 1), the exponents of this particle are dependent on the prosodic context, i.e. whether the syllable with which it is in junction is CVC in structure (e.g. sman-k'aṅ, ka-sbug, ḥbras-ljoṅs) or CV (e.g. lhas-sa, rgyal-rtse, dgon-pa). For these latter examples alternative phonetic forms to those given above have been recorded :—

Tone One	lɛ:sa:	- -	- - -
Tone Two	{ ˈɟaŋzɛ:	-	ˈdʒugyĩ
	ˈgomba:		(ḥgro-gi-yin)

In ft, in fact, these alternative phonetic forms have been more often recorded than those (lɛ:sələ, etc.) given at (II). The alternative forms are sometimes symbolized in the Tibetan text as lhas-sa-*la*, rgyal-rtse-*la*, etc., and sometimes specifically indicated by the use of such phonetic spellings as lhas-sar/lhas-saḥi, rgyal-rtser, etc.

One and Tone Two words, e.g. lhas-sa-*la* (1W), and rgyal-rtse-*la* (2W). The Nouns lhas-sa (Tone One) and rgyal-rtse (Tone Two) do not behave in this way.

There is one respect in which words which are grammatically analysable into monosyllabic Noun + Particle differ from words of the type considered hitherto ; for them the fourth order of exponents of Tone (voice quality) is statable. Clear voice may be stated as an exponent of Tone One and breathy voice of Tone Two.

The differences between words grammatically analysable as disyllabic Noun + Particle and those analysable as monosyllabic or trisyllabic Noun + Particle, or for that matter words analysable in terms of the other grammatical categories of the Nominal phrase, are those of detail only ; with appropriate differences in exponent, words of all grammatical types may be stated in terms of a two-term Tonal System applicable to the word as a whole no less profitably than the type of word considered in detail above.

8

THE 'BROKEN PLURALS' OF TIGRINYA

By F. R. PALMER

THE paradigms that may be set up for the nominals in Tigrinya [1] in terms of the category of number (established on syntactical and further morphological grounds) consist of two members, conveniently termed 'singular' and 'plural'. The morphological analysis for the forms placed in this grammatical relationship may, for some of them, be given in terms of 'external flection' or 'suffixation', but for many forms, including those in commonest use, the differences of syllabic pattern, and other differences throughout the entire forms, justify the use of the traditional term 'broken plural'. It is the purpose of this paper to make a phonological analysis to handle the morphological relation between the broken plurals and the singular forms with which they are grammatically paired.

The traditional treatment of such relations, in terms of internal vocalic change,[2] involves a considerable number of separate, unconnected 'morphophonemic' statements. The lack of integration in these statements is a result of a phonological analysis based on the script, which is designed to handle the entire data of the language with a single and limited set of symbols, and does not take into account the special requirements of the grammar. In this paper, instead of a monosystemic phonology of this kind, the approach is essentially 'polysystemic',[3] the phonological statement being made to cover only the data relevant to the present inquiry, and fully conditioned by the grammatical requirements.

It might be objected that this approach is unsound, since the grammatical statements are based upon, and therefore posterior to, the phonological statements. Such a view of the priority of phonology is not here accepted, the levels of analysis being regarded as interdependent.[4] Far from grammar being based on phonology, it is theoretically possible to make a grammatical statement without any reference to phonology at all. This may be illustrated by considering the following examples.[5]

---

[1] My research assistant was Mr. Mesgenna Almedom of Shuma Negus in the Hamasien district of Eritrea, who has spent most of his adult life in Asmara. Research was carried out in 1951–3, both in London and in Eritrea. Other speakers were used, but the linguistic statements are based on his speech.

[2] cf. W. Leslau, *Documents Tigrigna*, Paris, 1941, pp. 30 ff. The remarks that follow do not, however, apply to Leslau's analysis, which is neither directly based on the script, nor phonemic.

[3] cf. J. R. Firth, 'Sounds and Prosodies', *TPS*, 1948, p. 151.

[4] cf. J. R. Firth, 'Modes of Meaning', *Essays and Studies (The English Association)*, 1951, pp. 118–49, esp. pp. 119–21.

[5] Both the transcription and the translation are provided solely for the identification of the form, for the convenience of the reader, and are no part of the analysis presented here. The transcription does not belong in any way to the phonological analysis. It is based largely on the Ethiopic script used by my assistant. Most of the symbols have roughly the phonetic values indicated in the I.P.A. alphabet, except that t is used for [t'], c for [ʧ'], ʦ for [ts'], q for [k'], j for [ʤ], y for [j], ħ for [ħ], ʕ for [ʔ], ɣ for [ʕ], and k^w, g^w, and q^w for the labiovelars. Separate symbols are not used, as in the script, for the fricative (post-vocalic and non-geminated) k and q.

Source: F. R. Palmer, 'The "broken plurals" of Tigrinya', *BSOAS*, 17 (1955), 548–66. Reprinted by permission of the School of Oriental and African Studies and the author.

Singular.	Plural.	
mᵕflᵕs	mᵕfalᵕs	(' wild pig ')
dᵕrho	dᵕrahu	(' chicken ')

The arrangement of these four forms is based entirely on syntactical and lexical grounds, the lexical grounds involving analysis at the levels of context of situation and collocation, and the syntactical grounds involving concord, notably, but not solely, with the verb. The four forms are related in two directions. First **mᵕflᵕs** is paired with **mᵕfalᵕs** and **dᵕrho** with **dᵕrahu**, each pair forming a single lexical entry. Secondly, **mᵕflᵕs** and **dᵕrho** are both singular forms, and **mᵕfalᵕs** and **dᵕrahu** both plural forms. If the lexical identification is symbolized as Q and R for each pair, and singularity and plurality as S and T respectively, the following restatement, without loss of grammatical or lexical information, is possible :—

Singular.	Plural.	
QS	QT	(' wild pig ')
RS	RT	(' chicken ')

Although Q, R, S, and T are established without reference to a phonological analysis, a set of phonetic exponents can be given for each one of them. These are :—

Q   [m], [f], [l], and [s].

R   [d], [r], [h], and lip rounding and backness of vowel in the final syllable.

S   Syllabic pattern two syllables, the first one closed. Vowel qualities (i) half open central, (ii) in the region half close to half open.

T   Syllabic pattern three syllables, the first two open. Vowel qualities (i) half open central, (ii) fully open front, (iii) in the region half close to close.·

The conclusion to be drawn from this illustration that it is possible to make grammar independent of phonology, is not that phonology is unnecessary, or that it is desirable to make grammatical statements without considering the requirements of phonology, but that a phonological statement made without considering the needs of grammatical analysis, and so obscuring the relationships indicated above, is not conducive to an economic statement of the facts. For instance, an overall analysis, which, like the transcription, recognizes seven vowels in Tigrinya, and then requires a morphophonemic alternation of ᵕ and ə in the first example given above, and of o and u in the second, is to be avoided.

In order to undertake the phonological analysis it is necessary to assume :—

(1) that the singular and plural forms, identifiable both as word isolates and as elements of larger pieces, can be established ;

(2) that they can be placed in their paradigmatic pairs.

The justification for these assumptions is to be found in the analysis at all levels. The justification at levels other than the phonological must be taken for granted ; the phonological grounds are, of course, contained in the analysis itself.

The phonological analysis presented here is in terms of structure and system.[1] This involves the setting up of structures consisting of the elements of structure, consonant, and vowel. For some of these elements of structure, systems are to be established, the value of each term in the systems being determined solely by its place within the system. Those elements of structure for which systems are to be established are symbolized C and V. For other elements of structure no systems are to be set up. These elements, whose function is purely structural, are symbolized c and v. For instance, for the singular forms **mɐflɐs** and **bɐrmil** a single structure, CVCCVC, is to be set up. Six systems are required, one for each element of structure, and in five of these systems (all except the second) the consonant or vowel term of **mɐflɐs** is different from that of **bɐrmil**. The structure of the plural form **mɐfalɐs** is to be stated as CVCvCVC, no system of terms being set up for the vowel of the second syllable,[2] since the phonetic exponent of this vowel is always of a single quality, open front.

The analysis of the broken plurals of Tigrinya is based almost entirely on the relations between the two types of structure set up for the singular and plural forms and on the vowel systems established within those structures. No detailed reference is made to the consonant systems since the description of the consonants (the 'radicals') is to be placed in the lexical rather than the grammatical statement. It is assumed that analysis at the lexical level has been completed. In the symbolization used here the consonant elements are numbered, the numerals indicating the grammatical identification of the consonant elements of the singular and plural form. Thus the structures of **mɐflɐs** and **mɐfalɐs** will be symbolized $C_1VC_2C_3VC_4$ and $C_1VC_2vC_3VC_4$. The relative position of these elements is an important feature of the relations between the structures.

Several divisions and sub-divisions of the data are required. The first major division is made in terms of two types of plural form :—

I. Without prefix, the initial consonants of the singular and plural forms being grammatically identified.

II. With prefix, the initial consonant of the singular form being identified with the second consonant of the plural form.

I

The pairs of syllabic structures required for the statement of the systems may be divided into three sets. Typical pairs in each set may be stated as :—

1. Singular $C_1VC_2C_3VC_4$ Plural $C_1VC_2vC_3VC_4$
2.   ,, $C_1VC_2C_3V$,, $C_1VC_2vC_3V$
3.   ,, $C_1VC_2VC_3$,, $C_1VC_2vCvC_3$

[1] cf. W. S. Allen, 'Retroflexion in Sanskrit', *BSOAS* xvi, 3, p. 556, n. 2.

[2] Syllabic division is made in terms of syllable types **CV** and **CVC** only, where **C** stands for C and c and **V** for V and v.

Four types of element are to be distinguished. First, there are those consonant elements which are numbered. As stated, no detailed description of these will be given. Secondly, there are those elements symbolized by v, for which no systems are to be set up. The exponent of v in the second syllable of all plural forms is in all cases open front,[1] and the exponent of v in the third syllable of the plural of 3 is half close central. Thirdly, there are the elements symbolized V, and fourthly the consonant element, in the plural form of 3, which is not numbered. It is with the third and fourth types, for both of which systems are to be established, that the analysis here is concerned. In each structure two such systems are required, and these will be referred to simply as the 'initial' and the 'final' systems. In all cases the initial system is the vowel system of the initial syllable, and the final system is the vowel system of the final syllable, except in the plural of 3, where it is the third consonant system.

In addition to the syllabic structures, two types of consonant articulation are relevant to the statement of the systems. The abstraction of these features and the establishment of different systems in terms of them is not justified on purely phonetic grounds, that is to say, not simply because they permit the handling of what in a phonemic analysis would be regarded as allophonic differences, but because different systems, with different numbers of terms, are required for them. The two types of articulation may be described as 'labiovelarity', that is, simultaneous velar closure and lip rounding, and 'laryngality', which includes voiced and voiceless pharyngals, glottal stop, and 'h'. The initial and final systems set up in these terms are to be established independently of each other, i.e., in the analysis of a single form, systems that are different in terms of labiovelarity and laryngality may be required initially and finally.[2] The data will, therefore, be redivided (the divisions cut across those of 1, 2, and 3).

A   Non-laryngal, non-labiovelar
B   Non-laryngal, labiovelar
C   Laryngal, non-labiovelar
D   Laryngal, labiovelar

There is one feature of the plural forms that must be excluded from this analysis. It concerns the recognition of phonetically different alternative forms of the plural, for which only individual, i.e. lexical, rules can be given. Examples are :—

Singular.	Plural.	
kɐnfɐr	kɐnafər kɐnɐffɐr	'lip'
mɐflɐs	mɐfaləs	'wild pig'
kɐrmɐd	kɐrɐmmɐd	'kind of tree'

---

[1] Or half open central in the alternative form—see below.

[2] In a full phonological analysis labiovelar and laryngal consonant systems are required. Labiovelarity and laryngality are then prosodic in that they jointly characterize the consonant systems and the initial or final systems—initial and C_1 or C_2, final and C_3 or (structure 1 only) C_4..

Phonetically the entries in the second and third columns differ in two respects :—

(1) the vowel quality of the second syllable—open and front in the second and half open and central in the third ;

(2) the consonant articulation following this vowel—the greater length or ' tenseness ' in the examples in the third column are to be regarded as the exponents of ' gemination '.

These differences will be ignored in the analysis, not only because no grammatical rules can be given for them, but also because there is no need to set up different systems for structures defined in terms of them. The two terms may be regarded as ' prosodically equipollent '. Only in the transcription used for the identification of the examples will any indication of the difference be made.

It is convenient to divide first into A, B, C, and D (in terms of labiovelarity and laryngality), and to consider the structural pairs 1, 2, and 3 under each of these headings.

A. Non-laryngal, Non-labiovelar

For structures 1 and 2 vowel systems alone are involved, and these two structures may be taken together. The analysis of the final systems is the more difficult, and will be taken first. The relevant data are the vowel qualities of the final syllables, and the correspondences of these qualities in the singular and plural forms. They may be set out as follows :—

1. (Singular $C_1VC_2C_3VC_4$.   Plural $C_1VC_2vC_3VC_4$)

	Singular	Plural
(i)	Half close central	
	Half open central	Half close central
	Open front	
(ii)	Close back	Close back
(iii)	Close front	Close front

2. (Singular $C_1VC_2C_3V$.   Plural $C_1VC_2vC_3V$)

	Singular	Plural
(i)	Close back	
	Half close back	Close back
	Open front	
(ii)	Close front	Close front
	Half close front	

e.g.		Singular	Plural		
1	(i)	qənfəz	qɵnafəz		' porcupine '
		kɵnfɵr	kɵnafɵr	kɵnɵffɵr	' lip '
		fənjal	fənajəl	fənɵjjəl	' cup '
	(ii)	tərmuz	tɵramuz	tɵrɵmmuz	' bottle '
	(iii)	bɵrmil	bɵramil	bɵrɵmmil	' barrel '

		Singular	*Plural*		
2	(i)	dəmmu	dɐmamu		' cat '
		məlso	mɐlasu		' kind of bread '
		manta	manatu	manɐttu	' twin '
	(ii)	sɐldi	sɐladi		' money '
		sərre		sɐrɐrri	' trousers '

If the plural forms were treated alone, it would be possible to set up a three-term system for structure 1 and a two-term system for structure 2. For the grammatical statement, however, the relevant features of the vowel qualities of the plural forms are :—

(a) they are all close or half close, and differ in being front, back, and central ;

(b) the front, back, or central quality can be directly related to a set of qualities in the singular form.[1]

Instead, therefore, of setting up two systems for the singular forms and two for the plural (one for each different structure), five systems in all may be set up, each comprehending the vowels of the paired singular and plural forms. The phonetic exponents of the terms within the systems are statable in degrees of openness and closeness, and the systems themselves are characterized phonetically as front, back, and central. The vowel quality of the plural form is in all cases the exponent of the closest term in each system, here symbolized by 3. The other terms will be symbolized, in order of openness, by ʌ and a. The five systems may be schematized as (the phonetic exponents are given in brackets) :—

1 (i) Central	1 (ii) Back	1 (iii) Front	2 (i) Back	2 (ii) Front
3 [ə]	3 [u] [2]	3 [i]	3 [u]	3 [i]
ʌ [ɐ]			ʌ [o]	ʌ [e]
a [a]			a [a]	

The relations between the singular and plural forms may be stated by recognizing, in the singular form, any one of the terms within one of the systems, but in the plural form, only the closest term, (3), in that system. Two points, both concerning the term a need explanation, first that [a] is the exponent of terms in two different systems, and secondly that, although the phonetic quality of [a] is front, it is the exponent of terms in systems that are described as central and back. The first point is explained by the recognition that not only are the structures, within which these two systems set up, different (the final syllables being closed in 1 and open in 2), but also the grammatical relations differ since in 1 there is a correspondence of [a] in the singular with

---

[1] Except where the vowel quality in the singular form is open front, but on this see below.

[2] It is necessary to set up here *unitary* systems (of one term—not including zero, which would mean two terms) which are not usually justified, but are required here in view of their exact parallelism with the two- and three-term systems.

[ə] in the plural form, and of [a] with [u] in 2. It would be wrong, therefore, to treat these terms as phonologically identical, even though their phonetic exponents are exactly the same. The second point raises no more than a problem of terminology, resulting from the traditional phonetic description which classes [a] with [i] and [e] as ' front '. The analysis here requires that [a] should be associated with [ə] and [ʊ] in closed syllables, and in open syllables with [u] and [o]. The use of negative expressions such as ' non-back-close, non-front-close ' in place of ' central ' for 1 (i), and of ' non-front-close, non-front-half-close ' in place of ' back ' for 2 (i) would overcome the difficulty, but the expressions are so clumsy that it is preferable to retain ' central ' and ' back ' with the reservation that they are applicable to systems with one term whose exponent is open front.

The initial systems may be handled in a similar way. For structures 1 and 2 the relevant data may be set out as follows :—

	Singular	*Plural*
(i)	Half close central Half open central	} Half open central
(ii)	Open front	Open front

e.g. (All from 1.   A similar set from 2 could be given.)

	Singular	*Plural*		
(i)	dəngəl	dʊnagəl dʊnʊggəl	' virgin '
	mʊfiʊs	mʊfaləs	' wild pig '
(ii)	wancəl	wanʊccəl	' young baboon '

For these initial syllables it is openness instead of closeness that is the feature of the plural form. Systems may, therefore, be set up with the term whose exponent is that of greater openness recognized as the only term of the plural form. This term will be symbolized by a. The other term (there are no three-term systems) will be symbolized by $\wedge$. In the diagram below the more open terms are placed at the bottom of the column, in order that the arrangement may be congruent with that of the final systems, but it must be remembered that it is the more open term that is the first term in the system. Two systems may be set up :—

$$\text{(i) Central} \qquad \text{(ii) Open}$$
$$\wedge \ [\text{ə}]$$
$$a \ [\text{ʊ}] \qquad\qquad a \ [\text{a}]$$

The description of system (ii) as ' open ' may appear to raise a difficulty since the terms in system (i) are arranged in degrees of openness, and the use of openness to characterize both a system and terms within a system may appear to lead to confusion. But phonetic features are relative, and openness as an exponent of a term in a system is openness relative to other terms in the system. The full openness that is the exponent of system (ii) is therefore quite different from openness as the exponent of terms within the other system. The problem is again [1] a terminological one, the phonetic description of [a] as ' open front ' being the cause of the difficulty.

There are many syllabic structures, other than those already given (which will now be numbered 1 (*a*) and 2 (*a*)), for which the same systems and sets of relations may be set up. These differ from the others in two ways, either that there is a structural difference in the singular form alone, or that there are parallel differences in both singular and plural forms. In either case the differences are irrelevant for the setting up of the systems.

Thus to the structures under 1 may be added :—

1 (*b*) Singular $C_1VC_2C_3VC_4V$. Plural $C_1VC_2vC_3VC_4$
  (*c*) ,, $C_1VC_2C_3VC_4V$. ,, $C_1VC_2vC_3VC_4V$

e.g.   *Singular*   *Plural*

1 (*b*)   **dɐbtɐra**   **dɐbatər**   ' magician '
  (*c*)   **mantile**   **manatile**   ' rabbit '

In both cases a *word* final vowel system can be established, but in neither case is it relevant to the analysis of the initial and final systems. In 1 (*b*) this final V is to be set up for the singular only, while in 1 (*c*) it is to be recognized in both singular and plural, as are the consonant systems. In accordance with the analysis suggested here, the systems to be set up and the terms in those systems are, for the first example initially central and *a*, and finally central and ʌ, and for the second initially open and *a*, and finally back and ɔ.

Forms with even greater differences of syllabic structures may be handled in the same way. In the following example the *word* initial syllable and the *word* final vowel are not included in the analysis of the ' initial ' and ' final ' systems (in the sense prescribed here). In the symbolization the elements which, like the numbered consonant elements, are of relevance for structure only, and for which no systems are set up, are shown in brackets.

1 (*d*) Singular $(CV)C_1VC_2C_3VC_4(V)$. Plural $(CV)C_1VC_2vC_3VC_4(V)$

        Singular   *Plural*

        mɐsɐngɐle   **mɐsɐnagɐle**   ' chest, box '

For this example central systems are to be set up initially and finally, *a* being the term in the initial system and ʌ in the final, in the singular form.

Similarly to the structures under 2 may be added :—

2 (*b*) Singular $C_1VC_2(V)C_3V$. Plural $C_1VC_2vC_3V$

e.g.   *Singular*   *Plural*

        wɐʈɐʈo   **wɐʈaʈu**   ' he-goat '
        dəqala   **dɐqalu**   ' bastard '

A vowel system could here be set up for the second syllable of the singular forms, but it could not then be related to any feature of the plural form, and is not, therefore, to be handled in the grammatical analysis. In the following

---

[1] cf. pp. 138-9. The problem cannot be solved by calling the system ' front ', since later in this analysis a front system with [i] and [e] as the exponents of the terms is required (p. 145).

structure the entire *word* initial syllables are excluded from the analysis in terms of ' initial ' and ' final '.

2 (c) Singular $(CV)C_1VC_2C_3V$. Plural $(CV)C_1VC_2vC_3V$

e.g.

Singular	Plural	
ṭɐbɐnja	ṭɐbɐnaju	' gun '

All the structures treated above contain more elements than those originally considered. The same set of systems, however, can still be set up for a pair of structures, where there are fewer elements in the singular. In the following structures a single consonant element in the singular is to be related to two such elements in the plural.

2 (d) Singular C_1VC_2V. Plural $C_1VC_2vC_2V$

e.g.

Singular	Plural	
cɐru	cɐraru	' bird '
sɐwa	sɐwawu	' beer '

The analysis in terms of systems is exactly as before.

The analysis of structures type 3 must be quite different from that of 1 and 2, since it involves relations between consonant and vowel elements, and cannot be dealt with entirely in terms of vowel systems. The pair of structures illustrated earlier is, in fact, the only one :—

3   Singular $C_1VC_2VC_3$. Plural $C_1VC_2vCvC_3$

For the final systems it is necessary to set up a relation between a vowel system of four terms in the singular form (exponents [i], [e], [u], and [o]),[1] and a consonant system, established in third consonantal position in the plural, of two terms (exponents labiovelar semi-vowel and palatal semi-vowel). No system is to be set up for the vowels of the final syllable of the plural forms.

It is not possible to establish systems to comprehend the relevant features of both singular and plural forms, since consonant and vowel terms are not to be placed in the same system. It is, however, possible to set up two vowel systems characterized as back and front, relatable to consonant elements which may equally be characterized as back and front.

The back vowel system (required for the singular structure) is of three terms, here symbolized by 3, ᴧ, and α. The exponent of the relevant consonant element in the plural structure is a labiovelar semi-vowel.

e.g.

	Singular	Plural		
3	nɐgus	nɐgawɐs	nɐgɐwwɐs	' king '
ᴧ	ʃɐton	ʃatawɐn		' oven '
α	kɐdan	kɐdawɐnti [2]		' clothes '

---

[1] If the singular structure CVCVC were considered alone a seven-term system could be set up for the V of the second syllable. Where, however, central vowels [ə] and [ɐ] are the exponents of the terms the related plural form is cvCVC ; this is dealt with in part II. Where [e] is the exponent, there is no corresponding broken plural.

[2] There are several plural forms of structure 1 with the suffix -ti which is there to be treated as a lexical feature. For its *grammatical* relevance here, however, see p. 142.

The front vowel system has one term only. The exponent of the consonant element is a palatal semi-vowel.

e.g.	Singular	Plural	
	mɐdid	mɐdayəd	' grindstone '

In these examples the relation between the relevant elements of the singular and plural structures may be described either as ' back-back ' or as ' front-front '. Quite commonly a ' front-back ' relation is also to be recognized. In the following examples the front vowel quality of the final syllable of the singular forms is to be regarded as the exponent of a term in a front system, whereas the labiovelar semi-vowel articulation in the plural form is to be treated as the exponent of a back consonant element. It is to be noted that although examples of this front-back relation are not rare,[1] in no case is the reverse (back-front) to be recognized.

	Singular	Plural	
	qɐmiʃ	qɐmawəʃ	' shirt '
	ḥaric	ḥarɐwwəc	' flour '

For the initial systems the analysis is largely as for 1 and 2.

e.g.		Singular	Plural	
(i) (Central)	ʌ	nɐgus	nɐgawəs nɐgɐwwəs	' king '
	a	mɐdid	mɐdayəd	' grindstone '
(ii) (Open)	a	saʃun	saʃawən	' box '

For one set of forms this analysis of the initial systems cannot be employed since the vowel quality of the plural form is close, instead of half open.

e.g.	Singular	Plural	
	kədan	kədawənti	' clothes '
	məsar	məsawərti	' axe '

For a single example the relevant vowel quality is not only close, but also back and rounded, in both singular and plural forms :—

	Singular	Plural	
	ruʃan	ruʃawənti	' storied building '

It would be possible to treat the vowel qualities of the first two examples as exponents of the closer term in the initial central system, and to set up, for the last example, an initial back system. But it would then be necessary to point the anomaly that closeness, and not openness, is the feature of the plural. It is simpler not to handle these initial syllables in terms of the initial systems at all but, instead, to recognize vocalic elements that are the same in both singular and plural. There is no need to list these examples as ' exceptions ' since they belong to an easily identifiable class. In addition to the close quality of the vowel of the initial syllable of the plural form, they are characterized by

---

[1] There is a single example of such a relation for structure 2 : *Singular* mɐgʷdi *Plural* mɐgʷadu ' lid ', where the relevant vowel quality of the singular is the exponent of a term in a front system, and the quality of the plural is the exponent of a term in a back system.

(*a*) close or half close vowel quality in the initial syllable of all the singular forms,

(*b*) fully open front quality in the second syllable of all the singular forms,

(*c*) the suffix -**ti** in all the plural forms.

Finally there are some forms whose structures differ from those of 3, but whose analysis involves consonant-vowel relations, but in the reverse order, the relevant element being consonant in the singular and vowel in the plural. The exponents of the consonant elements are again the two types of semi-vowel, but the exponents of the vowel element are always back and rounded.

Singular $C_1VC_2C_3VCV$ or $C_1VC_2VC_3CV$. Plural $C_1VC_2vC_3V$

e.g.

	Singular	*Plural*	
	ʃancəwa	ʃanaʃu	' mouse '
	ɟanɟəya	ɟunaɟu	' fly '
	wəkarya	wəkaru	' jackal '

The relations may again be stated as back-back (the first example only) and front-back, but there is no example of front-front. Although the consonant-vowel relation is in the reverse order from that of 3, still no back-front relation is to be recognized. It is interesting to note that although the first example is described as back-back, the exponent of the term of C_3 is, in the singular a palatal, and in the plural an alveolar, ejective affricate. If palatal articulation were treated as the exponent of a front system of consonant terms,[1] in this example also it would be possible to recognize frontness in the singular and non-frontness, if not backness, in the plural forms.

B. NON-LARYNGAL, LABIOVELAR

The analysis of the non-laryngal, labiovelar systems follows closely that of A. The systems are similar to those of A, though with different exponents for the terms, except that a single three-term final system is set up to correspond to the back and central systems of A.[2]

The final systems required are :—

1 (i) (Back-central)	2 (i) (Back)	2 (ii) (Front)
3 [u]	(3) [u] [3]	(3) [i]
ʌ [o]	ʌ [o]	ʌ [e]
α [a]	α [a]	

---

[1] cf. p. 150.

[2] The fact that no front system is set up should not be regarded as important. Such a system would be required for singular forms not paired with broken plurals. System 1 (i) below might, on phonetic grounds, be labelled ' back', but since it is a three-term system with [a] as the exponent of the third term, it patterns with the central rather than the back system of A. In fact integration of the systems of A and B can be achieved by considering that the central and back systems of A are paralleled by a single system in B.

[3] The round brackets indicate that the term is to be set up only by reference to the plural form.

The grammatical relations are stated by the recognition of ɜ as the only vowel term of the plural form. The following examples are all taken from structures 1 (*a*) and 2 (*a*) with the exception of the last one (structure 2 (*d*)), which is the only example for the front system.

		Singular	*Plural*		
1	ɜ	mʉnkʷəb	mʉnakʷəb	mʉnʉkkʷəb	' shoulder '
	ʌ	ḥangʷɐl	ḥanagʷəl		' brain '
	a	dəkkʷan	dʉkʷakʷən	dʉkʷʉkkʷən	' shop '
2 (i)	ʌ	gʷɐggo	gʷɐgʷagu		' kind of bread '
	a	dəkkʷa	dʉkʷaku		' stool '
(ii)	ʌ	ḥəqʷe	ḥaqʷaqʷi		' back '

For the initials two systems, as in A, are required, though the exponents of the terms in the first system are all back quality vowels.

(i) (Central) [1]   (ii) (Open)

ʌ [u]

a [o]   *a* [a]

e.g. (All from structures 2 (*a*).)

		Singular	*Plural*	
(i)	ʌ	dəkkʷa	dʉkʷaku	' stool '
	a	tʉkʷla	tʉkʷalu	' wolf '
(ii)	*a*	kʷatra	kʷataru	' pigeon '

No labiovelar systems are to be set up for structures 3.

C. LARYNGAL, NON-LABIOVELAR

The laryngal systems differ from those of A in two respects. First, the final central system of 1 is of two terms, instead of three. Secondly, a single system of two terms corresponds to the initial central and open systems of A. In addition, a single example justifies the setting up of a front initial system. There are no examples for such a system in A or B.

The final systems required are :—

1 (i) (Central)	1 (ii) (Back)	1 (iii) (Front)	2 (i) (Back)	2 (ii) (Front)
ɜ [ə]	ɜ [u]	ɜ [i]	(ɜ) [u]	ɜ [i]
ʌ [a]			ʌ [o]	
			a [a]	

ɜ is, as in A, to be recognized as the only vowel term of the plural.

e.g. (All taken from structures 1 (*a*) and 2 (*a*) for simplicity.)

		Singular	*Plural*	
1	(i) ɜ	mʉftəḥ	mʉfatəḥ	' key '
	ʌ	mʉṭḥan	mʉṭaḥən	' mill-stone '
	(ii) ɜ	sanbuʕ	sanabuʕ	' lung '
	(iii) ɜ	ʕawliχ	ʕawaliχ	' olive '

[1] Phonetically describable as ' back ' this system is labelled ' central ' since it patterns with the central system of A. cf. n. 2, p. 143.

		Singular	Plural	
2	(i) ʌ	dɐrho	dɐraḥu	' chicken '
	a	qʷɛlχa	qʷɐlaʒu	' child '
	(ii) 3	ʕarḥi	ʕaraḥu [1]	' calf '

The initial systems include, as already stated, a front system based on a single example. This is important, since it is wholly congruent with the rest of the analysis. The exponent of the more open term in this front system is half close front, which again emphasizes the point that, in Tigrinya, [a] is never to be treated as the exponent of a term in a front system.[2]

The systems to be set up are :—

(i) (Central-Open)	(ii) (Front)
ʌ [ə]	ʌ [i]
a [a]	(a) [ɵ]

As elsewhere a is to be recognized as the term of the plural.

e.g. (All from structures 2 (a).)

		Singular	Plural	
(i)	ʌ	χɵtro	χataru	' water-jar '
	a	maʕdo	mɐʕadu	' brush '
(ii)	ʌ	χillu	χelalu	' foal '

The analysis of structures 3 is as under A. Two examples only, one illustrating the front-front relation and the other the back-back, were noted :—

	Singular	Plural	
	wɵḥij	wɐḥayɵj	' stream '
	dɵχul	dɵχawɵl	' ram '

For three examples, while the singular form is of structure 2, the plural form is that of 3 :—

Singular $C_1VC_2C_3V$.   Plural $C_1VC_2vCvC_3$.

	Singular	Plural	
	dɐrho	dɐrawɵḥ [3]	' chicken '
	qʷɛlχa	qʷɐlawɵʒ	' child '
	sɵsḥa	sɵsawɵḥ	' deer '

For these a back vowel system, as in the analysis of 2, is to be set up, but related to a back consonant element as in 3.

There are two examples which resemble those mentioned under A 3 in which the vowel quality of the initial syllable of the plural form was close or half close.[4] These two examples, while having all the other features of those in A 3, differ in the essential feature, that the vowel quality of the initial syllable in both singular and plural is fully open. Unlike the examples of A 3, they do not, therefore, require separate treatment.

---

[1] With front-back relation, cf. p. 142.   [2] cf. pp. 138–9 and 140, and n. 1.
[3] For different plural forms of the first two examples see above.   [4] p. 142.

	Singular	Plural	
	ɣarat	ɣarawətti	'bed'
	ḥamat	ḥamawətti	'mother-in-law'

D. Laryngal, Labiovelar

For structures 1 and 2 there is only one example which may be characterized as initially laryngal and labiovelar, and none that may be so characterized finally. On the basis of the analysis of A, B, and C, it would be reasonable to recognize here the more open term in a system.

	Singular	Plural	
	ʕagʷdo	ʕagʷadu	'round hut'

For structures 3, three examples permit the establishment of a final system with two terms :—

3 [u]
ʌ [a]

	Singular	Plural	
3	mɐgʷəʕ	mɐgʷawəʕ	'mortar'
3	mɐpʷəḥ	mɐpʷawəḥ	'handcuffs'
ʌ	qʷɐqʷaḥ	qʷɐqʷawəḥ	'francolin'

II

The second part of this paper deals with plurals with prefix (phonetic exponent, glottal stop and open front vowel).

Three types of syllable structure are required for the singular forms :—

(1) CVCCv   (Example bərki 'knee')
(2) CVCVC   (Example tɐrɐs 'horse')
(3) CVC   (Example bet 'house')

If these forms were considered without reference to the corresponding plural forms, two-term vowel systems phonetically describable as 'central' could be set up for the initial syllable of 1 and for both syllables of 2,[1] and a seven-term vowel system for 3. No system is to be established for the final vowel of 1. The phonetic exponent of this vowel is front close only. In isolation, examples of structure 1 have no exponents to distinguish them from examples of I 2 such as ʕarhi and sɐldi. In addition, however, to the grammatical difference illustrated by the different analysis given in this paper, it is essential to recognize a phonological difference, that is indicated by the forms with possessive suffixes, e.g. :—

ʕadgi (II)	ʕarḥi (I 2)	'donkey/calf'
ʕadgəka	ʕarḥika	'your donkey/calf'
ʕadgu	ʕarḥiyu	'his donkey/calf'

The final vowel of 1 is, then, to be regarded as a structural element only.

[1] See p. 141, n. 1.

Three types of syllable structure are required for the plural forms too :—

(1) cvCCVC (Examples ʕafras ' horses ', ʕaɣruk ' friends ')
(2) cvCCvCcv (Example ʕatkəlti ' plants ')
(3) cvCvCvC (Example ʕafatəl ' threads ')

Except for the consonant systems, which are not given in detail here, only one system is to be set up, a two-term vowel system in 1, with front open and back close as the exponents of the terms. The exponents of the remaining elements are as follows :—

> Initial cv of all structures—glottal stop and open front
> Second v of 2—half close central
> Final cv of 2—voiceless dental stop and front close
> Second v of 3—open front
> Third v of 3—half close central.

In this part of the paper labiovelarity need not be considered relevant to the analysis. This does not mean that it is ignored, but the same pattern of relations would be required for those examples which could be characterized as labiovelar as for those which could not, and that, therefore, labiovelarity will be assigned to the description of the phonetic exponents, and not to the phonological and grammatical analysis. Laryngality, on the other hand, is relevant to the establishment of the relations for one part of the analysis (section 1 below).

It is convenient to divide the analysis into three parts, numbered in accordance with the numbering of the structures of the singular forms.

1. Although two-term vowel systems could be set up for the singular structure CVCCv and the plural structure cvCCVC, this would involve the establishment of relations between terms in systems on the one hand, and structures on the other. To avoid this, it is convenient to recognize as structurally different CvCCv ([ə]) and CvCCv ([ʊ]), and cvCCvC ([u]) and cvCCvC ([a]), where the bracketed symbols indicate the exponents of the relevant vowels.[1]

For forms which are wholly non-laryngal three pairs of related structures may be established :—

(i) Singular $C_1vC_2C_3v$ ([ə]). Plural $cvC_1C_2vC_3$ ([a])
(ii) ,, $C_1vC_2C_3v$ ([ʊ]). ,, $cvC_1vC_2vC_3$
(iii) ,, $C_1vC_2C_3v$ ([ʊ]). ,, $cvC_1C_2vC_3cv$

e.g.

	Singular	*Plural*	
(i)	bərki.	ʕabrak	' knee '
(ii)	bʊtri.	ʕabatər	' stick '
(iii)	tʊkli.	ʕatkəlti	' plant '

---

[1] The same symbols will be used even for the very different qualities in syllables with labiovelar or laryngal articulation. For the latter even the transcription uses a instead of ʊ, but this will be ignored in the analysis and one set of symbols used.

Some similar pairs of structures may be set up for laryngal forms with the proviso that the exponents of elements within the same syllable in the plural form are never *both* laryngal articulation *and* open vowel quality, except in the initial syllable. This means that, where laryngal articulation is an exponent of C_1, pattern (ii) is not to be established, and where it is the exponent of C_2 or C_3, pattern (i) is not set up. In each case, however, an additional pattern is to be recognized :—

Laryngal C_1 : Singular $C_1vC_2C_3v$ ([ɐ]). Plural $cvC_1C_2vC_3$ ([u]).

Laryngal C_2 or C_3 : Singular $C_1vC_2C_3v$ ([ə]). Plural $cvC_1vC_2vC_3$

Examples of the patterns (i), (ii), and (iii), where they apply, and the additional patterns (marked with an asterisk) are :—

Laryngal C_1

	Singular	*Plural*	
(i)	ʕəgri	ʕaʕgar	' foot '
*	ɣarki	ʕaɣruk	' friend '
(iii)	ḥamli	ʕaḥməlti	' vegetable '

Laryngal C_2 or C_3

	Singular	*Plural*	
*	zəbʕi	ʕazabəʕ	' hyena '
*	nəhbi	ʕanahəb	' bee '
(ii)	saʕni	ʕasaʕən	' sandal '
(ii)	wɐrḥi	ʕawarəḥ	' month '
(iii)	zɐrʕi	ʕazrəʕti	' seed '

2. The only pattern to be set up is :—

Singular $C_1VC_2VC_3$. Plural $cvC_1C_2vC_3$ ([a]).

e.g.

	Singular	*Plural*	
	fɐrɐs	ʕafras	' horse '
	həbɐy	ʕahbay	' baboon '
	ḥàsər	ʕaḥsar	' straw '

3. One plural structure only is to be paired with the singular structure CVC, but the consonant elements are to be related in two different ways :—

(a) Singular C_1VC_2. Plural cvC_1CvC_2 ([a])

(b) Singular C_1VC_2. Plural cvC_1C_2vC ([a])

For many examples the analysis is similar to that of I 3. A back and a front system of vowels for the singular forms and a back and a front consonant element for the plural forms may be set up.

A back vowel system of two terms ɜ and ʌ (exponents [u] and [o]), and a back consonant element (exponent labiovelar semi-vowel) are required for the following examples. Both are of pattern (a).

		Singular	*Plural*	
ɜ		ɣuf	ʕaɣwaf	' bird '
ʌ		ʕom	ʕaʕwam	' tree '

A front vowel system of two terms (exponents [i] and [e]) may similarly be set up. In the first example below, which is of pattern (*b*), the exponent of the consonant element is a labiovelar semi-vowel, so that a front-back relation must again be recognized. In the second, which is of pattern (*a*), the exponent of the consonantal element is a palatal semi-vowel, so that the relation is front-front.

Singular	*Plural*	
ʕid	ʕaʕdaw	' hand '
bet	ʕabyat	' house '

For all other forms of pattern (*b*) the exponent of the final consonant element is a voiceless dental stop.

e.g.

Singular	*Plural*	
ṭub	ʕaṭbat	' breast '
ʃəm	ʕaʃmat	' name '

The treatment of pattern 1 in terms of laryngality is not applicable to patterns 2 and 3 only because, for 2 and 3, there are no examples of laryngal C_2 or C_3, though there are many examples of laryngal C_1. The plural structure of 2 and 3 is cvCCvC ([a]) only, and in accordance with the statement concerning laryngality, such a structure may be established for laryngal C_1 but not for laryngal C_2 or C_3. It is interesting to add that, for many speakers, where laryngal articulation is an exponent of C_1, the exponents of the prefix are palatal semi-vowel and half close central vowel, instead of glottal stop and open front. Thus, for these, the exponents of elements in the same syllable are never both laryngality and open front vowel quality, even in the word initial syllable,[1] except where the laryngality is solely that of the glottal stop of the prefix.

e.g.	*Singular*	*Plural*	
1.	ʕəgri	yəʕgar	' foot '
	ḥamli	yəḥməlti	' vegetable '
	ʒarki	yəʒruk	' friend '
2.	həbɐy	yəhbay	' baboon '
3.	ʒuf	yəʒwaf	' bird '

There are many forms which are not accounted for in either part of this paper, but for most of these some integration with the analysis presented is possible. For most of them it is necessary to set up unique patterns of the singular and plural structures, but then to handle them in terms of the systems of this analysis. Thus the following examples may all be analysed in terms of the systems of I 2 (in all three the systems are the vowel systems of the word initial and word final systems), all the other elements being regarded solely as structural features that are common to both singular and plural.

---

[1] cf. p. 148.

Singular	*Plural*	
nəʕəʃto	nɐʕaʃtu	' small '
ʕarḥədo	ʕarḥadu	' young she-goat '
baldɐngʷa	baladɐngu	' bean '

In the next two examples a single consonant element in the singular corresponds to two in the plural, as in I 2 (*d*). The first example will otherwise conform to the analysis of I 1, and the second is a further illustration of vowel-consonant relations (back-back) as in I 1 and II 3.

Singular	*Plural*		
kʷəlit	kʷɐlalit	kʷɐlɐllit	' kidney '
sur	sɐrawər	sɐrɐwwər	' root '

For others it would be convenient to handle the consonants as well as the vowels in front and back (or non-front) systems. It was suggested earlier that palatal articulation might be treated as the exponent of a term in a front system.[1] For the analysis of the following examples palato-alveolar friction is to be classed with palatal semi-vowel as the exponent of a front term, and alveolar friction with labiovelar semi-vowel as ' non-front '

	Singular	*Plural*	
(i)	gaʃʃa	ʕagayəʃ	' guest '
(ii)	kəʃʃa	ʕakyaʃ	' sack '
(iii)	ɣaʃʃa	ɣayasu	' foolish '
(iv)	qɐʃʃi	qɐsawəsti	' priest '

In the singular forms two front elements [2] (exponent of both, voiceless palato-alveolar friction) are to be recognized. In the plural similarly two elements are to be recognized, one of them with a semi-vowel as its exponent. The relation of the two pairs of consonant elements in terms of back and front may then be stated as :—

	Singular	*Plural*
(i)	Front and front	Front and front
(ii)	Front and front	Front and front
(iii)	Front and front	Front and non-front
(iv)	Front and front	Non-front and non-front

The structural patterns of (i), (ii), and (iv) are unique, but that of (iii) is the pattern set up in I 2.

The important features of the analysis presented here are

(1) that it is based solely upon the data relevant to the problem, an overall phonological analysis being explicitly rejected ;

(2) that it is both phonological and grammatical, and the phonology is not set out without reference to the grammatical requirements ;

---

[1] p. 143.

[2] I do not regard these as examples of ' gemination ', but of a cluster of two consonant elements.

(3) that it is in terms of structures and systems, which entails the recognition of consonant and vowel elements, and, where appropriate, the establishment of closed systems of consonant and vowel terms.

It is not claimed that the analysis leads to a simple statement. It is claimed that, instead of a set of unrelated statements, a single set of relations for part I and a limited number of such sets for part II have been established. Above all an attempt has been made to produce a statement that is appropriate to the complex but systemic patterns of the broken plurals of Tigrinya.[1]

---

[1] cf. J. R. Firth, "Sounds and Prosodies", *TTS*, 1948, p. 151 : ' The suggested approach will not make phonological problems appear easier or oversimplify them. It will make the highly complex patterns of language clearer both in descriptive and historical linguistics.'

9

A PHONOLOGICAL ANALYSIS OF THE SZECHUANESE MONOSYLLABLE

By N. C. SCOTT

A RECONSIDERATION of the material used for my article ' The mono-syllable in Szechuanese '[1] in the light of the technique of prosodic analysis being developed in the Department of Phonetics of the School of Oriental and African Studies [2] has led me to believe that it is susceptible of a more rigorous and satisfying treatment, in which some of the apparently eccentric features take a normal place.

The material consists of the spoken forms of all the isolated monosyllables of their native language known to two speakers referred to as Su (a native of Fengtuhsien) and Ch. (a native of Iping), whose pronunciations differ in certain respects. The monosyllables will be sufficiently well identified for the purposes of this paper by the ' systematic transcription ' used in the previous article, to which reference may be made for its phonetic interpretation.

In the present analysis, the structure of any monosyllable is considered to be either CVπ or Vπ. The phonological description of a monosyllable requires, for one of the first category, the statement of a member of the consonant system, and for those of both categories, the statement of a member of the vowel system and of a number of features referred to as prosodies. I find it necessary to recognize (a) prosodies of the syllable as a whole, (b) prosodies of syllable-initial, (c) prosodies of the syllable-final. These may be referred to as syllable-prosodies, initial-prosodies, and final-prosodies. The words ' initial ' and ' final ' are used here as phonological terms, and not as they are traditionally used by sinologists.

1. *Consonants.*—Two systems of consonants are recognized.

(a) Three occlusives, *P, T, K*. The only phonetic implications of these taken by themselves are bilabial, dental to alveolo-palatal, and velar plosion respectively.

(b) Three fricatives, *F, S, H*. The only phonetic implications of these taken by themselves are labio-dental, alveolar to alveolo-palatal, and velar friction respectively.

2. *Vowels.*—Three vowels are recognized, *ι, ε, a*. The phonetic implications of these are grades of openness : *ι*, grade 1, close ; *ε*, grade 2, between close and open ; and *a*, grade 3, open.

3. *Prosodies of the syllable as a whole.*—(a) Tone. For a phonetic description of the tonal features, see ' MS '. Syllables marked there as having Tone 5

---

[1] *BSOAS*, XII, 1, 1947, 197–213 (hereafter referred to as ' MS ').
[2] See J. R. Firth, ' Sounds and prosodies ', *TPS*, 1948, 127–52.

Source : N. C. Scott, ' A phonological analysis of the Szechuanese monosyllable ', *BSOAS*, 18 (1956), 556–60. Reprinted by permission of the School of Oriental and African Studies and the author.

are those considered here as having a final-prosody of glottalization (see below). It is possible to assign them to Tone 2 [1] and to regard each syllable as having one of four tonal prosodies. I do not propose to deal further with tone in the present paper, and the mark for the tonal prosody will be omitted from the phonological formulae.

(b) Every syllable as a whole is considered to have the prosodic feature of either frontness (y) or backness (w). For typographical convenience, the symbols for these will be shown on the line in the first place of the phonological formula.

In the pronunciation of syllables with frontness-prosody, the articulation is of a dominantly front type. They will be referred to as y-syllables. In the pronunciation of syllables with backness-prosody, the articulation is of a dominantly back type. They will be referred to as w-syllables. In the pronunciation of both y- and w-syllables, there is absence of lip-rounding unless the syllable has labio-palatalization or labio-velarization as an initial prosody or as a final prosody or as both. In the last case, there is lip-rounding throughout the utterance. The vowel-sound in the pronunciation of y-syllables with grade 2 vowel is of a fully front type when the syllable has y or ɥ initial prosody, and also when (except for glottalization) ' absence ' is the feature in the prosodies of syllable final. See below. Although in pronunciation the front or back quality is most obvious in the vowel-sound, it is not confined to it. See under final-nasalization below.

Examples [2] of y-syllables are $y^v P \iota^v$ (bi), $y^h S \epsilon$ (se), $y^h H \epsilon^n$ (hen), $y P a^n$ (ban), $y^{hw} K a^n$ (kwan).

Examples of w-syllables are $w^w P \iota^w$ (bu), $w^{hw} T \epsilon^w$ (to), $w P a^n$ (bang), $w^w K a$ (gwa).

4. *Prosodies of the syllable-initial.*—The following prosodic features are considered to be operative for the syllable-initial. In the phonological formulae, the symbols for these will be shown in superior position after the symbol for the prosody of the syllable as a whole.

(a) Aspiration (h) or its absence (unmarked),
(b) Palatalization (y), labio-palatalization (ɥ), labio-velarization (w), or the absence of all three (unmarked),
(c) Nasalization (n), or its absence (unmarked),
(d) Affrication (s), or its absence (unmarked).

(a) In the pronunciation of syllables having initial-aspiration, there is necessarily absence of voicing during the stop or constriction, voice beginning only after the opener position is reached. Examples are $w^h T a$ (ta), $w^{hw} S \iota^w$ (su), $y^{hvs} T \iota^y$ (kyi).

---

[1] The speaker referred to Tone 5 as ' upper 2 '

[2] In the examples, the phonological formula is given first, followed in brackets by the ' systematic transcription ' used in ' MS '.

In the pronunciation of syllables without initial-aspiration, there is voicing from the start, except in the case of those with occlusive consonant and absence of initial-nasalization, in which voice is usually absent during the stop, beginning with the release. Examples are wTa (da), $w^wS\iota^w$ ($\dot{z}u$), $y^{ʸs}T\iota^ʸ$ (gyi), $y^{ʸn}P\iota^ʸ$ (mi).

(b) In the pronunciation of a syllable with initial-palatalization, there is a close front element throughout the earlier part of the utterance, the lips being unrounded. When the syllable has also initial-affrication, the closure and following constriction are in the alveolo-palatal region. When the consonant is S, the friction is of alveolo-palatal type. Examples are $y^ʸ\iota^ʸ$ (yi), $y^{ʸs}T\epsilon^w$ ($gyeu$), $w^{hʸ}Sa^n$ ($hyang$), $w^{hʸ}Pa^w$ ($pyau$).

In the pronunciation of a syllable with initial-labio-palatalization, there is a close front element throughout the earlier part of the syllable with lip-rounding either from the start or increasing. When there is also initial-affrication, the closure and following constriction, and when the consonant is S, the constriction, are in the alveolo-palatal region. Examples are $y^ʸ\iota^ʮ$ (ywi), $y^{ʸs}T\epsilon$ ($gywe$), $w^{ʸs}T\iota^{wn}$ ($gyung$).

In the pronunciation of syllables with initial-labio-velarization, there is a close back element with lip-rounding throughout the earlier part of the utterance. Examples are $w^wK\iota^w$ (gu), $y^wK\epsilon^ʸ$ ($gwei$), y^wTa^n ($dwan$), $w^{hw}Ka^n$ ($kwang$).

All y-syllables with grade 1 vowel are considered to have either y- or $ʮ$-initial prosody, which, in pronunciation, is e.g. reflected in the articulation of the stop of $y^{hʸ}T\iota^ʸ$ (ti) as compared with that of y^hTa^n (tan), a syllable that has none of the initial features y, $ʮ$, or w. All w-syllables with grade 1 vowel are considered to have w-initial prosody. The pronunciation of $w^{hw}T\iota^w$ (tu) has lip-rounding and depression of the front of the tongue from the start.

(c) In the pronunciation of syllables with initial-nasalization, there is a bilabial, dental, or velar nasal followed by the homorganic plosive, according as the consonant of the syllable is P, T, or K. There is no nasality following the stop unless the syllable is one with the final prosody of nasalization. Examples are $y^{ʸn}P\iota^ʸ$ (mi), $y^{ʸn}T\epsilon^n$ ($lyen$), w^nKa^w ($ngau$).

(d) In the pronunciation of syllables with initial-affrication, which is restricted to syllables with consonant T, the plosion is followed by homorganic friction. When the syllable has y- or $ʮ$-initial prosody, the closure and following constriction are in the alveolo-palatal region ; for other types of syllable-initial, they are in the alveolar region. Examples are $y^{hʸs}T\iota^ʸ$ (kyi), $y^{ʸs}T\iota^ʮ$ ($gywi$), $y^sT\epsilon$ (dze), $w^{ws}T\epsilon^w$ (dzo).

In ' MS ', attention was drawn to the fact that Su pronounced syllables written with ny- in the ' systematic transcription ' with friction, and syllables written with ly- without friction. In the present analysis, syllables of the former type are considered to have initial-affrication, which is absent from syllables of the latter type. Thus, $y^{ʸns}T\epsilon^n$ ($nyen$), and $y^{ʸn}T\epsilon^n$ ($lyen$). For Ch., initial-affrication excludes initial-nasalization.

5. *Prosodies of the syllable-final.*—The following prosodic features are considered to be operative for the syllable-final. In the phonological formulae, the symbols for these will be shown in superior position following the vowel-symbol.

(a) Palatalization (y), labio-palatalization ($ч$), labio-velarization (w), or the absence of all of these (unmarked),

(b) Nasalization (n) or its absence (unmarked),

(c) Retroflexion (r) or its absence (unmarked),

(d) Glottalization (q) or its absence (unmarked).

(a) In the pronunciation of syllables with final-palatalization, there is a close front element with absence of lip-rounding in the latter part of the utterance ; in that of syllables with final-labio-palatalization, a close front element with lip-rounding ; and in that of syllables with final-labio-velarization, a close back element with lip-rounding. It is to be noted that y-syllables with grade 1 vowel and $ч$-initial may have either y- or $ч$-final. The phonological formula for the syllable written as *gywi* in 'MS' is $y^{чs}Tι^y$ for Su ; for Ch., it is $y^{чs}Tι^ч$. Other y-syllables with grade 1 vowel have y-final, and w-syllables with grade 1 vowel have w-final. Examples of syllables with y-final are $y^yPι^y$ (*bi*), $y^wKε^y$ (*gwei*), y^hKa^y (*kai*). Examples of syllables with w-final are $w^wTι^w$ (*du*), $yKε^w$ (*geu*), w^yPa^w (*byau*).

(b) In the pronunciation of y-syllables having final-nasalization, there is nasality in the latter part of the utterance, and if there is oral occlusion (see 'MS') it will be dental. In the pronunciation of w-syllables having final-nasalization, the utterance ends in a velar nasal. w-syllables with grade 1 vowel having final-nasalization have also final-labio-velarization ; y-syllables with grade 1 vowel and final-nasalization have also final-palatalization, unless they have $ч$-initial, in which case they may have either y- or $ч$-final. For Ch., the syllable written in 'MS' as *gywin* is to be considered as $y^{чs}Tι^{yn}$, for Su it is to be considered as $y^{чs}Tι^{чn}$. Examples of y-syllables with final-nasalization are $y^yTι^{yn}$ (*din*), $y^yTε^n$ (*dyen*), y^hPa^n (*pan*). Examples of w-syllables with final-nasalization are $w^wTι^{wn}$ (*dung*), wKa^n (*gang*).

(c) The syllables identified in 'MS' as si^{1-4} (Wade *sŭ*) are here considered to have a final-prosody of retroflexion. In pronunciation, the raising of the tongue-tip is maintained after the alveolar constriction. They are analysed as $y^hSι^r$, with Tones 1–4. The syllable identified in 'MS' as zi^5 is here analysed as $ySι^r$ with Tone 2. The syllables identified in 'MS' as zi^{1-4} (pronounced as a half-open front vowel with retroflexion) are here analysed as $yε^r$ with Tones 1–4.

(d) Pronounced by Ch., syllables with final-glottalization end with a glottal stop and have mid-level pitch. They are here assigned to Tone 2.

Su makes no difference in pronunciation between such syllables and syllables without final-glottalization having Tone 2. Examples are $y^hS\epsilon^q$ (*se⁵*), $w^q\epsilon^{wq}$ (*yo⁵*), $yP\alpha^q$ (*ba⁵*), $y^{hvs}T\epsilon^q$ (*kye⁵*).

In ' MS ', whenever it was possible without ambiguity, a single formula was given to cover the reading of the same single character by the two speakers. Thus *sei* was not shown in Table I, the syllabary, though this would have been appropriate for Ch. and it was necessary to make the rule that *se* with Tones 1–4 would be pronounced by him as if written *sei*. The present analysis makes it possible to deal with the two speakers separately within the systems established, and the formulae make clear the nature and extent of the likeness and difference of the forms. Thus, for the syllables just mentioned, the analysis for Su would give $y^hS\epsilon$ and for Ch. $y^hS\epsilon^y$. On the other hand, it was necessary in ' MS ' (p. 205) to identify the forms used in reading a particular character as *gwe* for Su and *go* for Ch. The formulae in terms of the systems established here are $y^wK\epsilon$ and $w^wK\epsilon^{wq}$, which indicate the relation of the forms while still making clear the differences.

IO

' OPENNESS ' IN TIGRE :
A PROBLEM IN PROSODIC STATEMENT

By F. R. PALMER

A N essential part of the prosodic approach is the abstraction of those features that may be regarded as syntagmatic.[1] One feature of this kind is ' vowel harmony ' ; prosodic analysis is well equipped to deal with this in terms of ' frontness ' and ' backness ', or ' openness ' and ' closeness ', these being treated as characteristic of the entire word or of a considerable part of it.

In the phonological analysis of Tigre [2] a prosodic feature of this kind may be abstracted, the relevant phonetic observation being that there are sequences of open front vowels, and that within those sequences there are no half open central vowels.[3] It is this feature that is referred to in the title as ' openness '.

The prosodic statement of openness is, however, complicated by the further observation that not only sequences of vowels, but also sequences of vowels and consonants are involved ; there is ' vowel-consonant harmony ' as well as ' vowel harmony '.[4] Yet the open vowel qualities observable in sequences of both kinds are phonetically identical.

The aim of this paper is to make a systematic investigation into the problems of the prosodic analysis of openness in Tigre, and to suggest a solution. For clarity and consistency the data considered are entirely drawn from the nominals, though a very similar statement could be made for the verbs.[5]

Since two features are involved, the phonological analysis must recognize not a single set of prosodies, but two such sets, the first statable entirely in terms of vowel qualities, the second in terms of vowel-consonant relations as well.

The prosodies of both types are to be established as prosodies within the word. The analysis presented here itself provides one of the criteria for the phonological definition of the word in Tigre.[6] The phonological delimitation of the word can be closely related to analysis at other levels, and does, in fact, correspond almost exactly to grammatical word division and to the ' institutionalized ' word as recognized by those Tigre speakers who can read and write their language. Only one problem of word division is raised ; this is dealt with in part III of this paper.

Both sets of prosodies will be treated as prosodies of syllables or of groups of syllables. The first problem, therefore, is that of syllable definition, and part I of this paper is concerned with establishing the syllable. Part II (in

---

[1] cf. J. R. Firth, ' Sounds and prosodies ', *TPS*, 1948, 129.

[2] One of the ' North Ethiopic ' Semitic languages, spoken in Eritrea. My assistant was Mr. Lijam Ishaq of Mehleb (Mensa dialect). Research was undertaken in the field.

[3] ' Vowel ' and ' consonant ' are used throughout as phonetic terms. In phonological statements V and C are used.

[4] cf. J. R. Firth, op. cit., 141.

[5] The word classes ' nominal ' and ' verb ' being established on morphological and syntactical grounds.

[6] See below, pp. 170–2.

Source : F. R. Palmer, ' " Openness " in Tigre : a problem of prosodic statement ', *BSOAS*, 18 (1956), 561–77. Reprinted by permission of the School of Oriental and African Studies and the author.

three sections, A, B, and C) deals with the statements required for the two sets of prosodies ; part III raises the problem of word definition, and part IV considers some of the theoretical problems raised.

I

The phonological analysis of the syllable depends largely on the treatment of the (phonetically) half close central vowels. For half close central and the absence of a vowel immediately after a consonant are mutually exclusive, the occurrence of the one or the other being predictable in terms of the structure of the entire word. In fact, the Ethiopic syllabary that has been adopted for writing Tigre does not distinguish between consonant plus half close central vowel and consonant without a vowel, both being represented by the ' sixth order '. This does not lead to any ambiguity, except in the case of two syllabic structures, to which only a small number of words belong, that the script does not differentiate.[1]

At the phonetic level it may be stated :—

(i) That there are no clusters of more than two consonants ;

(ii) that no consonant clusters are to be found initially or finally in the word [2] ;

(iii) that half close central vowels are to be found only where absence of a vowel would imply word-final or word-initial consonant clusters, or clusters of more than two consonants ;

(iv) that half close central vowels are not to be found word-finally, or (in common with the other vowels) word-initially.

Two possible phonological statements of the syllable will be considered.

(1) The phonological statement of the syllable that may be most directly related to phonetic observation is in terms of two types of syllable CV (' open ') and CVC (' closed '). In such a statement the mutually exclusive half close central vowel and absence of a vowel are regarded as related to different phonological categories, the former being an exponent of a term in the V systems of both types of syllable, and the latter being a feature of the final C of the syllable type CVC. If the relation of mutual exclusiveness between half close central vowel and absence of vowel is to be handled at all in such an analysis, it must be stated :—

(i) That there are two kinds of V system, one containing a term whose exponent is half close central, the other containing no such term ;

(ii) that V systems of the former kind are to be established only where absence of V would imply syllables of types other than CV or CVC.

---

[1] See below, p, 160.

[2] But there are verbal forms with either a long consonant, or a consonant cluster (the first a voiceless dental plosive) initially ; cf. W. Leslau, ' Grammatical sketches in Tigré ', *JAOS*, LXV, 1945, 168, and ' Supplementary observations on Tigré grammar ', *JAOS*, LXVIII, 1948, 132, with whom I agree. The rejection of Leslau's observation by E. Ullendorff, *The Semitic languages of Ethiopia*, London, 1955, 199, ' tᵊbäggäsä . . . does in fact sound tᵊbäggäsä ' is contrary to my own observation.

The first of these points may be illustrated by the word structure CVCVCV. Of the three V systems only the first contains a term whose exponent is half close central. Vowel qualities of several kinds are the exponents of terms in all three systems, but half close central (as illustrated by the first two examples below) is the exponent of a term in the first system only.

e.g. :—

gərade [1]	[gəra:de:]	scimitar
dəqala	[dək'a:la:]	bastard
kəbəro	[kəbəro:]	drum
badela	[ba:de:la:]	spade

The second point may also be illustrated by the structure CVCVCV. Absence of the first V would imply the syllabic structure CCVCV, which cannot be interpreted in terms of CV and CVC, whereas absence of the second or third V would imply CVCCV or CVCVC, structures that may be interpreted as CVC-CV and CV-CVC. It is, therefore, only in the first syllable of structures of this type that the V system of the type which contains a term whose exponent is half close central is to be established.

(2) A second and more appropriate statement is in terms of open syllables only. These are (provisionally at least) of two kinds CV and Cə, the exponent of ə being either half close central vowel or ' nil ',[2] according to its place in the structure of the word. It is convenient to refer to Cə, no less than CV, as a ' syllable ', even when the exponent of ə is nil, and to refer to ə as a ' syllabic '. The relation between half close central vowel and absence of vowel is now treated in terms of the alternative phonetic exponents of a single phonological category. The exponent of ə may be stated in terms of the place of the syllable in the word as follows :—

Initial	half close central
Final	nil
Medial (i)	nil
(ii) *only* when preceded or followed by another Cə syllable for which the exponent of ə is nil	half close central

e.g. :—

(a) gən	[gən]	(CəCə)	border
(b) kərəʃ	[kərəʃ]	(CəCVCə)	stomach
(c) fətəl	[fətəl]	(CVCəCə)	thread
(d) mənka	[maŋka:]	(CVCəCV)	spoon

---

[1] I follow the transliteration used by W. Leslau in his ' Verb in Tigré ' and ' Grammatical sketches in Tigré ', *JAOS*, lxv, 1945 (published together as *Grammar of Tigré*, American Oriental Society Offprint No. 18), with the substitution of ꝗ, ẓ, ḫ, ṭ, ṣ, c, ʃ, j, and ʊ for ', ', ḥ, ṭ, ṣ, c̣, š, ǧ, and đ respectively. An I.P.A. transcription is added in square brackets. The transliteration differs from the Ethiopic in presupposing a CV/CVC analysis, which is convenient for a reading convention.

[2] I use ' nil ' in the statement of exponents for absence of vowel immediately after a consonant.

(e) dəngəl   [dəngəl]   (CəCəCəCə)   virgin
(f) dənkəla   [dənkəla:] ⎱   ⎰ small antelope
(g) kərəmba   [kərəmba:] ⎰   (CəCəCəCV)   ⎱ cabbage

Half close central as the exponent of ə in the initial syllable is illustrated by
(a), (b), (e), (f), and (g), and nil as the exponent of ə in the final syllable by
(a), (b), (c), and (e). An example of nil as the exponent of ə in a medial syllable
is provided by (d), and an example of half close central as the exponent of ə
in such a syllable by (c)—the following syllable is Cə, and since it is final the
exponent of its ə is nil. In (e) there are two medial syllables, but the exponents
of the syllabics can only be nil and half close central, in that order, for since
the exponent of ə in the final syllable is nil, the exponent of ə in the preceding
(third) syllable is half close central (in accordance with (ii)), and, therefore, the
exponent of ə in the second syllable is nil (in accordance with (i)). In (f) and
(g) similarly there are two medial syllables, but while it follows from what has
been stated that the exponent of one of the syllabics is half close central and
the exponent of the other is nil, there is no indication whether the sequence
begins with nil (as in dənkəla) or with half close central (as in kərəmba).

Most commonly the exponent of the first syllabic in such sequences is nil.
Other examples are :—

        məsməsa   [məsməsa:]   (CəCəCəCV)   reason
        gəndəʒe   [gəndəʕe:]   (CəCəCəCV)   kind of tree

The forms in which half close central is the exponent of the first syllabic in
such sequences are of three kinds :—

(i) Those which may be treated as divisible into stem and prefix mə or
suffix ti, such that only the stem, not the entire word, may be analysed in
terms of the statements made above ; e.g. :—

        məhəngag   [məhənga:g]   (Cə/CəCəCVCə)   scratch
        ʃəgərti   [ʃəgərti:]   (CəCəCə/CV)   onion

(ii) Those in which prosodies describable as ' gemination ' or ' homorganic
nasality ' are involved, these prosodies being prosodies of two syllables, the first
always Cə, with the statement that, where these prosodies are set up, the
exponent of ə in the first of the two syllables is always nil ; e.g. :—

        ʃərəbbe   [ʃərəbbe:]   (CəCəCəCV)   drinking glass
        narəgge   [na:rəgge:]   (CVCəCəCV)   bitter orange
        kərəmba   [kərəmba:]   (CəCəCəCV)   cabbage
        qələnqal   [k'ələnk'a:l]   (CəCəCəCVCə)   euphorbia [1]

(iii) Plural forms of a single pattern only ; e.g. :—

        ʕəqərnət   [ʔak'ərnət] ⎱   ⎰ horns (Sing. qər)
        ʕəsəgdət   [ʔəsəgdət]   ⎰   (CVCəCəCVCə)   ⎱ necks (Sing. səgad)

Provided, therefore, that these phonological and grammatical features are

---

[1] If, in my analysis, gemination were not indicated, the first two forms might be interpreted
as *ʃərbəbe and *nargəge, but in the Ethiopic script the ambiguity is of a different kind, since
single and geminated consonants are not differentiated ; these forms could rather be interpreted
as *ʃərbe and *narge.

taken into account, analysis in terms of CV and Cə, with the exponent of ə wholly statable in terms of the place of the syllable in the word structure may be employed for all the nominal forms in Tigre. Syllabic analysis of this type is adopted in the remaining parts of this paper.[1]

II

In the completed statement two kinds of prosodic system are required. The terms of the one system, involving ' vowel harmony ', will be referred to as a and $\underline{a}$, and the terms of the other, involving ' vowel-consonant harmony ', will be referred to as ϕ and $\underline{\phi}$.[2] Since openness is a feature (though not the only feature) of both a and ϕ, the analysis will be greatly complicated if the data considered for the statement of one prosody differ in terms of the other. All ϕ pieces will, therefore, be excluded in the exposition of the $a/\underline{a}$ system, and all a pieces in the exposition of the $\phi/\underline{\phi}$ system. Part II is divided into three sections, the first (A) dealing with a and $\underline{a}$ (but excluding all ϕ pieces), the second (B) dealing with ϕ and $\underline{\phi}$ (but excluding all a pieces), and the third (C) integrating A and B and dealing with pieces that are both a and ϕ prosodic.

A. The first prosodic feature is exemplified by the following morphologically related forms [3] :—

sɐlsɐlɐta	[salsalata:]	her bracelet
sɐlsɐlɐtu	[sɐlsɐlɐtu:]	his bracelet

In the first form there is a sequence of front open vowels, the last being greater in duration,[4] whereas in the second form there is a sequence of three short half open central vowels and a final long back vowel. It is for the phonological description of these vowels that the $a/\underline{a}$ prosodic system is required.

For the further definition of a and the delimitation of the a piece, the following phonetic observations are relevant :—

(i) A short open front vowel is always followed, within the same word, by a long open front vowel, with no long vowel of any other quality between them ;

(ii) a short half open central vowel is

EITHER followed, within the same word, by a long vowel other than open front, with no long open front vowel between them,

OR not followed, within the same word, by any long vowel ;

[1] Leslau (*Grammar of Tigré*, 2) says ' in many cases we do not know whether a consonant is to be pronounced with the vowel ə or without vowel ', but such ambiguity is rare, except where there is gemination, and in fact only one of Leslau's interpretations is incorrect (he states that the plural forms mentioned above are of the pattern 'aqtəlät when, in fact, the pattern is 'aqtəlät, as Leslau himself observes in his later ' Supplementary observations on Tigré grammar ', 129).

[2] For $\underline{a}$ read ' non-a ' and for $\underline{\phi}$ read ' non-ϕ '.

[3] Noun + possessive suffix.

[4] The recognition of a phonetically short and a phonetically long open front vowel is central to the argument of this paper. The distinction was noted by Leslau, ' Supplementary observations on Tigré grammar ', 127, but the only suggestion of ' vowel harmony ' that I have noted is in R. Sundström, ' Some Tigre texts ', Monde orientale 8 (1914), 1. Ullendorff, op. cit., 168, and *BSOAS*, 14.1 (1952), 210, rejects Leslau's observations on purely *a priori* grounds, but is, in fact, mistaken ; some of Leslau's examples were confirmed by my own observation, notably ḥal ' maternal aunt ' and ḥāl ' maternal uncle ' (Leslau's transcription, ḥɐl and ḥaḷ in mine).

(iii) neither short open front vowels nor short half open central vowels are found word-finally.

e.g. :—

(a) sɐlsɐlɐta	[salsalata:]	her bracelet
(b) mɐnkahu	[maŋka:hu:]	his spoon
(c) nɐbit	[nɐbi:t]	wine
(d) sɐmbuka	[sɐmbu:ka:]	her boat
(e) dɐbela	[dɐbe:la:]	he-goat
(f) tɐkobɐta	[tɐko:bata:]	her mat
(g) sɐlsɐlɐt	[sɐlsɐlɐt]	bracelet
(h) baldɐngɐt	[ba:ldɐngɐt]	bean

Observation (i) is illustrated by (a) and (b). In both there is a sequence of several short open front vowels or one short open front vowel and a long open front vowel. There is also a long close back vowel in (b), but it is *after* the long open front vowel. The first part of observation (ii) is illustrated by (c), (d), and (e). In each case a short half open central vowel is followed by a long vowel of quality other than open front (close front, close back, and half close front respectively). In (d) and (e) there is also a long open front vowel, but it is *after* the other long vowel in each case. (f) exemplifies both observations ; a short half open central vowel precedes a long half close back vowel, and a short open front vowel precedes a long open front vowel. The second part of (ii) is illustrated by (g) and (h) ; all the vowels of (g) and the last two vowels of (h) are half open central, and they are not followed by any long vowel, the only long vowel being in (h), but *preceding* the two short vowels.[1]

The data may now be treated in terms of a and a̱ pieces, such that

(i) a pieces do not include short half open central vowels, and a̱ pieces do not include short open front vowels ;

(ii) the final articulation of an a piece (but only the final articulation) is a long open front vowel, and the final articulation of a a̱ piece (but only the final articulation) is a long vowel of quality other than open front—close front, half close front, close back, or half close back, *except that* the final articulation of a word-final a̱ piece may be a consonant (a word-final articulation can only be a consonant or a long vowel, since there are no word-final short vowels, in accordance with observation (iii) and the statement in part I that the exponent of the syllabic ə in a word-final syllable is nil).

The phonological implications are as follows :—

(1) An additional syllabic, to be symbolized ɐ, is required, for the treatment of the short half open central and short open front qualities. For with the exception of half close central, which has already been established as an exponent of the syllabic ə, these are the only vowel qualities to be found non-finally in the prosodic pieces ; they may not, therefore, be treated as terms

---

[1] It must be again stressed that ' vowel ' is used as a phonetic term, not to be confused with the phonological syllabic or V.

in a system which also includes terms whose exponents are the long vowel qualities, since these are not found non-finally in the piece. Moreover, one of the two qualities is only to be found in α pieces, and the other only in a̱ pieces ; they may not, therefore, be regarded as the exponents of two terms in any one system, since they are treated as different prosodically.

(2) V systems are required only in the final syllable of each prosodic group of syllables. For a̱ a four-term system is required (there being four vowel qualities finally in the piece), and for α a one-term system (long open front being the only quality). The setting up of a one-term system, and not another syllabic, is based upon the recognition of the exact parallelism of this one-term system, as an element of structure, with the four-term system of a̱.[1]

(3) Prosodic groups of syllables are to be established, each consisting of one CV syllable preceded by any number of syllables (including none) of the types Cə and Cʋ in any order, *with one exception*—that a word-final group may end not with CV, but with Cə (the word-final articulation is a consonant, the exponent of ə being nil).

The analysis of the forms already mentioned, in terms of their prosodies and their syllabic structure, is as follows :

selseleta	[salsalata:]	α(CʋCəCʋCʋCV)
menkahu	[maŋka:hu:]	α(CʋCəCV)a̱(CV)
nebit	[nʋbi:t]	a̱(CʋCVCə)
sembuka	[sʋmbu:ka:]	a̱(CʋCəCV)α(CV)
debela	[dʋbe:la:]	a̱(CʋCV)α(CV)
tekobeta	[tʋko:bata:]	a̱(CʋCV)α(CʋCV)
selselet	[selselʋt]	a̱(CʋCəCʋCʋCə)
baldenget	[ba:ldʋngʋt]	α(CV)a̱(CəCʋCəCʋCə)

A phonological statement in terms of α and a̱ is now possible, but there are other features of vowel harmony within pieces, which must be taken into account and will lead to a prosodic sub-system. The relevant phonetic observation is that there are three qualities of half open central vowels, and three qualities of half close central vowels, a fronted variety of each preceding long front vowels, a retracted variety preceding long back vowels, and a wholly central variety followed by no long vowel within the same word. Examples are the first vowels of the following forms, those of (*a*) and (*b*) being fronted, those of (*c*) and (*d*) retracted, and those of (*e*) and (*f*) wholly central.

(*a*)	nebit	[nɇbi:t]	wine
(*b*)	felit	[fɇli:t]	half-grown calf
(*c*)	tekobet	[te̱ko:bet]	mat
(*d*)	negus	[ne̱gu:s]	king
(*e*)	feres	[feres]	horse
(*f*)	meded	[meded]	grindstone

A prosodic system of three terms *w*, *y*, and ζ may be established and the a̱ prosodic data treated in terms of three types of prosodic piece, such that

[1] cf. my ' " Broken plurals " of Tigrinya ', *BSOAS* ,xvii, 3, 1955, 553, n. 2.

(i) y pieces include central vowels of fronted quality only, w pieces include central vowels of retracted quality only, and ζ pieces include vowels of wholly central quality only ;

(ii) the final articulation (but only the final articulation) of a y piece is a long front vowel, the final articulation (but only the final articulation) of a w piece is a long back vowel, and the final articulation of a ζ piece is a consonant, a ζ piece being always word-final.

The analysis is simplified if, instead of a two-term system and a three-term sub-system, a system of four terms a, y, w, and ζ is established. V systems are then required in the final syllables of a, w, and y groups, a one-term system for a and two-term systems for w and y. An advantage of this type of statement is that those word-final $\underline{a}$ prosodic groups that end in a C∂, instead of a CV syllable, are differentiated from all other groups by being described as ζ prosodic.

A revised statement of the forms mentioned is as follows :—

sɐlsɐlɐta	a(CɐC∂CɐCɐCV)
mɐnkahu	a(CɐC∂CV)w(CV)
nɐbit	y(CɐCV)ζ(C∂)
sɐmbuka	w(CɐC∂CV)a(CV)
dɐbela	y(CɐCV)a(CV)
tɐkobɐta	w(CɐCV)a(CɐCV)
sɐlsɐlɐt	ζ(CɐC∂CɐCɐC∂)
baldɐngɐt	a(CV)ζ(C∂CɐC∂CɐC∂)

The conclusions of this section may now be set out.

(1) Syllabic structure is to be stated in terms of CV, C∂, and Cɐ, ɐ no less than ∂ being a syllabic. This is a modification of the statement in part I.

(2) (a) A prosodic system of four terms is set up—a, y, w, and ζ (y, w, and ζ also being regarded as a sub-system of $\underline{a}$), each a prosody of a group of syllables ('group' being interpreted to include a single syllable).

(b) The number of prosodic groups and their order within a word are various, except that only one ζ group may be established for any one word, and in word-final position only.

(c) With the exception of ζ, each prosodic group consists of a CV syllable preceded by any number of C∂ and Cɐ syllables (including none) in any order ; a ζ group consists of one C∂ syllable preceded by any number of C∂ and Cɐ syllables (including none) in any order.

(d) A V system of two terms is required for y and w, and a V system of one term for a ; no V systems are required for ζ.

(3) (a) The exponents of the prosodies are to be stated in terms of

(i) the type of piece final long vowel quality (a 'constant' [1] feature of any prosodic piece) ;

(ii) the two types of short vowel quality within the piece (these are not

---

[1] cf. R. H. Robins, 'Formal divisions in Sundanese', *TPS*, 1953, 134.

' constant ' features ; qualities other than those stated are excluded from the piece, but qualities of either kind are not necessarily included).

In these terms the exponents of the prosodies are :—

α (i) open front
   (ii) half close central (neither fronted nor retracted) and open front

y (i) front (close or half close)
   (ii) fronted half close central and fronted half open central

w (i) back (close or half close)
   (ii) retracted half close central and retracted half open central

ζ (i) none
   (ii) half close central and half open central, both neither fronted nor retracted

(b) The exponents of the syllabics are stated, for each prosody, in the following table [1] :—

	ə	ɐ
u	half close central	open front
y	fronted half close central	fronted half open central
w	retracted half close central	retracted half open central
ζ	half close central	half open central

(c) The exponents of the terms in the V systems are stated, for each prosody, in the following table :—

	ə	ɐ
α		open front
y	close front	half close front
w	close back	half close back

B. The second prosodic feature is exemplified by forms such as :—

| fɐrɐɣ | [faraʕ] | clan |
| fɐrɐs | [fɐrɐs] | horse |

Both vowels of the first form are open front, while both vowels of the second are half open central. It is for the phonological description of these vowels that the ϕ/ϕ prosodic system is required.

For the definition of ϕ and the delimitation of the ϕ piece, the following phonetic observations are relevant :—

(i) A short open front vowel is always followed, within the same word, or *immediately* preceded by, a pharyngal or an ejective consonant (this does not preclude the possibility that such a vowel may be followed by more than one such consonant, or both immediately preceded by one and followed by one or more), the types of consonant being voiced pharyngal fricative, voiceless pharyngal fricative, ejective dental plosive, ejective alveolar affricate, ejective palato-alveolar affricate, and ejective velar plosive ;

(ii) a short half open central vowel [2] is never followed or immediately preceded by a pharyngal or ejective consonant.

---

[1] For ə an alternative exponent is, of course, nil.
[2] In this section ' half open central ' includes the fronted and retracted varieties noted in A.

e.g. :—

(a)	ʃɐnɐt	[ʃɐnat']	haversack
(b)	fɐləs	[faləts']	wood
(c)	rɐmɐc	[ramatʃ']	embers
(d)	wɐrəq	[warək']	gold
(e)	fɐrɐʑ	[faraʕ]	clan
(f)	wɐrəḥ	[warəḥ]	month
(g)	fɐrɐs	[fɐrɐs]	horse
(h)	fɐrəd	[fɐrəd]	revolver
(i)	jɐhɐt	[dʒɐhɐt]	direction
(j)	cɐbɐl	[tʃ'abɐl]	ashes
(k)	ʑɐstɐr	[ʕastɐr]	sky
(l)	ḥɐsḥɐs	[ḥats'ḥats']	pebbles
(m)	ʃɐrit	[ʃari:t']	line
(n)	sɐnduq	[sandu:k']	box, case

Observation (i) is illustrated by (a) to (f), the final consonants exemplifying all the ejective and pharyngal articulations, and observation (ii) by (g) to (i); other than the half close central vowels (the exponents of the syllabic ə), all the vowels of (a) to (f) are short open front, and all the vowels of (g) to (i) are short half open central. In (j) and (k) the first vowels, being immediately preceded by a pharyngal or ejective consonant, are short open front, but the second vowels, being neither immediately preceded nor followed by such consonants, are short half open central. In (l) the short open front vowel is not only preceded by a pharyngal consonant, but also followed by both a pharyngal and two ejective consonants. (m) and (n) are similar to (a) to (f), but are added to show that the presence of a long back or front vowel, so important in the statement of α, is irrelevant in the statement of φ; the first vowels of these forms are short open front.

The data may now be divided into φ and ϕ pieces, such that

(i) φ pieces do not include short half open central vowels, and ϕ pieces do not include short open front vowels;

(ii) a ϕ piece neither includes, nor within the word precedes, a pharyngal or ejective consonant, and the final consonant of a φ piece (but not necessarily only this consonant) is either pharyngal or ejective; a vowel immediately following such a consonant is included in the piece (this is based on the observation that a short open front vowel may be immediately preceded by a pharyngal or ejective consonant, and for the simplicity of the phonological statement all vowels immediately following such consonants, including the nil exponent of the syllabic ə, are treated as part of the φ piece).

The phonological implications are as follows :—

(1) Short half open central and short open front are, as in section A, to be treated not as the exponents of terms in a system, but of the syllabic ɐ in prosodically different syllables.

(2) Two kinds of C system are required, one of six terms with ejective

and pharyngal consonants as the exponents of the terms, and the other of eighteen terms, the exponents of the terms being neither ejective nor pharyngal (these are listed at the end of the section).

(3) Prosodic groups consist of any number of CV, Cə, and Cɐ syllables in any order. The type of C system is partially determined by the prosody, an eighteen-term system being established for all ϕ syllables, and a six-term system for the last syllable in a ϕ group ; the other systems of a ϕ group may have either six or eighteen terms.

(4) A ϕ prosodic group never precedes a ϕ group within the same word ; all words are, therefore, either wholly ϕ prosodic, or wholly ϕ prosodic, or consist of a group of ϕ syllables and a group of ϕ syllables, *in that order*.

Since it is only in the non-final syllables of ϕ groups that the C system is not determined by the prosody, it is only in such syllables that there is need to differentiate the two kinds of system. In the symbolization used here, the six-term system will be indicated by a subscript—C_6. This will be used not only where there is ambiguity, but also in the final syllable of the ϕ groups where no ambiguity is possible. The eighteen-term system is symbolized simply as C.

Some of the forms already illustrated may be analysed as follows :—

ʃənɐt	[ʃənat']	$\phi(C\partial C\text{ɐ}C_6\partial)$
wɐrəḥ	[warəḥ]	$\phi(C\text{ɐ}C\partial C_6\partial)$
cɐbɐl	[tʃ'abɐl]	$\phi(C_6\text{ɐ})\phi(C\text{ɐ}C\partial)$
sɐnduq	[sandu:k']	$\phi(C\text{ʊ}C\partial CVC_6\partial)$
ḥɐʒḥəʒ	[ḥats'ḥəts']	$\phi(C_6\text{ɐ}C_6\partial C_6\text{ɐ}C_6\partial)$
fɐrəd	[fɐrəd]	$\phi(C\text{ɐ}C\partial C\partial)$

The conclusions of the section are now set out.

(1) (*a*) A prosodic system of two terms ϕ and ϕ is set up, each a prosody of a group of syllables.

(*b*) The number of prosodic groups within a word is limited to one or two ; if two, the groups are ϕ and ϕ, in that order.

(*c*) Two types of C system are required, one of six, the other of eighteen terms.

(*d*) Each prosodic group consists of any number of CV, Cə, and Cɐ syllables, in any order, but a ϕ group contains only eighteen-term C systems and the final syllable of a ϕ group has a six-term C system.

(2) (*a*) The exponents of the prosodies are to be stated in terms of :—

(i) The type of consonantal articulation within the piece (a constant [1] feature) ;

(ii) the type of short half open central or open front vowels within the piece (not a constant feature).

In these terms the exponents of the prosodies are :—

ϕ (i) ejective or pharyngal articulation of the piece-final consonant
     (ii) open front

---

[1] cf. n. 1, p. 164.

ɸ̱   (i) absence of any ejective or pharyngal articulation within the piece

(ii) half open central

(b) The exponents of the syllabic ɐ are, for ɸ short open front, and for ɸ̱ short half open central.

(c) The exponents of the terms in the six-term C system are (listed under ejective and pharyngal) :—

ejective	*pharyngal*
dental plosive	voiced fricative
alveolar affricate	voiceless fricative
palato-alveolar affricate	
velar plosive	

The exponents of the terms in the eighteen-term system are :—

voiceless labio-dental fricative

voiced bilabial plosive

voiced bilabial nasal

voiceless dental plosive

voiced dental plosive

voiced dental nasal

voiceless alveolar fricative

voiced alveolar fricative

voiced alveolar trill

voiced alveolar lateral

voiceless palato-alveolar fricative

voiced palato-alveolar affricate

voiceless velar plosive

voiced velar plosive

voiced labiovelar semi-vowel

voiced palatal semi-vowel

glottal plosive

breath (' h ')

C. So far analysis in terms of α and α̱ has been presented only for ɸ pieces (in A), and an analysis in terms of ɸ and ɸ̱ only for α̱ pieces (in B). In fact, however, the phonological conclusions of both A and B may be extended to cover data of all prosodic types, except in the treatment of the short half open central and short open front vowels.

The treatment of these vowels affects the statement of the exponents of both the syllabic ɐ and of the prosodies. In terms of α and α̱, and ɸ and ɸ̱, four kinds of prosodic piece are possible—αɸ, αɸ̱, α̱ɸ, and α̱ɸ̱. The quality of short half open central or short open front vowel in pieces of three of these kinds has already been stated :—

αɸ̱ (section A) open front

α̱ɸ (section B) open front

α̱ɸ̱ (sections A and B) half open central (fronted, retracted, or neither according to the prosodic sub-system w, y, and ζ).

The quality of vowel in prosodic pieces of the fourth kind is now added :—
$a\phi$ open front. e.g. :—

      ʃənɐʈa   [ʃənat'a:]   her haversack

The implications of this are :—

(1) That the exponents of the syllabic ɐ must be stated with reference to both prosodic systems jointly.

(2) That in an integrated analysis the terms in the prosodic systems cannot be established by reference to the quality of the short half open central or short open front vowels (since half close central is an exponent of $\underline{a}$ only when the data are restricted to ϕ pieces, and of ϕ when the data are restricted to $\underline{a}$ pieces), but only by reference to their ' constant ' exponents—for a and $\underline{a}$ the quality of the piece final long vowels, and for ϕ and $\underline{\phi}$, features of the consonant articulation.

The statement of the V systems (in section A), together with the exponents of the terms, is valid for ϕ no less than $\underline{\phi}$ pieces, and the statement of the C systems (in B), together with the exponents of the terms, is valid for a no less than $\underline{a}$ pieces. The statement of the exponents of the syllabic ə (other than nil) in section A is also valid for ϕ no less than $\underline{\phi}$ pieces.

Analysis in terms of both prosodic systems is illustrated by the following examples :—

(a)	kɐnfɐra	[kanfara:]	$\overbrace{\text{CɐCəCɐCV}}$ ϕ above / a below	her lip
(b)	mɐftəħ	[maftəħ]	$\overbrace{\text{CɐCəCəC}_6\text{ə}}$ ϕ above / ζ below	key
(c)	sɐmbuka	[sɐmbu:ka:]	$\overbrace{\text{CɐCəCVCV}}$ ϕ above / w a below	her boat
(d)	sɐnduqa	[sandu:k'a:]	$\overbrace{\text{CɐCəCVCV}}$ ϕ above / w a below	her box
(e)	ħɐyɐt	[ħajɐt]	$\overbrace{\text{CɐCɐCə}}$ ϕ $\underline{\phi}$ above / ζ below	lion
(f)	ħayut	[ħa:ju:t]	$\overbrace{\text{CVCVCə}}$ ϕ $\underline{\phi}$ above / a w ζ below	lions

$$\overset{\phi}{\overbrace{\text{CVCə}}}$$

(g) **kis**   [kiːs]   CVCə   pocket

$$\underset{y \quad \zeta}{\smile}$$

$$\overset{\phi}{\overbrace{\text{CɐCəCVCə}}}$$

(h) **Ɂɐkyas**   [Ɂakjaːs]   CɐCəCVCə   pockets

$$\underset{a \qquad \zeta}{}$$

$$\overset{\phi}{\overbrace{\text{CɐCəCV}}}$$

(i) **mɐnka**   [maŋkaː]   CɐCəCV   spoon

$$\underset{a}{\smile}$$

$$\overset{\phi}{\overbrace{\text{CɐCɐCəCVCə}}}$$

(j) **mɐnɐkkit**   [mɐnɐkkiːt]   CɐCɐCəCVCə   spoons

$$\underset{y \qquad \zeta}{}$$

The interesting feature of (a) to (d) is the first vowel of each form which is short open front in all except (c) where it is half close central. (a) is entirely a prosodic and (b) entirely ϕ prosodic. (c) and (d) illustrate the different extent of a and ϕ pieces ; although the final vowel of (c) is long open front, the first vowel is in a w piece and so half open central (retracted) in quality, but the final consonant of (d) is ejective, and the whole form is ϕ prosodic, and the first vowel open front in quality. (e) to (j) exemplify pairs of words related in the grammatical category of number ; the prosodic features of the singular forms often differ considerably from those of the plural forms.

The conclusions of the phonological analysis are briefly :—

(1) (a) Two prosodic systems, each independent of the other, are to be established.

(b) Syllabic structure is in terms of the syllabics ə and ɐ, V systems determined by the $a/\underset{\tiny\_}{a}$ prosodic system, as stated in A, and C systems determined by the ϕ/ϕ prosodic system, as stated in B.

(2) (a) The exponents of the terms in the prosodic systems are as stated in A and B, but in an integrated analysis only the 'constant' exponents are to be stated.

(b) The exponents of the terms of the V and C systems are as stated in A and B respectively.

(c) The exponents of the syllabic ə are stated in terms of the a, y, w, and ζ system, as in A ; the exponents of the syllabic ɐ are to be stated in terms of both prosodic systems as summarized in C.

III

The implications with regard to word division in the phonological analysis set out are :—

(i) That there can be no word division within a single prosodic piece ;

(ii) that there is always word division at the end of a ζ piece ;

(iii) that there is always word division between a ɸ and a φ piece.

To the extent that the recognition of the word is used to establish the prosodies, the analysis cannot be used to justify word division without circularity, but if only those phonological statements that do not depend upon word division are taken into account, some statements about word division are possible.

(i) a, w, and y pieces may be defined in terms of the quality of a single long vowel and any number of preceding short vowels. No word division is possible within prosodic pieces of these kinds.

(ii) A ζ piece may be established by the recognition of its wholly central short vowels. Any sequence of a piece containing such vowels and a piece defined as a, y, or w is indicative of word division. e.g. :—

> sɐlɐs Sɐnas   [sɐlɐs ʕɐnaːs]   three men

(iii) A ɸ piece may be defined in terms of its half open central vowel qualities, and a φ piece in terms both of its short open front vowel qualities and its final ejective or pharyngal consonant. Any sequence of two pieces so defined is indicative of word division. e.g. :—

> kɐrɐs ʃɐʁɐb   [kɐrɐʃ ʃɐʕɐb]   inside She'eb

But since openness is a feature of both a and φ, it must be added that word division in terms of (ii) cannot be established if the ζ piece is φ prosodic, and word division in terms of (iii) cannot be established if the ɸ piece is a prosodic. This may be illustrated by the following forms, all single words :—

(a)	tɐstay	[tastaːi]	bull
(b)	ḥɐrmaz	[ḥarmaːz]	elephant
(c)	mɐftɐḥ	[maftɐḥ]	key
(d)	mɐfaːtɐḥ	[mafaːːtɐḥ]	keys

The first vowel of all four forms is short open front. In (a) this establishes the whole form as a prosodic, and, therefore, a single word, but in (b) the vowel is also in a φ prosodic piece, and its open quality does not, therefore, preclude the word division *ḥɐr/maz. Similarly the vowel in (c) establishes the whole form as ɸ prosodic and so a single word, but the vowel of (d) is also in an a piece ; its open quality does not preclude the word division *mɐfa/tɐḥ.

There is one very important exception to statement (i) above. A phrase such as the following may on grammatical grounds be treated as three words :—

> mɐbrɐhɐt la Sɐnas   [mabrahat laː ʔɐnaːs]   the man's lamp

Phonologically, however, mɐbrɐhɐt la is a single a prosodic piece—a sequence of three short open front vowels and one long open front vowel. Yet it would not be reasonable to treat mɐbrɐhɐt la as one word and Sɐnas as another grammatically, in view of the relation of Sɐnas ' a man ' and la Sɐnas ' the man '. But the prosodic unity of the words is important ; it marks the syntactical feature linking **mᵊbrᵊhᵊt** with **la Ɂᵊnas**, the relation of the ' genitive ' or ' possessive '. The prosody a extends beyond the word only when the second word is **la** ; in such a case it is of grammatical significance.

IV

One important theoretical problem is raised by the paper.[1] It is whether, in the statement of the phonetic exponents of the phonological categories, there is to be any ' overlap ' of the phonic data, or whether these data are to be regarded as mutually exclusive, and specifically whether the data allotted to the exponents of the terms of the C and V systems and the syllabics may or may not include those allotted to the terms of the prosodic systems.

In this paper it has been assumed that such overlap is permissible. For instance, ejection and openness are stated as exponents of the prosody ϕ, but the exponents of the terms in one of the C systems are stated as ' ejective dental plosive ', etc., and the exponent of the syllabic ɐ as ' open front '.

The alternative to such an approach is to regard the phonic data as mutually exclusive, so that data allotted to one phonological category may not then be allotted to another.[2] Such a view implies that the data are ' additive ', in that the sum of the data allotted will correspond without residue to the total relevant phonic data. The difficulties involved in such an approach may be illustrated from this paper.

(1) It is possible so to allot the data that the exponents of y and w are frontness and backness respectively. The exponents of the terms in the V systems may then be stated simply as ' close ' and ' half close '. This is extremely neat, but there are difficulties (a) in the treatment of the short vowels, and (b) in any attempt to integrate with this a statement of the a prosody.

(a) The short vowels are ' retracted ' or ' fronted ', not fully back or fully front. In the case of the long vowels the possibility of ' addition ' is obvious :—

$$\text{front} + \text{close} = \text{front close}$$
$$\text{back} + \text{close} = \text{back close}$$
$$\text{etc.}$$

With the short vowels, such straightforward addition is not possible. The statements are rather of the kind

$$\text{front} + \text{half close} = \text{fronted half close}$$
$$\text{back} + \text{half open} = \text{retracted half open}$$
$$\text{etc.}$$

If there is still ' addition ' then a different kind of ' frontness ' and ' backness ' is being added.

(b) If a is to be handled together with y and w, it is by no means clear what

---

[1] For the understanding of this problem I am indebted to Professor J. R. Firth, who has discussed it with me and permitted me to see the MS of an article as yet unpublished. ·

[2] cf. W. S. Allen, ' Retroflexion in Sanskrit ', *BSOAS*, xvi, 3, 1954, 556 ff.

are its exponents. To consider first the syllabic ɞ, if it were accepted that its exponent is ' half open ', as for y and w, then

$$\text{open} + \text{half open} = \text{open front}.$$

This is clearly strange, and not phonetically justifiable, but it is difficult to see how any other allotment of the data could improve upon this statement. The problem of the term of the V system is very similar.

(2) If the ejective consonants were considered, it would be possible so to allot the data that ejection, voicelessness, and voice were exponents of prosodies with dental, palatal, palato-alveolar, and velar ' occlusion ' as the exponents of terms in C systems. This statement would cover the analysis of the four ejective consonants and eight of the voiceless and voiced plosive, fricative, or affricate consonants. But such an analysis could not handle the pharyngal consonants, which so clearly form a prosodic group with the ejectives, for one of these is voiceless, and the other voiced ; they would, therefore, be exponents of terms in a prosodically different system from the ejective consonants.

It is not, then, to be assumed that there is a limited set of relevant phonic data, all of which are to be allotted, and allotted only once, to one or other of the phonological categories. The statement of exponents is intended solely to justify the linguistic statements ; through the exponents there is ' renewal of connexion ',[1] establishing contact between the theoretical framework and the language events for which the framework was designed.[2] They fulfil this and no other function ; they have no status independently of it.

[1] cf. W. S. Allen, op. cit., p. 556, n. 6.

[2] It follows from this that linguistic statements are not necessarily to be rejected if they involve circularity ; cf. on a similar, but philosophical, problem A. J. Ayer, *Thinking and meaning*, London, 1947, 28, ' We interpret one symbol by another ; but it is only because the circle is broken by our actual experiences that any descriptive symbol comes to be understood '.

II
SOME ASPECTS OF THE PHONOLOGY OF THE NOMINAL FORMS OF THE TURKISH WORD

By NATALIE WATERSON

(PLATES I–II)

THE relations within the suffixed forms of the Turkish word have hitherto been treated as a series of unconnected statements as a result of the phonological and grammatical levels of analysis being made in phonemic terms.[1] ' Vowel Harmony ', which implies a separating out of the vowels from the rest of the word structure, ' Consonant Alternance ', and ' variant ' forms with the implication of consonants ' changing ' from one form to another, all these are statements not related to the structure of the word, and bring in their train some irregularities in the grammatical statement where none need arise.

The analysis given here [2] is limited to the Turkish word belonging to the nominal class and applies to words of native Turkish origin and loanwords of similar structure, unless otherwise stated. It is hoped to show how the ' prosodic ' approach [3] enables one to take more fully into account the features observed at the phonetic level and enables a more complete and integrated statement to be made of the structure of the Turkish word and the relevant grammar. Nominal forms of the word will be considered with ' productive ' suffixes.[4] It is not intended to present a complete phonology of the word but only those aspects which are concerned with what has in the past been treated as Vowel Harmony, Consonant Alternance, and the ' insertion ' and ' dropping ' of letters.[5] Stress and intonation patterns which would have to be given for a complete phonological statement are not dealt with here.

A necessary part of the analysis is the setting up of structures in terms of the elements of structure consonant, vowel, and prosody. Consonant elements are symbolized by C, and vowel elements by V. Syllable structure is stated in terms of the following types : V, CV, VC, CVC and VCC, CVCC [6] where the

---

[1] For levels of analysis see J. R. Firth, ' The technique of semantics ', *TPS*, 1935, 36–72, and ' Modes of meaning ', *Essays and Studies* (English Association), 1951, 118–49, especially 119–21. Also R. H. Robins, ' The phonology of nasalized verbal forms in Sundanese ', *BSOAS*, xv, 1, 1953, 138–45.

[2] This is an analysis of Istanbul Turkish in slow, careful style. I was very fortunate in having the help of Professor Fahir Iz of Istanbul University, who kindly consented to act as my informant when he held a lectureship at SOAS. It is a great pleasure to acknowledge the sacrifice of his time in this work.

[3] J. R. Firth, ' Sounds and prosodies ', *TPS*, 1948, 127–52.

[4] Forms of the nominal including suffixes of the type for deriving nouns from verbs and verbs from nouns are not included in the analysis.

[5] As two examples of such treatment see J. Deny, *Grammaire de la langue turque* (*dialecte osmanli*), Paris, 1921, and N. McQuown and Sadi Koylan, *Spoken Turkish* (Holt Spoken Language Series), Ling. Soc. of America, 1946.

[6] This structure is not to be confused with the structure (C)VCəC which is a dissyllabic structure. See p. 182.

Source : Natalie Waterson, ' Some aspects of the phonology of the nominal forms of the Turkish word ', *BSOAS*, 18 (1956), 578–91. Reprinted by permission of the School of Oriental and African Studies and the author.

first C of the final group is a continuant and the second C is a plosive or affricate or where the first C and second C are both fricatives. For syllable division in polysyllabic words, the C unit is taken with the following V, e.g. CV-CVC. Where two Cs come together, the syllable division comes between them, e.g. CVC-CVC, and where three Cs come together, the division comes between the second and third C of the group, e.g. CVCC-CVC.

The orthography recognizes an eight term vowel system ; four back vowels, represented by *a ı o u*, and four front vowels, represented by *e i ö ü*, of which *o u ö ü* are rounded and *a ı e i* are unrounded. Rules are given for the distribution of these vowels, the phenomenon being termed ' Vowel Harmony '.

In the prosodic analysis presented here, on the basis of phonic data and supported by palatographic evidence,[1] the following word [2] prosodies are set up :

(*a*) **y** prosody characterizing words having front vowels, and consonants with some degree of palatalization.[3]

(*b*) **w** prosody characterizing words having back vowels, and consonants which are not palatalized.[4] All Turkish words within the limits stated earlier (on p. 174), with very few exceptions, will be classed as either **y** prosody or **w** prosody. A generalized statement of monosyllabic [5] word structure will be as follows :—

$$y/w(C)VC(C)$$

Exx.[6]

tunç	ʷCVCC	*ast*	ʷVCC	*bal*	ʷCVC	*ot*	ʷVC
denk	ʸCVCC	*üst*	ʸVCC	*bin*	ʸCVC	*ön*	ʸVC

A further abstraction (*c*) o prosody, is made where labiality is a feature of the whole syllable, i.e. where there is lip rounding throughout the articulation of the whole syllable, e.g. *kol*, where there is lip rounding throughout the articulation of *k*, *o*, and *l*, and (*d*) non-o prosody (ǫ) where there is absence of labiality throughout the whole syllable or where labiality is initial or final

---

[1] See Appendix pp. 185–6 and Plates I and II for palatograms showing the difference in articulation of a few consonants with front and back vowels.

[2] ' Word ' here includes both what is called the unsuffixed form and the suffixed form. For division into base and suffix see p. 177. See also note 1 above.

[3] Seen on palatograms as having a generally greater degree of contact of tongue on palate.

[4] In phonemic analyses, the consonants and vowels are considered separately, and apart from *k* and *l*, which have long been singled out for special notice, the difference in articulation of consonants with back and with front vowels does not appear to have been noted in Western publications. Soviet linguists have recognized this difference in articulation but treat it as allophonic, after the way of Russian Phonetics. See N. A. Baskakov, *Karakalpakskij jazyk* II. *Fonetika i morfologija. Čast' pervaja*, Moscow, 1951 ; S. Ramazanov and Kh. Khismatullin, *Tatar tele grammatikasy*, Kazan, 1954, and Grammatical Supplement to N. K. Dmitriev (ed.), *Russko-Čuvašskij slovar*, Moscow, 1951.

[5] The prosodies for polysyllabic words will be the same, the formulae are given for monosyllabic words for simplicity of statement.

[6] Examples are given in the Turkish orthography which is in general an adequate guide to the phonetic realization if one bears in mind note 4 above. In the few instances that it is inadequate, examples are given in I.P.A. in brackets after the orthographic form.

only, e.g. *bal*. Thus, in addition to being classified as **y** or **w**, all words are also classified as **o** or **ǫ**. Taking again the monosyllabic structure, a generalized statement will be as follows :—

$$y^{o/ǫ}\text{(C)VC(C)} \qquad\qquad w^{o/ǫ}\text{(C)VC(C)}$$

Exx.   *tunç* $\overset{o}{w}$CVCC   *ast* $\overset{o}{w}$VCC   *bal* $\overset{o}{w}$CVC   *ot* $\overset{o}{w}$VC

       denk $\overset{o}{y}$CVCC   *üst* $\overset{o}{y}$VCC   *bin* $\overset{o}{y}$CVC   *ön* $\overset{o}{y}$VC

A two term Vowel system is set up (1) α (phonetic exponent openness)[1] and (2) ı (phonetic exponent closeness). The phonetic features of frontness, backness, rounding, and non-rounding are abstracted as word prosodies and are not therefore required to be stated as terms in the V system.

o prosody ' operates ' with ı in all syllables of the word but with α only in the first syllable,[2] e.g. :—

    yolumuz $\overset{o}{w}$Cα-Cı-CıC   but *yollarımız* $\overset{o}{w}$CαC-Cα-Cı-CıC

    önü $\overset{o}{y}$α-Cı   but *önünden* $\overset{o}{y}$α-CıC-CαC

ǫ prosody ' operates ' with α and ı in all syllables of the word, e.g. :—

    kalabalık $\overset{o}{w}$Cα-Cα-Cα-CıC   *kızımdan* $\overset{o}{w}$Cı-CıC-CαC

but a syllable with ᵒı may follow a syllable with ǫα if there is labiality at the initial of the syllable with ı, e.g. :—

    çabuk $\overset{o}{w}$Cα- $\overset{o}{}$CıC   *karpuz* $\overset{o}{w}$CαC- $\overset{o}{}$CıC [3]

It is not necessary to mark the limits of **y/w/o/ǫ** prosodies in the formulae as rules have been given to show their ' extent '.

In previous analyses the quality of the vowel of the suffix was said to depend on the last preceding vowel, hence certain loanwords with the letters *a, o,* or *u* in the spelling of the last vowel, and having front vowel suffixes, are treated as not following the laws of Vowel Harmony. If such words are carefully examined, however, it will be observed that the final consonants are palatalized and the sounds represented by the letters *a o u* are not the same as when *a o u* are followed by back type consonants, but are more fronted in character, or there may be a palatal glide preceding the final consonant. Such words will be classified as **wy** words, i.e. **w** beginning and **y** ending, instead of being all **w** or all **y** as words of native Turkish origin.

---

[1] In the orthography open vowels are represented by *o a ö e*, and close vowels by *u ı ü i*.

[2] In loanwords and onomatopoeic words **o** can operate with α in all syllables of the word, e.g. loan : *komposto* $\overset{o}{w}$CαC-CαC-Cα and onomatopoeic word : *şorolop* $\overset{o}{w}$Cα-Cα-CαC.

[3] Some alternative forms are possible in structures of this type, e.g. *kapı/kapu* $\overset{o}{w}$Cα-Cı $\Big/$ $\overset{o}{w}$Cα- Cı.

Exx.

	Unsuffixed form		Suffixed form	
saat	[sɑ'aʈ]	ʷCV-VʸC [1]	saati [sɑa'ʈi]	ʷCV-V-ʸCV
rol	[roḷ]	ʷCVʸC	rolü [ro'ḷy]	ʷCV-ʸCV
hâk	[hɑ:c]	ʷCVʸC	hâki [hɑ:'ci]	ʷCV-ʸCV

In this analysis, the word is accepted as institutionalized and the categories of base and suffix are taken as established at the grammatical level. These categories are supported by evidence at the phonological level, i.e. the base is always initial in the word, there is a greater number of terms in the initial and final C systems, and a greater number of values for V. A suffix can never be initial in the word, there is a smaller number of terms in the C systems in suffix initial and final, and a smaller number of values for V. The Turkish word can include several suffixes, e.g. *kollarımızdan*, base *kol*, suffixes *lar/ımız/dan*.

The prosodic treatment of certain phonetic features observed at the junction of base and suffix makes it possible to show that words which are identical at the phonetic level and in their written form but are different at the phonological and grammatical levels, have different structures.[2] The analysis given here is restricted to the ' base plus one suffix ' form of the word, except where necessary to consider more than one suffix to complete the statement of the structure of the suffix under discussion. The analysis of base plus more than one suffix would involve no new principles, so is not dealt with here.

Integration of base and suffix in the larger unit, the word, is recognized in two ways :—

(1) By prosodies extending over the whole word, i.e. y/w/o/ǫ, which have already been dealt with. This applies to all suffixed forms without exception.[3] Such an analysis makes possible a clearer and more economical statement than the two-fold and four-fold suffix vowel alternances.

(2) By prosodies of the junction of base final and suffix initial. In order to set up these prosodies, systems for base final and suffix initial must be given and this cannot be done unless syllabic structure is stated in terms of the types given on p. 578, para. 3. Syllabic structure does not necessarily coincide with division into base and suffix(es), e.g. taking the example above *kollarımızdan*, the syllabic structure is CVC-CV-CV-CVC-CVC. Phonological statements are not made about the initial systems of base and final systems of suffix except in so far as they are relevant.[4] There are six of the type (2) prosodies, viz. H, J, S, Ə, N, and Z, and these and the type (1) prosodies enable one to handle all suffixed forms of the word within the limits given in this article ; the features observed at the phonetic level at the junction of base

---

[1] It is not intended to indicate in the formulae exactly where w prosody ends and y prosody begins but only to show that there is a w beginning and y ending.

[2] See J. R. Firth, ' Sounds and prosodies ', *TPS*, 1948, 143. ' Even if *'s true* and *strew* should happen to be homophonous, the two structures are different : *ç'cvw* and *'cvw.*'

[3] See p. 176 for the treatment of some loanwords.

[4] See pp. 182–3 on *benim*, *bizim*.

and suffix are taken into account and a more systematic statement is made than the customary ' alternances ' or the ' insertion ' or ' dropping ' of letters. These prosodies are marked in the main, only in the generalized formulae as it is clear from the structure of base final and suffix initial (and sometimes also final) which prosody is ' operative '.

H prosody. H prosody at the phonological level is an expression of the structure base plus consonant initial suffix, where a plosive system ' p ' is set up for suffix C initial, i.e. C_p----. p is a two term system with values t and ʧ.[1] Words with the following suffixes are examples of such structure : locative, ablative, agentive, diminutive.[2]

Base final structure is ------C/V. For Base final V a two term system is set up, α and ι.[3]

For Base final C [4] a three term system is set up, p, k, and f, i.e. ----$C_{p/k/f}$. Under system p are grouped plosives and affricates, under system k are grouped voiced continuants, and under f fricatives.

p system. There are four terms in the p system, for which h and non h (ḥ) sub-systems are set up. The values for the terms in p/h are **p t k ʧ** which are voiceless in syllable initial and in syllable final position, e.g. :—

ipler $V\underline{C}_{ph}$–CVC,[5] *ipi* V–$\underline{C}_{ph}V$, *oklar* $V\underline{C}_{ph}$–CVC, *oku* V–$\underline{C}_{ph}V$, *atlar* $V\underline{C}_{ph}$–CVC, *atı* V–$\underline{C}_{ph}V$, *saçlar* $CV\underline{C}_{ph}$–CVC, *saçı* CV–$\underline{C}_{ph}V$. The values for the terms in p/ḥ are **p t k ʧ** which are voiced in syllable initial and voiceless in syllable final,

---

[1] Values are given in I.P.A.

[2] In this analysis words with *daş/taş* would be treated as compound words rather than suffixed forms as *daş/taş* is always w prosody, e.g. *arkadaş* ʷVCCV-CVC, *meslektaş* ʸCVCCVC-ʷCVC. However, H prosody operates here as for C_p---- suffixes and the analysis therefore suggests that this is a transitional stage of a word being used as a suffix.

[3] This applies to all base final V structures. See p. 176.

[4] Where there is a long vowel in Base final, represented in the orthography by vowel + ğ, e.g. *dağ* [dɑ:] *tuğ* [tu:] *iğ* [i:], Base final structure is treated as (C)VC because the integrating prosodies at the junction of Base final and Suffix initial are the same as for Base final C, and not as for base final V. This structure will fit into the k system of Base final C. *dağ* [dɑ:] is a monosyllable with the structure CVC. Here ğ represents what is known to have been a voiced velar plosive in an earlier stage of the Turkish language. The vowel is long only in syllable final position, i.e. in absolute final and pre-consonantal position, e.g. *dağ* [dɑ:] *dağda* [dɑ:'da] but short in pre-vocalic position, with a voiced transition from the first vowel to the next, e.g. *dağı* [dɑ'ɨ] The phonetic exponents of Base final C in this CVC structure are therefore vowel length in syllable final and voiced glide in syllable initial position. In rapid colloquial (which is not being dealt with here) the forms *dağı* and *dağa* may be pronounced as one syllable [dɑ:] making no difference between the three forms *dağ*, *dağa*, and *dağı*.

Some loanwords of Arabic origin having a long vowel in Turkish where the Arabic had ع غ or ء are similarly treated as having CVC structure. Here the phonetic exponents of base final C are long vowel in syllable final and glottal stop in syllable initial, e.g. :—
cami [ʤɑ:mi:] (Redhouse's *Turkish dictionary*, London, 1880, gives خامع) CVCVC̣ and *camii* [ʤɑ:mi:ʔi] CVCV-ÇV *menşe* [mĕnʃɛ:] (Redhouse gives منشأ) CVCCVC̣ and *menşei* [mĕnʃɛ:ʔi] CVCCV-ÇV.

[5] Base final C is underlined to show its position in syllable initial and syllable final.

e.g. *dipler* CV$\underline{C}_{ph}$–CVC, *dibi* CV–$\underline{C}_{ph}$V, *kulaklar* CVCV$\underline{C}_{ph}$–CVC, *kulağı* [1] CVCV–$\underline{C}_{ph}$V, *kanatlar* CVCV$\underline{C}_{ph}$–CVC, *kanadı* CVCV–$\underline{C}_{ph}$V, *pabuçlar* CVCV$\underline{C}_{ph}$–CVC, *pabucu* CVCV–$\underline{C}_{ph}$V.

f system. h and ẖ sub-systems are similarly set up for the f system. There are four terms in the f/h sub-system, values **f s ʃ h** which are voiceless in syllable initial and syllable final position, e.g. *raflar* CV$\underline{C}_{fh}$–CVC, *rafı* CV–$\underline{C}_{fh}$V, *taslar* CV$\underline{C}_{fh}$–CVC, *tası* CV–$\underline{C}_{fh}$V, *taşlar* CV$\underline{C}_{fh}$–CVC, *taşı* CV–$\underline{C}_{fh}$V, *şahlar* CV$\underline{C}_{fh}$–CVC, *şahı* CV–$\underline{C}_{fh}$V. There are three terms in the f/ẖ sub-system, values **f s ʃ** which may be voiceless or voiced in syllable absolute final, but are voiced in final (pre-consonantal position) and in syllable initial, e.g. *evler* V$\underline{C}_{fh}$–CVC, *evi* V–$\underline{C}_{fh}$V, *tuzluk* CV$\underline{C}_{fh}$–CVC, *tuzu* CV–$\underline{C}_{fh}$V, *garajlar* CVCV$\underline{C}_{fh}$–CVC, *garajı* CVCV–$\underline{C}_{fh}$V.

k system. ẖ only. This is a five term system, values **y r l m n**, voiced in syllable initial and syllable final (pre-consonantal) and voiceless or voiced in syllable absolute final, e.g. *günler* CV$\underline{C}_{k}$–CVC, *günü* CV–$\underline{C}_{k}$V, *şeyler* CV$\underline{C}_{k}$–CVC, *şeyi* CV–$\underline{C}_{k}$V, *kardan* CV$\underline{C}_{k}$–CVC, *karı* CV–$\underline{C}_{k}$V, *kollar* CV$\underline{C}_{k}$–CVC, *kolum* CV–$\underline{C}_{k}$VC, *hamamda* CVCV$\underline{C}_{k}$–CV, *hamamı* CVCV–C_{k}V.

The phonetic exponents of H prosody are absence of voice at the junction of suffix initial and base final C when the systems of base final C are p/h, p/ẖ and f/h, and voice when base final C systems are k and f/ẖ and when base final is V.

H
$$\overbrace{\text{----V}/C_{p/k/f} \qquad C_{p}\text{----}}$$

Exx. *uncu* $\overset{o}{\text{w}}_{1}C_{k}$–$C_{p}$1   *topçu* $\overset{o}{\text{w}}C\alpha C_{ph}$–$C_{p}$1   *babacığım* $\overset{o}{\text{w}}C\alpha C\alpha$–$C_{p}$1C1C

unda $\overset{o}{\text{w}}_{1}C_{k}$–$C_{p}\alpha$ *taşta* $\overset{o}{\text{w}}C\alpha C_{fh}$–$C_{p}\alpha$ *evcik* $\overset{o}{\text{y}}\alpha C_{fh}$–$C_{p}$1C

eşekçik [2] $\overset{o}{\text{y}}\alpha C\alpha C_{ph}$–$C_{p}$1C

---

[1] When the terms for p/ẖ are ʸ/ʷk, there is voicelessness and plosion in syllable final position and voice with absence of plosion in syllable initial, unless a nasal precedes. In a **y** prosody word, there is a palatal glide and in a **w** prosody word, there is a velar glide (with no friction), both glides being represented in the orthography by *ğ*.

e.g. *kulakta* ʷCVCV$\underline{C}$-CV   *kulağı* ʷCVCV-$\underline{C}$V
      köpekte ʸCVCV$\underline{C}$-CV   *köpeği* ʸCVCV-$\underline{C}$V
      denkte ʸCVC$\underline{C}$-CV   *dengi* ʸCVC-$\underline{C}$V

These glides are the phonetic exponents of one of the four terms of the Base final p/ẖ sub-system and are therefore C in the structure.

[2] Structures with base final C_p with the value **k** may have no phonetic exponent for base final C in the form with suffix *-cik*, e.g. *eşekçik* or *eşecik*, structure VCV$\underline{C}$-CVC.

This prosodic treatment of the phonetic features of voicelessness and voice at the junction of base final and suffix initial is economical as it is not necessary to have voiced and voiceless alternances of initial plosive and affricate suffixes.

J prosody. J prosody is an expression of word structure base plus V initial suffix, excluding suffixes with the structures $VC_{r/n}$ (for which see below) and VC^n (for which see pp. 586–7). Words with the following suffixes are examples of such structure : accusative, dative.

A two term system is set up for suffix initial V, α and ı. Structures set up for base final are C and V.[1]

$$J$$
$$\overbrace{\text{------C/V} \quad \text{V-----}}$$

With base final V, the phonetic exponent of J prosody is yotization at the junction of base and suffix. With base final C, there is no phonetic exponent, e.g. :—

$$babayı \quad \overset{o}{w}CαCα\text{-}ı \quad sütü \quad \overset{o}{y}C_1C\text{-}ı$$

It may at first sight seem pointless to recognize a prosody which has no phonetic exponent in a particular structure, but the reason for doing so becomes clear when it is seen that there are forms of words whose written and spoken forms are identical but whose structures at the phonological and grammatical levels are different.[2]

Variant forms with *y* are not postulated nor is it necessary to set up *n* variants.[3]

S prosody. S prosody is an expression of word structure base plus $VC_{r/n}$. There are only two forms as examples of such structure, those with the 3rd per. sg. possessive suffix [4] for which the structure VC_n is set up, and the distributive suffix, for which the structure VC_r is set up. V has a two term system α and ı, α combining with r final and ı with n final. Base final structures are C and V.

$$S$$
$$\overbrace{\text{-----C/V} \quad VC_{r/n}}$$

With base final V, the phonetic exponent of S prosody is sibilance, palato-alveolar with suffix structure VC_r and post alveolar with suffix structure VC_n. With base final C there is no phonetic exponent.[5]

In the structure VC_n, C is dental nasal in syllable initial and syllable final, except in absolute final, when there is no exponent for C.

Exx.   *altışar* $\overset{o}{w}αCC_1\text{-}αC_r$ *dörder* $\overset{o}{y}CαCC\text{-}αC_r$

            babası $\overset{o}{w}CαCα\text{-}ıC_n$ *sütü* $\overset{o}{y}C_1C\text{-}ıC_n$

---

[1] Systems for C are not given unless relevant.

[2] See pp. 184–5 for examples of such forms.

[3] See S prosody above.

[4] 3rd per. *plur.* possessive suffix *-ları* is analysed into plur. suffix *-lar* which comes under Z prosody on p. 183, and 3rd per. sg. poss. suffix VC_n.

[5] There is an exception to this, *yarımşar*, $CVCVC\text{-}VC_r$, i.e. the exponent is sibilance with base final C.

With the treatment of VC_n as a C final structure instead of V final, there are no variant n forms for the accus., loc., abl., gen., and dat. case suffixes,[1] e.g. :—

J   S   J

akşamı VCCVC-V   *babasını* $CVCV-VC_n-V$

and similarly the prosody is H in such structure with C_p---- suffix, as with other C final structures, e.g. :—

H   S H

akşamdan $VCCVC_k-C_pVC$ *babasından* $CVCV-VC_{n(k)}-C_pVC$ [2]

ϑ *prosody.* ϑ prosody is an expression of word structure base plus consonant initial suffix when the system for suffix initial C is nasal, i.e. C_n----- [3] where C has a two term nasal system, values **m** and **n**. Words with the following suffixes are examples of such structure : 2nd per. sg. and plur. poss., 1st per. sg. and plur. poss., *-msi*, *-mtrak*, *-nci*. Structures set up for base final are C and V.

ϑ

$\overbrace{\qquad\qquad}$

----C/V C_n----

With base final C, the phonetic exponent of ϑ is syllabicity characterized by closeness with $y/w/o/\varrho$ prosodies, i.e. with whichever prosodies are operating in the word. There is no phonetic exponent with base final V.

Exx. *atımız* ${}^{\overset{o}{w}}\alpha C\text{-}C_n\imath C$ *babamız* ${}^{\overset{o}{w}}C\alpha C\alpha\text{-}C_n\imath C$ *altıncı* ${}^{\overset{o}{}}\alpha CC\imath\text{-}C_nC\imath$

      kızın ${}^{\overset{o}{w}}C\imath C\text{-}C_n$ *odan* ${}^{\overset{o}{w}}\alpha C\alpha\text{-}C_n$ *beşinci* ${}^{\overset{o}{y}}C\alpha C\text{-}C_nC\imath$

This treatment makes it unnecessary to consider the vowel in this type of suffix as ' dropping out ' after a base final V, or alternatively, as a vowel being ' inserted ' after base final C.

---

[1] The pronominal forms *bu, şu, o, kendi,* and the suffix *-ki* are similarly treated as C final structures, with a 1 term system for C, dental nasal in all positions except absolute final, when there is no phonetic exponent, e.g. *bunu* CV-CV, *bunlar* CVC-CVC, but *bu* CVC. *Burada, şurada,* etc., are treated as compound words, as *bu, şu* have their absolute final forms. This analysis agrees with the history of the Turkish language. The treatment of these pronominals as having base final C structure instead of the customary base final V structure has the same advantage as for the 3rd per. sg. poss. suffix in that no *n* variants have to be set up. *su* ' water ' is the only noun which has up to the present been considered irregular ; that is because of its form *suyu* instead of the expected *susu* for 3rd per. sg. poss., and the form *suyun* instead of the expected *sunun* for gen. suffix (see p. 183). Here there is no reason for it to be considered irregular, as it is treated as a base final C structure. The phonetic exponent of base final C is a palatal glide in syllable initial but there is no phonetic exponent in syllable final position, e.g. *suyun* CV-CVC, *sular* CVC-CVC. Cf. Uzbek *cyb* [**suw**] ' water ', also CVC structure, where the phonetic exponent of base final C is bilabial frictionless continuant in syllable initial and syllable final.

[2] As final C of VC_n is a nasal, it is classed as a continuant and comes under the k sub-system. See p. 178.

[3] Not to be confused with C_n in the structure VC_n, where C_n is suffix final and has no phonetic exponent in absolute final position.

It is important not to confuse Ə prosody with the dissyllabic base structure CVCəC, which has also hitherto been treated as ' dropping' a vowel in some of its suffixed forms, viz. with suffixes with V initial. In the base structure CVCəC, the second C and the third C are continuants. The phonetic exponent of the syllabic (ə) is close vowel with $y/w/o/\varrho$ prosodies, e.g. :—

burun ^{w}C₁CəC,[1] *beyin* ^y_oCɑCəC, *alın* ^w_oɑCəC, *oğul* ^w_oɑCəC.[2]

When the syllabic structure is such that the first C of the group is final in the syllable, and the second C is initial in the following syllable, there is no phonetic exponent for ə, e.g. *burnu* CV-Cə-CV but *burundan* CV-CəC-CVC. *Burnu* is different from e.g. *türkü* which has the syllabic structure CVC-CV aₙd *türkten* CVCC-CVC.

Some loanwords in Turkish, mostly of Arabic origin, in which the 2nd and 3rd Cs of the base are continuants, fit into the same pattern, e.g. :—

	şehirden	CVCəC-CVC	*şehri*	CVCə-CV
	isimden	VCəC-CVC	*ismi*	VCə-CV
	kasırdan	CVCəC-CVC	*kasrı*	CVCə-CV
	nefisten	CVCəC-CVC	*nefsi*	CVCə-CV
	nesilden	CVCəC-CVC	*nesli*	CVCə-CV
and	*filimden*	CVCəC-CVC	*filmi*	CVCə-CV[3]

Similarly some loanwords, mostly of West European origin, which have initial CC structure, in Turkish have the structure əCC--- or CəC---, e.g. :—

istim ' steam ' əC-CVC

sipor or *ispor* ' sport ' Cə-CVC or əC-CVC

The structure of words like *sipor* may be ^{y}CəʷCVC [si'por] or ^{w}CəCVC si'por], i.e. the syllabic is not necessarily w prosody with a w prosody word and in this way is different from the V system.

N prosody. N prosody is an expression of word structure base plus suffix VCⁿ. In the suffix structure VCⁿ[4] ı is the only term in the V system and C is a nasaļ system, phonetic exponent dental nasal except in y prosody

---

[1] The phonetic exponents of ı and ə here are the same, i.e. close, back, rounded vowel.

[2] The phonetic exponents of the first C are voiced frictionless glide in syllable initial position, *oğul* [o'ul], and vowel length in syllable final position, *oğlu* [oː'lu]. Cf. *dağ, dağı,* etc., on p. 178, n. 4.

[3] Note also words like *rükünden* CVCəC-CVC, *rüknü* CVCə-CV, where the second C of the base is a plosive, and *vakit* CVCəC, *vakti* CVCə-CV, where both are plosives, which have the same syllabic structure as the examples given above. Loanwords like *sarp, fevk, zamk*, where the 2nd C of the base is a continuant and the 3rd C is a plosive have similar structure to native Turkish words (see pp. 174–5), i.e. CVCC. In words of Arabic origin having final CC structure, where the Cs are homorganic, the second C has no phonetic exponent in syllable final position, e.g. *hissi* CVC-ÇV, *histen* CVCÇ-CVC, *sırrı* CVC-ÇV, *sırdan* CVCÇ-CVC, *muhikki* CVCVC-ÇV, *muhikten* CVCVÇ-CVC, *muhilli* CVCVC-ÇV, *muhilden* CVCVÇC-CVC, *gammı* CVC-ÇV, *gamdan* CVCÇ-CVC, *hakkı* CVC-ÇV, *haktan* CVCÇ-CVC.

[4] In this structure Cⁿ is always in absolute final position and is different from Cₙ in the structure VCₙ. See p. 181, n. 3.

structures with bilabial base initial in the pronominal class, where the phonetic exponent is bilabial nasal, e.g. *benim* $CVC\text{-}VC^n$, *bizim* $CVC\text{-}VC^n$. Structures set up for base final are C and V.

$$\overbrace{\text{-----C/V} \qquad VC^n}^{N}$$

With base final V the phonetic exponent of N prosody is dental nasality ; with base final C there is no phonetic exponent.

Exx.   *babamın* $\overset{\circ}{w}C\alpha C\alpha\text{-}{}_1C^n$ *atın* $\overset{\circ}{w}\alpha C\text{-}{}_1C^n$

Words with the genitive suffix are examples of this structure.

Z prosody. Z prosody is an expression of the structure base plus consonant initial suffix where C initial is a three term system, values l, m, and s, i.e. $C_{l/m/s}\text{----}$. Words with the following suffixes are examples of such structure : *-lar, -li, -lik, -siz, -si,* interrog. *mi*.[1] Structures for base final are C and V.

$$\overbrace{\text{-----C/V} \qquad C_{l/m/s}\text{----}}^{Z}$$

There is no phonetic exponent of Z prosody with base final C or V except the 'negative' one of absence of the exponents of the other five prosodies, H, J, Ə, N and S.

Exx.   *kediler* $\overset{\circ}{9}C\alpha C_1\text{-}C\alpha C$ *kalaylı* $\overset{\circ}{w}C\alpha C\alpha C\text{-}C_1$ *kuruşluk* $\overset{\circ}{w}C_1C_1C\text{-}C_1C$

       kalaysız $\overset{\circ}{w}C\alpha C\alpha C\text{-}C_1C$ *kalay mı* $\overset{\circ}{w}C\alpha C\alpha C\text{-}C_1$ *çocuksu* $\overset{\circ}{w}C\alpha C_1C\text{-}C_1$

In the analysis dealing with H prosody [2] the phonetic exponents of p/ḥ were given as voicelessness in syllable final and voice in syllable initial position. Plosive ' p ' systems and non-plosive ' p ' systems may be set up for base final C, with h and ḥ sub-systems for the p system. In structures where base final p/ḥ is in syllable initial, i.e. structures with J, Ə, N, and S prosodies, the phonetic exponent of p/ḥ is voice. In structures where base final p/ḥ is in syllable final position, i.e. structures with H and Z prosodies, the phonetic exponent of p/ḥ is voicelessness. Therefore a further prosody ' v ' may be set up in structures where p/ḥ is a term in the base final C system. The phonetic exponents of v prosody are voice in structures with J, Ə, N, and S prosodies and voicelessness in structures with H and Z prosodies, e.g. :—

Jv	Sv	Əv
pabucu $CVCVC_{ph}\text{-}V$	*pabucu* $CVCVC_{ph}\text{-}VC_n$	*pabucum* $CVCVC_{ph}\text{-}C_n$

---

[1] The post-position *ile* does not come under this group. Its spoken forms, i.e. *-la/-le, -yla/-yle,* permit it to be treated as a suffix. In that event, another prosody, ' i ' has to be set up to cover its junction with base final. Suffix structure is C_1V. The phonetic exponent of i prosody with base final V will be yotization, e.g. *usturayla* $VCCVC\underline{V}\text{-}C_1V$ and with base final C there will be no exponent, e.g. *vapurla* $CVCV\underline{C}\text{-}C_1V$.

[2] See pp. 178–9.

$$\overset{\text{Hv}}{pabuçtan\ CVCVC_{p\underline{h}}-C_p VC}\qquad \overset{\text{Zv}}{pabuçlar\ CVCVC_{p\underline{h}}-CVC}\qquad \overset{\text{Nv}}{pabucun\ CVCVC_{p\underline{h}}-VC^n}$$

v prosody is an expression of word structure base and suffix only where base final is p/ḫ but this is no reason for not setting up a **v** prosody, as the phonetic features of voicelessness and voice can be related not only to syllabic structure but also to the different types of junction of base and suffix.

The ' operation ' of the syllabic in the base structure (C)VCəC may similarly be set up as a prosody ' ə ', whose phonetic exponent in structures with H and Z prosodies is close vowel with $y/w/o/\varrho$ prosodies and in structures with J, Ə, N, and S prosodies, absence of syllabicity of base final CəC, e.g. :—

$$\overset{\text{Hə}}{burundan\ CVCəC_k-C_pVC}\qquad \overset{\text{Zə}}{burunluk\ CVCəC-CVC}\qquad \overset{\text{Jə}}{burnu\ CVCəC-V}$$

$$\overset{\text{Sə}}{burnu\ CVCəC-VC_n}\qquad \overset{\text{Əə}}{burnum\ CVCəC-C_n}\qquad \overset{\text{Nə}}{burnun\ CVCəC-VC^n}$$

The main features of the analysis given are :—

(1) That various phonetic features of the word are related to word structure by the prosodic approach instead of being given as sets of segmental unit lengths. This gives greater clarity and economy and ' variant ' forms and ' alternances ' become unnecessary.

(2) Structures are stated in terms of the elements of structure of which the three principals are consonant, vowel, and prosody. Systems for C and V are set up where relevant. By the nature of this analysis an overall system is not applicable.

(3) Words different at the phonological and grammatical levels but identical at the phonetic level and in written form are shown to have different structures, i.e. the analysis at the phonological level is made in order to clarify the grammatical statement. A few examples of such words are listed below.

$$\overset{\text{J}}{atı\ acc.\ VC-V}\qquad \overset{\text{S}}{atı\ 3rd\ per.\ sg.\ poss.\ VC-VC_n}$$

$$\overset{\text{Ə}}{atın\ 2nd\ per.\ sg.\ poss.\ VC-C_n}\qquad \overset{\text{N}}{atın\ gen.\ VC-VC^n}$$

$$\overset{\text{Ə\ J}}{atını\ 2nd\ per.\ sg.\ poss.\ +\ acc.\ VC-C_n-V}\qquad atını\ 3rd\ per.\ poss.\ sg.\ +\ acc.$$

$$\overset{\text{S\ J}}{VC-VC_n-V}$$

$$\overset{\text{Ə\ H}}{atından\ 2nd\ per.\ sg.\ poss.\ +\ abl.\ VC-C_n-C_pVC}\qquad atından\ 3rd\ per.\ poss.$$

$$\overset{\text{S\ H}}{sg.\ +\ abl.\ VC-VC_{n(k)}-C_pVC}$$

$$\overset{\text{Z\ J}}{atları\ pl.\ +\ acc.\ VC-CVC-V}\qquad atları\ pl.\ +\ 3rd\ per.\ sg.\ poss.\ =\ 3rd\ per.\ poss.$$

$$\overset{\text{Z\ S}}{pl.\ VC-CVC-VC_n}$$

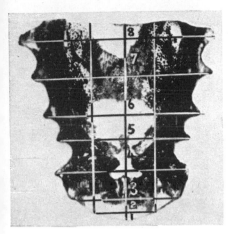

1. *kül*

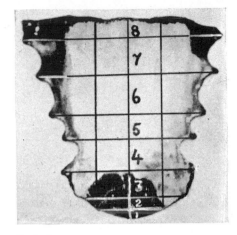

2. *kul*

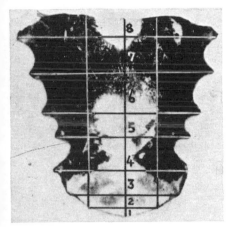

3. *gir*

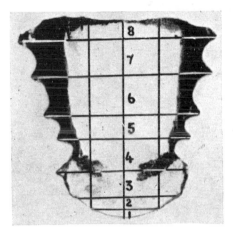

4. *kır*

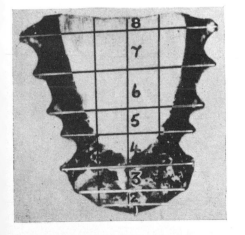

5. *ün*

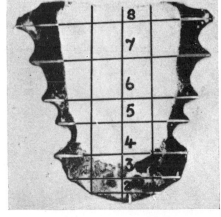

6. *un*

PLATE I

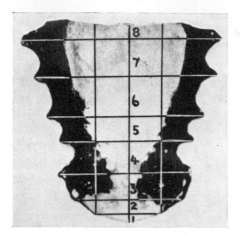
7. *üz*

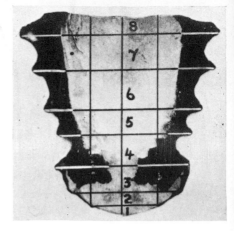
8. *uz*

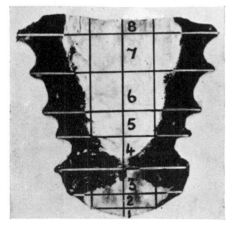
9. *üç*

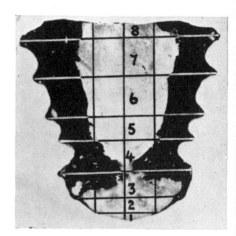
10. *uç*

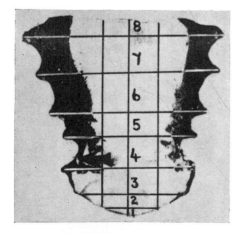
11. *işi*

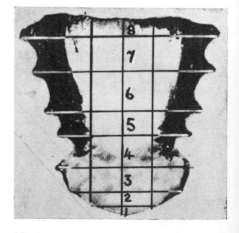
12. *kışı*

PLATE II

ə J
atına 2nd per. sg. poss. + dat. VC–C$_n$–V   *atına* 3rd per. sg. poss. + dat.
S   J
VC–VC$_n$–V

Appendix

An extensive palatographic study was made of words with front vowels and words with back vowels and it was observed that the articulation of consonants varied, those with front vowels having a different articulation from those with back vowels. A few palatograms are illustrated.[1] Pairs of words were selected to show the difference in the articulation of consonants with front and with back vowels. The amount that can be shown on a palatogram is necessarily limited and words have to be selected which have non-interfering articulations.[2] Six pairs of words are shown. Odd numbers are palatograms of words with palatal articulation (y prosody words) and even numbers are palatograms of words with non-palatal articulation (w prosody words). The palatograms are described with reference to the Palatogram Figure given below.[2]

The Palatogram Figure [3]

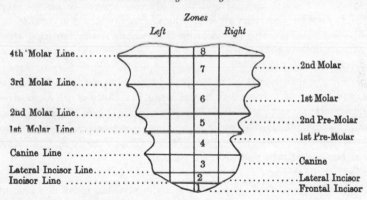

Zones

Left   Right

4th 'Molar Line......... | 8
7 |.........2nd Molar
3rd Molar Line..........
6 |...........1st Molar
2nd Molar Line...........
5 |..........2nd Pre-Molar
1st Molar Line ....
4 |.............1st Pre-Molar
Canine Line ....
3 |...........Canine
Lateral Incisor Line...........
Incisor Line .... | 2 |.............Lateral Incisor
1 |.................Frontal Incisor

1. *kül* [cyl̪]   2. *kul* [kul̪]

The black areas show where contact was made by the tongue during the articulation of the words.

---

[1] These palatograms were made by Yıldız Serpen, a native speaker of the Istanbul dialect. It is a pleasure to acknowledge her participation in this rather arduous work. Her willingness and enthusiasm greatly contributed to its success.

[2] For the technique of palatography see J. R. Firth, ' Word-palatograms and articulation ', *BSOAS*, XII, 3 and 4, 1948, 857–64, and J. R. Firth and H. J. F. Adam, ' Improved techniques in palatography and kymography ', *BSOAS*, XIII, 3, 1950, 771–4.

[3] I am pleased to acknowledge the assistance with the technical side of the palatographic work given by Mr. H. J. F. Adam, Chief Technician at SOAS, who also drew the Palatogram Figure.

In *kül* the only zones left untouched are zone 8, left zone, i.e. the area between the median line and the line marked ' left ' on the Palatogram Figure, and right zone, i.e. the area between the median line and the line marked ' right ', and a small area in the post-palatal zone (7) left and right zones. Also the left and right zones of part of the mid-palatal zone (6) and nearly the whole of the prepalatal zone (5) and part of the post-alveolar zone (4) left and right zones, and a small area in the alveolar zone (3), and most of the left and right zones of the denti-alveolar zone (2), and the whole of the dental zone (1).

In *kul* there is by contrast very little tongue contact. The contact for *k* in zone 8 is a thin wipe-off behind the 4th molar line right across the palate, and there is some contact in the left and right alveolar zones, i.e. the areas to the left and the right of the left zone and right zone, of the post-palatal zone (7), and a slight contact in the left alveolar zone of the mid-palatal zone (6). The contact for *l* extends from the dental (1) through the denti-alveolar (2) to the alveolar zone (3), and extends from the right zone to the left zone and slightly into the left alveolar zone.

3. *gir* [ɟiɾ].   4. *kır* [kɨr]

The contact for *g* is similar to the contact for *k* in *kül* above. The contact in the post-alveolar zone (4) extends slightly into the alveolar zone (3), more particularly in the left alveolar and right alveolar zones. In *kır* the contact in the left alveolar and right alveolar zones is narrow and the contact in the post-alveolar zone (4) is also very narrow. The contact extends into the alveolar zone (3) only in the right and left zones.

5. *ün* [yɲ].   6. *un* [un]

In *ün* the contact in the left alveolar and right alveolar zones is wider than in *un*, and the contact extends from the dental (1), through the denti-alveolar (2) and alveolar (3) and partly into the post alveolar (4) zone. In *un* the contact in the left and right alveolar zones is much narrower and the contact extends from the dental (1), through the denti-alveolar (2) and partly into the alveolar (3) zone but not into the post-alveolar zone (4).

7. *üz* [yʒ]   8. *uz* [uz]

The contact in the left alveolar and right alveolar zones is wider in *üz* than in *uz*. The contact in *üz* in the right zone and right alveolar zone of the alveolar zone (3) extends slightly beyond the lateral incisor line into the denti-alveolar zone (2), and in the left alveolar zone and left zone comes further forward to the lateral incisor line than in the corresponding zones in *uz*. In *uz*, at no point does the contact in the right and right alveolar zones and left and left alveolar zones go beyond the lateral incisor line.

9. *üç* [ytʃ].   10. *uç* [utʃ]

The contact in the alveolar zone (3) in *üç* extends further forward to the canine line than in *uç*. The contact in the left alveolar and right alveolar zones is greater in *uç* than in *üç*.

11. *işi* [iʃi].   12. *kışı* [kɨʃɨ]

In *işi* there is contact in the post-alveolar zone (4) which extends slightly into the alveolar zone (3) in the left alveolar zone and also a certain amount into the left zone. In the right alveolar zone, the contact also extends slightly into the alveolar zone (3) but does not extend into the right zone. In *kışı* there is no contact in the alveolar zone (3) and the contact in the post-alveolar zone (4) only extends to just beyond half way to the canine line. The contact in the left alveolar zone of the post-alveolar zone (4) extends very slightly into the left zone in *kışı* and the contact in the right alveolar zone extends very slightly into the right zone.

12
ASPECTS OF PROSODIC ANALYSIS

By R. H. ROBINS

The object of this paper is to give some account and illustration of what would seem to be certain of the general principles of Prosodic Analysis, as being developed among the group of linguists working in London in association with.Professor J. R. Firth. Prosodic analysis falls under the general rubric of phonology, and this in turn comes within the compass of descriptive linguistics.

The modern era of general and descriptive linguistics may perhaps be said to begin with the great Swiss scholar Ferdinand de Saussure, whose lectures, published postumously in 1916 (*Cours de linguistique générale*, Paris, 1949 (4th edition)), more than any one other factor served to broaden the academic study of language from its nineteenth-century preoccupation with the comparative and historical aspect, and to establish as well as christen the discipline of synchronic linguistics. In establishing synchronic linguistics de Saussure did much to inaugurate the application of structural analysis to language, which is emphasized by almost all schools of linguistics today.

Many of the main features of structural linguistics, on which the literature is now very extensive, can be traced back to de Saussure, whose ideas were developed on different lines by the Prague school and by Hjelmslev; cf. especially Karl Bühler, ' Das Strukturmodell der Sprache ', *TCLP*, 6 (1936), 3–12 ; Ernst A. Cassirer, ' Structuralism in modern linguistics ', *Word*, 1 (1945), 99–120 ; Louis Hjelmslev, ' The structural analysis of language ', *Studia linguistica*, 1 (1947), 69–78 ; *Prolegomena to a theory of language* (Tr. Whitfield, as Supplement to *IJAL*, 19/1 (1953), 13–17).

In developing the structural approach to language, de Saussure drew attention to the two dimensions that must be taken into account in linguistic analysis, the syntagmatic and the associative, in his own terms (*Cours*, pp. 170–5) Rapports Syntagmatiques and Rapports Associatifs, the former referring to the relations obtaining between elements in parallel to the stream of speech (' in praesentia '), the letter to the relations (' in absentia ') between different elements in the language that are associated in some way with the items at various points in stretches of speech. This latter set of relations was more appropriately designated Paradigmatic by Hjelmslev (*Actes du quatrième congrès international de linguistes*, 1936, p. 140), thereby avoiding the latent psychologism of de Saussure's term.

In connection with these two sets of relations, syntagmatic and paradigmatic, it is desirable to keep apart on the same lines the terms *Structure* and *System*, so often used almost interchangeably, and to employ *structure* and its

Source : R. H. Robins, ' Aspects of prosodic analysis ', *Proceedings of the University of Durham Philosophical Society*, I, Series B (Arts), No. 1 (1957), 1–12. Reprinted by permission of the University of Durham Philosophical Society and the author.

derivatives (*structural*, etc.) to refer to the syntagmatic relations and pieces in parallel with stretches of utterance in a language, and to reserve *system* and its derivatives (*systemic*, etc.) for the paradigms of comparable and contrastive elements relevant to the various places in structures (see further · Robins (1953b), p. 109, Allen (1954), p. 556. Thus syllables, words, and sentences constitute structures, and the relations between and within them are structural relations ; the familiar vowel triangles and quadrilaterals of languages, and sets of consonants or consonant clusters applicable to particular places in syllables or words are examples of phonological systems, and the word classes (parts of speech) of a language and its sets of inflectional categories are grammatical systems.

During the period in which de Saussure's thought was making its impact on linguistics, the synchronic study of phonology was expressing itself in the development of the phoneme theory, or, as we might better put it from the standpoint of today, the various phoneme theories. The dominance of the phoneme concept on phonology at the present time may be seen in the array of phoneme derived terms currently in use, particularly in the writings of American linguists (phonemic, allophone, phonemicize, rephonemicize, etc.).

The origin of the phoneme as a linguistic concept must be seen in the search for economical ' phonetic transcriptions ' of the type of Sweet's Broad Romic and Daniel Jones's Broad Transcription [cf. Henry Sweet, *Handbook of phonetics* (Oxford, 1877), 100–8, 182–3 ; Daniel Jones, *Outline of English phonetics*, 6th edition (Cambridge, 1947), 48–51]. Since these early days different interpretations and theoretical developments have made such growth that the need has been felt to formulate explicit statements of principle in regard to phonemic analysis ; one may instance in particular Trubetskoy's ' Grundzüge der Phonologie ', *TCLP*, 7 (1939) (tr. Cantineau, Paris, 1949) ; Bloch's ' A set of postulates for phonemic analysis ', *Lg.*, 24 (1948), 3–46 ; Daniel Jones's *The phoneme : its nature and use* (Cambridge, 1950) ; and the all too neglected monograph by W. Freeman Twaddell, *On defining the phoneme*, Language Monograph 16 (1935).

During the development of the phoneme theories, considerable discussion took place on the status of the phoneme as an analytical term, on the classical lines of the philosophical disputes between realists, conceptualists, and nominalists. According to the realist view espoused by Jones and others [cf. Jones, ' Concrete and abstract sounds ', *Proc. 3rd Int. Cong. Phon. Sci.* (1936), 1–7], the phoneme has actual existence as an ' abstract sound ' or structural entity in the language to which it belongs ; on the conceptualist view, favoured by Trubetzkoy for a time [cf. ' La Phonologie actuelle ', *Psychologie du langage* (Paris, 1933), 227–46 ; ' Zur Allgemeinen Theorie der Phonologischen Vokalsysteme ', *TCLP*, 1 (1929), 39–67. But note his later views, *Principes de phonologie* (tr. Cantineau), 41–6], the phoneme is a mental entity or conception as against the sound, which is a physiological and acoustic entity. The nominalist attitude, in contrast to both the above viewpoints, is that the phoneme, like any other element of scientific analysis, is no more than an appropriate term or operational fiction, with which to handle the mass of observations and to make orderly statements about the gross data, in the case of phonetics, the sounds of a language (cf. Twaddell, op. cit., 33–6).

It might be said that this controversy is of no concern to linguists as such ; but it has a relevance to linguistic work, not as an aspect of philosophical thinking, but as one of method and attitude to linguistic science. In a fairly recent statement of the realist position, Pike writes (*Phonemics*, Ann Arbor, 1947, pp. 57–8) : ' It is assumed in this volume that *phonemes exist as structural entities or relationships*, and that *our analytical purpose is to find and symbolize them*. This implies that there is only one accurate phonemic analysis of any one set of data ' (author's italics). This says in effect that phonemes exist in some way in languages apart from the work of the analyst, who is finding an existing structure or system lying behind the phenomena of utterance, and that this structure or system is organized in phonemes, which the linguist must discover and in his description and symbolism represent as accurately as he can.

Methodologically there is much to be said for the nominalist point of view. Such an attitude, which has been somewhat flippantly labelled ' hocus-pocus ' in contrast to the ' God's truth ' or realist position (cf. Fred W. Householder in *IJAL*, 18 (1952), pp. 260–8) does not imply any levity towards language as an object of study, nor any scientific irresponsibility or disregard of the need for the most meticulous observation and painstaking analysis that is possible. All that adherents of this view of the subject would claim is that existence or reality are not properly predicable of anything other than the actual phenomena or data under observation. Terms and concepts used in analysis are in the nature of a set of words, and no more, employed by the analyst to talk about his data, and in so talking to make summary statements and analyses which account for and explain not only the data from which they are made, but also further data from the same field, in the case of the linguist, from the same language. Phonemes, like all other technical terms in linguistics, take their place as part of the linguist's ' language about language ', and no more than that. In linguistics we are, in fact, putting language to an unfamiliar and relatively uncomfortable task, that of talking about itself. To summarize, one may quote Firth ' Personality and language in society ', *Sociological review*, 42 (1950), p. 42) : ' In the most general terms we study language as part of the social process, and what we may call the systematics of phonetics and phonology, of grammatical categories or of semantics, are ordered schematic constructs, frames of reference, a sort of scaffolding for the handling of events. . . . Such constructs have no ontological status and we do not project them as having being or existence. They are neither immanent nor transcendent, but just language turned back on itself '.

The attitude summed up here is relevant to the purpose of this paper. If the terms and categories employed by the linguist are, as it were, imposed on the language in the process of analysis, it follows that linguistic structures and systems must likewise be thought of not as pre-existing or discoverable in any literal sense, but rather as the product of the linguist in working over his material. No one analysis, or mode of analysis, is the only one accurate or sacroscant, but any account of the language, in any terms, is an adequate statement and analysis, provided that, and to the extent to which, it comprehensively and economically explains what is heard (and read) in the language, and ' renews connection ' with further experience of it. Questions of truth and falsity of ' what is there ' and ' what is not there ', only arise on the view here set out at the level of the barest phonetic observation and recording, before any analysis has taken place.

The last few paragraphs may seem like an unnecessary methodological digression, but it is necessary to make it clear that in developing phonological analysis on prosodic lines there is no suggestion that phonemic analysis is wrong, invalid, or untrue. In terms of the general theory of linguistic analysis just outlined, such statements have no meaning. Nor is it suggested that phonemic analysis is inapplicable or unhelpful.

It is, however, legitimate to claim that from its origin the phoneme concept has been primarily tied to transcription, the representation of a language in terms of its phonic material by means of discrete and consecutive letters or symbols on paper (cf. the sub-title of Pike's book *Phonemics, A technique for reducing languages to writing*), and that in consequence of this, phoneme theories have necessarily concentrated on minimal contrast in identical environment, emphasizing the paradigmatic aspect of phonological relationships at the expense of the syntagmatic or structural aspect (in the narrower sense of *structural* referred to at the beginning of this paper). Where a language is unwritten, or where the orthography is far from adequate as a key to pronunciation, a phonemic analysis may well be indispensable as the basis of a workable transcription unburdened with the excess of different symbols required in a narrow impressionistically ' accurate ' phonetic transcription. But phonological analysis need not stop at or be based on phonemic transcription.

The aim of prosodic analysis in phonology is not that of transcription or unilinear representation of languages, but rather a phonological analysis in terms which take account not only of paradigmatic relations and contrasts, but also of the equally important syntagmatic relations and functions which are operative in speech. These syntagmatic factors should be systematized and made explicit in phonology, no less than paradigmatic contrasts.

The theory of prosodic analysis was put forward in a paper read to the Philological Society by Firth in 1948, and since then applications of the method there presented and theoretical developments have been undertaken with reference to a variety of individual languages. An attempt will be made here to state the principles of this sort of analysis very briefly and then elaborate them in the light of recent work and with the aid of examples.

Prosodic analysis is, in fact, an abbreviated designation of an analysis that makes use of two types of element, Prosodies and Phonematic Units (cf. Firth (1948), pp. 150–2, Allen (1954), p. 556) ; the latter are not phonemes or phonemic units, and the analysis is carried out in terms other than phonemic. In this analysis, abstractions adequate to a full analysis of the phonological working of the language are made from the phonic data, or the raw material of the actual utterances, and these abstractions fall into the two categories of prosodies and phonematic units. Phonematic units refer to͞those features or aspects of the phonic material which are best regarded as referable to minimal segments, having serial order in relation to each other in structures. In the most general terms such units constitute the consonant and vowel elements or C and V units of a phonological structure. Structures are not, however, completely stated in these terms ; a great part, sometimes the greater part, of the phonic material is referable to prosodies, which are, by definition, of more than one segment in scope or domain of relevance, and may in fact belong to structures of any length, though in practice no prosodies have yet been stated as referring to structures longer than sentences. We may thus speak of syllable prosodies, prosodies of syllable groups, phrase or sentence-part prosodies, and sentence prosodies ; and since grammatically defined elements may also be characterized by prosodic features (cf. Sharp (1954), pp. 168–9) we may have in addition word and morpheme prosodies. A structure will thus be stated as a syntagmatic entity comprising phonematic or segmental units and one or more prosodies belonging to the structure as a whole.

This abstract statement of principle may be illustrated from the application of prosodic analysis to Siamese (Henderson * (1948)), a basically monosyllabic and tonal language with fairly rigid patterns of syllable structure. Phonological analysis of a Siamese sentence involves among others, the following prosodic and phonematic elements :

Sentence Prosody : Intonation ;

Prosodies of Sentence pieces : Length Stress and Tone relations between component syllables ;

Syllable Prosodies : Length, Tone, Stress, Palatalization, Labiovelarization ;

Prosodies of Syllable Parts : Aspiration, Retroflexion, Plosion, Unexploded closure.

Phonematic Consonant and Vowel units, in such classes as Velar, Dental, Bilabial, Nasal, Front, Back, Rounded, Unrounded.

After this very summary and incomplete illustration, more may be said in explanation and justification of the methods of prosodic analysis. Phonemic analysis essentially involves the allotment of all the phonic material that is regarded as relevant to individual segments or segmental phonemes, except for the special case of suprasegmental phonemes which are of limited application (cf. below, p. 198. But a great deal of the phonic material of languages seems clearly to belong to structures longer than single segments, and is very probably so perceived by the native speakers. Broadly speaking this may come about in two ways.

In the first case a feature may be spread or realized phonetically over a structure, such as a syllable, as a whole ; examples of this type of syllable prosody are stress, pitch, and length, nasalization, in languages in which a nasal consonant is always followed by a nasalized vowel and a nasalized vowel is only found after a nasal consonant, and palatalization and velarization, when front or palatally articulated consonants are associated in the syllable with front type vowels and back type consonants with back articulated vowels, as in some Slavonic languages. In languages with ' vowel harmony ' as a feature of word structure, for example Turkish and Hungarian, this is well treated as a prosodic feature of the word as a whole or word prosody ; these word prosodies may be put in such categories as Front, Back, and Lip-rounded, and apply to the words concerned as structures, the articulation of the consonants being determined by the relevant prosodies no less than that of the vowels (cf. Waterson (1956), pp. 578–80). Intonation sequences or ' tunes ' that are associated with sentences or with divisions within sentences (clauses and the like) are stated as prosodies of sentences or of sentence parts. The typical English intonation tunes 1 and 2, as described by Daniel Jones (*Outline*, pp. 258–76), are obvious examples.

Features of the type that have just been instanced can, of course, be analysed phonemically, but in such an analysis there is the risk of misrepresenting or distorting important aspects of the phonic material. Where a feature belongs in ·the manner described above to a syllable (for example) as a whole, this of necessity involves the phonemicist in saying that at one point in the syllable, say the consonant, the distinction between (say) palatalization and non-palatalization is phonemic or relevant [in Prague terms pertinent (cf. Trubetz-koy, *Principles* (tr. Cantineau, p. 34)], while the same feature in the vowel, being a constant concomitant of the consonantal feature, must be relegated to non-significance, non-pertinence, or 'redundancy'. Yet at what point are we to tell, if at any point, that the feature involved is perceived and so functions for the native listener ? It is not of course, implied that linguistic analysis can or should be based on the Sprachgefühl or sentiment linguistique of native speakers ; but it is desirable that the analysis should not be in violent disagreement with it. This may be illustrated from Jones's treatment of the palatalized (soft) and non-palatalized (hard) consonants in Russian (Daniel Jones, *The phoneme*, pp. 50–3, cf. pp. 25–6). Any phonemic analysis of Russian, it would appear, must recognize as phonemic the difference between the two sets of consonants in that language ; this being so, the concomitant differences in the quality of adjacent vowels will necessarily be non-distinctive phonemically. But we are told that the difference between a palatalized and a non-palatalized consonant is in many words easier to recognize by the difference in the adjacent vowel than in the consonant itself. Thus we are involved in listening to the non-distinctive or irrelevant feature in order to catch what is distinctive or relevant. An analysis of palatalization and non-palatalization as syllable prosodies with phonetic realization in the syllable as a whole helps to avoid this rather paradoxical form of statement, though it is obviously necessary to differentiate, by the concept of Focus (cf. Allen (1957), p. 943), or otherwise, palatalized syllables with initial palatalized consonants, those with final palatalized consonants, and those with both.

We must not be slaves to our machines in preference to the observations of the human ear, for which in the first instance speech is given utterance, but it may be relevant to notice that the tracings of the kymograph show scant regard for the phonemic segmentation of each and every phonetic feature that requires phonological notice. In kymograph tracings made of the utterances of a Georgian speaker (Robins (1952), pp. 66, 70 ; see also the kymograph tracings below, Figures 1 and 2) it is clearly shown that the glottalized consonants, p', t', tʃ', k', and q', are followed in the syllable by vowels of a constricted or glottalized tamber, a feature also noticeable in listening. Glottalization in such syllables may be treated as a feature of the syllable and abstracted as a syllable prosody.

The above examples are intended to illustrate the first case of prosodic treatment mentioned earlier, in which prosodies are abstracted as elements of structures in view of the extended realization of a feature therein.

In the second case may be mentioned features which are not realized phonetically over the whole or large part of a structure, but which nevertheless serve to delimit it, wholly or partly, from preceding and following structures, thus entering into syntagmatic relations with what goes before or after in the stream of speech. By virtue of their syntagmatic relations in structures, such features may be treated as prosodies of the structures they help to mark or delimit (cf. Firth (1948), p. 129 ; for examples of prosodies of both types, with respect to monosyllables, see Scott).

Examples of these demarcative prosodies are found in the analysis of Siamese mentioned above. In Siamese, as in some other languages of Southeast Asia, the audible release of stop consonants, or plosion, is confined to syllable initial position, final stop consonants being unexploded. In this language, therefore, plosion serves as a syntagmatic signal of syllable initiality and helps delimit the syllable. So also do aspiration, affrication, and some other articulatory features (Henderson * (1949), pp. 192–3). These are abstracted as prosodies of syllable initiality ; though they may be realized phonetically at one place in the syllable, their relevance extends over the whole structure which they serve to mark off and bind together as a functional unit. In a similar manner features invariably associated with the final place in syllable structures may be abstracted as prosodies of syllable finality.

Obviously phonetic features which in one language are treated as prosodic may not be so treated, or may be so with reference to different structures, in other languages. It is the task of the analyst to decide what and how many prosodic elements and phonematic units he requires, to state the syntagmatic and paradigmatic relations relevant to the phonology of the language as completely, economically, and elegantly as he can.

The grammatical unit referred to as the word, fundamental to the traditional distinction between syntax and morphology, is in many languages marked off in speech, to a greater or lesser extent, by prosodic features of this second type. In English no word in normal speech has more than one full stress. Orthographically hyphenated words like *home-made*, which in certain contexts bear two full stresses, may for that reason be regarded structurally as two words, behaving phonologically like other comparable sequences of two words (cf. ' This parsnip wine is ¹home-¹made/¹well ¹brewed ' and ' This is a ¹home-made/¹well brewed parsnip wine ') and the difference between *greenhouse* and *green house*, *blackbird* and *black bird*, *Maryport* and *Mary Port*, can be at least partially explained in these terms. On the other hand the converse is not true ; in connected discourse many words are not fully stressed, and certain words, such as the definite and indefinite articles, never bear stress in the forms in which they are most frequently found in speech (ð ɔ and ə (n)). In at least two languages, which are quite unrelated, Swahili and Sundanese, full stress is confined in words of more than one syllable to the penultimate syllable (a few exceptions to this rule occur in Sundanese and may be covered by a separate statement (cf. Robins (1953b), pp. 125–6). In these languages, stress, which is a prosody by extension of the syllable which it characterizes, is a prosody by demarcation of the word whose boundaries it helps to delimit. Similar prosodic significance may be assigned to the word-initial stress of Hungarian and Czech.

In some languages particular aspects of consonantal articulation, which would be regarded as allophonic or phonemically irrelevant in a phonemic analysis, exhibit this demarcative function. In English word divisions falling between a final consonant and an initial vowel (e.g. *an ocean*, *an aim*) are, potentially at least, distinguishable from word divisions falling between vowel and consonant (e.g. *a notion*, *a name*). The distinguishing features, which include greater duration and laxer articulation of the word-final consonant as against the tenser and shorter articulation of the word-initial consonant, may be treated as prosodic word markers, and set English off as prosodically different in this respect from French, where the feature of liaison in similar phonetic contexts is no respecter of grammatical word divisions.

Some further examples of the application of prosodic analysis to various languages may serve to illustrate both types of prosody that have been referred to in the preceding paragraphs. (It may be felt that these examples are mostly drawn from relatively little known languages. This should not be taken as implying that prosodic analysis is more readily applicable to such languages than to more familiar ones ; the choice of languages is governed by the fact that the linguists whose work is being described are, or have been, members of the staff of the School of Oriental and African Studies in the University of London, with the consequent concentration of their attention in the main on languages coming within the purview of the School. It is greatly to be hoped that the attention of linguists in Great Britain will progressively be turned to the languages that form the basis of our general educational system.) The well known feature of Sanskrit word structure usually referred to as Cerebralization has been re-examined prosodically (Allen (1951b)). This feature, which concerns the relations between certain retroflex consonants in Sanskrit words, is generally expressed in such terms as these (A. A. Macdonnell, *Sanskrit grammar*, second edition, London, 1911, p. 28) : ' A preceding cerebral ṛ, ṝ, r, ṣ (even though a vowel, a guttural, a labial, y, v, or Anusvāra (a nasal consonantal unit whose precise phonetic value is obscure (cf. Allen (1953a), pp. 39–46)) intervene) changes a dental n (followed by a vowel or n, m, y, v) to cerebral ṇ'. It is an unsuitable metaphor to say that one sound operates at a distance over intervening sounds to exert a force on another sound, and change it from something which in fact it never was (in the words concerned) into something else. It is indeed generally desirable that synchronic description and analysis should as far as possible avoid the use, even metaphorically, of terms and concepts more appropriate to the diachronic study of the history and development of languages and linguistic features (cf. C. F. Hockett, ' Two models of grammatical description ', *Word*, 10 (1954), pp. 210–34).

In the re-examination of retroflexion in Sanskrit, it is suggested that an R-prosody, or prosody of retroflexion, be abstracted from the words concerned as a structural feature. This prosody was no doubt marked by a retroflex articulation not only of the lingually articulated consonants but also of the intervening vowels, though the traditional treatment makes no mention of this. Such a retroflex ' colouring ' of vowels in juxtaposition to retroflex consonants is certainly a feature of many Indian languages today (cf. Allen (1957b), p. 942).

The analysis proposed requires no concept of action at a distance of one sound on another, but simply posits a non-linear, non-segmental feature, retroflexion, as part of the structure of the words, or portions of the words, concerned, realized at all points where it is phonetically possible, that is where the tongue tip is one of the organs of articulation.

Mention has already been made of the relevance of prosodic abstractions in several languages to grammatical units. It is interesting in this connection to see that in more than one language what may appear at first sight as a miscellany of separate phonetic features characterizing a particular grammatical category can all be shown to be the exponents of a single prosodic feature, which thus serves as the marker of a category in the grammar of the language. Such a congruence between the different levels of analysis (cf. Firth, ' The technique of semantics ', *TPS*, 1935, pp. 36–72) of a language, as it operates between speakers, is surely an important desideratum of our linguistic operations. Two examples may be cited from widely separated languages. In Bilin (Palmer (1957)), a language of Eritrea, the morphology of the very complex tense system of the nine verb classes that have been set up for that language may be analysed in terms of a single set of statements involving the prosodies of centrality, frontness, backness, and openness, realized in the consonantal and vocalic articulations of the verb forms concerned. In Sundanese (Robins

(1953a)), two types of verb root are found for nearly all verbs, and these two types are used both by themselves, roughly speaking as active and passive verbs respectively, and as bases for a very large number of derived forms involving prefixation, infixation and suffixation, with extensive functions in the language. The relation between these two verbal roots can be simply stated by showing that the active form is always characterized by an N- prosody, or prosody of nasalization, the precise realization that the N-prosody takes being determined by the phonological structure, involving other prosodic components, of each type of verb.

One may find instances, which future research is likely to multiply, of prosodic treatment bringing into the analysis phonetic features either not noted before or dismissed as phonologically (i.e. phonemically) irrelevant. Examples of the demarcative prosodic function of some ' allophonic ' features have already been given. Fixed place word stress for example, and consonantal features invariably associated with syllable initial or syllable final position, are frequently treated as differentially irrelevant since they are positionally determined, but they are, for just that reason, prosodically relevant and functional. That phonemic analysis may let slip many phonologically relevant features is illustrated from the following observation by Leonard Bloomfield, *Language*, London, 1935 (p. 84) : ' Practical phoneticians sometimes acquire great virtuosity in discriminating and reproducing all manner of strange sounds. In this, to be sure, there lies some danger for linguistic work. Having learned to discriminate many kinds of sounds, the phonetician may turn to some language, new or familiar, and insist upon recording all the distinctions he has learned to discriminate, even when in this language they are non-distinctive and have no bearing whatever '. *Distinctive* in the context of phonemic analysis often means *capable of differentiating one word from another* (cf. Bloomfield, op. cit., pp. 77–8 ; Jones in *TPS*, 1944, pp. 127–32), the implication being that phonetic differences not serving such a purpose are functionally and phonologically irrelevant. This implication is unjustified. In addition to the examples already given we may consider the phonological status and functions of the glottal stop in Sundanese (Robins (1953b)). This is a frequent phonetic component of utterances in the language, and a failure to use it properly may lead to misunderstanding and would certainly mark the speaker as a foreigner ; but it is not a phoneme on a par with the other phonemes that would be set up in a phonemic analysis of the language, and it would not be easy to devise a satisfactory allophonic treatment of its occurrences (though structurally the two are very different, cf. Jones's remarks on the glottal stop in English (*Outline*, pp. 138–9)). The Roman orthography currently in use in Java today for Sundanese, which comes very near to a phonemic transcription, has no symbol for the glottal stop, except in certain, mostly Arabic, loan words, where it is represented by an apostrophe. As a prosodic element, however, the Sundanese glottal stop has several functions in words other than loans, and in various contexts serves as a syntagmatic marker of the junction of syllables, morphemes, words, and clauses.

Between like vowels, syllable division, when not marked by any other consonant, is marked by the glottal stop. Between unlike vowels, not separated by any other consonant, the glottal stop is only found at points corresponding to certain morpheme boundaries within a word, whose morphological structure it thus helps to indicate. A glottal stop between a consonant and a vowel signals either a morpheme boundary or a word boundary ; a glottal stop between a vowel and a consonant, usually in conjunction with other features, signals a clause division within the sentence.

The glottal stop in Sundanese is, in fact, an example of a phonetic feature which should be treated less as a member of a paradigm of consonants than as a marker of certain syntagmatic relations between one structure and another, at both the phonological and grammatical levels. It is the syntagmatiç or structural dimension of language that phonemic analysis may be felt to neglect, or to subordinate to the paradigmatic dimension of overall contrast in identical environment, a lack of balance that prosodic theory and practice attempts to redress.

After the description and illustrations of prosodic analysis that have been given, mention should be made of some relatively recent developments in phonemic theory that partially at least seem to cover the same ground in phonology.

One of the first phonetic features of a strictly non-segmental character to be brought into phonemic analysis was that of pitch, whether in the category of intonation or in the category of tone, in the so-called tone languages (cf. Pike, *Tone languages* (Ann Arbor, 1948), p. 3). In either case pitch phenomena clearly belong to the syllable as a whole, though in transcription pitch is frequently marked over the vowel letter. Pitch (or tone), stress, and sometimes length (as distinct from shortness) are now fairly generally treated (at least in America) as Suprasegmental Phonemes, a self-explanatory and self-justificatory category which would seem at first sight to apply to the same field as syllable prosodies of the first type mentioned above, where the phonetic feature treated prosodically was phonetically realized over the whole syllable (p. 193). The terms *prosodic phoneme*, and *prosodeme* are sometimes used instead of *suprasegmental phoneme*, with no difference in technical meaning.

There are, however, two differences. Firstly, in prosodic analysis any phonetic feature whose realization extended over the whole or greater part of a syllable could be eligible for treatment as a syllable prosody of this type, irrespective of the nature of its articulation. Examples have already been given of nasalization, palatalization, and glottalization, as well as pitch, stress, and length, being prosodically analysed. But suprasegmental phonemic treatment has in practice been confined to these last three phonetic features, and Pike explicitly limits the term *suprasegmental* to ' quantitative characteristics . . . some modification of a sound which does not change the basic quality or shape of its sound waves ' (*Phonemics*, p. 63 ; for a suggestion that other features might be treated suprasegmentally, see G. L. Trager in *Language, culture, and personality*, ed. L. Spier, Menasha, 1941, pp. 131–45), i.e. pitch, stress, and length, and nothing else. Secondly, suprasegmental is simply non-segmental, with the implied domain of the syllable ; a syllable prosody is an abstraction of a specific order in a separate dimension (the syntagmatic), taking its place in a system of prosodies intended to cover the analysis of syntagmatic relations generally, within linguistic structures.

The demarcative aspect of prosodies (see pp. 194–5 , above) is foreshadowed by the Grenzsignale of the Prague school and the Juncture Phonemes of some American linguists. It is certainly the case that the Prague discussion of these junction features (see Trubetzkoy, *Anleitung zu Phonologischen Beschreibungen*, Brno, 1935, pp. 30–2 ; *Principes* (tr. Cantineau), pp. 290–314) was one of the first factors drawing the attention of linguists to the neglected syntagmatic aspect of phonology, but the Prague treatment of them, left where Trubetzkoy left it does not fully exploit the analytic and structural potentialities of these features, and the status of the Grenzsignale, partly phonemic (phonematische) and partly non-phonemic (aphonematische), remains rather in a phonological limbo, as a sort of appendage rather than a fully integrated part of a complete theory.

Structurally similar features to those treated under the category of Grenz-signale by Trubetzkoy are analysed in terms of Juncture Phonemes. It may be said that this aspect of phonemic analysis is somewhat complicated by the involvement of two separate questions : firstly, the phonological analysis of the features and their functions in the language, and secondly, their symboliza-tion in a unilinear transcription. Juncture phonemes, like other phonemes in current theories, are also subject to the general rule that the phonemic analysis and transcription of a phonetic element or feature at any point necessarily implies the same analysis of that feature at all other points in structures, despite the quite different relations that it may contract at different places. Alone among phonemicists, it would seem, Twaddell explicitly challenged the assump-tions that phonological relations were the same throughout all places in the structures of a language, and that the needs of a full phonological analysis and those of an economical transcription could be satisfied with one and the same procedure and with the same basic elements or concepts (*On defining the phoneme*, pp. 54–5. For this reason phonemic analysis may be considered basically ' monosystemic ' (Firth (1948), pp. 127–8)).

Perhaps symptomatic of the unsettled state of juncture analysis in phonemic terms are the wholly contrasting natures of the juncture phonemes of Harris and of Hockett (cf. Zellig S. Harris, *Methods in structural linguistics*, Chicago, 1951, pp. 79–89 ; Charles F. Hockett, ' A manual of phonology ', *IJAL*, 21.4, part 1, 1955, pp. 167–72). For Harris juncture phonemes are zero phonemes, with no phonetic realizatión, put into the analysis to complete the picture, and the border phenomena involved in the analysis are assigned to the allophones of the phonemes in the new environment created by the insertion of the juncture zero phonemes. For Hockett, on the other hand, juncture phonemes are bundles of all the phonetic features, of whatever nature, associated with the boundaries or borders to be analysed.

In general, juncture phonemes tend to be associated with word and morpheme boundaries in American phonemics, just as suprasegmental phonemes are generally confined to the domain of the syllable. In this way junctures have a particular relevance to current American linguistic theory, which holds that grammatical features and grammatical units cannot be used as part of the defining environment of phonemes. (The principal opponent among American linguists to this methodological attitude is Pike ; see his ' Grammatical prerequisites to phonemic analysis ', *Word*, 3, 1947, pp. 155–72, and ' More on grammatical prerequisites ', *Word*, 8, 1952, pp. 106–21.) It is, therefore, highly advantageous if convenient grammatically defined elements, such as word and morpheme, can be for the most part matched by phonemically defined juncture marked stretches of the same length, even though the correlation between the two in a language may not be complete. As has already been said, prosodic analysis sees no objection to the use of analysis at the grammatical level for the stating of contexts in analysis at the phonological level, and prosodies may be abstracted and stated of grammatical elements as well as of more purely phonological elements (p. 192, above ; cf. Palmer (1955), pp. 548–9).

Finally mention should be made of Phonemic Long Components, which are intended as a means of stating syntagmatic relations and structural implications between successive segmental phonemes in stretches of utterance (cf. Harris, *Methods*, pp. 125–49). There are at least three differences between abstractions of this type and the prosodies of prosodic analysis : firstly, abstraction of a component from a phoneme in one environment implies its abstraction from that phoneme in all other environments (op. cit., p. 128) ; secondly, long components are not all associated with specific phonological or grammatical structures ; thirdly, no one phonetic feature can be stated as the mark or exponent of the long component over its domain in the way that prosodies statable of a whole structure are associated with phonetic features exhibited by that structure as a whole (op. cit., p. 129).

The remarks on certain recent developments in phonemic analysis in the last few paragraphs must not be taken as a comprehensive review of contemporary phonemic theories, and still less as a disparagement of the work of other linguists. They are merely intended to help place prosodic analysis in its context of relations with current phonological doctrine and methods elsewhere.

I3

PHONOLOGICAL (PROSODIC) ANALYSIS OF THE NEW CHINESE SYLLABLE (MODERN PEKINGESE)

by M. A. K. Halliday

A. 1. Pekingese is distinguished, from other East Asian languages and (to a lesser extent) from other forms of New Chinese, by the extreme limitation of its syllabic structure. The number of distinct syllables (the syllable here being a phonological unit) employed by a typical Pekingese speaker is within a few of four hundred; with their distribution among the four syllabic tones of the language the number is something over 1,250.[1]

A. 1.1. In terms of traditional Chinese phonology the Pekingese syllable may be considered as consisting of an initial and a final, the final being further subdivided into three parts. If we designate the four parts in general phonetic terms as consonant; semi-vowel, vowel, and nasal consonant or close vowel, the Pekingese syllable then consists of either (i) these four elements or (ii) certain combinations of three or two of these elements, both in the order given. Possibilities of manner and place of articulation for the four elements are then as follows :

(i) (Initial) consonant : Plosive, affricate, fricative, nasal (continuant) or liquid ; labial, labio-dental, dental, alveolar, palato-alveolar or velar ; or zero.

(ii) Semi-vowel : Front spread, back rounded or front rounded ; or zero.

(iii) Vowel : Open [2] ; half open : front spread, central, back rounded or back spread ; close : front spread, back rounded or front rounded ; or apical (sometimes regarded as zero).

(iv) (Final) nasal consonant or close vowel : Nasal consonant : alveolar or velar ; close vowel : front spread or back rounded ; or zero.

---

[1] Certain combinations (i) of tone with initial consonant and (ii) of tone with syllabic type do not occur. Thus for certain syllabic types we are able to set up a three-term tone system. For other combinations of tone and syllable which are absent it is impossible to account systematically.

[2] Five qualities may be recognized (phonemically, variants of the a-phoneme ; in phonetic transcription [ɛ] [æ] [a] [ɑ] [ɔ]).

Source : M. A. K. Halliday, " Phonological (prosodic) analysis of the new Chinese syllable (modern Pekingese) ", *Appendix to Secret history of the Mongols* (1959), 192-204. Reprinted by permission of the author.

A. 1.2. Only a very limited number of the theoretically possible syllabic combinations do in fact occur : the totality of such forms constitutes a phonological system, with the syllable as the unit. Below is given a statement of this system in prosodic terms.[1] The statement is based on phonetic observations, primarily of the speech of Mr. Lien Shihmin [2] but also of that of various speakers, made by myself in Peking in 1947–49. Three points may perhaps be stressed : (i) The statement is made with the syllable as unit : it is not an analysis of speech (contextualized utterance) but of the syllable spoken in isolation. (ii) The aim of the statement is to set up a transcription suitable for the purposes of the present work (that is, for adaptation for use in a descriptive grammar of the " Secret History "). (iii) The statement is offered as one possible method, chosen for simplicity and comprehensiveness, of ordering the material.

A. 2. We may recognize three points or positions in the syllable : these will be represented as C(onsonant) V(owel) F(inal).[3] To C corresponds the combination of articulatory features represented in linear phonetic transcription as (initial) consonant plus semi-vowel ; to V and F those represented as vowel and (final) nasal consonant or semi-vowel respectively. Each position admits of three prosodies as general features of articulation : the y-feature (tongue forward and raised), the w-feature (lips rounded) and the a-feature, with neither of these characteristics.

[1] Actually prosodic-phonemic ; the shorter term points the contrast but may be misleading. For a phonemic analysis of Modern Pekingese, see Lawton M. Hartman, ' The Segmental Phonemes of the Peiping Dialect ', Charles F. Hockett, ' Peiping Phonology ', and Helen Wong, ' Outline of the Mandarin phonetic system '.

[2] Mr. Lien was 33 years old, born and educated in Peking and a university graduate. I am most grateful to him for his interest and assistance in my study of Pekingese phonetics.

[3] An alternative designation would be I(nitial) M(edial) F(inal), by which the positions would be explicitly represented as terms in a successive system. C, V are however preferred as (i) usual in prosodic analysis (F being retained to avoid the ambiguity of C_2 as positional category by the side of $C_2 = (C = $ two-term system)), and (ii) precisely avoiding the implication of succession, since, while certain features of articulation undoubtedly stand to one another in successive relation, others are to be recognized as overlapping and characteristic of the syllable as a whole.

The three positions form a hierarchy such that the direction of prosodic force or determination in the syllable is (i) inwards, rather than outwards ($C\rightarrow$ and $\leftarrow F$, not $\leftarrow V\rightarrow$) and (ii) forwards, rather than backwards ($C\rightarrow$ overcomes $\leftarrow F$) ; the hierarchy in descending order is thus $\dot{C}$ F V. For this reason the prosody of position C may be regarded as the prosodic feature of the syllable as a whole.[1] In this way we arrive at the following statement of possibilities : $\dfrac{y/w/a}{CV_{y/w/a}F_{y/w/a}}$, or, where S = syllabic prosody, $\dfrac{S_3}{CV_3F_3}$.

A. 3. In fact the systems of y- and w-feature syllables are more restricted than is that of neutral syllables. The latter form a seven-term system :

$$\frac{a}{a\,a}\quad\frac{a}{a\,y}\quad\frac{a}{a\,w}\quad\frac{a}{y\,y}\quad\frac{a}{y\,w}\quad\frac{a}{w\,y}\quad\frac{a}{w\,w}$$

which may be summarized as $\dfrac{a}{a\,a}$ plus $\dfrac{a}{a/y/w\ \ y/w}$. The former recognize only four terms each :

$$\frac{y}{a\,a}\quad\frac{y}{a\,y}\quad\frac{y}{a\,w}\quad\frac{y}{w\,w}\,;\quad\frac{w}{a\,a}\quad\frac{w}{a\,y}\quad\frac{w}{a\,w}\quad\frac{w}{y\,y},$$

which may be summarized as $\dfrac{y}{w\,w}$ plus $\dfrac{y}{a\ a/y/a}$; $\dfrac{w}{y\,y}$ plus $\dfrac{w}{a\ a/y/w}$.

Thus (i) if F = a, then V = a ; the type $CV^{y/w}F^a$ does not occur ; (ii) in close syllables (C = y/w), V = $either$ a or the other term in the close system ; the types C^yV^yF, C^wV^wF do not occur ; (iii) in close syllables, a marked prosody in V excludes the other marked prosody in F ; the types $C^{y/w}V^yF^w$ and

---

[1] The backward direction of determination is well seen in the difference in the articulation of V in the syllables sun and suŋ, or in sin and siŋ, where F n, ŋ are y-, w- prosodic respectively. The dominance of $C\rightarrow$ over $\leftarrow F$ is seen in the articulation of open vowel in the following series, where five qualities can be distinguished (ranged from front to back) :—

jian   jan   ja   jaŋ   juaŋ
jia   jua
jiaŋ   juan

$C^{y/w}V^wF^y$ do not exist. So that of a possible 27 syllabic types, 15 occur.[1] These are :

$$\frac{a}{a\,a}\quad\frac{a}{a\,y}\quad\frac{a}{a\,w}\quad\frac{a}{y\,y}\quad\frac{a}{y\,w}\quad\frac{a}{w\,y}\quad\frac{a}{w\,w}\quad\frac{y}{a\,a}\quad\frac{y}{a\,y}\quad\frac{y}{a\,w}\quad\frac{y}{w\,w}\quad\frac{w}{a\,a}\quad\frac{w}{a\,y}\quad\frac{w}{a\,w}\quad\frac{w}{y\,y}$$

A. 3.1. In each syllable type there is a limited number of possibilities in each position. The total possibilities for each position in all syllabic types are as follows :

(i) C :

 Place of articulation (5) :
  L(abial inc. labio-dental) D(ental-alveolar) V(elar R(etro-flex) P(alatal).
 Manner of articulation (5) :
  p(losive) a(ffricate) f(ricative) n(asal) l(iquid)
 Condition of articulation (C = p a f only) (2):
  h (= voiceless ((p a f), aspirate (p a))) o (= unaspirate ((p a f), voiced (f) voiceless (p a))).

(ii) V :

 Level of articulation (3) :
  h(igh) m(id) l(ow).

(iii) F :

 Condition of articulation (F^y, F^w only) (2) :
  o(ral) n(asal).

A. 3.2. The terms in the system of each position for each prosodic type are as follows :

(i) C :

 a-prosodic syllables (26)
 y-prosodic syllables (11)
 w-prosodic syllables (21).

---

[1] Thus the value of the terms a, y, w will be seen to vary. In a-syllables, for example, V^y forms a three-term system and has a different value from V^y in a w-syllable where it forms a two-term system. It is of course represented as V^y in both cases, since the marking of the syllable prosody gives the required information.

(ii) V :

a-prosodic (3)

y-prosodic (1)

w-prosodic (1)

(iii) F :

a-prosodic (1)

y-prosodic (2)

w-prosodic (2)

A. 3.3. These terms, distributed in syllabic types, are as follows :

1. $\dfrac{a}{a\ a}$: $C_{20}V_3$. C = L(except Lfo)DVR

But where C = R(except Rl)Daf there V = V_3

in all other instances V = V_2 (Vml)

except that where C = Rl, there V = V_1 (Vh)

and where C = V, there V = V_1 (Vl).

2. $\dfrac{a}{a\ y/w}$: $C_{19}V_2$. C = L (except Lfo)DVR V = ml.[1]

3. $\dfrac{a}{y\ y/w}$: $C_{19}V_1$. C = L(except Lf)D(except Daf)P.

But where C = Dp, there $^yF = F_1$ (Fo).

4. $\dfrac{a}{w\ y/w}$; $C_{25}V_1$. C = LDVRP

But where C = L(except Lfo)Pnl, there F = F_1 (^{w}Fo).

5. $\dfrac{y}{a\ a}$: $C_{11}V_2$. C = L(except Lf)D(except Daf)F, V = ml.

But where C = LDpPn, V = V_1 (Vm).

6. $\dfrac{y}{a\ y}$; $C_{11}V_1F_1$. C as no. 5, V = 1, F = n.

---

[1] The series C = D(except Dnl)VR, V = m, F = ^{y}Fo, is defective : of thirteen possibilities, seven do not occur, one occurs only as (historically) a fusion of two syllables and the remaining five occur each uniquely (i.e. having only one corresponding lexical unit). Compare CD Vm ^{y}Fn, of which of seven possibilities two do not occur and the remaining five are unique occurrences. The groups CLp Vm ^{w}Fo and CLfh Vl $^{y/w}$Fo are absent.

7. $\dfrac{y}{a\ w}$: $C_{11}V_2$. C, V as no. 5.

But where C = LD, there V F = V_1F_1 (Vl, Fo),
and where C = P and V = m, there F = F_1 (Fo).

8. $\dfrac{y}{w\ w}$: $C_7V_1F_1$. C = DP.[1]

9. $\dfrac{w}{a\ a}$: $C_{21}V_2$. C = LfoDVRP, V = ml.

But where C = DP, V = V_1 (Vm).

10. $\dfrac{w}{a\ y}$: $C_{19}V_2$. C = LfoDVRP (except Pnl), V = ml.

But where C = D, there V = V_1 (Vl)
where C = LVR and V =m, there F = F_1 (Fo).
and where C = P, there V F = V_1 F_1 (Vl, Fo).

11. $\dfrac{w}{a\ w}$: $C_7V_1F_1$. C = LfoVR(except Rfo), V = l, F = n.

12. $\dfrac{w}{y\ y}$: $C_{11}V_1F_1$. C = D(except Dnl)VR(except Rfo).[2]

A. 4. For the purposes of alphabetic transcription it is simpler to distinguish all possibilities in each position regardless

[1] This group might be included under syllabic type $\dfrac{y}{a\ w}$ of which it is a systematic variant: $\dfrac{y}{a\ w}$ syllables CP Vm F have tones 3, 4, $\dfrac{y}{w\ w}$ syllables tones 1, 2. It is true that $\dfrac{y}{a\ w}$: CD Vm F does not occur, whereas $\dfrac{y}{w\ w}$: CD VF does—but this uniquely, in the character diǝu (possibly an archaizing pronunciation ; the regular form may have been (homophonous with) a swearword) (on the uniqueness of archaizing forms, see Demiéville, op. cit., p. 37). Cf. no. 12, $\dfrac{w}{y\ y}$ below.

[2] This group might be included under syllabic type $\dfrac{w}{a\ y}$ of which it is a systematic variant: $\dfrac{w}{a\ y}$ syllables C Vm F have tones 3, 4, $\dfrac{w}{y\ y}$ syllables tones 1, 2. $\dfrac{w}{a\ y}$: CRah Vm F does not occur, while $\dfrac{w}{y\ y}$: CRah V F does ; on the other hand CRfo Vm F occurs as $\dfrac{w}{a\ y}$ and not as $\dfrac{w}{y\ y}$. These two non-occurrences must be regarded as gaps in the system of tone-syllable combinations. Cf. no. 8 above.

of their restricted distribution in given syllabic types. The symbols required may be broken down as follows :

(i) C : 27

L : 5   h/oLp/f (4), Ln (1)

D : 7   h/oDp/a (4), Df (1), Dn (1), Dl (1)

V : 4   h/oVp (2), Vf (1), Vn (1)

R : 5   h/oRa/f (4), Rl (1)

P : 6   h/oPa/f (4), Pn (1), Pl (1).

In addition, syllabic prosody, being abstracted from position C, requires distinct symbolization (which may however be synthetic with C) for the three terms a/y/w.

(ii) V : 5 (including V prosody)

a-prosody : 3   h/m/l

y-prosody : 1

w-prosody : 1

(iii) F : 5 (including F prosody)

a-prosody : 1

y-prosody : 2   o/n

w-prosody : 2   o/n.

A. 5. In the transcription used here as a basis for a transcription of the language of the " Secret History " the following symbols have been employed :

(i) C :

L : h/oLp/f : p b f w		Ln : m
D : h/oDp/a : t d x z	Df : s Dn : n Dl : l	
V : h/oVp : k g	Vf : h Vn : ŋ	
R : h/oRa/f : č j š ř		Rl : Ɪ
P : h/oPa/f : ci ji si yi	Pn : ni Pl : li.[1]	

[1] It is desirable that the symbols of the palatal series should be distinct from those employed in the dental and velar series in Modern Pekingese, while some parallel with the retroflex series may well be maintained. This difficulty is variously overcome in the different transcriptions in current use, most successfully in GR, where however the irregularity of j/ch might well have been avoided. The use of a diacritic for the retroflex series seems justifiable here. It is unfortunate that the limitations of the Roman alphabet impose the use of s in both the dental and the retroflex/palatal series, but no alternative seems to present itself.

Syllabic prosodies :

a-prosody :　unmarked.
y-prosody :　addition of i after C [1]
w-prosody :　addition of u after C.

(ii) V :

a-prosody : h/m/l : (zero)　ə　a
y-prosody :　　　　　i
w-prosody :　　　　　u

(iii) F :

a-prosody :　　　　　(zero)
y-prosody : o/n :　i　n
w-prosody : o/n :　u　ŋ

Notes to the transcription :

(i) In syllables with C = P, i is written once only (that is, the second i, indicating y-prosody of either the syllable or V, is omitted) ; thus ci, cin, cian (not cii, ciin, ciian) etc.

(ii) Syllabic types $\dfrac{y}{w\ w}$ and $\dfrac{w}{y\ y}$ are not recognized in the transcription, such syllables being regarded and transcribed as $\dfrac{y}{a\ w}$ and $\dfrac{w}{a\ y}$ respectively. (Thus the formal ambiguity of $\dfrac{y}{w\ w}$ syllables with those of type $\dfrac{a}{w\ w}$ where C = P, caused by the omission of the second i, does not arise : ($\dfrac{y}{w\ w}$: ciu becomes) $\dfrac{y}{a\ w}$: ciəu, but $\dfrac{a}{w\ w}$: ciu etc.)

(iii) In the articulation of w-prosodic syllables and those with w-prosodic V, where C = P, there is initial lip-rounding ; the combination iu thus represents the complex articulation of y- and w-prosodic features.

---

[1] See notes to transcription below.

(iv) In the articulation of C = Vn (ŋ), Mr. Lien had glottal release.[1] C = Vn only occurs in a-prosodic syllables with a-prosodic V.

(v) In the articulation of C = Rl (̆), there is prothetic retroflex vowel. The only occurrence of this C is in the syllabic type $\frac{a}{a\,a}$. Rl has been included in the C system (as in one Chinese transcription, the New Latinized Script) in preference to that of F because of the more restricted character of the latter.

(vi) In the articulation of V = m, at least four distinct qualities may be noted, determined by the prosodic features of C and F : front spread (in y-syllable with ${}^aF$, in w-syllable with ${}^aF$ where C = P and in a-syllable with ${}^yFo$), central (in a-syllable with ${}^{y/w}Fn$, that with ${}^yF$ being slightly front of that with ${}^wF$), back spread (in a-syllable with ${}^aF$ except where C = L) and back rounded (in w-syllable with ${}^aF$ except where C = P, and in a-syllable with ${}^aF$ where C = L and a-syllable with ${}^wFo$).

A.6. The total syllabary is given in the following table, where syllables enclosed in parentheses are those of unique or irregular occurrence, while empty parentheses indicate gaps in the system.

---

[1] Other speakers velar nasal, others one or the other. The articulation as voiced velar fricative, noted by Karlgren, ' A Mandarin Phonetic Reader in the Pekingese dialect ', who adds " this initial is dropped by many, perhaps most Pekingese ", (p. 8) seems to have died out.

$\dfrac{a}{a}$: V = l m h

	p	b	m	f	t	d	n	s	z	x	l	k	g	h	ŋ	č	j	š	ř
a	pa	ba	ma	fa	ta	da	na	sa	za	xa	la	ka	(ga)	(ha)	ŋa	ča	ja	ša	( )
ǝ	pǝ	bǝ	em	(fǝ)	eṭ	ep	en	es	ez	ex	el	ek	eg	eh	eŋ	eč	ej	eš	ǝř
					eṭ			s	z	x								š	ř / ľ

$\dfrac{a}{ay}$: V = l m

	p	b	m	f	t	d	n	s	z	x	l	k	g	h	ŋ	č	j	š	ř
ai	pai	bai	mai	fai	tai	dai	nai	sai	zai	xai	lai	kai	gai	hai	ŋai	čai	jai	šai	řau
an	pan	ban	man	fan	tan	dan	nan	san	zan	xan	lan	kan	gan	han	ŋan	čan	jan	šan	řan
ei	pei	bei	mei	(fei)	(ṭei)	(dei)	nei	(zei)	(zei)	(nex)	lei	(kei)	(gei)	(hei)	neŋ	( )	(jei)	(šei)	( )
en	pen	ben	men	fen	ten	(nep)	nen	(tes)	(tez)	(nex)	(nep)	ken	gen	hen	neŋ	čen	jen	šen	řeŋ

$\dfrac{a}{aw}$: V = l m

	p	b	m	f	t	d	n	s	z	x	l	k	g	h	ŋ	č	j	š	ř
au	pau	bau	mau	fau	tau	dau	nau	sau	zau	xau	lau	kau	gau	hau	ŋau	čau	jau	šau	řau
aŋ	paŋ	baŋ	maŋ	faŋ	taŋ	daŋ	(naŋ)	saŋ	zaŋ	xaŋ	laŋ	kaŋ	gaŋ	haŋ	(ŋaŋ)	čaŋ	jaŋ	šaŋ	řaŋ
eu	(peu)	(beu)	(meu)	(feu)	(ṭeu)	(deu)	(neu)	nes	nez	nex	leu	keu	geu	heu	(ŋeu)	(čeu)	(jeu)	šeu	(řeu)
eŋ	peŋ	beŋ	meŋ	feŋ	teŋ	deŋ	neŋ	nes	nez	nex	leŋ	keŋ	geŋ	heŋ	ŋeŋ	čeŋ	jeŋ	šeŋ	řeŋ
eq	peq	beq	meq	feq	teq	deq	neq				leq	keq	geq	heq	ŋeq	čeq	jeq	šeq	řeq

$\dfrac{a}{yy}$:

	p	b	m	f	t	d	n	s	z	x	l	k	g	h	ŋ	č	j	š	ř
i	pi	bi	mi		ti	di	ni				li					ci	ji	si	
in	pin	bin	min				(nin)				lin					cin	jin	sin	

$\overline{y\ w}$:

piŋ biŋ miŋ tiŋ diŋ ciŋ jiŋ siŋ yiŋ niŋ liŋ

$\frac{a}{w\ y}$:

wun tun dun xun zun sun (nun) lun kun gun hun čun ǰun šun řun ciun jiun siun yiun

$\frac{a}{w\ w}$:

pu bu fu wu mu tu du xu zu su nu lu ku gu hu ču ǰu šu řu ciu jiu siu yiu niu liu

wuŋ tuŋ duŋ xuŋ zuŋ suŋ nuŋ luŋ kuŋ guŋ huŋ čuŋ ǰuŋ ( ) řuŋ ciuŋ jiuŋ siuŋ yiuŋ

$\frac{y}{a\ a}$: V = l m

cia jia sia yia ( ) (lia)

piə biə miə tiə diə ciə jiə siə yiə niə liə

$\frac{y}{a\ y}$:

pian bian mian tian dian cian jian sian yian nian lian

$\frac{y}{a\ w}$: V = l m

piau biau miau tiau diau ciau jiau siau yiau niau liau

ciaŋ jiaŋ siaŋ yiaŋ niaŋ liaŋ

(miəu) (diəu) ciəu jiəu siəu yiəu niəu liəu

$$\frac{w}{a\ a}\ :\ V = l\ m$$

wua

enua

kua gua hua ( ) ǰua šua (ɣua)

enu ɣuŋ enuŋ čuŋ enuŋ šuŋ ɣuŋ

enua enuŋ ɣuŋ enⱴ enⱴ enⱴ

enx enⱴ enz enx enz enⱴ

ens enz enx enⱴ enɣ

$$\frac{w}{a\ y}\ :\ V = l\ m$$

wuai

kuai guai huai (čuai) (ǰuai) šuai ( )

wuan tuan duan xuan zuan suan nuan luan kuan guan huan čuan ǰuan šuan ɣuan ciuan jiuan siuan yian

iens ienz ienx ienⱴ ienɣ

ienz ienx ienⱴ ienɣ

kuei guei huei čuei ǰuei šuei ɣuei

liuŋ niuŋ niuŋ ɣiuŋ enuŋ siuŋ enuŋ jiuŋ enuŋ cuŋ enⱴ

$$\frac{w}{a\ w}\ :$$

wuaŋ

kuaŋ guaŋ huaŋ čuaŋ ǰuaŋ šuaŋ ( ).[1]

[1] Types $\frac{a}{y\ w}$, $\frac{a}{w\ y}$ might be eliminated, syllables of these types being regarded as $\frac{y}{a\ w}$, $\frac{w}{a\ y}$ respectively : the series piaŋ biaŋ etc. (Fn) would then be paralleled by čiau jiou etc. (Fo), and wuan tuan etc. by wuai tuei etc. I should regard this form of statement as more systematic and therefore preferable in an analysis of the Modern Pekingese syllable made for the purposes of Modern Pekingese alone.

The above (15 − 2 =) 13 syllabic types contain respectively 43, 65, 73, 20, 11, 19, 43, 16, 11, 25, 28, 39 and 7 syllables, making a total syllabary of 400.[1]

14

Some Problems of Segmentation in the Phonological Analysis of Terena

JOHN T. BENDOR-SAMUEL

INTRODUCTION

1.1. SCOPE OF THIS PAPER. That speech, like the State, is one and indivisible is generally recognized, yet linguists agree that the necessities of linguistic analysis demand segmentation. However, there seems to be little agreement as to how such segmentation is to be carried out on the various levels of linguistic analysis and there is as yet no agreement as to whether segmentation on one level of analysis should match segmentation on another level.

The discussion of material which bears upon this fundamental but unresolved problem is therefore likely to be of interest to linguists. It is the purpose of this paper to present some features of the phonological analysis of Terena[1] in which segmentation plays a major role.

In the discussion of these features the more usual phonemic type of segmentation is contrasted with a prosodic type. The former type, with its segmental, junctural, and supra-segmental phonemes can be characterized as VERTICAL segmentation since it is based on a linear, "beads-on-a-string" sequential approach. In contrast to it, segmentation in the prosodic style of analysis can be characterized as HORIZONTAL segmentation since, although there is still much vertical segmentation, there is recognition to a much greater degree of phonetic features which either extend over or have implications over more than one linear segment. This Terena material, it is argued, illustrates that a vertical phonemic type segmentation of these particular features does not present as clear or as neat an analysis as a more horizontal prosodic type segmentation. Furthermore, the more horizontal type segmentation makes it possible to state congruences between the

[1] The Terena Indians, numbering approximately 5000, live in eleven villages in southwestern Mato Grosso, Brazil. Their language is classified as Arawakan; cf. N. A. McQuown's classification in the *American Anthropologist* LVII (1955), pp. 501–570. The data for this paper were gathered from January to April, 1959, while residing at Chacara União, near Miranda, Mato Grosso, working under the auspices of the National Museum of Brazil.

Source: J. T. Bendor-Samuel "Segmentation in the phonological analysis of Terena", *Word*, 16.3 (1960), 348–55. Reprinted by permission of The Linguistic Circle of New York, Inc., and the author.

phonological analysis and the grammatical analysis. These parallelisms are obscured by the vertical type segmentation.

The main section of the article (section 2) deals with the analysis of certain nasal features. These are described phonetically and followed by a full discussion of various phonemic-type treatments. The phonemic treatments of these features are then contrasted with a prosodic-style analysis. The third section of the article discusses the question whether a prosodic analysis of certain other features is desirable. These sections will be preceded by a very brief outline of those elements of the phonological system which impinge upon this problem.

1.2. OUTLINE OF THE TERENA PHONOLOGICAL SYSTEM. The following phonemes result from a phonological analysis of Terena:[2]

stops	p	t	k		fricatives	s	ʃ	h	hy
laterals	l	r			glottal	ʔ			
nasals	m	n			semi-vowels	y	w		
	vowels		i	e	a	o	u		

The stops and fricatives are voiceless and have no sub-members except that *t* has a sub-member *tʰ*, voiceless aspirated alveolar stop, occurring only before *i*. The phonemes *h* and *hy* are grouped with the fricatives for both functional and phonetic reasons. *hy* is considered a true fricative in that there is friction produced with the passage of air through the gap between the blade of the tongue and alveolar area. *h* functions phonologically in the same way as *hy* and *s* and *ʃ*.

Two types of syllable are found, CV and V. There are, apart from the features under discussion in this paper, no consonant clusters and all syllables are open. Vowel clusters occur both within the morpheme and between morphemes when a syllable of CV structure is followed by a V syllable. Long consonants and vowels are found but only in connection with the stress system of the language.

It is against this background that the phonetic features discussed in this paper must be interpreted.

THE NASAL FEATURES OF FIRST PERSON FORMS

2.1. THE NASAL FEATURES. A phonemic analysis of Terena establishes as full phonemes a bilabial nasal and an alveolar nasal. The evidence for this

---

[2] See the phonemic analysis by M. Harden in "Syllable Structure in Terena," *International Journal of American Linguistics* XII (1946), pp. 60–63. The two additional vowel phonemes set up by Miss Harden are accounted for by the *hy* phoneme in this analysis. Otherwise the two analyses are the same.

is clear-cut and obvious, viz.: ¹ima³ 'her husband', ¹ipara 'his gift', ¹ina 'then', ¹iha 'his name', i¹sane 'his field', etc.

However, other nasal features are not so easily interpreted by phonemic procedures. The features in question are nasalized vowels and semi-vowels and the consonantal sequences of nasal followed by stop or fricative, namely: mb, nd, nz, nʒ and ŋg. Phonetically, the non-nasal elements of the nasal consonantal sequences under discussion, i.e. b, d, g, z and ʒ are identical with the stops and fricatives, p, t, k, s and ʃ found elsewhere in Terena except for the voicing. Similarly, the nasalized vowels and semi-vowels have the same qualities as their oral counterparts.

These nasal features are linked grammatically in that they mark the category of first person. They do not occur otherwise except for a very few words almost all of which are clearly words borrowed from Portuguese. The grammatical category of first person is actualized phonetically in the same way irrespective of the word class of the indivdual words. The phonetic actualization is as follows:

(a) the nasalization of all vowels and semi-vowels in the word up to the first stop or fricative. In words without stops or fricatives all vowels and semi-vowels are nasalized, together with

(b) a nasalized consonantal sequence replacing the first stop or fricative in the word as follows: mb replaces p, nd replaces t, ŋg replaces k, nz replaces both s and h and nʒ replaces both ʃ and hy. Examples:

e¹moʔu 'his word'	ẽ¹mõʔũ 'my word'	¹ayo 'his brother'
¹ãỹõ 'my brother'	¹owoku 'his house'	¹õw̃õŋgu 'my house'
¹piho 'he went'	¹mbiho 'I went'	a¹hyaʔaʃo 'he desires'
ã¹nʒaʔaʃo 'I desire'		

2.2. INTERPRETATION AS TWO SEGMENTS. One possibility would be to analyze these nasalized vowels as comprising vowel and nasal consonant. The nasalized vowels and semi-vowels could then be treated as submembers of the vowel and semi-vowel phonemes with their distribution limited, in the case of the vowels, to occurrence immediately preceding this nasal consonant, and in the case of the semi-vowels to occurrence immediately after this nasal consonant. A word such as ãỹõ 'my brother' would then be analyzed as aNyoN, using N as a symbol to distinguish this nasal phoneme from the other nasal phonemes, m and n. Phonetically this interpretation would not be implausible, since there is often a very marked degree of nasalization in such words.

Carrying this type of interpretation one stage further the nasalized consonantal sequences could be analyzed as comprising a naṣal consonant

---

³ All Terena material in this paper is in phonetic and not phonemic transcription.

followed by a voiced stop or fricative. These stops and fricatives could be treated as sub-members of the series of stops and fricatives already established. This nasal consonant might be linked with the *N* already discussed, and in which case *N* would have sub-members, *m* before *p*, *n* before *t*, *s* and *f*, *ŋ* before *k* and *N* before semi-vowels and laterals. This solution would set up one additional phoneme *N* and add sub-members to all vowels, semi-vowels, stops and fricatives. Alternatively, if the *m* of *mb*, the *n* of *nd*, *nz* and *nʒ*, the *ŋ* of *ŋg* and the *N* were not grouped together, the *m* could be assigned to the *m* phoneme occurring elsewhere and the *n* treated similarly, and the *ŋ* treated as a sub-member of *n* occurring only before *k*. There would, thus, be one additional phoneme *N* and submembers added to *n* as well as to all vowels, semi-vowels, stops and fricatives.

Perhaps the chief advantages of this type of analysis lie in the economy of phonemes needed. However, there would be one serious objection. This solution sets up closed syllables and consonant clusters which are wholly alien to the rest of the syllable structure of the language.

Another sequel to this type of analysis would be the necessity, in the case of words in which *h* or *hy* is the first member of the stop-or-fricative series to occur, to set up allomorphs so as to deal with the fact that these words in first person constructions have *h* and *hy* replaced by *nz* and *nʒ* respectively. Thus, for example, a form like ˈahya 'desire' would have an alternate form *aʒa* occurring with the infix -*N*- 'first person' as in ˈaNʒa 'my desire'.

2.3. INTERPRETATION AS ONE SEGMENT. Another possibility would be to analyze the nasal features as single units. There would be set up as full phonemes five nasalized vowels, two nasalized semi-vowels and five nasalized consonants, *mb nd nz nʒ* and *ŋg*. This analysis has certain advantages. It preserves the dominant syllable pattern of the language and does not require the postulation of consonant clusters. Furthermore, from the purely phonetic point of view, word-initial sequences like *mb* sound very much like pre-nasalized stops; the degree of nasalization before the oral release is often very small. Also, when sequences such as iˈwuʔiʃo 'he rides' and iˈwuʔinʒo 'I ride' are compared, the rhythm and length of the last two syllables of these words are similar. They may be contrasted with iwuˈʔiʃːo in that, apart from the difference in stress, there is a very marked difference of length in the last two syllables. It is very noticeable that these nasal consonantal sequences function like single consonants and not like long consonants.

The chief disadvantage of this analysis is that it adds twelve full phonemes to the stock of phonemes and this may well be regarded as cumbersome.

At the grammatical level this solution would make it necessary to handle the first person as a series of phoneme replacements, which is also rather cumbersome.

2.4. OTHER PHONEMIC INTERPRETATIONS. It would, of course, be possible to mix these two types of interpretation. For example, nasalized vowels could be considered full phonemes while nasalized consonantal sequences could be regarded as sequences of two phonemes.

Another possibility would be to interpret the nasalized vowels and semi-vowels as vowel or semi-vowel plus suprasegmental phoneme of nasalization. This could be harmonized with the interpretation of the consonantal sequences as nasal plus consonant. In effect this would seem to be another type of interpretation as two segments. Some type of componential analysis would provide yet another interpretation of these nasal features. These types of analysis could be considered partially horizontal and it is interesting to compare them with the prosodic type analysis below.

2.5. PROSODIC INTERPRETATION. Another approach to the problem is from a rather different theoretical standpoint, that of prosodic analysis.[4] Instead of making the statement of the phonology by means of phonemes, two other linguistic units are employed, namely the phonematic unit and the prosody. Phonetic features which either extend over or have implications over more than one place in the syllable are allotted to specific prosodies, while other phonetic data are assigned to phonematic units. Prosodies may be stated for the syllable or the word.

This type of approach might set up the following phonematic units for the statement of this particular problem: stops *p*, *t* and *k*, fricatives *s*, *f*, *h* and *hy*, semi-vowels *w* and *y* and vowels *i*, *e*, *a*, *o* and *u*, and a prosody of nasalization which could be termed *n*-prosody. This prosody would probably be regarded as a prosody of the word rather than the syllable since its phonetic exponents[5] may extend beyond any one syllable. The phonetic exponents of this *n*-prosody would be as follows:

(a) Lowering of the velum throughout the word until the first stop or fricative, together with

(b) Vibration of the vocal chords during the articulation of the first stop or fricative, together with

---

[4] For an introduction to the theory of prosodic analysis see J. R. Firth, "Sounds and Prosodies", *Transactions of the Philological Society*, 1948, pp. 127–152; and R. H. Robins, "Aspects of Prosodic Analysis", *Proceedings of the University of Durham Philological Society*, volume I, Series B, No. 1 (1957).

[5] The term "phonetic exponent" is used for the phonetic actualization of the phonological categories.

(c) Narrowing of the opening between the alveolar ridge and tongue, with grooving of the tongue, producing increased friction when *h* or *hy* are the first fricative.

Thus, the word can be said to be marked by a prosody of nasalization which can be symbolized as, for example, in: $\grave{e}^{l}m\ddot{o}\mathcal{P}\ddot{u}^{n}$VCVCV 'my word'.

One advantage of this type of a solution is that the syllabic pattern of the language is preserved and that we are not faced with the necessity to postulate consonant clusters in order to account for the phonetic data. Furthermore, sequences which phonetically share nasalization are merely treated as related exponents of one phonological category.

2.6. COMPARISON OF THE PHONEMIC AND THE PROSODIC TYPE SOLUTIONS. When the various phonemic and prosodic analyses are compared it seems clear that the chief difference between them centers in the way in which segmentation is carried out. What distinguishes all the phonemic analyses is that they all proceed vertically, whereas prosodic analysis is partially vertical and partially horizontal. Take, for example, the word $\tilde{a}\tilde{y}\tilde{o}$ 'my brother'. The phonemic analysis (which interprets the nasal features as a sequence of two phonemes) segments the word into five phonemes: vNcvN. The nasalized vowels and semi-vowels are regarded as sub-members of the vowel and semi-vowel phonemes and the feature of nasalization is thus segmented into five parts. The phonemic analysis thus assigns the nasal features under discussion to three distinct phonemes. In contrast with this, a prosodic analysis, proceeding partially vertically and partially horizontally, considers the nasalized vowel $\tilde{a}$ as the phonetic exponent of the phonematic unit *a* on the one hand and as the (partial) exponent of the *n*-prosody on the other.

The phonemic type analysis has the advantage of a certain over-all simplicity of statement in that all phonetic phenomena are assigned to one type of phonological unit, the phoneme. Segmentation is consistently vertical. This is achieved at the cost of subdividing what can be considered one single phonetic phenomenon. The prosodic type analysis has the advantage of treating the phonetic features of nasalization, which is itself the exponent of one particular grammatical category, the first person, as one feature phonologically. In this case it can therefore be said to give a more integrated analysis of the language as a whole.

THE *y* FEATURE OF SECOND PERSON FORMS

3.1. A PHONEMIC INTERPRETATION. A somewhat similar problem is raised by the phonetic exponents of the grammatical category of second person. In phonemic terms the second person is shown as follows:

(a) All words beginning in any vowel except *i* are prefixed by *y*-. Examples: *o*ˡ*topiko* 'he cut down', *yo*ˡ*topiko* 'you cut down', ˡ*ayo* 'her brother', ˡ*yayo* 'your brother'.

(b) All other words are marked by the following vowel replacements (generally affecting the first vowel of the word): *a* and *o* are replaced by *e*; *u* and *e* are replaced by *i*. If the first vowel of the word is *i* these rules apply to the second vowel; if both the first and the second vowels of the word are *i*, the rules apply to the third vowel, and so on. Examples: *ku*ˡ*rikena* 'his peanut'; *ki*ˡ*rikena* 'your peanut'; ˡ*piho* 'he went', ˡ*pihe* 'you went'.

(c) Occasionally, when the first two or more vowels of the word are *e* (or, less commonly, *u*) all are replaced by *i*. In the case of two-syllable words with both vowels *e*, this is always so. Examples: ˡ*nene* 'his tongue', ˡ*nini* 'your tongue'; ˡ*xerere* 'his side', ˡ*xiriri* 'your side'.

(d) In certain two-syllable words, almost exclusively nouns, instead of the vowel replacement already described, a vowel cluster comprising the replacive vowel followed by the original vowel is found. Examples: ˡ*tuti* 'his head', ˡ*tiuti* 'your head', ˡ*paho* 'his mouth', ˡ*peaho* 'your mouth'.

A further phonetic feature may be mentioned. In the case of vowel initial words prefixed by *y*- the first vowel is found somewhat raised and further front than in other utterances of the word.

There is, of course, no problem in the phonemic analysis of these phenomena. No new phonemes are required; syllable patterns remain unaltered. Nor is it difficult to frame a grammatical statement which would cover the data. However these two statements remain unconnected.

3.2. A PROSODIC INTERPRETATION. All these phonetic exponents of second person have much in common since they all involve some type of fronting and raising. Furthermore not infrequently this fronting and raising extends beyond one linear place in the word. Can, then, a prosodic type analysis be set up so as to give a more integrated statement of these features than the phonemic analysis? Such an analysis could be framed along the following lines.

There is a *y*- prosody with the following phonetic exponents: either,

(a) In the case of all words beginning with a vowel phonematic unit other than *i*, a narrowing of the opening between the tongue and the palate with vibration of the vocal chords, together with slight fronting and raising of the first phonematic unit; or

(b) In the case of all other words except certain two-syllable words, a fronting and raising of the first vowel, except that when that vowel is *i* the second vowel is fronted and raised, etc. This feature of fronting and raising may extend for two or three syllables when the vowel of such syllables is *e* or *u*; or

(c) In the case of certain two-syllable words this fronting and raising is only partial for the first syllable and results in a vowel cluster.

In certain respects this type of analysis is attractive. On the phonological level these various phonetic phenomena, all involving fronting and raising, are grouped together. Then, too, on the grammatical level one category is matched by one parallel phonological feature. There would, in fact, be three word prosodies, *n*, *y* and zero, corresponding to the categories of first, second and third person. All singular words except particles would be marked by one of these three. Such a congruence of the phonological and grammatical categories of the language is particularly interesting and attractive.

However one serious problem is raised. Identical phonetic features would be assigned to different phonological categories, i.e. sometimes to one phonematic unit and prosody and sometimes to another phonematic unit and prosody. For example, the *e* of *ˡyeno* 'you walked' (contrast *ˡyono* 'he walked') would be regarded as the phonetic exponent of both the phonematic unit *o* and the *y* prosody. But the *e* of *ˡyeno* 'his wife' (contrast *ˡyino* 'your wife') would be regarded as the phonetic exponent of the phonematic unit *e* and the zero-prosody. In this way a different analysis would be made of two sounds which are in fact identical. Few linguists would accept such an analysis. At this point the prosodic style analysis would be rejected not on the grounds of the kind of segmentation involved but because it leads to this type of intersection.

SUMMARY

4. The validity of horizontal as well as vertical segmentation seems assured though, doubtless, linguists will differ in their opinions as to when it is most appropriate to segment in these different ways. A prosodic type analysis may at some points give a more integrated account of the phonetic data than a phonemic analysis. Furthermore those whose canons of excellency in linguistic analysis include the desirability of stating the congruences between the grammatical and phonological levels of analysis may well find in the prosodic type analysis a useful tool of descriptive linguistics.

Summer Institute of Linguistics
Santa Ana, California

15

VOWEL HARMONY IN IGBO

By J. CARNOCHAN

In the descriptions of a number of languages spoken in widely different areas of the world, one comes across references to vowel harmony ; in the Efik[1] and Twi[2] languages of West Africa, in Telugu, in Bengali, and in some Turkic languages. One of my colleagues at the School, Mrs. N. Waterson,[3] has drawn my attention to the use of prosodic marks in the writing of Turkic languages as a device for handling vowel harmony. In Kazan and in Kirghiz, writers using the Arabic script for these languages have made use of special diacritics to mark ' fronting ' or ' backing ' in the pronunciation of the word as a whole where it has been found that the normal pointing of the Arabic script is not adequate. Until the late Professor Ida C. Ward turned her attention to the study of Igbo the vowel letters used for writing this language were six, a, e, i, o, ọ and u. J. Spencer[4] said that this was not satisfactory because although rules could be given for the relationship between the vowels of the verb roots and the prefixes and suffixes where four of the letters were concerned, ' no rules can be given for i and u roots, as some take a and others e.' Professor Ward made a fresh phonetic study of Igbo and found it necessary to distinguish eight vowels, not six.[5] She suggested the use of eight vowel letters in the new orthography.

In advocating this new orthography Professor Ward said, ' A further advantage of the eight vowel letters is that a vowel harmony which is essential to Ibo can be shown in writing, as it cannot adequately be indicated in the old. Before the discovery of the eight-vowel system, vowel harmony was only imperfectly understood and in some cases was considered as an apparently arbitrary phenomenon incapable of explanation.'[6] This was a very important step forward in the study of the language and provided a useful spelling convention, but although Professor Ward showed how the rule applied in certain grammatical contexts;[7] the study of vowel harmony remained largely at the word level. The eight vowel letters are arranged and numbered in this way :—

1. i		5. u
2. e		6. ǝ
3. ɛ		7. o
4. a		8. ɔ

[1] See Ida C. Ward, *The phonetic and tonal structure of Efik*, Heffer, 1933, chapter v.
[2] See Ida C. Ward, *The pronunciation of Twi*, Heffer, pp. 6 ff.
[3] See also Natalie Waterson, *Some aspects of the phonology of the nominal forms of the Turkish word*, BSOAS, XVIII, 3, 1956.
[4] J. Spencer, *A first grammar of the Ibo language*, 1901, second edition 1927.
[5] See Ida C. Ward, *An introduction to the Ibo language*, Heffer, 1936, pp. 1 ff.
[6] See Ida C. Ward, *Ibo dialects and the development of a common language*, Heffer, 1941, p. 3.
[7] See *Introduction to the Ibo language*, pp. 2–5.

Source : J. Carnochan, ' Vowel harmony in Igbo ', *African Language Studies* I (1960), 155–163. Reprinted by permission of the School of Oriental and African Studies and the author.

Professor Ward says of them, ' A system of vowel harmony in Ibo requires that the vowels in a word of two or more syllables should be either those numbered with odd ńumbers (above), or those which are numbered with even numbers. Odd and even numbers, with few exceptions, do not occur in one word.' In *The phoneme ; its nature and use*, Professor D. Jones deals briefly with vowel harmony in Igbo and omits to mention the exceptions. He says in section 509 ' The vowels of Igbo fall in fact into two classes, and only vowels belonging to the same class can occur in a given word '. Indeed, there are a good many exceptions ; Professor Ward's text of twenty-two lines ' The Journey and Law of the Tortoise ',[1] for example, has nineteen such items (some being repetitions of the same word), including litara, merela, zitara, eboci, tiya, ecela, zigara and loruru. The fact that vowel harmony could be stated for some words and not for others, and could be stated for some grammatical structures and not for others, suggested that a fresh appraisement of the phenomena would be of value. This present article is based on the pronunciation of Mr. J. O. Iroaganachi, who speaks a central dialect of Igbo, and who was an Assistant at the School for a number of years. The writer has also had the advantage of working with other Igbos, both in London and in Nigeria.

Regularly recurring differences of phonetic detail observed in examples of different grammatical structures preclude the possibility of making an over-all statement for vowel harmony in Igbo and I find it necessary to give a number of separate accounts of this phenomenon. ' Une langue forme un système où tout se tient ' is a principle which can no longer be seriously held in modern linguistics and a polysystemic approach[2] does no more than recognize the complexity of the language under discussion. My attitude towards linguistic analysis derives from the theories and teaching of Professor J. R. Firth, to whose *Collected papers*[3] the reader is referred. Much of what I have to say is at one or other of three levels, grammatical, phonological or phonetic. I hold the view that it is by means of the silent and unpronounceable abstractions of phonology that one can relate the ever changing phonetic detail of the speech stream to the grammatical statement.[4] Elements of structure established at the phonological level are of two kinds, phonematic and prosodic. Vowel harmony in Igbo is a method of considering the relation between vowel qualities in successive syllables in words spoken in isolation, or in examples of selected grammatical constructions. Further research has suggested that more light can be thrown on the analysis of Igbo by regarding this syntagmatic relation in terms of prosodic elements of structure.

I shall illustrate different sorts of relation by using examples of short verbal pieces. As my purpose is to draw attention to the vowels, it is preferable to use the same consonants as far as possible and I have drawn on many of the same examples as Professor Ward. In some cases the vowels are the same from syllable to syllable (see Table I) ; in others the relation is one of the degree of openness[5] or closeness

---

[1] *Idem*, pp. 209–11.

[2] This is seen not only in the different treatment of noun and verb examples (pp. 161–162) compared with those of singular pronoun and verb in Tables II and III, but also in the different phonological treatment of what may be called the same vowel sounds, on the one hand in the verb stems where a V element is established and, on the other hand, in the endings, where a syllabic element (ə) is set up.

[3] J. R. Firth, *Collected papers in linguistics*, 1935–55.

[4] For a different view, see W. S. Allen, *Structure and system in Abaza*, TPS, 1956, p. 145.

[5] See F. R. Palmer, ' *Openness* ' in Tigre : *a problem in prosodic statement*, BSOAS, XVIII, 3, 1956.

of vowel articulation from syllable to syllable (see Table II) ; in yet other cases this is coupled with lip rounding for both syllables, or lack of lip rounding (see Table III).

In Table I the eight examples are of thé same grammatical structure, 1st person singular, Tense 1, Aspect 1. The vowel sound in the second syllable of each example is the same as in the final syllable ; together they constitute one alternance. There are not two separate independent alternances, one in one syllable and a different one in the other. For this reason, I give a phonological formula for them all : mCVrə. In the second syllable I establish a V element of structure and recognize an alternance here of the V elements in a paradigmatic system. In the final syllable, however, I do not recognize a V element, with a separate alternance, since there is no separate alternance. In this syllable I recognize a syllabic : ə. This V-ə phonological notation indicates the interdependence of the syllables and correlates with hearing the same vowel sound in both syllables.

TABLE I

1st pers. sing., Tense 1		Phonological formula mCVrə	
1. m siri	I cooked	2. m sere	I said
3. m sɛrɛ	I quarrelled	4. m sara	I washed
5. m zuru	I stole	6. m zere	I bought
7. m zoro	I hid	8. m zɔrɔ	I got up

Table II sets out the 2nd person singular Tense 1 forms, parallel to those in Table I. In the four examples on the left, the initial syllable is written with the letter i, corresponding in the pronunciation to a close front vowel, with spread

TABLE II

2nd pers. sing. Tense 1		Generalized phonological formula R/L [ICVrə]	
1. i siri	you cooked	2. e sere	you said
3. i sɛrɛ	you quarrelled	4. e sara	you washed
5. i zuru	you stole	6. e zere	you bought
7. i zoro	you hid	8. e zɔrɔ	you got up

lips. In the other four examples, the first syllable is pronounced with a half-close front vowel with spread lips, written here with the letter e.

The initial syllable, the pronoun, in all these eight examples is pronounced with, to use H. Sweet's terminology,[1] a high vowel, the particular degree of closeness correlating with the vowel harmony of the example as a whole. Phonologically, then, I do not propose to distinguish between the [i] and [e] vowel sounds by means of two V elements, but by means of two prosodic elements, R-prosody and .L-prosody, which will take into account certain features of closeness or openness of the other vowel sounds in each example as well. The generalized phonological formula in Table II shows that I am setting up one V elemeñt of structure, with the symbol I, for the initial syllable, the pronoun, whether it is pronounced with a close front vowel or with a half-close front vowel. This difference, which is part of the vowel harmony of the example as a whole, is dealt with by R-prosody where there

---

[1] H. Sweet. *A primer of phonetics*, Clarendon Press, 1890.

is more raising of the tongue for the vowel articulation and L-prosody where there is more lowering. By placing the R or L outside the square brackets, I am indicating that it is an element of structure of the example as a whole.

It is felt to be hardly necessary to give eight examples of the impersonal form, Tense 1 ; two will be sufficient.

    1. ɛ siri it is cooked   2. a sere it is said

The situation here is much the same as for the examples in Table II, the initial syllable, the pronoun, having two pronunciations differing in the degree of raising of the tongue, this distinction being part of the vowel harmony of each example as a whole. The generalized phonological formula for the impersonal examples, Tense 1, is R/L [ACVrə], where A is the low V element (as opposed to I (see Table II), the high V element).

Two examples of the 3rd person singular, Tense 1 form, show a similar relation between degree of raising of the tongue from one example to the other and the vowel harmony within each example.

    1. o siri he cooked   2. ɔ sere he said

Before dealing with the generalized phonological formula here, I would like to give in Table III another set of eight examples, 3rd person singular, Tense 2.

TABLE III

3rd pers. sing. Tense 2		Generalized phonological formula R/L [(A)w (CVA)y/w]	
1. o siɛ	he cooks	2. ɔ sea	he says
3. o tɛɛ	he rubs	4. ɔ saa	he washes
5. o zuo	he steals	6. ɔ zeo	he buys
7. o goo	he buys	8. ɔ bɔɔ	he cuts up

The final vowel sound in each example has a low tongue position, either about half-open (as in examples 1, 3, 5 and 7), or open (in examples 2, 4, 6 and 8). In examples 1, 2, 3 and 4 the vowel sounds are front and this is so not only for the final vowel in each example, but also for the vowel in the preceding syllable. In examples 5, 6, 7 and 8 the final vowels are back and this is so for the preceding vowel in each example also.

Thus frontness of vowel quality and spread or neutral lips, with absence of lip-rounding, are characteristics of siɛ, sea, tɛɛ and saa in examples 1 to 4 and these features are exponents of the y-prosody shown outside the round brackets in the phonological formula. In the same way, exponents of w-prosody in zuo, zeo, goo and bɔɔ are backness of vowel quality and lip-rounding. The inclusion of CVA inside the round brackets indicates that I consider that y- or w-prosody, as the case may be, is an element of structure of the two syllables as a whole. In the pronunciation of the examples, the lip-rounding or the absence of lip-rounding, as the case may be, is as much a part of the consonant articulation as it is of the vowel articulation. I will now give the phonological structure of the eight examples in Table III, but will continue to generalize the C elements, as to go further into detail in this respect is not relevant to my purpose.

    1. o siɛ R[(A)w (CIA)y]   2. ɔ sea L[(A)w (CIA)y]
    3. o tɛɛ R[(A)w (CAA)y]   4. ɔ saa L[(A)w (CAA)y]
    5. o zuo R[(A)w (CIA)w]   6. ɔ zeo L[(A)w (CIA)w]
    7. o goo R[(A)w (CAA)w]   8. ɔ bɔɔ L[(A)w (CAA)w]

It will be seen from these structures that my phonological analysis recognizes two V elements : A, a low V element, and I, a high V element. The rounding or unrounding of the vowel sound in pronunciation is considered together with the rounding or unrounding of the consonant articulation, where there is one, and stated phonologically as a prosody of the syllable or, where appropriate, of the word and symbolized as y or w outside the round brackets. The other dimension of vowel quality, the degree of raising of the tongue, as between close and half close and between half open and open, is considered for the vowel sounds in each example as a whole. In the examples already quoted in this article, the vowel sounds are for any one example, either all close and half open, or all half close and open. Each example is therefore characterized as R, that is, pronounced with the more raised vowel sounds associated with I and A, or as L, that is, pronounced with the more lowered vowel sounds associated with the two V elements.

I will now return to the phonological structure of examples of the 3rd person singular, Tense 1, and compare them with the impersonal examples.

1. Impersonal ɛ siri R[(A)y (CIrə)y]
2. 3rd pers. sg. o siri R[(A)w (CIrə)y]
3. Impersonal a sere L[(A)y (CIrə)y]
4. 3rd pers. sg. ɔ sere L[(A)w (CIrə)y]

Here the difference in pronunciation between the half open front vowel [ɛ] and half open back vowel [o] is treated phonologically as a y/w syllable-prosody alternance. So is the difference between the open front vowel [a] and the open back vowel [ɔ]. The difference between [ɛ] and [a] and between [o] and [ɔ] is linked to the differences between [i] and [e] in both syllables of the verb words siri and sere and in each example treated as a prosody of the whole, in terms of R or L.

The approach that I have used necessitates going beyond what has been regarded in Igbo as ' vowel harmony ', but it enables me to set up relations of a phonological nature between the parts of the examples and so to link the details of pronunciation with the grammatical categories established. The examples discussed so far have been of such a nature that R or L can be stated for each whole example, but there are, of course, many more complex cases and some of these are examined below. The texts pronounced for me by my assistant included some folk stories, from one of which the following is a short extract.

Otu mgbɛ, otu nwanye metara otu nwa. Otu eboce, nwanye a gara yɔrɔ uri ɔ ga-ɛdɛ n'ahe n'eboce ahya. Nwa ya agwa ya ka ɔ yara idɛ, na mgbɛ ɔ yɔrɔ ahya, ya ɛdɛwɛ. Ya akpochiɛ nthe, gwɛɛ uri aɦe, dɛɛ n'ahe. Ya akwakɔtaa abɔ ahya ya, gawa ahya.

' Once upon a time there was a woman who had a daughter. One day, the woman went and gathered some indigo to paint on her body on market day. Her daughter told her that she should postpone this, and should begin to put on the indigo when she returned from market. She paid no attention, ground up the indigo, and painted it on her body. She gathered up her market baskets, and set off for market.'

This short extract illustrates three modifications to the new orthography which are needed to write the central dialect. One is the use of the letter h after a consonant to denote aspiration of the syllable, e.g. in nthe 'ear'. The second is the use of the tilde to denote nasality of the syllable, e.g. in aɦe 'this' (compare ahe 'body'). The third is the use of ɣ instead of the orthographic gh for a voiced velar fricative, e.g. in yoro 'gathered'. In this dialect, gh indicates an aspirated syllable, as in aghe 'a leopard'.

Consideration of the pronunciation of the folk stories by my assistant led to the examination of a number of other similar examples of each grammatical structure covering what I believe to be the full phonological range. For instance, the pronunciation of . . . . metara otu . . . in the first sentence could be approximately shown by [. . . metaro:tu . . .]. There was no phonetic syllable [ra]. This led to an investigation of other examples of the same grammatical structure, Verbal Phrase – Nominal Phrase, Tense 1. In all cases it was found that there was a lengthened duration of the vowel quality of the first syllable of the noun word, as in the example above. Where the last letter of the verb was i or e, there was a palatal feature at the junction, e.g. o siri ane 'she cooked some meat', can be shown as [oʃirja:ne]. Similarly, where the last letter of the verb was u or e, there was lip-rounding at the junction, e.g. o gburu aghe 'he killed the leopard', is shown as [ogburwa:ghe]. It is not possible to say in listening to Igbo connected speech where one word ends and the next begins and certainly in listening to the examples just cited, where phonologically R-prosody is an element of the first part and L-prosody of the last part, it would seem that the first vowel quality to be associated with L-prosody is heard in the pronunciation of the last syllable of the first word, R[(A)w (CI)w] L[w(rA)y (CI)w].

I would next like to consider the Nominal Phrase – Verbal Phrase pieces, Tense 1. There is an intonational feature associated with such structures, which may be regarded as correlating with the category, Tense 1. It is that no matter what is the internal structure of the nominal phrase, whether it is just a noun word, or a noun and pronoun, or of a more complex nature, the syllable immediately preceeding the verb word is either on a low pitch of the voice, or on a pitch falling to low. This is not a feature of ' noun ' as such in the examples I shall give, but a prosodic element of the clause or sentence as a whole, where the clause or sentence includes Tense 1 as a grammatical element. There are other regularly recurring intonational features in other sentences in Igbo which are best considered as correlating with other tenses.

In the examples below, the nominal phrases are all proper names except nwanye 'the woman'.

1. **Oti gburu aghe.** ' Oti killed the leopard.'

Here Oti is the nominal phrase and gburu the verbal phrase. R-prosody is an element of structure of both phrases.

2. **Oti gara ahya.** ' Oti went to market.'

Here R-prosody is an element of the nominal phrase and L-prosody of the verbal phrase, gara.

3. **Nwanye dɛrɛ uri.** ' The woman painted on the indigo.'

L-prosody is an element of the nominal phrase and R-prosody of the verbal phrase, but the L-R structure does not correspond here with the word division. The last vowel of the noun is pronounced with a close front quality, not a half close front quality, and is shown in [ŋwa:ɲidɛru:ri].

4. **Nwanye gara ahya.** ' The woman went to market.'

Here L-prosody is an element of both the nominal phrase nwanye and the verbal phrase gara and the final vowel sound of the noun is half close.

5. **Ogu gburu aghe.** ' Ogu killed the leopard.'

Here R-prosody is an element of both the nominal phrase **Ogu** and the verbal phrase **gburu**, and the final vowel sound of the noun is close.

6. **Ogu gara ahya.** ' Ogu went to market.'

Here R-prosody is an element of the nominal phrase and L-prosody of the verbal phrase. The final vowel sound of the noun is close.

7. **Aghe gburu aghe.** ' Aghe killed the leopard.'

Here L-prosody is an element of the nominal phrase and R-prosody of the verbal phrase, but the final vowel sound of the noun is close, not half close.

8. **Aghe gara ahya.** ' Aghe went to market.'

L-prosody is here an element of both the nominal phrase **Aghe** and the verbal phrase **gara** and the final vowel sound of the noun is half close.

For these eight examples the V element of the final syllable of the nouns **Oti, nwanye, Ogu** and **Aghe** is the high V element, I. R-prosody is stated for **Oti** and for **Ogu** and L for **nwanye** and **Aghe**. The final vowel sound of **Oti** and **Ogu** is close in quality in all four examples in which they occur, whether R is stated for the following verbal phrase, as for **gburu** in examples 1 and 5, or L as for **gara** in examples 2 and 6. But where L-prosody is stated for the nominal phrase, as for **nwanye** and **Aghe**, the case is different. The final vowel sound in these words is half close where the prosody of the following verbal phrase is L, but is close where the prosody of the following verbal phrase is R, as for **dɛrɛ** in example 3 and **gburu** in example 7.

When one turns to examples of the same grammatical structure, but where the final V element of the nominal phrase is the low element A, the matter is more straightforward. I will give eight examples.

1. **Igwɛ dɛrɛ uri**   ' Igwɛ painted the indigo '.
2. **Igwɛ gara ahya**   ' Igwɛ went to market '.
3. **Adha dɛrɛ uri**   ' Adha painted the indigo '.
4. **Adha gara ahya**   ' Adha went to market '.
5. **Ugho dɛrɛ uri**   ' Ugho painted the indigo '.
6. **Ugho gara ahya**   ' Ugho went to market '.
7. **Ɔgɔ dɛrɛ uri**   ' Ɔgɔ painted the indigo '.
8. **Ɔgɔ gara ahya**   ' Ɔgɔ went to market '.

R-prosody is an element of phonological structure for **dɛrɛ** and L-prosody for **gara**. I can detect no difference in quality of the vowel sound of the second syllable in **Igwɛ** in sentence 1 from sentence 2. The vowel sounds of the other nouns **Adha, Ugho** and **Ɔgɔ**, too, seem no different when followed by **dɛrɛ** than when followed by **gara**. In sentences of this structure and where the final V element of the nominal phrase is the low element A, the exponents of R- and L-prosodies are co-extensive with word division. This observation is restricted to the Nominal Phrase – Verbal Phrase piece of the sentence, that is, in the examples given, to the initial noun and the verb that follows.

CONCLUSION

The concept of vowel harmony in Igbo has been based on two sets of four different vowels, without any link being stated between the members of each set. If, perhaps, it cannot be said that too much has been made of the vowels, it is true that too little has been made of the harmony. Phonematic elements of structure are, of course, not to be ignored. It is important to the partial analysis discussed above to state whether the V element is A or I. It is also important to state the grammatical framework within which the phonology is presented. The chief emphasis which the present writer makes, however, is on syntagmatic features, on those unifying elements of structure which can be said to characterize the word or piece as a whole. These features are made abstractions, and stated as R-prosody, and L-prosody, elements of structure of the word or piece, and as y-prosody and w-prosody, elements of structure of the syllable. In the stream of Igbo speech one hears, perhaps within a closely knit grammatical piece, perhaps within a word, vowel qualities in successive syllables that do not come within the ' rules ' of vowel harmony. The rules admittedly apply to the word, but the prosodic approach, by taking account of syntagmatic features and stating some of them in terms of R- and L-prosody, is equipped to deal not only with those structures that fall within the scope of the vowel harmony rules, but also those that fall outside.

16

VOWEL HARMONY IN LHASA TIBETAN [1]:
PROSODIC ANALYSIS APPLIED TO INTERRELATED
VOCALIC FEATURES OF SUCCESSIVE SYLLABLES

By R. K. SPRIGG

I. THE CLOSURE SYSTEM

IN his phonemic analysis of Lhasa Tibetan in *Love songs of the sixth Dalai Lama* Jaw Yuanrenn (Y. R. Chao) notices ' variations ' of some of the phonemes, and ascribes some of these ' variations ' to differences in tempo or to chance : of the phoneme that he writes as ' e ' he says ' 有 時 候 也 變 成 ι, 例 如 10 首 3 句 *khrel gzhung* tʂʻelɕuŋ 讀 作 tʂʻιlɕuŋ ' [it may sometimes change to ι, e.g. in song 10, line 3, *khrel gzhung* tʂʻelɕuŋ is pronounced tʂʻιlɕuŋ] ; of the phoneme ' ɑ ', ' 快 讀 的 時 候 會 變 成 ə, 例 如 4 首 2 句 *lam buhi* lɑmpʻø 讀 作 ləmpø ' [it may change to ə in rapid speech, e.g. in song 4, line 2, *lam buhi* lɑmpʻø is pronounced ləmpø] ; and of the phoneme ' o ', ' 偶 爾 讀 成 u, 例 如 36 首 3 句 *rlung po* luŋpo 讀 作 luŋbu ' [it may occasionally be pronounced u, e.g. in song 36, line 3, *rlung po* luŋpo is pronounced luŋbu] [2] ; but a phonological analysis of the speech of Rinzin Wangpo (*rig-'dzin dbang-po*) (R.), a Lhasa-dialect-speaking Tibetan, overwhelmingly suggests that vowel alternations such as these should be attributed to vowel harmony.[3]

The Lhasa-Tibetan vowel harmony is of the type in which degrees of vowel

---

[1] This article is based on a paper, ' Vowel harmony in Lhasa Tibetan ', read at the twenty-fifth International Congress of Orientalists, Moscow, in August 1960. Vowel harmony was chosen as the subject of this paper as a compliment to the late Professor Georges de Roerich (Ю. Н. Рерих), of the Institute of Peoples of Asia of the Academy of Sciences of the U.S.S.R., with whom its author had discussed this aspect of Tibetan phonology some ten years ago in India.

In the phonological analysis presented in this article, following F. R. Palmer, ' " Openness " in Tigre : a problem in prosodic statement ', *BSOAS*, XVIII, 3, 1956, 561, *vowel* and *consonant*, and their derivatives (vocalic, consonantal), are used as purely phonetic terms ; for phonological units of Syllable structure V and C are used. A particular term in a V system, e.g. A, may have one or more vowels stated as its phonetic exponents. With *vowel* used in this phonetic sense the term vowel harmony refers to a relationship not of structural units but of vocalic, and therefore phonetic, features ; but Lhasa Tibetan is also a vowel-harmony language in the traditional use of this term : ' the peculiar restriction . . . of tolerating only certain combinations of vowels in successive syllables ' (L. Bloomfield, *Language*, London, 1950, 181). There is thus a twofold sense in which the title of this article is appropriate to the material presented in it.

[2] *Love songs of the sixth Dalai Lama Tshangs-ɑ̄byangs=rgya-mtsho*, translated into Chinese and English with notes and introduction by Yu Dawchyuan, and transcribed by Dr. Jaw Yuanrenn (Y. R. Chao) (Academia Sinica, Series A, No. 5, Peiping, 1930), 8–9. I am indebted to my colleague Mr. H. Simon for a translation of the relevant passages.

[3] R. was born and educated in Lhasa. He was employed as Research Assistant by the School of Oriental and African Studies for the period December 1948–September 1949, in London. The material obtained from R. was checked against the utterances of other speakers of the Lhasa dialect in Kalimpong (West Bengal) and in Gyantse (Tsang Province, Tibet) during the session 1949–50.

Source : R. K. Sprigg, ' Vowel harmony in Lhasa Tibetan : prosodic analysis applied to inter-related vocalic features of successive syllables ', *BSOAS*, 24 (1961), 116–138. Reprinted by permission of the School of Oriental and African Studies and the author.

closure are interrelated. These vowel-closure features are treated here as exponents of terms in a prosodic system named, since it has to do with interrelated degrees of vowel closure, the Closure system.[1]

Prosodic analysis, with its emphasis on syntagmatic relations, would seem to be particularly well suited to dealing with interrelated vocalic features of successive syllables [2]; and in order to illustrate the advantages that are claimed for it over other types of phonological analysis, and particularly over phonemic analysis, the account of the Closure system is followed on pages 249–252 below, by a brief comparison with a representative phonemic analysis of the same material.

The Closure system comprises two terms : Close, Open. It is applicable to certain groups of two successive Syllables, which are termed Closure Pieces, i.e. Pieces for which the Closure system is statable.[3] These Closure Pieces may be coextensive with a Word, provided, of course, that it is disyllabic ; but commonly they are contained within a Word, a Word, that is, of three or more Syllables.

The relevant vowel-closure features of the two Syllables comprised in the Piece are treated as features of the Piece as a whole unit, in much the same way as certain other phonetic features, pitch features, for example, and duration features, are ascribed not to individual phonematic units (terms in C and V systems) but to Syllable units and Word units as wholes.

Since the Closure system comprises only the two terms Close and Open, a given example of the Closure Piece must be either an Open Closure Piece (or Open Piece, oP) or a Close Closure Piece (or Close Piece, cP).

A Closure Piece can in all circumstances be identified as Close or as Open through the application to it of phonetic criteria. A particular vocalic feature or set of coarticulated features of either the first or second Syllable of the Piece may be adequate for the purpose of identifying the Piece, and may therefore serve as a phonetic criterion without reference to features of the other Syllable (pp. 243–4) ; or it may be necessary to cite as a phonetic criterion vocalic features drawn from both Syllables of the Piece (pp. 245–6), or even to include intervocalic consonantal features in the criterion (pp. 246–7).

The material presented in this article lends itself to drawing a distinction between phonetic criteria, whose function is to provide grounds for identification, and phonetic exponents, whose function is to substantiate the abstractions made at the phonological level, and to ensure ' renewal of connexion '.[4] The

---

[1] For ' prosodic system ' see J. R. Firth, ' Sounds and prosodies ', *TPS*, 1948, 127–52. Subsequent publications that distinguish prosodic and phonematic categories are listed at *BSOAS*, XIII, 4, 1951, 945, and *BSOAS*, XVII, 1, 1955, 134.

[2] See also Palmer, ' " Openness " ', 561, and J. Carnochan, ' Vowel harmony in Igbo ', *African language studies*, I, 1960, 156.

[3] When used as phonological terms Syllable, Word, Piece, Closure, etc., are distinguished by capital letters.

[4] Palmer, ' " Openness " ', 577.

aim that determines which phonetic features are cited as phonetic criteria of a phonological term (e.g. the Close or the Open term of the Closure System), is thus very different from the aim that determines which features should be stated as exponents of that term, though it may be that the same feature, or set of coarticulated features, or sequence of features, will appear among both exponents and criteria, but where, however, two or more terms of a system have some exponents in common (pp. 243–6), the common features clearly cannot be stated as criteria.

The exponents of the two Terms of the Closure system are stated first ; and the distinction between phonetic exponent and phonetic criterion is then illustrated by listing those features from the statement of exponency that can also serve as criteria, and by supplementing them with other, and especially consonantal, features, wherever identification of the Close or Open term is impossible from the features stated as exponents (pp. 245–6).

A Closure Piece can be classified grammatically, on formal grounds, as of one of five types : (a) Noun ; (b) Noun + Particle ; (c) Adjective + Particle ; (d) Particle + Particle (Verbal) ; (e) Verb + Particle.[1] The following examples of each of these five grammatical types of Closure Piece have been chosen because they clearly show what is taken to be an alternation of exponent for one and the same V term ; but, simply because attention is, for the purposes of exposition, focused on only one Syllable of each Piece rather than on both simultaneously, it must not be overlooked that each of these alternative exponents has a harmonizing degree of vowel closure characterizing the remaining Syllable of its Piece. Thus, in example (i) of section (a), the alternation of half-openness (ε) with half-closeness (e) as exponents of the particular V term of the first Syllable (skad) in both the oP example skad-cha and the cP example skad-bsgyur must not be allowed to obscure the fact that the matching degrees of vowel closure of the second Syllable in each (ə and u respectively) are of equal significance for the Closure system ; but, since it is the alternation in exponency that provides the phonological problem considered in this article, the alternative exponents have nevertheless been abstracted from each Piece, and are symbolized in the right-hand column below.[2]

---

[1] Since the Piece is either coextensive with, or contained in, the Word, it follows that more than one grammatical category can be exemplified in the Word as well as the Piece : the examples given at (b), (c), and (e) below can also serve as examples of Noun-+-Particle, Adjective-+-Particle, and Verb-+-Particle, Words. The examples bzhes-kyi-yod-pas and rgyab-kyi-yin-pas at (d) are also examples of the Verb-+-Particle Word. The examples at (a), on the other hand, exemplify a single grammatical category, the Noun, and are termed Noun Words ; the second Word of the examples at (e, ii), gnang, exemplifies the Verb category only, and is termed a Verb Word.

[2] It has been assumed that it is legitimate to treat a given phonetic feature as available for statement as an exponent of more than one term, whether prosodic or phonematic. In this particular instance it is the feature half-openness (ε) that is shared by the V term of the Syllable skad with the exponent of the Open term of the Closure system, which embraces vowel features of both Syllables of the Piece (ε — ə). For a discussion of whether such an overlap is permissible, see Palmer, ' " Openness " ', 576–7.

(a) Noun

(i)
oP	cɛ:dʑə	*skad-cha*	speech	ɛ [1]
cP	ce:ʈu:	*skad-bsgyur*	interpreter	e

(ii)
oP	phø:gɛ:	*bod-skad*	Tibetan	ɛ
cP	dʈu:ge:	*'brug-skad*	Bhutanese	e

(b) Noun + Particle

oP	pha:lə	*bar-la*	between	ɑ
cP	phʌ:tə	*bar-du*	as far as	ʌ

(c) Adjective + Particle

oP	$\begin{cases} \text{maŋbɵ} \\ \text{maŋgɵ} \end{cases}$	*mang-po(go)* [2]	many	a
cP	dʑʌŋgɵ	*ljang-khu*	green	ʌ

(d) Particle + Particle (Verbal)

oP	-jøβɛ:	*bzhes-kyi-yod-pas*	do you eat	ɛ
cP	-jumbe:	*rgyab-kyi-yin-pas*	shall you print	e

(e) Verb + Particle

(i)
oP	$\begin{cases} \text{tɕa:bə-} \\ \text{tɕaɹɐ-} \end{cases}$	*bcar-ba(ra)-yin*	I visited	ɑ/a
cP	tɕʌ:gə-	*bcar-gyi-yin*	I shall visit	ʌ

(ii)
oP	nɑ̃:ɹo:	*gnang-rog gnang* [3]	please give	ɔ
cP	lɐbɹo:	*bslabs-rog gnang*	please teach	o

The above examples have been included in order to demonstrate that the Closure system is applicable to Pieces of any of the above five types ; but this article is from this point onwards restricted to a detailed study of type (e), Verb + Particle.

II. VERB-+-PARTICLE TYPE OF PIECE

For the sake of clarity in exposition it is again useful to take first examples of Pieces that contain Syllables whose V terms have alternative exponents, like *bcar* (ɑ/a and ʌ) and *rog* (ɔ and o) already illustrated, though by no means all Verb Syllables and Particle Syllables have V terms with alternative exponents.[4] Only four, in fact, of the Particle Syllables that can be exemplified

[1] The phonetic transcriptions, in the International Phonetic Alphabet but with the addition of v̄ (non-velarity), show no more detail than is relevant to this account of vowel harmony ; pitch features, therefore, have not been symbolized.

[2] The forms in round brackets are phonetic spellings, put immediately after the regular orthographic form with which they alternate.

[3] The spaces between words, for which there is no warrant in Tibetan orthography, reflect the delimitation of words on formal (phonological and grammatical) grounds.

[4] Referring to Syllables by their phonological formulae rather than by their orthographic forms, though theoretically preferable, would in practice result in unjustified complications, and would pose more questions than it answered, as may be seen from a comparison of *gnang*, the orthographic form of one of the Verb Syllables, with its phonological formula ^{1}ŋ^{ə}vNV, in which the indices indicate the prosodic classification of this syllable as Tone One (of a two-term Tone system, referable to the Word), as ŋ (of an eight-term Quality system, referable to a monosyllabic or disyllabic Piece), as ə (of a three-term Labiality system, referable to a monosyllabic Piece), and as v (of a three-term Glottality system, referable to a monosyllabic Piece), while N specifies the N term of a C phonematic system, and V the sole member of a V system.

in the Verb-+-Particle type of Piece have V terms with alternative exponents : the Interrogative-Particle Syllable *pas/gas/ngas/ras* (henceforth referred to simply as *pas*), the Nominalizing-Particle Syllable *rog*, the Dubitative-Particle Syllable *a*, and the Negative-Particle *ma/mi*.[1] The Closure system is illustrated first from Pieces containing *pas* and *rog*.

A. Pieces containing *pas* and *rog*

First to be considered are examples of the Close Piece. In each of these the V term of the second Syllable (*pas* or *rog*) has its closer degree of vowel closure, half-closeness (e and o respectively) ; and a harmonizing vowel-closure feature characterizes the first Syllable, the Verb Syllable. This harmonizing vowel-closure feature is either (i) closeness (i, ι, y, ɷ, u) or (ii) half-closeness combined with backness and spreading (ɤ) :

(i) { first Syll. : closeness (i ι y ɷ u) [2]
{ second Syll. : half-closeness (e o)

rang bod-pa yin-'pas (**jumbe:**)	are you a Tibetan
gzigs-mo gzigs-pas (**si:be:**)	did you see the show
gsol-ja zhus-pas (**ɕy:be:**)	did you serve tea
khang-pa 'di skyid-po 'dug-gas (**dɷge:**)	is it an attractive house
rgyal-rtse-la bzhugs-pas (**ɕu:be:**)	did you stay in Gyantse
zin-rog (**sinɹo:**) *gnang*	please catch it
dris-rog (**ʈʂi:ɹo:**) *gnang*	please ask him
phul-rog (**phy:ɹo:**) *gnang*	please offer it
zhu-rog (**ɕɷɹo:**) *gnang*	please request
blug-rog (**lu:ɹo:**) *gnang*	please pour it out

(ii) { first Syll. : half-closeness + backness + spreading (ɤ)
{ second Syll. : half-closeness (e o)

khang-pa mdas ge rgyab-pas (**jɤbe:**)	have you swept this room [3]
bod-skad bslabs-rog (**lɤbɹo:**) *gnang*	please teach (me) Tibetan

In the Open Piece, on the other hand, the V terms of the second Syllables *pas* and *rog* have as exponent their more open degree of vowel closure : half-openness (ɛ and ɔ respectively) ; and harmonizing vowel-closure features,

---

[1] Prosodic analysis enables two or more phonetic forms, which may or may not be differently symbolized in the orthography, to be associated with a single phonological structure, as exponents of units of that structure under differing prosodic conditions. Thus, the phonetic forms **be:, ge:, ɳe:,** and **ɹe:** can all be stated as exponents of the C and the V terms of the Interrogative-Particle Syllable variously symbolized in Tibetan orthography as *pas, gas, ngas,* or *ras*, in one or other of eight prosodically differing types of disyllabic Piece covering not only the relevant features of this Particle Syllable, but also associated features of the preceding (Verb) Syllable. Similar prosodic statements provide grounds for associating various phonetic forms with the single phonological structures symbolized as *ma/mi* (Negative Particle), *pa/ba/ga/nga/ra* (Past Particle, Nominalizing Particle), and *gi/gyi/kyi*.

[2] The term closeness is used for a tongue position higher than half-close ; it therefore includes ι and ɷ.

[3] C. A. Bell, *Grammar of colloquial Tibetan*, Alipore, 1939, 136.

which may be summarized as non-close, characterize the first Syllable (Verb) :
openness (ɑ, a, ɒ), half-openness (ɛ, ɔ), half-closeness + frontness (e, ø) :

    first Syll. : non-closeness (a ɑ ɒ ɛ ɔ e ø)
    second Syll. : half-openness (ɛ ɔ)

snyug-se (ser) yod-pa gnang-ngas (naɲɛ:)	have you any dark yellow [1]
rtswa-chag yag-po ster-ras (tɛɹɛ:)	did you give plenty of fodder [2]
Connaught Hall-*la bsdad-pas* (dɛ:bɛ:)	did you stay at Connaught Hall
rkang thang-la yong-ngas (jʊŋɛ:)	did you come on foot [3]
rgyal-rtse-la phebs-pas (phe:bɛ:)	did you come to Gyantse
gsol-ja bzos-pas (sø:bɛ:)	did you make tea
gnang-rog (nɑ̄:ɹo:) *gnang*	please give
phye-rog (tɕhɛɹo:) *byed*	would you open
bstan-rog (tɛ̄:ɹɔ:) *gnang*	please show
nyo-rog (ɲɔɹo:) *byed*	would you buy
yong-rog (jɔ̄:ɹo:) *byed*	would you come
phebs-rog (phe:ɹo:) *gnang*	please come
skyon-rog (cø̄:ɹo:) *gnang*	please print

In Pieces in which the second Syllable is either *pas* or *rog*, then, the exponents
of the two terms Close and Open are :

	First Syllable	Second Syllable
Close		
(i) closeness (i ɪ y u ɵ)		
(ii) half-closeness + backness + spreading (ɤ)		half-closeness (e o)
Open		
non-closeness, except ɤ as above (a ɑ ɒ ɛ ɔ e ø)		half-openness (ɛ ɔ)

    Two exceptions have been observed : ɹβɛ:, *red-pas*, and tɕhɔɲɛ:, *byung ngaɤ*,
e.g.

ycig-pa red-pas (ɹβɛ:)	is it the same
phebs-lam-la sku mnyel-po ma-byung-ngas (-dʑɔɲɛ:)	I hope you had a good journey [4]

In these two examples one would have expected to find either half-closeness
(e) as a feature of the second Syllable harmonizing with the closeness (ɪ ɵ)
of the first, or, alternatively, a vowel other than ɪ or ɵ, but not i, u, y, or ɤ,
as a feature of the first Syllable harmonizing with the half-openness (ɛ) of the
second.

    tɕhɔɲɛ: and -dʑɔɲɛ: can only be treated as exceptions ; but it is possible
to account for the irregularity of ɹβɛ:. The V term of the Syllable *red* has

---

[1] ibid., 165.
[2] Based on Sir Basil Gould and Hugh Edward Richardson, *Tibetan sentences*, O.U.P., 1943, 11.
[3] ibid., 102.
[4] Gould and Richardson, *Tibetan language records, etc.*, Kalimpong, 1949, C 29.

alternative exponents: (i) closure between close and half-close, with some centrality (ι), as above in *red-pas*, and in ɹιbɑ:, *red-pa*, ' it is, is it not ' ; and (ii) half-closeness + frontness, with or without long duration (e e:). This alternation in exponency can be dealt with through a prosodic system that takes into account not only differences in closure and degree of frontness, but also duration and pitch, as a result of which *red* is classified as a Close/Open-Piece (c/oP) Verb (section B below).[1]

The behaviour of the other two Particle Syllables that have V terms with alternative exponents, *a* (Dubitative) and *ma/mi* (Negative), differs from that of *pas* and *rog* as regards degrees of closure (*a* : a/ʌ ; *ma/mi* : a(ɛ)/ι), and also in the fact that the order of grammatical categories in Verb-+-Particle Words in which either of these two sub-categories of Particle is colligated with the Complement sub-category of Verb is, exceptionally, not Verb—Particle but Particle—Verb, e.g. *a-yin, a-yod, ma-red, mi-'dug*. Moreover, Words exemplifying these Particles contribute to solving the problem posed by ɹιβɛ: and tɕhoɳɛ:/-dʑoɳɛ:.

The exponent of the V term of *a* is half-openness (ʌ) in the Close, and openness (a) in the Open, Piece ; that of the V term of *ma/mi* is closeness (ι) in the Close, and either openness (a) or half-openness (ɛ) in the Open, e.g.

a	cP	*chang'di yag-po a-yin* (ʔʌjῐ)	I doubt whether this beer is all right
	oP	*la a-yod* (ʔajø)	I am not sure that I have
		mang-po zhe-po a-yong (ʔajɔ̃)	I should not think there are very many
ma/mi	cP	*tsha-bɑ tsha-sa'i mi-'dug-gas* (mιndøge:)	is it not a warm spot too
	oP	*mang-po zhe-po mi-yong* (mɛjɔ̃:)	there are not very many [2]
		la ma-red (maɹe)	no, he is not

Openness (a) as a feature of the first Syllable of *ma-red* (maɹe) and *ma-byung* (madʑõ) is an oP criterion. It supports the classification of *red* as a c/oP Verb (pp. 235-6) ; it conflicts with the cP criterion closeness (õ̃) of the second Syllable of *ma-byung*, and therefore supports the classification of *byung* as irregular (p. 235).

No other single Particle Syllable has alternative exponents for its V term ; but there is an alternation in the exponency of their V terms for combinations

---

[1] For a corresponding alternation in vowel duration to the e(:) and ι of the V term of *red*, with or without a correlated alternation in vowel quality, cf. dn(:), *'dug*, and døge:, *'dug-gas* (u:/ɷ) ; jø(:), *yod*, and jøβɛ:, *yod-pas* (ø:/ø) ; mɛ:, *med(mad)*, and mɛβɛ:, *med(mad)-pas* (ɛ:/ɛ), all of them examples of the Complement sub-category of Verb (*red, 'dug, yod, med(mad), yin, min(man), byung, yong*).

[2] The difference in exponency of the V term of *ma/mi* in Words in which the Verb Complement is represented by *yong* and *red* is associated with the presence of initial palatality (-ɛj-) and non-palatality (-aɹ-) in the Verb Syllable, and would require a further prosodic statement.

of the Nominalizing Particle *pa/ba(ga/nga/ra)* with either the Genitive Particle *gi/gyi/kyi/-'i* or the Agentive Particle *gis/gyis/kyis/-s* : half-close (e) in the Close Piece, half-open (ε) in the Open (and therefore phonetically identical with *pas*), e.g.

cP
{
 ma yin-pas (**jɯmbe:**)   through our not being
 zhing-kha 'di btab-pa'i (**tɤbe:**)   in order to sow this field [1]
 don-dag-la
}

oP
{
 byas-pas (**tɕhɛ:bɛ:**)   on my saying
 London-*la phebs-pa'i* (**phe:bɛ:**)   your reason for coming to London
 sku-don
}

The Particle Syllables *pas*, *rog*, *a*, and *ma/mi*, and the Nominalizing Particle *pa/ba(ga/nga/ra)* when combined with *gi/gyi/kyi/-'i* or *gis/gyis/kyis/-s*, can be contained in both the Close and the Open Piece ; and, apart from the exceptional behaviour of Pieces containing *byung*, their V terms have as exponents alternative degrees of closure accordingly (e/ε, o/ɔ, ʌ/a, ɩ/a(ε)). None of the other Particle Syllables that can be contained in the Verb-+-Particle type of Piece resembles them in this latter respect (alternation in the exponency of their V terms) [2] ; but the majority of these Particle Syllables can, like *pas*, *rog*, *a*, etc., be contained in both Close Piece and Open Piece. All such Particle Syllables are therefore termed Close/Open-Piece (c/oP) Particle Syllables to distinguish them from a minority that has still to be considered (Close-Piece Particle, p. 239), and to mark the fact that they may be contained in both prosodic types of Closure Piece (the remaining Particle Syllables are in fact confined to the Close Piece).

The following Particles are c/oP ; most of them, listed in section (i), are written with the vowel letters *e* ('*greng-bu*) and *o* (*na-ro*), and with *a* (for which Tibetan orthography has no name) when not immediately followed by the letter *b* ; but a few of them, listed in section (ii), are, however, written with *i* (*gi-gu*) and *u* (*zhabs-kyu*) :

(i) *e*, *o*, *a* (except when followed by *b*)

se/ze, *med(mad)* ; *rog*, *dwogs* (or *rdog*), *do*, '*gro(gro)*, *yong*, *yod*, *dgos(dgo*, *go)*, *myong(nyung)*, *song*, *long* ; *pa/ba(ga/nga/ra)* (Nominalizing), *pa/ba(ga/nga/ra)* (Past), *pas/gas/ngas/ras*, *pa/ga/nga*, *mkhan(nyan)*, *ga(ka*, *kag)*, *ta*, *(b)stangs*, *shag/zhag*, *sa*, *a* (Imperative), *a* (Dubitative), *byas*, *tsang*, *na*, *ya/yag*, *ma/mi*, *nas(ni)*.

(ii) *i*, *u*

shig, *bzhin*, *(ni)*, *mi/ma* ; '*dug*, *byung*, *(nyung)*.

---

[1] Bell, *Grammar*, 53.

[2] With the possible exception of the Nominalizing Particle *dwogs*, or *rdog*, e.g. *yin-dwogs kha-po red* ' he may perhaps be ', '*gro-rdog kha-po red* ' I might perhaps have to go ' (Gould and Richardson, *Records*, C 42), and the Perfective Particle *med(mad)*, e.g. (oP) '*byor-mad-pa-no* (**dʑoːmɛ:-**) ' have you not received ', (cP) *bzhugs-mad-pa-no* ([?] ***ɕuːmɛ:-** or ***ɕuːme:-**) ' is he not staying ', for neither of which does the available material provide sufficient evidence.

B. Pieces containing Close/Open-Piece (c/oP) Verb Syllables

There are also Verb Syllables that resemble *pas*, *rog*, *a*, and the other c/oP Particle Syllables, in that they too are not restricted to the Close or the Open Piece but may be contained in either. These Verb Syllables are also therefore termed Close/Open-Piece (c/oP), to distinguish them from certain other Verb Syllables that behave differently, and to mark the fact that they may be contained in either type of Piece.

All the Verb Syllables that have so far appeared in this article in examples of the Open Piece (pp. 233, 235) are c/oP ; but in spite of the fact that they have so far been exemplified only in the Open Piece, as c/oP Verb Syllables they can of course equally well be contained in the Close Piece. The Particle Syllables *pas* and *rog* thus provide a means of identifying c/oP Verb Syllables ; for in Pieces containing a c/oP Verb Syllable, and in no other Pieces except *byung-ngas*, the V terms of *pas* and *rog* always have their more open exponents (ε ɔ). The following Verbs, all of which have already been exemplified, are therefore c/oP : *gnang*, *ster*, *bsdad*, *yong*, *phebs*, *bzos*, *phye*, *bstan*, *nyo*, *skyon*, and *red*, but not *byung*.

Pieces containing c/oP Verb Syllables may usefully be considered at this point, because the majority of them, like *pas* and *rog*, have V terms with alternative exponents. A pair of examples is given for each Verb ; in the first example of each pair each Verb is exemplified in an Open Piece, and in the second in a Close Piece. The alternative exponents of its V term are symbolized in the right-hand column ; the exponents of the Close and Open terms of the Closure system are stated subsequently.[1]

'then	oP	tha-mag 'then-pa-red (thɛmbə-)	he smoked	ε/ι
	cP	,, 'then-gyi-'dug (thɪŋgɪ-)	he smokes	
thon	oP	thon-pa-red (thəmbə-)	he set out	ø/ʏ
	cP	thon-gyi-'dug (thyŋgʏ-)	he sets out	
'gro	oP	'gro-ba-red (dɹɔbə-)	they go	ɔ/ɵ
	cP	'gro-gi-'dug (dɹɵgʏ-)	they are going	
bsdad	oP	bsdad-pa-yin (dɛːbə-)	I stayed	ɛː/eː
	cP	bsdad-kyi-yin (deːgə-)	I shall stay	
klog	oP	klog-pa(ga)-yin (lɔːbə-/lɔːgʙ-)	I read	ɔː/oː
	cP	klog-gi-yin (loːgʏ-)	I shall read	
yong	oP	yong-ba(nga)-yin (jɒŋbə-/jɒŋʙ-)	I came	ɒ/ɵ
	cP	yong-gi-yin (jɵŋgʏ-)	I shall come	
gnang	oP	gnang-ba(nga)-red (naŋbə-/naŋʙ-)	he gave	a/ʌ
	cP	gnang-gi-red (nʌŋgə-)	he will give	
bcar	oP	bcar-ba(ra)-yin (tɕɑːbə-/tɕaɹʙ-)	I visited	ɑː/ʌː
	cP	bcar-gyi-yin (tɕʌːgə-)	I shall visit	a/ʌː

[1] Only the difference in degree of vowel closure is relevant here ; but, since there are no generally accepted symbols for e.g. closeness, half-closeness, other features (frontness, spreading, etc.) are unavoidably symbolized as well.

The alternative degrees of vowel closure are, then, as follows :

	oP	cP		
(i)	half-close	close	ɵ(:)/ʏ(:)	*thon mchod*
(ii)	half-open	close	ɛ/ɩ ɔ/ɵ	*'then 'gro*
(iii)	,,	half-close	ɛ:/e: ɔ:/o:	*bsdad kloq*
(iv)	open	close	ɒ/ɵ	*yong*
(v)	,,	half-open	a/ʌ ɑ:(a)/ʌ:	*gnang bcar*

The Particle exemplified in all the Open Pieces in the last paragraph but one is *pa/ba(ga/nga/ra)* (Past), henceforth referred to simply as *pa*. It has already been classified as c/oP (p. 237). The Particle exemplified in the Close Pieces, on the other hand, *gi/gyi/kyi*, henceforth referred to simply as *gi*, is one of the minority of Particles that can be exemplified only in the Close Piece, whence they are termed Close-Piece (cP) Particles. This sub-category of Particle comprises six members : *gi, rtsis, dus, rgyu, mus, thabs*. These Particles are therefore sufficient to identify examples of the Closure Piece in Tibetan texts as Close ; and the reader must treat them as such, whatever the Closure class of the Verb may be. It is significant that all six are written with one or other of the vowel letters *i* and *u*, and with *a* when immediately followed by *b* (but *i* and *u* in a Particle Syllable are not of themselves sufficient to identify a Piece in a text as Close : the c/oP Particles listed in section (ii) on p. 237 are also spelt with these letters).

There are certain c/oP Verb Syllables, *phebs, bstan*, and *ster*, for example, whose V terms do not have alternative exponents in the Close and the Open Piece (except for the fast-tempo alternative forms tɛʀɵ- and chɛʀɵ- to the te:bɵ- and che:bɵ- of *ster-ba(ra)-red* ' he gave ' and *khyer-ba(ra)-red* ' he carried ' respectively, which give an alternation ɛ/e), e.g.

phebs	{	oP	*phebs-pa-red* (phe:bɵ)	he came	} e:
	{	cP	*phebs-kyi-'dug* (phe:gɩ-)	he is coming	
ster	{	oP	*ster-ba(ra)-red* (te:bɵ-/tɛʀɵ-)	he gave	} e:
	{	cP	*ster-gyi-red* (te:gɵ-)	he will give	
bstan	{	oP	*bstan-pa-red* (tɛmbɵ-)	he showed	} ɛ
	{	cP	*bstan-gyi-red* (tɛŋgɵ-)	he will show	

In spite of the fact that in this respect *phebs, ster, bstan*, and other Verbs like them, differ from the majority of c/oP Verbs, there is no doubt that they are c/oP : the degree of vowel closure of the V term of the Particle Syllables *pas* and *rog* in phe:bɛ:, *phebs-pas*, tɛʀɛ:, *ster-ras*, and tɛ̃:ʀɔ:, *bstan-rog*, half-open (ɛ ɔ), proves it.

The c/oP Verbs are too numerous for listing, unlike the c/oP Particles (p. 237) ; but the orthography provides a fairly reliable means of identifying them : they are regularly written with the vowel letters *e* and *o*, and with *a* when not immediately followed by *b*, the same orthographic features as, with certain exceptions, distinguish the c/oP from the cP Particles.

The c/oP Verb Syllables that do not have alternative exponents of their V terms are regularly symbolized (i) by *e* immediately followed by either *b*, *d*, or *s*, or by *r* or *l*, except that examples of this last type have a fast-tempo alternative form, mentioned above, e.g. tɛɹɐ-, cf. te:bɐ-, *ster-ba(ra)-red* ' he gave ' (the resulting tempo alternation ɛ/e is not to be confused with the Closure alternation) : *sleb* ' arrive ', *phebs* ' come ', *'gyel* ' fall ', *'phel* ' spread ', *rjed* ' forget ', *brjes* ' change ', *bzhed* ' fear ', *ster* ' give ', and possibly *bzhes* ' eat ' and *khyer* ' carry ' [1]; and (ii) by *a* immediately followed by *n* : *bstan* ' show ', *man* (a phonetic spelling ; cf. *min*) ' am not ', *phan* ' profit by ', *dran* ' recollect ', *nyan* ' listen to ', *san* ' listen to '. The only exception to be noted from R. is *skyed* ' give birth to, create ', for which he would accept ci:gɪ- as an alternative to ce:gɪ- in, for example, *skyed-kyi-'dug* ' they create ', with the result that for the V term of this Verb Syllable, a cP exponent (i), in *skyed-kyi-'dug*, alternates with an oP exponent (e), in, for example, *skyed-pa-red* (ce:bɐ-) ' they created '.

Another Lhasa-dialect-speaker, Paljor Phuntshok (*dpal-'byor phun-tshogs*) (P.), a nobleman of the Tsarong (*tsha-rong*) family, would accept the form ci:gɪ-, but not ce:gɪ-. Further, since the form phi:gɪ- was heard from other Lhasa-dialect-speakers for R.'s phe:gɪ- (*phebs-kyi-'dug*), for them some at least of the Verb Syllables listed in the previous paragraph as having V terms with a single exponent have alternative exponents. Possibly the orthography had something to do with R.'s insistence on regarding these Verb Syllables as having the same exponent for the V term in Open Piece and Close Piece alike ; for he gave the orthography as his reason for avoiding certain pronunciations that he agreed were current in the dialect. Thus, once they had been pointed out to him, R. readily accepted the alternatives ɔ:/o:, a/ʌ, and ɑ:/ʌ: as his own usage ; for there is no orthographic means of symbolizing the latter alternative of each pair independently of the former ; but he was reluctant to accept the alternative exponents ø/y, ø:/y:, ɛ/ɪ, ɔ/ɵ, and, at first, ɛ:/e: too ; for the latter member of each of these can be symbolized differently from the former, by *u* as opposed to *o* for ø(:)/y(:), ɔ/ɵ, and ɒ/ɵ, by *i* as opposed to *e* for ɛ/ɪ, and by *e* as opposed to *a* for ɛ:/e: ; and to use the closer degree of vowel closure in the Close Piece would, he insisted, result in orthographic and lexical confusion. R. said that it was for this reason that he made a point of avoiding such forms as thɔŋgy-, *mthong-gi-'dug* ' he sees ', ɕyŋgy-, *zhon-gyi-'dug* ' he mounts ', and tʳyɤ:gy-, *'phrod-kyi-'dug* ' he delivers ', which he agreed were to be heard from other speakers of the Lhasa dialect, in favour of thɒŋgɪ-, ɕøŋgɪ-, and tʳɤ:gɪ-, respectively ; for the form thɒŋgy-, for example, might be confused with the thɒŋgy- of *'thung-gi-'dug* ' he drinks '.[2]

For *phye-gi-'dug* ' he opens ', *rtse-gi-'dug* ' he plays ', and *len-gyi-'dug* ' he

---

[1] A phonetic form ɕɪgɪ- has been noted for *bzhes* in addition to ɕe:gɪ-, *bzhes-kyi-yod-pas* ' do you drink ' ; the latter form is perhaps to be regarded as a spelling pronunciation. Alternative phonetic forms chi:gɪ-, *khyer-gyi-'dug*, and chɹɐ-, *khyer-ba(ra)-red*, have also been noted that would require *khyer* to be classed as cP (p. 128).

[2] P. not only pronounced *mthong-gi-'dug* ' he sees ', thɒŋgydu:, but insisted that it and *'thung-gi-'dug* ' he drinks ' were homophonous.

takes ', on the other hand, in each of which the Verb Syllable is spelt with *e*, R. would accept **tɕhɪgɪ-** and **tɕhɛgɪ-**, **tsɪgɪ-** and **tsɛgɪ**, and **lʊŋgɪ-** and **lɛŋgɪ-**, as free variants ; for *gon-gyi-'dug* ' he wears ', he considered **khyŋgy-** to be appropriate to informal, and **khøŋgɪ-** to formal, occasions.

R.'s usage, however, as reflected in both scripted and unscripted recordings, does not always support his preferences. The following phonetic forms, for example, to which he preferred **khɔgɪ-**, **thøŋgɪ-**, and **tɕhøːgɪ-**, are taken from recordings, in which his pronunciation is necessarily less self-conscious than in examples that he volunteered after some reflection :

ha go-gi-med (**khɔgə-**)	I do not understand
du-ba thon-gyi-'dug (**thyŋgɪ-**)	smoke will come out [1]
kha zhed-drags skom-gyi-'dug (**kɔmgɪ-**)	I am very thirsty [2]
gsol-ja mchod-kyi-yin (**tɕhøːgy-**)	we will drink tea

Although R. believed that he did not distinguish cP and oP exponents for the V terms of *go*, *thon*, *skom*, and *mchod*, he was prepared to accept alternative exponents as his own usage for the V term of the Verb Syllables *'gro* and *yong*, e.g. *'gro-gi-'dug* (**dɹɔgy-**) ' he is going ', *'gro-ba-red* (**dɹɔbə-**) ' they are in the habit of going ' (ɔ/ɔ) ; *yong-gi-yin* (**jɔŋgə-**) ' I shall come ', *yong-ba-red* (**jɔŋbə-**) ' he came ' (ɔ/ʋ). Since both of these Verbs are frequently exemplified in the material, it is possible that frequency of use has something to do with whether or not R. was willing to accept alternative exponents for the V term of some Verb Syllables.

Thus far in this section attention has been focused on the Verb Syllable and alternations in the exponency of its V term ; for it is this alternation in the degree of vowel closure characterizing certain Verb Syllables and the Particle Syllables *pas*, *a*, *rog*, etc., that sets the phonological problem that the Closure system is designed to solve ; but the exponents of the Close and Open terms of the Closure system are not, of course, drawn from only one Syllable of the Piece but from both at once. There is, however, a good reason for leaving the stating of these exponents until this point : the exponents of the Close and Open terms are most easily stated for Pieces in which the Particle Syllable is either *pas* or *rog* ; for the degrees of closure in either Syllable are different in each type of Piece, and there is no overlap :

	First Syllable	Second Syllable
Close	i ɪ y u ɔ ɤ	e o
Open	e ø ɛ ɔ ɒ ɑ	ɛ ɔ

Pieces of that type provide the simplest introduction to the problem ; but in Pieces in which the Particle Syllable is a Syllable other than *pas* or *rog*, it is possible for the same degree of vowel closure to characterize the first Syllable, and, more commonly, the second Syllable, of Open and Close Piece alike. There is then an overlap of phonetic feature as between the Close and the Open Piece ; and the stating of exponents becomes more complicated :

---

[1] Gould and Richardson, *Sentences*, 97.   [2] ibid., 69.

the vocalic features e: and ɛ can characterize the first Syllable of both, as in the examples of *phebs*, *ster*, and *bstan* (p. 125) ; and ə, ɪ, and ɵ can characterize the second Syllable of both, e.g.

ə
- oP *ga-bar slab-pa gnang-ba-yin-na* (**naŋbə-**) — where did you learn
- cP *phyag-las su'i rtsa-la gnang-gi-yod-na* (**nʌŋgə-**) — whose place are you working at

ɪ
- oP *khang tshar-ni* (**tshɑːnɪ**) [1] — having finished filling
- cP *tshar-gyi-'dug* (**tshʌːgɪ-**) — he is finishing

ɵ
- oP *phyag-las ga-re gnang-dgos-red* (**naŋgɵ-**) — what work do you have to do [2]
- cP *bsgrigs-pa gnang-rgyu* (**nʌŋgjɵ**) — for setting up

The sum total of the exponents of Close and Open are, for Pieces in which the Verb Syllable is c/oP (for the remainder, see p. 133) :

First Syllable	Second Syllable

Close

closeness (iː ɪ y(ː) ɵ) [3]
half-closeness (eː oː [ø(ː)]) [4]
half-openness + backness + spreading (ʌ(ː))
half-openness + frontness + spreading + short duration (ɛ)
half-openness + frontness + spreading + nasality (ɛ̃ː)
[half-openness + rounding + short duration (ɔ)]
[half-openness + rounding + nasality (ɔ̃ː)]
[openness + rounding (ɒ)]

closeness (iː ɪ yː ɵ)

half-closeness + backness + spreading (ɤ)

medium centrality (ə)

Open

half-closeness (eː ø(ː))
half-openness (ɛ(ː) ɔ(ː))
openness (a ɑː ɒ)

closeness (ɪ u ɵ)
half-closeness + frontness (e ø)
half-openness (ɛ(ː) ɔ(ː))
openness (ɑː a)
medium centrality (ə)
open ,, (ɤ) [5]

---

[1] Fast-tempo alternative to **tshɑːnɛ**, *tshar-nas*. [2] Bell, *Grammar*, 174.

[3] **ciːgɪ-** (*bskyed-kyi-'dug*) provides the only example of i (p. 240).

[4] Features thought to have been influenced by the orthography (pp. 240–1) are enclosed in square brackets throughout.

[5] Except for *a-yod* (ʔajø), *a-yong* (ʔajõː, ʔajõ̃), *ma-red* (**maɹe**), *mi-yong* (**mɛjõː**), the first Syllable is also the Verb Syllable.

Some of the features given above are peculiar to either the Close or the Open Piece, and will therefore also serve as criteria of the appropriate term of the Closure system ; others are common to both. When characterizing the first Syllable, closeness (i ι y ɷ), half-closeness + backness + rounding (o), and half-openness + backness + spreading (ʌ), are peculiar to the Close Piece ; while openness + frontness (a), and openness + backness + non-rounding (ɑ:), on the other hand, together with half-openness, provided that it is further accompanied by long duration + non-nasality (ɛ: ɔ:) provide phonetic criteria of the Open term ; and so, probably, except in self-conscious utterances, do half-closeness + frontness + rounding (ø(:)), half-openness | rounding + either short duration (ɔ), or long duration + nasality (ɔ̃:), and openness + backness + rounding (ɒ). From the second Syllable, closeness + frontness (i: y:) and half-closeness + backness + spreading (ɤ) provide Close criteria (these features are also exponents of particular V terms of cP Particle Syllables, p. 239), e.g.

bzu-rtsis (sɒdzi:) *ra-po yod*   I am sort of about to make
bzhugs-gdan 'jag-mus (dʒʌ:my:) *yin-pa-no*   is he in residence
'di byed-thabs (tɕhιdɤp) *yod-ba* [sic]   there is no help for it [1]
-ma-red

These three examples also provide phonetic criteria of the Close term from the first Syllable (ɷ ʌ ι).

It might appear that those features of the second Syllable which both serve as exponents of the Open term and are not shared with the Close term, half-closeness + frontness (e ø), half-openness (ɛ ɔ), openness (a ɑ), and open centrality (ɤ), must necessarily also provide oP criteria ; but this is not so ; for half-openness (ɛ ɔ), openness (a ɑ), and open centrality (ɤ) can equally well characterize the second Syllable of the Close Piece (i.e. the Close Piece in which the Verb Syllable is Close-Piece). In other words these features can also be exponents of the V terms of c/oP Particle Syllables (p. 237), each of which can, by definition, be contained in either the Close or the Open Piece. The remaining second-Syllable feature, half-closeness (e ø), is, as it stands, too imprecise to be considered from the point of view of phonetic criteria ; but the more specific combination half-closeness + frontness + spreading + long duration (e:), which characterizes not a Particle Syllable but a Verb Syllable (p. 242, n. 5), e.g. *ma-red* (maɹe:) 'it is *not*', is restricted to the Open Piece, and does, therefore, provide an oP criterion. Half-closeness + frontness + spreading/rounding + short duration (e ø), on the other hand, does not : (oP) *bgres-byas* (dɹe:dʒe) 'having mixed up' ; (cP) *zhus-byas* (ɕy:ʑe) 'having asked for' ; (cP) *bzhugs-yod* (ɕu:ɥø) 'she is alive' ; (oP) *bzhugs-gdan 'jag-yod-pas* (dʒɑ:jø-) 'is he at home'.

If, however, *dwogs* (or *rdog*) and *med*(*mad*) were found to have cP alternative exponents (o e) (p. 237, n. 2), as may well be the case, then half-openness (ɛ ɔ)

---

[1] Bell, *Grammar*, 134.

could after all be stated as an oP criterion, e.g. *yod-dwogs* (jɐndɔ:), *gnang-rog* (nɑ̃:ɪɔ:), *'byor-mad-pa-no* (dʑɔ:mɛ:-), *bsdad-pas* (dɛ:bɛ:).

The fact that it is uncertain whether half-openness (ɛ ɔ) as a feature of the second Syllable can of itself be stated as an oP criterion is, of course, no obstacle to using the alternation in exponency of the V terms of *pas* (ɛ e) and *rog* (ɔ o) to determine whether a Closure Piece is Close or Open.

It is noteworthy that, as features of the second Syllable, closeness + backness + rounding (u), and closeness + some centrality (ɪ ɵ), do not, as one might perhaps have expected, provide cP criteria : these features can also characterize the second Syllable of the Open Piece, e.g.

phebs tshar-'dug (tshɑ:du), not **tshʌ:du*	(the doctor) has already left [1]
byas-bzhin (tɕhɛ:ɕĩ:), not **tɕhe:ɕĩ:*	therefore
khang tshar-ni (tshɑ:nɪ), not **tshʌ:nɪ*	having finished filling
klog-shig (lɔ:ɕɪ), not **lo:ɕɪ*	read it
phyag-phebs gnang-byung (nɑ̃:dʑɵ̃), not **nʌ̃:dʑɵ̃*	good morning
chibs-bsgyur gnang-song (nɑ̃:sɵ̃), not **nʌ̃:sɵ̃*	he went
go-nyung (khɔɲɵ̃), not **khɔɲɵ̃*	I had heard
bshad-go-red-se (ɕɛ:gɵ-), not **ɕe:gɵ-*	' you will have to explain '

The features so far cited as criteria have been drawn from a single Syllable, whether first or second ; where, however, a feature can be common either to the first or to the second Syllable of Close and Open Piece alike, it becomes necessary at least to cite as criteria features drawn from the vowels of both Syllables, and in some instances consonantal features as well. Since half-closeness + frontness + spreading (e:), half-openness + frontness + short duration (ɛ), and half-openness + frontness + long duration + nasality (ɛ̃:), together with the features that are suspected of being due to the influence of the spelling, [half-openness + frontness + rounding (ø(:))], [half-openness + rounding + short duration (ɔ)], [half-openness + rounding + long duration + nasality (ɔ̃:)], and [openness + rounding (ɒ)], are common to both Close and Open Piece as features of the first Syllable, it is essential to combine these with features of the second Syllable in order to secure criteria. Half-openness + frontness + nasality (ɛ̃:)', and half-closeness + frontness + rounding + nasality (ø̃:), as features of the first Syllable, together with any of the second-Syllable vowels ɪ, u, ɵ, e, ø, ɛ(:), ɔ(:), ɑ:, a, are oP criteria ; e.g.

par skyon-ni (cø̃:nɪ)	having printed
bstan-song (tɛ̃:sɔ̃)	he showed
min-na (mɛ̃:nə)	if I am not

oP criteria are also provided by either of the first-Syllable vowels e: or ɛ,

---

[1] Gould and Richardson, *Sentences*, 51.

or the suspect vowels [ø(:)], [ɔ], and [ɒ], when combined with any of the second-Syllable vowels u, e, ɛ(:), ø, ɔ(:), ɑ:, and a, but not with ι, ω, or ə ; e.g.

ga-nas phebs-pa (**phe:bɑ:**)   where did you come from

gsungs-'dug (**sɒŋdu:**)   they have said

thag ra-po mchod-ma-song (**tɕhø:ma-**)   they sort of did not decide

Where the second Syllable is characterized by the vowel features ι, ω, or ə, a combination of any one of these with one of the first-Syllable vowels just considered, e:, ɛ, [ø(:)], [ɔ], and [ɒ], cannot provide a cP or oP criterion except by including in the criterion features of the intervocalic consonant or consonants. The cP Particle Syllable gi is largely responsible for this complication ; for medium centrality (ə) can, under certain prosodic conditions, be an exponent of the V term of this Syllable ; and, since gi is confined to the Close Piece, medium centrality (ə) can by this means be part of the exponency of the Close term. For the V term of gi, ə alternates as an exponent with the vowels ι and y. These three exponents can be related to features of the preceding Verb Syllable and the following Particle Syllable, if any, harmonizing not with vowel-closure features but with labial features. Roughly speaking, for a detailed account of this alternation is not relevant to Closure, lip-rounding is a feature of gi (**gy**) where it is also a feature of the Verb Syllable (u ω o) ; lip-spreading is a feature of gi (**gι**) where spreading + closeness (i ι) is a feature of the Verb Syllable ; medium centrality (**gə**) is a feature of gi where any other lip position (e ɤ ʌ) characterizes the Verb Syllable. Clearly a prosodic system can be set up to deal with the harmonizing labial features of these two Syllables, just as it can for the associated closure features of the Verb and the Particle Syllable of the Closure Piece ; but the relevance of these labial features to the Closure system is that in Closure Pieces in which the Syllable preceding the cP Particle Syllable gi, the Verb Syllable, is characterized by half-closeness + frontness + spreading (e) or by backness + spreading (ɤ ʌ), and the Syllable following gi by features other than closeness + backness (u ω), then gi is generally characterized by medium centrality (ə), a feature that also characterizes the c/oP Particle Syllables pa, ta, sa, and na, e.g.

cP Particle : gi (**gə**)

    lo ga-tshod rtse thad-kyi-yod-na (**the:gə-**)   about how many years is it since . . .

    phyag-las su'i rtsa-la gnang-gi-yod-na (**nʌŋgə-**)   whose place are you working at

    bslab-kyi-yin (**lɤβgəjῑ:**)   I will learn [1]

c/oP Particle : pa (**bə**), ta (**də**), sa (**sə**), na (**nə**)

    lhas-sa rang-la bzhugs bzhugs-pa-yin-na (**ɕu:bə-**)   used you to live in Lhasa itself, or . . .

    chibs-pa thar-sa (**thɑ:sə**) med   ponies cannot cross by it [2]

[1] Gould and Richardson, Sentences, 67.   [2] Bell, Grammar, 154.

As a result, both Open and Close Piece may have identical vowel exponents in each Syllable : e: — ə/ɩ, ɛ — ə/ɩ, [ø: — ɩ], [ɔ — ɩ], [ɒ — ɩ] ; e.g.

e: — ə	oP	*ster-ba(ra)-red* (**te:bə-**)	he gave
	cP	*ster-gyi-yin* (**te:gə-**)	I shall give
		bsdad-kyi-yin (**de:gə-**)	I shall stay
e: — ɩ	oP	*phebs-ni* (**phe:nɩ**)	having come
	cP	*phebs-kyi-'dug* (**phe:gɩ-**)	he comes
ɛ — ə	oP	*bstan-pa-red* (**tɛmbə-**)	he showed
	cP	*bstan-gyi-yin* (**tɛŋgə-**)	I shall show
[ø: — ɩ]	oP	*skol-shig* (**kø:ɛɩ**)	boil it
	cP	*bskol-gyi-'dug* ([**kø:gɩ-**])	he boils

Intervocalic velarity must be specified in the cP criterion, and intervocalic non-velarity in the oP :

cP criteria

    (i) the vowels e:/ɛ, velarity, the vowels ə/ɩ (e:gə, e:gɩ, [ɛgə], [ɛgɩ], ɛŋgə, ɛŋgɩ) ;

    (ii) the vowels [ø:] [ɔ] [ɒ], velarity, the vowel ɩ ([ø:gɩ], [ɔgɩ], [ɒŋgɩ]) ;

oP criteria

    (i) the vowels e:/ɛ, non-velarity, the vowels ə/ɩ (e:$\overline{V}$ə, e:$\overline{V}$ɩ, ɛ$\overline{V}$ə, ɛ$\overline{V}$ɩ) [1] ;

    (ii) the vowels [ø(:)]/[ɔ], non-velarity, the vowel ɩ ([ø(:)$\overline{V}$ɩ], [ɔ$\overline{V}$ɩ]).[2]

Similarly, where the vowel of the first Syllable is e: or ɛ, or one of the controversial vowels [ø:], [ø], [ɔ], or [ɒ], and that of the second Syllable is ɔ, it is necessary to specify the intervocalic sequence of features velarity—semi-vowel (gj) for the cP criterion, and features other than this sequence for the oP ; e.g.

cP	*bstan-rgyu* (**tɛŋgjɔ**)	for showing
	la thad-rgyu (**the:gjɔ**) *red*	no, he has not gone yet
oP	*phebs-nyung-ngas* (**phe:ɲɔ-**)	did you ever come to
	ga-re byed-dgos-red (**tɕhɛgɔ-**)	what is one to do

In the course of the preceding two sections (A, B) all the relevant Particle Syllables have been classified, prosodically, as either Close/Open-Piece (c/oP), and therefore containable in both the Open and the Close Piece, or Close-Piece (cP), and therefore containable only in the Close Piece ; and some Verb Syllables have been classified as Close/Open-Piece (c/oP), and therefore containable in both the Open and the Close Piece. It now remains only to give an account of those Verbs which have not been classified as Close/Open-Piece.

C. Pieces containing Close-Piece (cP) Verb Syllables

The Particle Syllables *pas* and *rog* have already been used diagnostically, in section A, for classifying certain Verbs as Close/Open-Piece ; all the remaining Verbs that are exemplified in that section (in Pieces containing *pas* and *rog*), all of them in Close Pieces, are in fact confined to the Close Piece. These Verbs (*yin*, *gzigs*, *zhu/zhus*, *'dug*, *bzhugs*, *zin*, *dris*, *phul*, *blug*, *rgyab*,

---

[1] $\overline{V}$ symbolizes non-velarity.   [2] $\overline{V}$ɩ is not preceded by ɒ.

slab), and others like them, are therefore termed Close-Piece (cP) Verbs. No cP Verb Syllable can have alternative exponents of its V term, one for the Close and one for the Open Piece, because it cannot be contained in the Open Piece.[1] In the following examples, all of them, of course, Close-Piece, the Particle category is exemplified by *pa*, which is c/oP, and by *gi*, which is cP, so that these examples of cP Verb Syllables may be directly compared with the examples of c/oP Verb Syllables (p. 248) :

shi	*shi-ba-red* (ɕɪbə-)	he died	ι
	shi-gi-'dug (ɕɪgɪ-)	he dies	
bris	*bris-pa-red* (tʂi:bə-)	he wrote	i
	bris-kyi-'dug (tʂi:gɪ-)	he writes	
mthun	*mthun-pa-red* (thymbə-)	it matched	y
	mthun-gyi-'dug (thyŋgy-)	it matches	
phul	*phul-ba(ra)-red* (phy:bə-/phyʁɐ-)	he offered	y
	phul-gyi-'dug (phy:gy-)	he offers	
bskums	*bskums-pa-red* (kɔmbə-)	he drew up	ω
	skum-gyi-'dug (kɔmgy-)	he draws up	
bzhugs	*bzhugs-pa(qa)-red* (ɕu:bə-/ɕu:gɐ-)	he stayed	u
	bzhugs-kyi-'dug (ɕu:gy-)	he stays	
bslabs	*bslabs-pa-red* (lʁbə-)	he learnt	ɤ
	bslabs-kyi-yin (lʁbgə-)	I shall learn	

The cP Verbs are, unlike the six cP Particles, too numerous to list ; but the orthography regularly indicates them by the vowel letters *i* and *u*, and by *a* when immediately followed by *b* (cf. also the spelling of the cP Particle Syllables, p. 239), any of which orthographic features, when characterizing a Verb Syllable in a text, necessarily also indicates that where the Verb Syllable is contained in a Closure Piece, the Closure Piece must be Close, whatever the prosodic class of the following Particle Syllable may be.

The exponents of both the Close and the Open terms have been given for Pieces in which the Verb Syllable is c/oP (p. 242) ; the following exponents, which apply to Pieces in which the Verb Syllable is cP, should be added to those Close exponents :

First Syllable	Second Syllable
Close	
closeness (i ι y u ω)	closeness (i ι y u ω)
half-closeness + backness + spreading (ɤ)	half-closeness (e o ɤ)
half-openness + backness + spreading (ʌ)[2]	half-openness (ɛ ɔ)
	openness (a ɑ)
	centrality (ə ɐ)

[1] The V terms of some cP Verb Syllables do have alternative exponents, but in relation to differences in tempo, e.g. (i) *bzhugs-pa(ga)-red* ; ɕu:gɐɹe (fast tempo), ɕɔgbəɹe (slow tempo), ɕu:bəɹe (common tempo) ; (ii) *btsir-ba(ra)-yin* : tsi:bəjĭ (common tempo), tsɪɹɐjĭ (fast tempo).

[2] These features refer to the Particle Syllable *a*, e.g. ʔʌjĭ. The first Syllable is a Particle Syllable in *a-yin*, *mi-'dug*.

Some of the above features, incidentally, provide criteria for the Close
Piece over and above those given on p. 243. Closeness + backness (u), as
a feature of the first Syllable, can be incorporated in the previously stated
criterion, closeness (i ɩ y ɷ), to form a more comprehensive criterion : closeness
(i ɩ y u ɷ) ; and half-closeness + backness + spreading (ᵥ) can be merged
with the previously stated criterion half-closeness + backness + rounding (o)
to form a new criterion : half-closeness + backness (o ᵥ). The second-Syllable
combination of features half-closeness + backness + rounding can, similarly,
be merged with half-closeness + backness + spreading to form the new
criterion half-closeness + backness (ᵥ o).

It is not essential for the Verb to be colligated within Word boundaries
with the Particle category ; monosyllabic Words in which the Verb alone is
exemplified are both possible and common (p. 232). In Words such as these,
Verb Words, the degree of closure of the V term of those c/oP Verb Syllables
which have alternative exponents (pp. 238–9) is the same as that which is
appropriate to the Open Piece (e ø ɛ ɔ ɒ a ɑ), e.g.

bod-skad rgyab (ɟɑ:) *ma shes-na*, not *ɟʌ:	if they do not know how to speak Tibetan
klog (lɔ:) *thugs-pa*, not *lo:	being able to read
so-so'i lung-pa'i phyu-pa gon (khə̄:), not *khȳ:	wear one's own country's dress
sa-skya khul-la'i cig chibs-bsgyur gnang (nɑ̄:), not *nʌ̄:	he went to the Sakya area too

D. Conclusion

Two types of Piece are distinguished by this prosodic analysis of disyllabic
forms grammatically classifiable as Verb + Particle : Close, and Open ; both
Verb Syllables and Particle Syllables are then classified, according as they can
be contained in (i) both Close and Open Piece, or (ii) the Close Piece only,
as (i) Close/Open-Piece (c/oP) Verb, and Particle, Syllables, or (ii) Close-
Piece (cP) Verb, and Particle, Syllables.

One of the results of this analysis is that it becomes impossible to identify
the Verbal Particle *gi/gyi/kyi* with the graphically similar Nominal Particle
gi/gyi/kyi/-'i, an identification that has probably had much to do with the
attempts of some grammarians to incorporate what is in this article distinguished
as the Verb category in the Noun.[1] The Verbal Particle *gi/gyi/kyi* is a Close-
Piece Particle ; the Nominal Particle *gi/gyi/kyi/-'i* is not, e.g.

---

[1] Bell, *Grammar*, 43 : ' The Tibetan Verb . . . is in effect a Verbal Noun. Thus : *khos lug-sha
za-gi-'dug* . . . HE IS EATING MUTTON, *lit.*, BY HIM, AS REGARDS MUTTON, AN EATING IS '. Herbert
Bruce Hannah, *A grammar of the Tibetan language*, Calcutta, 1912, 239 : ' the so-called Tibetan
Verb is rather a kind of Noun, modified in its signification by the Verb *to be*, according to the
mood or tense of the latter '.

Even orthographically it is not possible to identify the Verbal Particle with the Nominal :
the form of the Verbal Particle *gi/gyi/kyi* that follows a vowel letter is *gi* ; but the form of the
Nominal Particle *gi/gyi/kyi/-'i* that follows a vowel letter is not *gi* but *-'i*.

sba-bu lags-kyis (**lɑːgɩ**), not ***lʌːgɩ**	by Babu La ; cf.
sba-bu lags-la (**lɑːlə**)	to Babu La
dbyin-ji'i skor-gyi (**kɔːgɩ**), not ***koːgɩ**	about English ; cf.
'di'i skor-la (**kɔːlə**)	about this
bod-kyi (**phøːgɩ**), not ***phyːgɩ**	of Tibet ; cf.
bod-la (**phøːlə**)	in Tibet

Setting up the Closure system is part of a conscious attempt to reconcile the categories required by analysis at the grammatical, lexical, phonological, and phonetic levels. The implications of this prosodic system for grammatical analysis have just been illustrated ; certain advantages are also claimed for it in phonological and lexical statement over, for example, a phonemic analysis.

Firstly, the close association of the two Syllables concerned, bound together by linking vowel-closure features, is given proper emphasis by treating these two Syllables as a unit, and by stating these closure features of both Syllables as an aspect of the whole unit, as an exponent of one or other term of the Closure system. In reading from a text, too, the Tibetan must take the second Syllable of the Closure Piece into account before he utters the first, just as, in intonation, he must be aware of the end of the Clause unit before he embarks on the beginning ; otherwise, he might mispronounce it.

Prosodic analysis also makes it possible to secure the considerable lexical advantage of associating the alternative degrees of vowel closure ɛ/ɩ, ɔ/ɷ, ø/y, ɔ/o, ɛ/e, ɒ/ɷ, a/ʌ, and ɑ/ʌ, as exponents of the same V term under alternative prosodic conditions (in the Close or in the Open Piece).[1] A phonemicist would also, no doubt, be aware of the advantages to be gained from such an association of alternative features, and would try to associate them as allophones of the same phoneme. He would succeed, under certain conditions, in assigning the alternative vowel qualities ɔ/o, a/ʌ, and ɑ/ʌ each to the same phoneme (say /oː/, /a/, and /aː/). Thus, where the vowel of the following syllable had any of the features symbolized by a, ɑ, ɔ, ɛ, ɐ, e, and u, the allophones of /oː/, /a/, and /aː/ would be, respectively, ɔː, a, and ɑː, e.g. **loːjɑː**, *klog-ya(g)*, ' for reading ', **naŋga** (*phyag-las*) *gnang-ka*, ' in order to work ', **tɕɑːgɐre**, *bcag-pa(ga)-red*, ' he broke ' ; and where the vowel of the following syllable had the features symbolized by i, y, and ɤ, their allophones would be, respectively, oː, ʌ, and ʌː, e.g. **loːdzi**, *klog-rtsis*, ' about to read ', **nʌŋdyː**, (*phyag-las*) *gnang-dus*, ' when you work ', *bzhugs-gdan 'jag-mus*, (**dʑʌːmyː**), ' in residence '.

This phonemic statement would run into difficulties where the vowel of the following syllable had the features symbolized by ɩ, ə, and ɷ ; for ɩ and ɷ may follow either of the proposed allophones ɔː and oː, a and ʌ, and ɑː and ʌː ; but this difficulty would not be insuperable : it could be disposed of by extending

---

[1] The analysis implied by Tibetan orthography is, incidentally, in agreement with the prosodic analysis in this respect (ɛ/ɩ is symbolized by *e*, ɔ/ɷ, ø/y, ɒ/ɷ, and ɔ/o by *o*, and ɛ/e, a/ʌ, and ɑ/ʌ by *a*), and therefore seems superior to the phonemic analysis of this material.

the environment of the allophones to include the intermediate consonant sounds. The allophones oː, ʌ, and ʌː would be appropriate to environments comprising the sequences gɪ and gjɒ, e.g. loːgjɒ, *klog-rgyu*, ' to be read ', *phyag-las gnang-rgyu* (nʌŋgjɒ), ' work to be done ', loːgɪduː, *klog-gi-'dug*, ' he is reading ', and the allophones ɔː, a, and ɑː to environments comprising the sequences dʒɒ̃, dɒ-, sɒ̃, ɲɒ̃, jɒ̃, gɒ, and mɪ, nɪ, ɛɪ, and ɛɪ̃ ; e.g. *phyag-las ga-re gnang-dgos-red* (naŋgɒre), ' what work do you do ',[1] loːɲɒɲɛː, *klog-myong-ngas*, ' have you ever read ', tɑ̃ːmɪndɒgeː, *btang-mi-'dug-gas*, ' has it not been sent ' ; while the allophones ʌ and ʌː would be appropriate to environments comprising the sequence gə, e.g. *dga'-gi-red*, gʌgəreː, ' you would do well to ', *bcar-gyi-yin*, tɛʌːgəjɪ̃ː, ' I will visit ', and the allophones a and ɑː to sequences comprising bə, də, sə, and nə, e.g. *phyag-las gnang-ba-red* (naŋbəre), ' he worked ', *bcar-na*, tɛɑːnə, ' if I visit '.

For the alternations ɔ/o, a/ʌ, and ɑ/ʌ, then, a phonemic analysis could achieve the same lexical aims as the prosodic analysis ; but this phonemic analysis would fail to associate the remaining alternative vowels ɛ/ɪ, ɔ/ɒ, ʋ/ɒ, ø/y, and ɛ/e each as a pair of allophones of the same phoneme. The reason for this failure is that one of the members of each of the pairs is phonetically identical with a vowel sound that would be allotted to another phoneme ; and that member would, therefore, also have to be allotted to that same phoneme : the alternative vowels ɪ, ɒ, y, and e of the pairs ɛ/ɪ, ɔ/ɒ, ʋ/ɒ, ø/y, and ɛ/e, e.g. sɪgɪduː, *zer-gyi-'dug*, ' he says ', dɹɒgyduː, *'gro-gi-'dug*, ' he is going ', tɕhyːgɪjøːbɑː, *mchod-kyi-yod-pa*, ' do you drink . . . or ' (cf. the oP examples : sɛbəɹe/sɛɹɛɹe, *zer-ba(ra)-red*, ' he said ' ; dɹɒbəɹe, *'gro-ba-red*, ' they are in the habit of going ' ; tɕhøːbəɹe, *mchod-pa-red*, ' they drank '), are phonetically identical with the vowels of *bzi*, *khrud*, and *phul*, as in *ra bzi-gi-'dug* (sɪgɪduː), ' he gets drunk ' (cf. the cP example *ra bzi-ba-red* (sɪbəɹe), ' he got drunk '), tɹɒgyduː, *khrud-kyi-'dug* ' he washes ' (cf. *khrud-pa* (tɹɒbə) *gnang-na*, ' if he washes '), phyːgɪjøː, *phul-gyi-yod*, ' I offer ' (cf. phyːbəjɪ̃, *phul-ba-yin*, ' I offered ').[2] The vowel ɪ of *zer-gyi-'dug* (sɪ-) would then have to be allotted to the same phoneme (say /i/) as the vowel ɪ of *ra bzi-gi-'dug* (sɪ-), and separated from the vowel ɛ of *zer-ba-red* (sɛ-), which would be allotted to another phoneme (say /ɛ/) ; the vowels ɒ and y of *'gro-gi-'dug* (dɹɒ-) and *mchod-kyi-yod-pa* (tɕhyː-) would, similarly, be allotted to the same phonemes (say /u/ and /yː/ respectively) as the vowels ɒ and y of *khrud-kyi-'dug* (tɹɒ-) and *phul-gyi-yod* (phyː-), and would be separated from the alternative vowels ɔ and ø of *'gro-ba-red* (dɹɔ-) and *mchod-pa-red* (tɕhø-) respectively, which would be allotted (say) to phonemes /ɔ/ and /øː/. *zer*, *'gro*, and *mchod*, and other similar forms, would have to be treated, for purposes of lexical reference, as bi-phonemic : *zer* : /i/ and /ɛ/ ; *'gro* : /u/ and /ɔ/ ; *mchod* : /yː/ and /øː/.

---

[1] Bell, *Grammar*, 174.

[2] On the inadmissibility in phonemic analysis of assigning successive occurrences of the same sound under the same phonetic conditions to different phonemes, see Bernard Bloch, ' Phonemic overlapping ', *American Speech*, XVI, 278–84, and *Readings in linguistics*, Baltimore, 1957, 93–7.

This phonemic analysis would thus result in two different, and inconsistent, treatments of the same phonetic feature, vowel harmony : some pairs of alternative vowels would be assigned to the same phoneme, as allophones ; other pairs would be split between two phonemes, an embarrassing contradiction that could only be disposed of by a complicated morpho-phonemic statement.

A third advantage of prosodic analysis is that it enables one to avoid the concept of assimilation, to which objections have been raised.[1] In this prosodic analysis each member of each of the pairs of alternative degrees of vowel closure, ε/ɩ, ɔ/ɷ, ɒ/ɷ, ɵ/y, ε/e, ɔ/o, a/ʌ, and ɑ/ʌ, is regarded as an equal exponent of the appropriate V term (I, E, O, etc.) under alternative prosodic conditions ; there is no need to assume that one member of each pair is, somehow, basic, or a norm, and is replaced in some contexts (in which it is not merely unattested but unattestable) by the other non-normal member. On the contrary, one degree of closure is the appropriate exponent of the V term when contained in the Close Piece (its cP exponent) and the other is the appropriate exponent of that same V term when contained in the (complementary) Open Piece (its oP exponent) ; e.g. the V term of the Syllable 'then (E) has closeness (ɩ) as an exponent in the Close Piece, and half-openness (ε) in the Open Piece. Each of these two exponents is attested in, and only in, the appropriate prosodic type of Piece ; neither is ever an unattestable phantom. The norm concept is clearly inappropriate : each alternative would be the norm in its appropriate context ; and there could never be a non-norm in that context.

There is a further obstacle in the way of applying the assimilation concept to the vowel-harmony material presented in this article. This concept would seem to require an assimilator and an assimilee. Thus, the vowel ε of the assimilee Syllable 'then as in tha-mag 'then-pa-red (thɛmbə-) ' he smoked ', would be said to have been replaced in tha mag 'then-gyi-'dug (thɩŋgɩ-) ' he smokes ', by the vowel ɩ under the influence of the vowel ɩ of the following assimilator Syllable gi. In this example the assimilation relationship is of the type assimilee-assimilator. In, for example, zin-pas, sɩmbeː, ' did you catch ', on the other hand, the relationship is of the type assimilator-assimilee : the vowel ε of the assimilee Syllable pas (as in bsdad-pas, dɛːbɛː, ' did you stay ') would be said to have been replaced by the vowel e under the influence of the vowel ɩ of the preceding assimilator Syllable zin. Difficulties arise when both Syllables of the assimilation are of the same assimilation type : assimilee-assimilee, e.g. bsdad-pas, dɛːbɛː, ' did you stay ' ; or assimilator-assimilator, e.g. zin-gyi-red, sɩmgɩ-, ' he will catch '. Where both Syllables are assimilators, which is assimilated to which ?

The classification of Verb Syllables and Particle Syllables as either Close-Piece (cP) or Close/Open-Piece (c/oP) is purely distributional, and is based

---

[1] W. S. Allen, ' Some prosodic aspects of retroflexion and aspiration in Sanskrit ', *BSOAS*, XIII, 4, 1951, 939.

on the possibility of being included in the Close, and the Open, Piece ; there is no attempt to assign to one Syllable responsibility for the degree of vowel closure of the other. On the contrary, the relevant features of both Syllables are treated as part of an exponent that applies to the disyllabic Piece as a whole. Features of the second Syllable of the Piece may be later on the time-track than features of the first ; but they are to such an extent integrated with them that both can best be treate as parts of a single articulation.

Bibliography

ALBROW, K. H.
- (1962) 'The phonology of the personal forms of the verb in Russian' *Archivum Linguisticum* 14, 146–56.
- (1966) 'Mutation in spoken North Welsh' *JRF*, 1–7.

ALLEN, W. S.
- *(1951a) 'Some prosodic aspects of retroflexion and aspiration in Sanskrit' *BSOAS* 13, 939–46.
- (1951b) 'Phonetics and comparative linguistics' *Archivum Linguisticum* 3, 126–36.
- (1953a) *Phonetics in Ancient India*, London: Oxford University Press.
- (1953b) 'Relationship in comparative linguistics' *TPS*, 52–108.
- (1954) 'Retroflexion in Sanskrit: Prosodic technique and its relevance to comparative statement' *BSOAS* 16, 556–65.
- (1956) 'Structure and system in the Abaza verbal complex' *TPS*, 127–76.
- (1957) 'Aspiration in the Harauti Nominal' *SLA*, 68–86.

ASHER, R. E.
- (1966) 'The verb in spoken Tamil' *JRF*, 15–29.

BENDOR-SAMUEL, J. T.
- *(1960) 'Some problems of segmentation in the phonological analysis of Terena' *Word* 16, 348–55.
- (1961) 'The verbal piece in Jebero' *Word* 17 Supplement (Monograph 4).
- (1962) 'Stress in Terena' *TPS*, 105–23.
- (1965) 'Phonemic interpretation in some West African languages' *Sierra Leone Language Review* 4, 85–90.
- (1966) 'Some prosodic features in Terena' *JRF*, 30–9.

BURSILL-HALL, G. L.
- (1961) 'Levels analysis: J. R. Firth's theories of linguistic analysis' *Journal of the Canadian Linguistics Association* 6, 124–35, 164–91.

CARNOCHAN, J.
- (1948) 'A study in the phonology of an Igbo speaker' *BSOAS* 12, 417–26.
- *(1951) 'A study of quantity in Hausa' *BSOAS* 13, 1032–44.
- (1952) 'Glottalisation in Hausa' *TPS*, 78–109.
- (1957) 'Gemination in Hausa' *SLA*, 149–81.
- *(1960) 'Vowel harmony in Igbo' *African Language Studies*, 155–63.
- (1961) 'Pitch, tone and intonation in Igbo' *Proceedings of the Fourth International Congress of Phonetic Sciences* (Helsinki), 547–54.
- (1964) 'Pitch, tone and intonation in Yoruba' *DJ*, 397–406.
- (1967a) 'Igbo' *Word Classes*, 1–23 (*Lingua* 17).
- (1967b) 'Towards a syntax for Igbo' *Journal of African Languages* 2, 222–6.

CHINEBUAH, I. K.
(1963) 'The category of number in Nzema' *Journal of African Languages* 2, 244–59.

DOLPHYNE, F.
(1967) 'A phonological analysis of Twi vowels' *Journal of West African Languages* 4, 83–9.

FIRTH, J. R.
(1934) 'The principles of phonetic notation in descriptive grammar' *Papers*, 3–6 (First published in *Congrès International des Sciences Anthropologiques et Ethnologiques*).
(1935) 'Phonological features of some Indian languages' *Papers*, 47–53 (First published in *The Proceedings of the Second International Congress of Phonetic Sciences*).
(1936) 'Alphabets and phonology in India and Burma' *Papers*, 54–75 (First published in *Bulletin of the School of Oriental Studies* 8).
(1937) [with B. B. Rogers] 'The structure of the Chinese monosyllable in a Hunanese dialect (Changsha)' *Papers*, 76–91 (First published in *Bulletin of the School of Oriental Studies* 8).
*(1948) 'Sounds and prosodies' *Papers*, 121–38 (First published in *TPS*).
(1957) 'A synopsis of linguistic theory' *SLA*, 1–32.

FROMKIN, V.
(1965) 'On system-structure phonology' *Language* 41, 601–10.

HAAS, W.
(1966) 'Linguistic relevance' *JRF*, 116–47.

HALLIDAY, M. A. K.
*(1959) 'Phonological (prosodic) analysis of the new Chinese syllable (modern Pekingese)' Appendix to *Secret History of the Mongols*, Oxford: Basil Blackwell, 192–204.

HENDERSON, E. J. A.
(1948) 'Notes on the syllable structure of Lushai' *BSOAS* 12, 713–25.
*(1949) 'Prosodies in Siamese' *Asia Major* 1, 189–215.
*(1951) 'The phonology of loanwords in some South-East Asian languages' *TPS*, 131–58.
(1952) 'The main features of Cambodian pronunciation' *BSOAS* 14, 149–74.
(1960) 'Tone and intonation in Western Bwe Karen' *Burma Research Society Fiftieth Anniversary Publication* 1, 59–69.
(1961) 'Tonal exponents of pronominal concord in Southern Vietnamese' *Indian Linguistics*, 86–97.
(1965a) *Tiddim Chin; A Descriptive Analysis of Two Texts*, London: Oxford University Press.
(1965b) 'Final -*k* in Khasi: a secondary phonology pattern' *Lingua* 14, 459–66.
(1966) 'Towards a prosodic statement of Vietnamese syllable structure' *JRF*, 163–97.

HILL, T.
(1963) 'Phonemic and prosodic analysis in linguistic geography' *Orbis* 12.
(1966) 'The technique of prosodic analysis' *JRF*, 198–226.

LYONS, J.
(1962) 'Phonemic and non-phonemic phonology: some typological reflections' *International Journal of American Linguistics* 28, 131–58.

MACAULAY, D.
(1962) 'Notes on some noun-initial mutations in a dialect of Scottish Gaelic' *Scottish Gaelic Studies* 9, 146–75.

MITCHELL, T. F.
(1953) 'Particle-noun complexes in a Berber dialect' *BSOAS* 15, 375–90.
(1957a) 'Some properties of Zuara nouns, with special reference to those with Consonantal Initial' *Mémorial André Basset*, 83–96.
(1957b) 'Long consonants in phonology and phonetics' *SLA*, 182–205.
(1958) 'Syntagmatic relations in linguistic analysis' *TPS*, 101–18.
(1960) 'Prominence and syllabication in Arabic' *BSOAS* 23, 369–89.

PALMER, F. R.
*(1955) The "broken plurals" of Tigrinya' *BSOAS* 17, 548–66.
*(1956) '"Openness" in Tigre: a problem in prosodic statement' *BSOAS* 18, 561–77.
(1957a) 'The verb in Bilin' *BSOAS* 19, 131–59.
(1957b) 'Gemination in Tigrinya' *SLA*, 134–48.
(1958a) 'The noun in Bilin' *BSOAS* 21, 376–91.
(1958b) 'Linguistic hierarchy' *Lingua* 7, 225–41.
(1958c) 'Comparative statement and Ethiopian Semitic' *TPS*, 119–43.
(1959a) 'An outline of Bilin phonology' *Proceedings of the Convegno di Studi Ethiopici* (Rome), 109–16.
(1959b) 'The verb-classes of Agau (Awiya)' *Mitteilungen des Instituts für Orientforschung* 7, 270–97.
(1962a) *The morphology of the Tigre Noun*, London: Oxford University Press.
(1964) 'Grammatical categories and their phonetic exponents' *Proceedings of the Ninth International Congress of Linguists* (Cambridge, Mass.), 338–44.

ROBINS, R. H.
(1952) [with Mrs. N. Waterson] 'Notes on the phonetics of the Georgian word' *BSOAS* 14, 55–72.
*(1953a) 'The phonology of the nasalised verbal forms in Sundanese' *BSOAS* 15, 138–45.
(1953b) 'Formal divisions in Sundanese' *TPS*, 109–42.
*(1957a) 'Aspects of prosodic analysis' *Proceedings of the University of Durham Philosophical Society* 1, 1–12.
(1957b) 'Vowel nasality in Sundanese: A phonological and grammatical study' *SLA*, 87–103.
(1963) 'General linguistics in Great Britain 1930–60' in Christine Mohrmann et al., Eds., *Trends in Modern Linguistics*, Utrecht: Spectrum, 11–37.

Scott, N. C.
(1948) 'The monosyllable in Szechuanese' *BSOAS* 12, 197–213.
*(1956) 'A phonological analysis of the Szechuanese monosyllable' *BSOAS* 18, 556–60.
(1966) 'Nasal consonants in Land Dayak (Bukar-Sadong)' *DJ*, 432–6.

Sharp, A. E.
(1954) 'A tonal analysis of the disyllabic noun in the Machame dialect of Chaga' *BSOAS* 16, 157–69.

Shorto, H. L.
(1960) 'Word and syllable patterns in Palaung' *BSOAS* 23, 544–57.
(1966) 'Mon vowel systems' *JRF*, 398–409.

Sprigg, R. K.
(1954) 'Verbal phrases in Lhasa Tibetan' *BSOAS* 16, 134–56, 320–50, 566–91.
*(1955) 'The tonal system of Tibetan and the nominal phrase' *BSOAS* 17, 134–53.
(1957) 'Junction in spoken Burmese' *SLA*, 104–38.
*(1961) 'Vowel harmony in Lhasa Tibetan: prosodic analysis applied to inter-related vocalic features of successive syllables' *BSOAS* 24, 116–38.
(1963a) 'Prosodic analysis, and phonological formulae, in Tibeto-Burman linguistic comparison' *Linguistic comparison in South East Asia and the Pacific*, School of Oriental and African Studies, University of London, 79–108.
(1963b) 'A comparison of Arakanese and Burmese based on phonological formulae' *Linguistic comparison in South East Asia and the Pacific*, 109–32.
(1964) 'Burmese orthography and the tonal classification of Burmese lexical items' *Journal of the Burma Research Society* 47.2, 415–44.
(1965) 'Prosodic analysis and Burmese syllable-initial features' *Anthropological Linguistics* Vol. 7, No. 6, 59–81.
(1966a) 'Phonological formulae for the verb in Limbu as a contribution to Tibeto-Burman comparison' *JRF*, 431–53.
(1966b) 'Lepcha and Balti Tibetan: tonal or non-tonal languages?' *Asia Major* (New Series), 12.2, 185–201.
(1967) 'Balti-Tibetan verb syllable finals, and a prosodic analysis' *Asia Major*, 13.1.

Wallis, E.
(1956) 'Simulfixation in aspect markers of Mezquital Otomi' *Language* 32, 453–9.

Waterson, N.
*(1956) 'Some aspects of the phonology of the nominal forms of the Turkish word' *BSOAS* 18, 578–91.